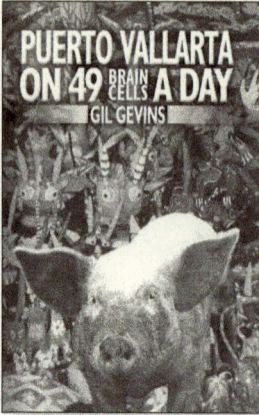

**Puerto Vallarta
On 49 Brain Cells A Day**

Refried Brains

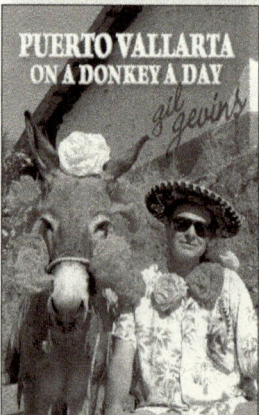

**Puerto Vallarta
On A Donkey A Day**

SLIME and PUNISHMENT

SLIME and PUNISHMENT

Gil Gevins

COATIMUNDI PRESS
Oakland, California

To Consuelo,
the world's greatest mother-in-law

PART I

ONE

I have always taken all of my oaths seriously. The Hippocratic oath. My wedding vows. The several times I have been sworn to silence by unfaithful friends. Even as a Boy Scout, if I swore it I meant it, earnestly and forever.

Then what happened? God only knows.

There were no omens. The day the foundations of my orderly life began to crumble dawned and proceeded to chug along like any other day, until I was unmasked by Pedro, the Puerto Rican orderly, in the hospital cafeteria. The cafeteria was where I ate my actual breakfast; my faux breakfast I shared at home with my wife, along with our faux marriage.

A typical August morning. The girls were sleeping in. Janice sat on her side of the outsized breakfast nook in our cozy sixteen-room Sands Point pseudo-Tudor mansion, and I sat on mine.

Janice ate a slice of dry seven-grain whole wheat toast and a plate of mixed organic fruit topped with two tablespoons of organic Canadian flaxseed and four ounces of low-fat (hormone-free) cottage cheese.

I ate a cup of black coffee, as I scanned without interest the front page of the Times.

"You have a busy day today, dear?"

"I'm not sure. It depends on how much time Captain America is prepared to waste on me."

"Brian?"

I nodded. Janice did not ordinarily refer to two-time NFL MVP's by their first names, but Brian Westin, the greatest narcissist in the history of team sports, was a constant blight on our lives, a relentless case of acne haunting us into middle age.

"Brian is so selfish," Janice said, taking a tidy bite of her toast.

"What else is new."

"Charles feels that it's partly your fault, that you haven't been strict enough in maintaining the proper doctor-patient relationship. You are supposed to be the authority figure, dear."

"Hmmm."

Charles, her older brother, was an arrogant insufferable prick who Janice had worshipped since birth. Though a successful doctor in his own right (I use that term loosely—he was in fact a psychiatrist) with a thriving practice in Manhattan, Charles was insanely jealous of me. The root of this pathology lay in the fact that, while he was one of the top ten shrinks in Manhattan, I was *the knee surgeon*, sought after by every over-paid athlete on the Eastern Seaboard, and beyond.

Ironically, my wife, whenever I dared level at Charles even the most minimal criticism, would accuse me of being jealous of Charles' wealth, which far outstripped our own. Charles did not earn via his practice even half what I did. He had, however, made huge sums utilizing his "financial genius" to trade successfully in the stock market.

I would have liked on these occasions to let my wife in on a dirty little secret. My attorney and close friend, Irving Waxman, happened to be the family attorney for two of Charles' ex-patients, CEO's of large New York based corporations. Both of these powerful gentlemen had confided in Irving that my sanctimonious brother-in-law had on multiple occasions made radically unethical use of insider information gleaned from their therapy sessions. When Charles, at every family gathering, would mention in passing another killing he'd made in the market, it required all of my self-control not to fling the truth in the hypocritical bastard's face.

What stopped me of course was Janice. In spite of her misplaced brother-worship, I loved Janice. She was my life's companion. She'd been a good wife and an exemplary mother. I could not stand even the thought of hurting her, and sullying the saintly image of her beastly brother would have done just that, caused her an enormous amount of pain.

"Yes," I said, "I probably am at fault. But these bigheaded athletes are difficult to manage. Even their coaches can't control them, and that's their job. Mine is merely to repair their knees."

Satisfied with the mea culpa, Janice changed lanes and said, "Dear, you really should eat something with your coffee. I worry about your gastritis. I bought that live-bacteria yogurt for you and it just sits there in the refrigerator."

"I'm not hungry first thing in the morning. You know that."

"But breakfast is the most important meal of the day. All of the nutritionists agree. And I hate to see good food go to waste."

"I don't believe it's being wasted," I said. "Surely all those live bacteria are feasting upon one other, even as we speak."

"That is not funny, Karl. The reason I asked about your schedule—I have two meetings to preside over today, both in the City, and I was wondering if you could make sure that the girls eat some real food for dinner."

"I don't know. Aside from Brian's visit, I have four surgeries scheduled. And a meeting with Edna."

"If we lived in the City," Janice pointed out, "we'd have far more time, and all of this scheduling wouldn't be such a problem."

This was another minor bone of contention between us. Janice had been pushing hard lately for us to move into Manhattan. Several years ago Charles' family had bravely migrated from their home across the bay in Kings Point to an enormous walnut-floored co-op on the East River, and Janice was convinced that we should follow in their trailblazing footsteps. Now that the girls were all grownup (Brenda was off to college in a few weeks, and Candace was about to begin her senior year of high school), Janice maintained that we had outgrown our rationale for living in the suburbs.

"But I like living here," I said. "I like looking at the trees out my window. I like the quiet and the clean air. I like…"

"But the culture, darling," Janice insisted. "Aside from the convenience of not having to commute, think of the culture. That was one of Charles' prime motivations for moving to the City, to be near the theatre, the ballet, the benefits."

And, I was dying to add, his Italian mistress. Another nasty little tidbit I'd picked up, from a neurosurgeon I knew. But once again, I swallowed my words.

Swallowed words: a leading cause, some say, of chronic indigestion.

TWO

Is it possible to recognize in oneself the first symptoms of insanity? I suppose I could ask my brother-in-law, but I think I already know the answer: probably not. In my case the first person to become aware of my altered mental state was Pedro, the Puerto Rican orderly.

Though I stood a thousand rungs higher than Pedro in the hospital hierarchy, he treated me much of the time as if I were an imbecile. Pedro may have been pulling my leg on these occasions, or not. But I didn't mind. I found his superior attitude refreshing.

It all began that morning in the bleak neon-lit cave known as the employee cafeteria. As a star surgeon I was entitled to dine upstairs, or anywhere else I pleased. But I preferred the basement cafeteria where the lingua franca was Spanish. Though medicine was my passion, the Spanish language had been, ever since a romantic incident in the East Village when I was at a young and impressionable age, something more than a hobby for me. Eating in the employee cafeteria allowed me to hone my language skills. Once I walked through those doors I never spoke a single word of English.

On that morning Pedro assaulted me the minute we sat down, as was our daily custom, at a table tucked into a corner of the enormous room. Typically, Pedro was the most care-free of men. Today his dark handsome face was creased with anxiety.

"Doc," he said in his slurred Caribbean Spanish, "we have to talk. I am very worried about you. You have the nose of a dog."

"I beg your pardon?"

"Your donkey is out of control," he clarified.

"My donkey? Do I own a donkey, Pedro?"

"Okay, Doc, I'll spell it out. You are so horny, you are going crazy. Like a Jamaican stepfather. Maybe worse."

Puerto Ricans and Jamaicans, I had learned, did not generally hold one another in high regard.

"Perhaps, we should lower our voices," I suggested.

"You need to get laid!"

"Not so loud!" I hissed.

Pedro ingested a large wad of scrambled eggs, knocked it back with some coffee and nodded his head. "I've been watching you, Doc. What's your problem? Why don't you do something?"

"I don't know what you're talking about. I'm a happily married man."

"*No mientes, cabron.* That's bullshit, and you know it. I saw you trailing that foxy nurse yesterday. You looked like a starving cat after a bird. And that boner. You coulda squashed a cockroach with that thing!"

Pedro was, lurid language and all, essentially correct. Dr. Karl Sanderson, famous for his rigid self-control, was on the verge of losing it altogether, like a cartoon boiler bursting at its metal seams. I needed to relieve the pressure, lighten the load, confess. If I'd been a Catholic, I would have sought out a priest. But I wasn't anything, so I settled for Pedro.

In hushed tones I reviewed for the orderly's benefit my current state of mind, or lack thereof. Yes, I'd been experiencing for several months now (or was it years?) a mounting wave of sexual desire. And yes, it was becoming increasingly unmanageable. But mine was not a straightforward situation. There were complications—the prickly issue of my marriage, for example.

"Shit man," Pedro sighed, "she's all the way out there on Long Island! What are you worried about?"

There was always, I told Pedro, the possibility of discovery. Something could always go wrong. You read about it all the time. A jealous girlfriend confronting the wife. An overheard conversation. An envious colleague. "The best laid plans often go astray, Pedro. You know, Murphy's Law?"

"Murphy? Who the fuck is Murphy?"

"I'm not sure. But the point is, I cannot run the risk of Janice finding out."

Pedro regarded me with pity. "I keep forgetting, because you speak Spanish so good, that down deep you're still a screwed-up white man. *Escuhame*, Doc. I'm telling you this for your own good. You think if you screw one of the nurses, your wife, living up there in the suburbs, is going to find out? I don't think so. And by the way, you want to know some cute nurses who go with you in a minute, I'll make a list."

"Really?"

"*Por supuesto!* You're the big-shot surgeon. Operates on all the quarterbacks. You're rich. A good-looking guy. Still young. How old are you—thirty-nine?"

"Forty-nine."

And that, as painfully trite as it might sound, lay precisely at the root of my illness, otherwise known as middle-aged dementia. Whether it was hormonally, psychologically or atavistically induced, I don't know, and at this point how could it matter. The end result was the same: I was desperate to have sex with a woman other than my wife, something which, unbelievably, I had never done.

Janice and I had been the stereotypical college sweethearts. We'd married and raised two daughters. Twenty-seven years later we were still married. I was well-off, physically fit, at the top of my profession and, by some accounts, not a bad-looking man. And, I was forty-nine years old. And, the only woman I had ever had sex with (no, scratch that: *used to* have sex with) was my wife.

Pedro was aghast. "Forty-nine? Shit, man, you don't look that old."

Old? Was forty-nine old? Was it only a repressed fear of death that was causing all of this hormonal havoc? Death.

One day I would surely die, and was that how I wanted to go out: practically a virgin? Sex between Janice and I, even at its "peak", had never been all that great. Janice was simply incapable of letting go. And so, if the truth be told, was I.

"All right, Pedro, for the sake of argument, let's say, hypothetically, I decide to…you know. You're the expert. Tell me what to do. But first, you must understand one thing. I will not hurt my wife. Under no circumstances can there be even the smallest chance of her finding out about…about…"

"Yeah, yeah, yeah," Pedro said. "What you want, mi amigo, is total discretion. I figured that out already. Let me chew it over. I'll let you know something soon. But if I was you, I'd grab one of them foxy nurses, one of them Mendez sisters, and just put it to her. You're too dumb to notice, Doc, but they worship the ground you operate on. Both of them."

"They do?"

"Yeah, well," Pedro admitted, "they probably don't know how old you are. But I'm not saying nothing," he added loyally.

THREE

That night I couldn't sleep, thinking of the Mendez sisters on the one hand and my wife, lying not two yards away, on the other.

If the Mendez sisters were really that fond of me, one reason had to be the fact that I was the only non-Hispanic doctor in the entire New York Hospital for Orthopedic Surgery who spoke to them in their native tongue. As I said, I've always had a love affair with that lyrical language, studying it first in high school and then in college, until my medical studies intervened, monopolizing all my time.

Once I began to practice, I made a point of conversing with the Spanish speaking staff as often as I could. My colleagues used to ridicule me, thinking my behavior absurd and demeaning. "Is he a surgeon or a social worker?" they whispered loudly behind my back. At one point brother Charles had attempted to convince me that I was compensating for feelings of deep-seated guilt related to the death of...someone—I can no longer recall who exactly. It must have been a close relative. Or perhaps a pet.

The hours trudged by. The Mendez sisters were a pair of Latina angels, with those perky young-adult breasts and... and...then there was Janice, who had begun to lightly snore. The awful thing about Janice was that there was nothing really wrong with her. Nothing I could point to and say, That bitch, she doesn't deserve my fidelity! She had kept her shape (long and lean, like mine), was active, attractive, positive, supportive, and so on.

Of all her laudable ives, first and foremost was active. Janice was incredibly, staggeringly active (except in bed, of course). She did aerobics. She played tennis. She chaired, co-chaired and re-chaired a string of charities. She was a conscientious mother. She was honest, fair, straightforward. In short (except for the misguided adoration of her sleazy brother), an exemplary human being.

If Janice had a fault, perhaps it was that at times she could be a little too well-intentioned. Her passion for political correctness, one could argue, did indeed border on the obnoxious. And her mania for health foods could, every now and then, take on the faintest of fascistic overtones.

The Mendez sisters, appropriately named Alba (Dawn) and Dulce (Sweet), probably knew nothing of political correctness. Nor, judging by the quantity of potato chips they seemed to be continually scarfing down their long lovely throats, did they appear to be overly concerned with nutrition. And, unlike Janice, they had not been educated at Vassar. They were merely a pair of charming, lovely young women who happened to possess two of the finest rear ends in the Greater Metropolitan Area.

The digital display on my nightstand showed a little after three. The night, like my marriage, seemed to be dragging on forever.

Yes, matrimonially speaking, Time was definitely an issue. And alongside it, growing like a family of fungi, the issues of Over-Familiarity, Routine and, last but not least, the issue of me being completely out of my frigging mind.

As I tossed in torment between painful tumescence one moment and pangs of guilt the next, I prayed silently to my pillow: "Please, Janice, hurt me. Have an affair with the pool boy. Curse the memory of my beloved mother. Drown a kitten. Vote Republican. Do something (anything) despicable for a change!"

An hour later I gave up on the whole idea of natural sleep and administered myself five milligrams of valium.

Pedro met me at an unpopular, overpriced Japanese restaurant twenty-seven blocks from the hospital. It was, by my lights, a nearly ideal rendezvous: no one I knew would be caught dead there, and no one Pedro knew would even suspect the place existed.

"Smells like shit in here," Pedro remarked.

"Yes," I said agreeably, "that's the seaweed."

"Seaweed?"

The waiter served us wee cups of warm sake. Pedro took a cautious sip and scowled. "What kind of place is this? The food smells like shit, and the booze tastes like piss."

"It's Japanese," I replied. "An acquired taste."

"Well you can acquire your own damn taste. Next time we go Italian."

A short while later, chewing suspiciously on the soggy tempura, Pedro launched into his pitch, which he began with enormous enthusiasm. "Okay, Doc, I am about to do you the biggest favor of your life!"

"*Gracias*, Pedro."

"*De nada*. I won three-hundred dollars at dominos last night," he said with seeming irrelevance.

"Congratulations."

"Gracias. So, me and the boys were talking around the table. The usual bullshit when guys get together, and I said, 'Hey, I got an interesting question.' 'What's that?' one of the guys says. 'Okay,' I say, 'suppose you're a gutless white wimp who wants to cheat on his wife, but...'"

"A gutless white wimp? Is that how you see me, Pedro?"

The orderly favored me with a brief pitying look and said, "'So, you're a guy who wants to cheat on the wife, but the wife, she's the daughter of Don Corleone. You get caught, kiss your nuts goodbye. So, the question is, where do I do this broad so there is absolutely no fucking way anybody is ever going to find out? That's the question.'"

"Brilliant."

"I know. And Doc, let me tell you something. These guys I play dominoes with? They are experienced men. Serious sex fiends. They get laid so much, they could open a tire factory with all the rubber they go through. They could start an elementary school with all the..."

"All right, Pedro, I get the idea. These friends of yours are among the most dissolute men on Manhattan Island. I understand. So, what's the point?"

"Funny you should mention islands, Doc."

"Why is that?"

"You," Pedro shouted, "are going to Cuba!"

"Pedro, for the love of God, lower your voice!"

FOUR

It was the last Saturday in August, another miserable muggy summer afternoon on Long Island—not that you would have known it in our house, where the silent central air maintained matters at an agreeably crisp seventy-five degrees.

In two days Brenda was scheduled to follow in her mother's athletic shoes and embark upon her new life as a freshman at Vassar. Janice, to mark the occasion, had planned a special family gathering, a type of premature Thanksgiving dinner, complete with premature turkey and an endless procession of low-fat trimmings. To make the occasion "extra-special" she'd invited Charles, his long-suffering wife, Ann, and Steven, their strange stuttering son, to share in the celebration.

When I first met her Ann had been a playful, perky bohemian bride fresh from Greenwich Village. Then twenty years of living with Charles had squeezed her nearly flat, like an exhausted tube of toothpaste. Steven, the same age as Candace, was a wonderfully bright and eccentric boy who spent most of his spare time playing baroque music and building clavichords. Shy, effeminate and largely devoid of social skills, he was a great disappointment to his father.

(It is an accepted medical fact, I should point out, that stuttering in boys is often attributable to sadistic overbearing fathers.)

I'd spent days pleading with Janice to make the party an "intimate family gathering", with just the four of us. But no, Janice had argued, having our "extended family" present would make the occasion more special, more "worthy of this major milestone" in our eldest daughter's life.

(Yes, on occasion my wife actually did speak this way, as if she were addressing the Kiwanis Club.)

The multi-course extravaganza was set to begin in half an hour. I sat in my study attempting to steel myself for an entire evening with Charles. If I'd been a drinking man, now would have been the time to knock back a few, but I'd never been that fond of alcohol.

A light knock sounded on the door.

"Enter."

"Hi, Dad, are you busy?"

"Never too busy for you, sweetie. What's up?"

Candace settled into a leather armchair, her face filled with compassion. "It's a trial for you, isn't it, Dad?"

"Well, you know, sweetie, time passes. Kids grow up. Sure, I'm a little sad to see Brenda leaving home, but it's just a part of life, after all. A parent has to accept…"

"No, Dad, I meant having dinner with Uncle Charles. He's such an ass-hole."

We were a bright family to be sure, a very bright family, if I may put it plainly. But Candace, in addition to being far too cute for anyone's good, was an actual genius and, to my secret delight, a bit of a rebel. She was bored by school and had expressed, to her mother's dismay, her intention of postponing or possibly even skipping college altogether. Though school left her cold, she read voraciously (a dizzying variety of books), and was a bona fide musical prodigy, though again, to her mother's complete stupefaction, her instrument of choice was the electric guitar.

"Candace is an under-achiever," Janice always informed me at report card time, her voice tinged with dread, as if she were announcing the onset of a degenerative disease.

"I don't know, dear," I always replied, "she's a wonderful musician, and she reads books even I can't understand."

"But her grades," Janice would moan, "her grades!"

Whenever my wife uttered those two words I was always reminded of Marlon Brando, the psychotic colonel in the film *Apocalypse Now*, moaning, "The horror, the horror!"

"Why are you smiling?" Janice would then demand. "An A-minus average is no laughing mater!"

Back in the present moment I attempted to put upon my face a look of parental dismay. "Number one, Candace, I will not hear that kind of language spoken in this house. And number two…ah…number two…"

"I love you, Dad," Candace said, "but you're a crumby actor."

"What do you mean?"

"Your mommy imitation—it sucks."

"Go put on a dress," I said. "This is not a jeans kind of occasion."

"I know things about Uncle Charles," Candace said darkly. "Ugly things. Steven confides in me."

"That's nice. Go put on a dress."

"All right, Dad, as long as I can wear that red cleavage thing. Then we can watch Uncle Charles trying not to stare at my tits."

"Candace!"

A college education? Pity the poor professors.

Charles and his family arrived as Janice and Essie (our occasional "African-American Domestic Assistant") were busy adding the final strokes to the evening's heart-healthy *espectaculo*. The girls were upstairs in their separate rooms, Brenda preparing for her grand entrance, and Candace playing the theme from *Phantom of the Opera* on her red guitar. It was left to me, praying all the while for an emergency call from the hospital, to answer the door.

And there they were, all three of them. Ann scuttled off at once to help with dinner. Steven, after asking, "C-c-c-c-an I g-g-g-o see Ca-ca-ca-ca?" zipped up the stairs, and I was left alone with Charles.

"This is a very special day for you," Charles proclaimed.

"It is?"

Charles had a real gift for disorientation. Excessively tall, he made a point of standing uncomfortably close to the person he was speaking to. Then, looming over his prey, he would sight down his long, narrow villain's nose as if it were a rifle, his loveless eyes boring into those of his victim, the thin bloodless lips curled smugly upward like a Gestapo colonel from central casting.

Though Charles succeeded in intimidating nearly everyone, he did not frighten me. To me, Charles was like a huge horsefly: repulsive, aggravating and disconcerting, to be sure, but nothing to be really scared of. It was merely a matter of dousing oneself with mental repellant and waiting for the large loathsome thing to buzz off and suck on someone else's psyche.

"Of course," Charles said. "Your baby girl is leaving the nest. One of life's major milestones."

"Of course." It must be genetic, I thought.

"Dinner is served!" Essie's melodious voice rang out from the dining room.

Saved by the bell.

FIVE

Our formal dining room could handle a dozen people with ease, but it was only with an audible groan that it's feng shui managed to contain my brother-in-law's outsized ego. The long teakwood table was set for seven. I sat in my rightful place at the head. From the standpoint of symmetry, the remaining diners should have been distributed evenly, three to a side. Charles, however, insisted upon occupying a position of authority equal to my own, and so was seated at the opposite end, rendering the entire table awkwardly askew. A portent of what was to come.

As Essie served the first course, a refreshing arugula salad with pine nuts, fresh mango slices, caramelized walnuts, goat cheese and beets, accompanied by a citrus/honey/mustard dressing, everyone proceeded to make a large fuss over Brenda.

My eldest daughter resembled her mother to an eerie degree: tall, thin, athletic (Brenda had captained her high school soccer team, while Janice had led her field hockey squad to the county championships), long straight honey-colored hair, aquamarine eyes, creamy complexion. Clones, I thought uneasily, looking from one to the other.

Brenda smiled stoically, and waited for the flood of hyperbolic praise to recede.

Abruptly, Charles stood up and raised his glass, beating me to the first toast—I'd planned on waiting at least until the soup. "Here's to you, Brenda!" the pompous ass proclaimed. "Never has an uncle felt so proud. To see the Meredith genes shining at their zenith like a morning star, expressed so exquisitely, so gracefully, so brilliantly in my marvelous niece fills me with wonder and awe. To you, Brenda!"

Everyone clinked glasses, where possible, and took half-hearted sips of the organic apple cider Janice (née Meredith) had procured for the occasion. The clinking, both real and symbolic, was followed by an awkward silence. Charles' over-the-top toast had thrown everyone off-stride. Janice stared blankly at her salad. Brenda went pink with embarrassment, as did her aunt. Candace rolled her eyes in disbelief. Steven, at this backhanded slap, cringed visibly. And I, having had my rightful role as the first toaster usurped, and my own genetic contributions so blithely swept under the rug, forced a smile and said, a little too loudly, "Here's to Brenda!"

Brenda favored me with a tight-lipped smile. What she was thinking, I had not a clue. I adored her of course, and was almost as proud of her as Charles pretended to be. Like her mother, Brenda had a generous nature. And she was as brilliant as she was beautiful. In one of the most competitive high schools in America, she had graduated second in her class. If only she would open up a bit. The rigid self-control she'd inherited from her mother (and me as well, I suppose) seemed unnatural in one so young.

Between the salad and the soup, Charles called cheerfully down the table: "So, Karl, been mending loads of knees lately?"

Mending. As if I were a cobbler repairing shoes, or a grandmother darning socks. Candace shot me a sympathetic smile.

"Yes, as a matter of fact," I replied, "I've been wading hip-deep in them. And how about you, Charles? Been shoring up your share of shattered egos?"

"How alliterational!" Charles smirked. "Didn't know you had a poetic streak, Karl."

"Alliterational is not a word, Uncle Charles," Candace said sweetly. "I think you meant to say alliterative."

God bless you, sweetheart!

Charles regarded his niece with a forced smile. "I was being facetious, Candace."

"Ungrammatically facetious, Uncle Charles? Or facetiously ungrammatical?"

"Steven," Janice said, before things got out of hand (Candace and her uncle had locked horns before), "I understand you've graduated from clavichords and are building a harpsichord now. That must be quite a challenge."

"Y-y-y-y-es, and n-n-n-n…"

What Steven wanted to say was that, yes, he was building a harpsichord, but that, no, it was not a challenge. It was, in fact, quite easy. He had already explained this to Candace earlier in her room. Steven's stuttering improved dramatically when he was alone with Candace, and deteriorated badly when he was around his father, particularly in public.

Ann, who had barely uttered a word all evening, intervened. "Steven builds the clavichords from kits," she began to explain, "and the harpsichord is also built…"

"Let Steven explain for himself," Charles cut in. "It's therapeutic."

Therapeutic? Sadistic was more like it. It took Steven, who in several years would find himself permanently enrolled in one of the top mental hospitals in the country, a full three minutes to get it all out—that after building three clavichords, the harpsichord was a "p-p-p-p-p-p-p-iece of ca-ca-ca-ca-ca-ca-cake."

"How nice," Janice said, as everyone, exhausted by the ordeal, sighed with relief. Essie, whose timing was excellent, chose that moment to serve the main course: enormous plates of *low-fat* turkey, stuffing, cranberry sauce, baby green beans and candied yams, all prepared without an iota of butter, salt or animal fat of any kind. Repressing a nearly overpowering urge to shower my plate with grease and salt, I wondered how in God's name one went about producing a low-fat turkey.

Everyone dug in gratefully, and for a short idyllic interval we were spared the need for further conversation.

"Jannie, absolutely scrumptious!" Charles exclaimed, breaking the silence.

"Thank you, Chuck," Janice replied, glowing like a radioactive mannequin.

"I don't know how you do it," Charles went on. "No butter, no salt, no cream, and yet…and yet…" Charles threw up his hands, as if at a loss for words.

Candace caught my eye and briefly clutched her throat, as if she were about to throw-up something as well. Though not displeased, I gave her a severe look; she was going over the line, on the verge of creating a scene.

"Yes, dear," I said dutifully, "you've really outdone yourself."

"Great, Mom, really great," Brenda agreed.

"D-d-d-de-licous!" Steven managed to get out. "Even b-b-better than la-la-la-…"

"Have you decided on a major yet, Brenda?" Charles asked, cutting his son off in mid-la.

"I'm leaning strongly towards pre-med," Brenda replied.

"Oh?" Charles said with a hint of alarm. "Have you settled upon a particular field or specialty?"

"Not yet," Brenda said. "I want to keep my options open."

"Very good," Charles said. "You don't want to rush into anything until you've explored all your options." Nearly everything Charles said had a subtext, and in this case it could not have been more clear: Hopefully, you won't decide to become a technician, like your father.

"The main thing," Charles went on, casting a significant glance at his sister, "is to have a career. All young women as intelligent as you should have a career."

Once again the pompous patronizing prick was taking a not so subtle jab at yours truly. When I started medical school, Janice had suspended her own studies in order to take on a fulltime job, supporting the two of us until I'd finished school and begun to earn a decent living. For this selfless act, I have always been sincerely grateful. But hers and Charles' insistence that she had given up a "promising career" for the sake of my studies always seemed to me to be stretching the point just a bit.

Janice had, after all, been majoring in Sociology, one of the most useless subjects known to mankind. What "promising career" was it then that she had forsaken: Parole Officer? To hear her or Charles describe her "enormous sacrifice" one would think she'd spent five years toiling in a coal mine, when in fact she'd been managing a comfortable law office; or that she'd turned her back on an all but certain Nobel Prize, in order to pursue a life of domestic drudgery.

The fact of the matter was, Janice had been rewarded for her five years of gainful employment with an entire lifetime of leisure, luxury and the freedom to do absolutely anything she wished. Not a bad bargain, if you think about it. Meanwhile, my two decades of practicing medicine, providing the sole support for our privileged family, seemed to count for naught.

"Oh, I'm definitely going to have a career, Uncle Charles," Brenda said.

"Our Brenda is going to do something really special with her life," Janice said with conviction.

"Yeah," Candace said, "I bet Brenda becomes a famous surgeon, just like Dad."

"I haven't decided yet," Brenda insisted.

"She has plenty of time to make up her mind," Charles decreed.

I was about to say something to the same effect when Essie burst into the dining room cradling a round silver platter. On her broad face was an expression of abject disgust.

"Here it is…the low-fat flan."

If Brenda was difficult to read, Essie was an open book. "These white people," she was thinking, "what the hell is wrong with them?"

SIX

Every fall, accompanied by my two best friends, I went on a fishing trip to a remote area in the heart of the Adirondack Mountains. None of us were avid fishermen; the idea was simply to get away—to get away from everything. No phones, no television, no newspapers, no patients, no clients and, last but not least, no families.

Our wives were not particularly happy with us going off like this, but we were all such exemplary husbands (effective income generators) that we were grudgingly permitted this one small annual lapse. Janice chalked it up to "prolonged adolescence", a condition she described as the "North American male's refusal to totally grow up". There was probably some truth in that; there was usually a substantial portion of truth in every depressing opinion my wife expressed.

Burt, pale, thin and nerdy, was a top-notch anesthesiologist with whom I worked on a regular basis. Irving, a short bear of a man whose beefy hands rarely strayed far from the next pastrami sandwich, was my attorney. At our last Sunday morning planning session, I informed them for the first time of my plan. Needless to say, it was none too well received.

"As your attorney," Irving said from behind his incredibly cluttered desk, "I strongly urge you to reconsider this irrational and foolhardy scheme."

It had been my idea to meet at Irving's Manhattan office. On a Sunday morning it was naturally deserted.

"What's your objection, Irving?"

"My objection?" Irving said in his courtroom voice. "My objection? All right. To begin with, let us throw morality out the window."

"Good idea," Burt agreed.

"Let us put aside the concepts of loyalty, steadfastness and self-restraint."

"Here! Here!"

"Let us examine," Irving said, "the one and only true flaw in your entire grand design."

I held my breath, believing that Irving had discovered a fatal weakness in my supposedly "foolproof" plan.

"By running off," Irving said, "to screw your brains out in Cuba, you will be…"

"Breaking the law?" Burt suggested.

"Let us leave the law out of this," Irving ruled from behind his enormous desk. "You will be…"

"Risking exposure to deadly diseases?" Burt offered.

"Health considerations aside," Irving said. "All other considerations aside, you, my feral friend, by taking this radically irresponsible step, will be fucking up our fishing trip!"

In the end, my friends had no choice but to play along, to pretend that I'd gone fishing with them in the mountains when in fact I would be, as Irving had so elegantly put it, screwing my brains out in Cuba. Over the years I had been asked to cover for both men on a couple of occasions when they had engaged in their own questionable behavior, and they could hardly, when push came to pelvic thrust, refuse to return the favor. For that very reason (not to mention our friendship), I knew that I could count on their complete discretion.

In a last desperate attempt to keep the threesome intact, Irving pleaded with me to "…fornicate with one of the nurses at the hospital, for Christ's sake!"

"Yeah," Burt said, "what's wrong with those Mendez sisters? Either one'd jump you in a minute."

"They would?" I found myself asking for the second time in two weeks.

"In a minute."

"I find that hard to believe," I said. "To begin with, they must realize that I'm married. And then…"

"Karl, Karl, Karl," Irving said. "Do you ever take a good look at yourself in the mirror?"

"Of course," I said, "every morning, when I shave. But what has that got to do with anything?"

"You look," Irving said, "but you don't see. If you saw, you'd realize that you look like a movie star."

"Like frigging Clint Eastwood," Burt agreed.

"It's a terrible waste," Irving said. "Burt and I, we're just a pair of frustrated, pot-bellied middle-aged putzes who can't get a decent looking broad's attention without waving a bar of gold under her tits. But you! You, who could take your pick of New York's finest, you…you…"

"Please," Burt begged, "don't screw up our trip. Screw a Mendez sister, instead. Screw them both."

"For our sake," Irving pleaded.

"Sorry. Too close to home. I'm not about to take that kind of chance. If Janice found out, I'd never forgive myself."

"Coward."

"Wimp."

"Flake."

The meeting with Burt and Irving came to a satisfactory, if somewhat incendiary, conclusion. In the end, they'd acquiesced, given me manly hugs and wished me luck with my new endeavor, as they continued to pepper me with insults.

But as I drove home, instead of feeling a sense of satisfaction at a job well done, I was suddenly engulfed by a storm of disturbing emotions so intense I had to pull my Volvo (I would have preferred a Mercedes, but Janice had insisted that somehow owning Volvos mysteriously made us better human beings) to the side of the road.

Sitting there in my air-conditioned, late-model politically correct vehicle, I broke out in a cold sweat. I began to tremble. Up until that moment, a substantial part of me had never really believed in the adulterous fieldtrip Pedro and I had planned; or rather, never believed that one Dr. Karl Sanderson, man-of-his-word surgeon, with twenty-five years of fidelity under his belt, would ever have the courage to carry it out.

It's only a titillating daydream, I'd been telling myself, a harmless middle-aged fantasy. But now my pact with Burt and Irving had made it official, and all at once I felt as if I were sliding off a cliff.

Hyperventilating inside the cozy Volvo, I made a panicked attempt at dissecting my fractured state of mind. There was, first and foremost, excitement, the thrill of a pending adventure. But there was also, in nearly equal measure, fear. Fear of the unknown. Fear of making a fool of myself. But most of all, fear of being found out, and the terrible guilt I would feel for mortally wounding my wife. And then, coursing through my veins like a powerful stimulant, there was the hormonal rush, the anticipation of sex with…whom? I imagined Cuban versions of the Mendez sisters eagerly spreading their thighs and suddenly I was on the verge of apoplexy. I could actually hear my heart thudding dangerously inside my chest. Thud! Thud! Thud!

Of course it wasn't really my heart. It was a policeman, rapping on the window. God only knows what I looked like, sitting behind the wheel gasping for air, parked in front of a fire-hydrant (naturally). I rolled down the window and attempted to breathe through my nose.

"Sir, are you all right?" the polite young officer inquired.

"Yes, yes, of course," I said breathlessly. "Why wouldn't I be?"

"Do you live around here, sir?"

For a moment I wasn't sure how to answer his question, so far had my mind flown from real-time reality. Quickly, I looked around to get my bearings. I was on a quiet street in Manhasset Estates, a well-heeled neighborhood I occasionally used as a shortcut home.

"No, not really," I admitted.

"Sir, have you been drinking?"

"Of course not. I'm a surgeon."

"Sir, please step out of the car."

SEVEN

Thirty minutes later, having passed the breathalyzer test, I was back at home, safely ensconced in my study. In order to rid myself of the polite but persistent policeman I'd had to invent a bogus justification for my mini-fit of hysteria, blurting out the first thing that came to mind: "My brother-in-law—I just learned that he was killed in a terrible accident. Nearly decapitated. His chest crushed like a potato chip. If only he'd been wearing his seatbelt. We were very close."

At each other's throats, as a matter of fact.

"I'm sorry to hear that, sir," the young man said. "Do you think you'll be all right to drive now?"

"He was only fifty-two, in the prime of life," I felt compelled to add, God knows why. "A wonderful human being. It seems so unfair."

"It's always like that," the nice policeman said. "The good ones die young. Are you sure you can drive?"

"Yes. I just need another moment to gather my wits."

"All right then. I'll be on my way. Sorry for your loss, sir."

Lying to the young policeman left a bad taste on my tongue. Sitting in the comfort of my study, staring out the French doors at the oaks and maples, I tried to remember the last time I had deliberately told a non-white lie…and couldn't; it had been so long. Well, that's all over, I told myself: the lies will be coming thick and fast now. The thought made me feel so rotten I took the nearly unprecedented step of pouring myself a medicinal glass of port.

The alcohol lifted my spirits at once. I loved sitting in my study on a quiet Sunday afternoon, listening to music, watching an old movie or simply staring out the window.

The foliage never failed to bring a feeling of peace and well-being after a long and stressful week. On average I performed three surgeries a day, some routine and some demanding. I loved to operate, but I also liked my quiet time.

Janice was out and about, playing tennis, or golf, or bridge—her multitude of activities sometimes melted together in my mind like the colors of an abstract painting. Brenda was off at college now and Candace was…somewhere. It was perfectly quiet in the big old house, and I sat there quietly myself, trying not to think about sex, or the plane ticket hidden artfully between the spleen and the pancreas in an anatomy text on a shelf behind my head.

Unaccustomed to the port, I fell asleep in my chair, only to be awakened sometime later by the sound of music floating down from the second floor. It was a duet: Candace on guitar, and Steven, if I wasn't mistaken, playing a small electric piano.

"You have to have a piano for writing music, Dad," Candace had explained to me a week before her fourteenth birthday. Despite what she believed, I was no pushover. She already owned three guitars and did not, as far as I knew, even know how to play the piano.

"Don't forget to save the receipt," had been my stern reply. "In case I can write it off as an entertainment expense."

The music they were playing was, to my ear, strange but appealing, the result of a musical tug-of-war in which Steven attempted to yank Candace in the direction of Bach and Vivaldi, while she endeavored to muscle her cousin over to the side of Buddy Guy and Muddy Waters. Every now and then a shout would override the music: "That's n-n-not a n-n-note!" Or, "For once, get off the fucking page, Steven!"

Candace had other friends she would have preferred "jamming" with on a Sunday afternoon. But despite her tough persona, she was really a sweet girl. She knew she was Steven's only friend, and made a point of spending time with him as often as she could. When they took a break to raid the fridge, I got up to join them.

"I liked that, ah, tune you were playing," I said.

"You d-d-d-id?" Steven asked in astonishment.

"Yes, it was kind of refreshing. Scarlatti plays the blues. You should make an album."

"We saw the greatest flick in the City, Dad."

"The l-l-latest S-s-scorceesee film."

"DeNiro was awesome."

"And J-joe Pesci p-p-played the b-best psycho!"

"Oh, I'll have to check it out." I preferred old movies, without all the bloody realism—I got enough of that at the hospital. But for the kids' sake I made a pretense of keeping up. "Was it, ah, very violent?"

"Over the top, Dad," Candace beamed. "Gore galore!"

"Well, maybe you should refrain from mentioning it to your mother."

"No problem, Dad. We'll tell her we saw the director's cut of Merry Poppins."

"Good idea. What's a…" I was about to ask what a "director's cut" was, but stopped myself, almost in time. The cousins looked at each other and burst out laughing.

"I wish my da-da-da-da-dad was more like you," Steven said with disarming directness. "He thinks C-c-candace is a b-b-b-ad influence on me."

"Candace is an angel. You suppose we could keep the shouted profanities to a minimum?" I asked my daughter.

"Sorry, Dad, didn't think you could hear me."

"Wrong answer."

Candace saluted me smartly. "Oui, mon capitain!"

"That's where you belong," I told her, "in the Foreign Legion."

"Among zee coarse brutes," Candace emoted, "zee blackguards, zee villains and zee cutthroats!"

"Why don't you adopt me," Steven suggested, amazingly, without a single stutter.

"Yeah, Dad, we've got lots of room. Rescue Steven from that slope-nosed ogre before it's too late."

I felt deep in the pit of my stomach a feeling of intense joy. What a marvelous pair of kids these were! Especially Candace. My marriage had lost its glow long ago. And Brenda, cool distant Brenda, had flown the familial coop. But Candace, all by her beautiful self, made my home life not only worthwhile, but a thing to be marveled at and cherished.

With a superhuman effort I made myself frown. "Listen," I told them, "life is not perfect, and neither are you. And neither are your parents. But in spite of our imperfections, we, your parents, are still the ones who bring you into this world, who nurture and protect you. And we, all of us, despite our imperfections, are entitled to a modicum of respect. Am I making myself clear?"

"Y-y-y-es, sir."

"He's still an ass-hole, Dad."

EIGHT

On my last day at work, over a super-fried breakfast of bacon and eggs in the employee cafeteria, Pedro handed me a small package wrapped in plain brown paper.

"What's this?"

"A little present," Pedro replied with a lewd wink. "Open it on the plane."

Once I'd finished tidying up the office, I buried Pedro's gift beside the plane ticket at the bottom of my briefcase. My hands ("the steadiest in the business") were trembling. I hadn't even left the office yet, let alone had sex with a stranger, and already the guilt was gnawing away at my neurons. For the hundredth time I wondered if I really had the nerve to carry out my plan, which was seeming more insane by the second.

On my way out the door, I was stopped by the phone.

"What's this I hear?" Brian Westin, the NFL's highest paid player, said without preamble. "You're taking a vacation? For how long? Do you realize the season started last week?"

"Brian, I always take a vacation this time of year. Seventeen days. It's been, what, ten years in a…"

"I'm experiencing a twinge," Brian cut in.

"Experiencing a twinge?"

"My left knee." Brian, like most thirty-year-olds in his profession, had problems with both his knees, but the left one had only required minor surgery, so far.

"Isn't that the good one, Brian?"

"Supposedly."

"Where exactly is the twinge located?"

"It's hard to say."

"Would you call it a generalized twinge, then, Brian?"

"Generalized? Yeah, that's exactly what it is!"

"Then you have nothing to worry about." I knew what he was after: an office visit, then and there. I had to head him off. "After that last bit of arthroscopic work, Brian, a generalized twinge is exactly what we want to feel. It's part of the normal healing process."

I was, of course, making this up as I went along. Brian was, besides being a massive egotist, a huge hypochondriac. A "twinge" was what football players felt on their good days. I knew there was nothing wrong with him, and I had no time for a visit. "You're fine," I assured him, "and if anything comes up while I'm gone, you can call Dr. Slodnic."

"Screw Slodnic!" Brian said with feeling. "No one touches these knees but Dr. Karl Sanderson. We have an exclusive contract. Bobby showed it to me." Bobby was his agent.

"I have a life, too, Brian."

"Not during the season you don't. It's in writing!"

"Well then, have Bobby call my attorney. And try to keep the scuttling to a minimum. And stay in the pouch, or the purse, or whatever they call it. Good-bye, Brian."

"Okay, Doc," Brian said, giving up for the moment on the idea of completely controlling my life. "I guess you're right. Catch a can of tuna for me, Doc. And don't drown or anything. The team needs you. Maybe you could cut the trip a little short this time and…"

Hanging up on Brian felt good. Almost at once, the phone began to ring again, but I was already gone.

It was far out of season and the plane, a direct flight from JFK to Kingston, Jamaica, was not crowded. But business class was, for whatever reason, almost full. The person sitting next to me, a well-groomed woman in her early forties, was polite but distant, which suited me perfectly. I was dying to open Pedro's package.

As I undid the paper I caught my seatmate casting an idle glance my way. I gave her a weak smile and removed from its wrapping a small booklet which looked a good deal like a home-made instruction manual for a telephone answering machine. On its cover, in English, were the bold hand-written words: HOW TO CHEAT ON YOUR WIFE IN CUBA.

Quickly, I flipped the booklet over, as if I were anxious to see the author's portrait on the back. To disguise my embarrassment, I turned to my neighbor, who may or may not have seen the title, and said, "So, what do you do?"

"I'm an attorney," she said. "My specialty is divorce." Then, with a thin smile, she handed me a business card. Ordinarily, I am not a superstitious man. Nonetheless…

I had two hours to kill in Kingston, so I busied myself buying a roast beef sandwich, a coke, several gallons of sun screen, a pair of dark glasses and a spiffy Panama hat.

From Kingston I caught a direct flight to Havana, where I was surprised by the modernity and efficiency of the airport. This airport, I would soon discover, was the only thing in Cuba (with the exception of the tourist hotels and the Ministry of Sports) one could attach to the words "modern and efficient" without being laughed off the street.

The uniformed individual at the immigration booth regarded me with what I felt was a certain lack of friendliness.

"Buenas tardes," I said in my Puerto Rican inflected Spanish, "could you please not stamp my passport?"

Pedro had pointed out in Section (1.1) of his handwritten manual that it was illegal for American citizens to set foot on Cuban soil, and that the local authorities, if asked nicely, would refrain from staining my passport with their incriminating stamps.

Once the unsmiling immigration officer had stamped my visa and cooperatively failed to stamp my passport, I found a government taxi (the last I would ever use) and told the driver to take me to the Hotel Nacional. En route, the driver mentioned seven times (I counted) that he, like all Cubans, were paid just enough to slowly starve to death, and depended on tips to feed his family, etc. I tipped him two dollars, grabbed my single suitcase and proceeded to check in to the hotel.

My room, as per Pedro's instructions, was only to be occupied for one night. Apparently, bringing girls to a hotel room was, along with an immense list of other activities, heavily frowned upon by the authorities. Before changing into my "tropical outfit" (Panama hat, Hawaiian shirt, Bermuda shorts and Mexican sandals), I took a shower and slathered myself in sun screen. My excessive caution, vis-à-vis solar radiation, had less to do with my fear of skin cancer than it did my fear of Janice: one did not typically acquire a great tan in late September in the Adirondacks, especially on one's arms and legs.

Out on the street, it was hellishly hot, the sun a painful blur. I set off at once in search of the several addresses with which I'd been provided by Pedro's sex-fiend pals—see Section (1.3). These addresses belonged to "privately owned" homes where one could rent a room. For whatever reason the authorities had no problem with tourists bringing girls to these places. Unless they were under eighteen, of course.

At the first house, no one was home. At the second, all the available rooms were rented. At the third, a small white stucco affair, I hit the jackpot. The owner, a frumpy seventy-something-year-old woman, greeted me at the front door. Her name was Eustacia and she spoke in a scratchy but friendly voice.

"I have two very nice private rooms in the back of the house," she said, before I could speak a word, "and one is available. *Es muy privado*," she added, in case I hadn't heard her the first time.

The entrance to the room was indeed private, located down a narrow walkway which ran along the side of the house and around a corner. The room itself was small, cozy and clean. And it was blessed with an old Russian air conditioner, which made a good deal of noise, but just managed to keep the room uncomfortably warm.

"Where does that door go to?" I asked.

"That opens into the hallway of my house," the old woman replied. "But you don't have to worry. Your privacy will be respected at all times. In the morning, you get coffee and orange juice. That's included in the rent. Twenty-five dollars a day. Payable in advance," she added with an ingratiating smile.

Eustacia and I, I thought wrongly, are going to get along just fine.

I paid her ten days in advance, and she nearly hugged me. In Cuba two-hundred and fifty dollars was a small fortune, not that she would get to keep much of it. The government's cut, I later learned, was eighty-five per cent.

"You need to give me your *pasaporte*," my new landlady said, "for bookkeeping purposes." When I handed it over, she seemed surprised. "You're an American?"

Afraid that she was going to return my money and eject me forthwith from the premises, I nodded my head. "Is that a problem?"

"No, no, no. It's your Spanish. You talk just like a Puerto Rican. Of course, now that I'm looking at you," she said, appraising me carefully from head to toe, "you are too tall, too white and too handsome to be a Puerto Rican."

"Um…gracias."

"Are you with the CIA?"

"No," I laughed, "I'm an orthopedic surgeon. I work with a great number of people who speak Spanish, however, and most of them are Puerto Rican."

"Oh, well, that must explain it. One more thing," she added, a severe note creeping into her creaky voice, "no one under eighteen."

"Of course not," I said, turning rose-red with embarrassment.

"Any chica you bring here, I have to see her I.D."

"*Si, señora.*"

"No exceptions!"

"*Por supuesto, señora.*"

"It's against the law. In case you were wondering."

NINE

Now that my government-approved sex-chamber was secured with cold cash, I thought of moving into it at once. But I feared that checking out of my hotel only two hours after checking in might arouse the interest of the authorities. So I decided to go for a walk, sit down somewhere cool and quiet, have a cold glass of juice and resume my perusal of Pedro's manual.

The hotel and Eustacia's house were both situated in the "newer" more "modern" part of town known as *Vedado*. It was a convenient location, but altogether lacking in character. I began to walk downhill towards the water in search of some local color, and a little relief from the murderous heat.

In Section (2.1), "Getting Settled", which I'd studied in depth at the Kingston airport, Pedro recommended taking things slowly until I had acquired some familiarity with the lay of the land. His actual words, of course, had been somewhat more colorful: "...so keep that big dog of yours on a leash till you figure out what the fuck is what."

Fifty meters down the street from the hotel a young man fell in step beside me. "How are you today, my friend?" he asked in heavily accented English. He was tall, black and handsome, and wore upon his head, despite the overpowering heat, a knit rainbow colored cap. In his right hand he carried a matching umbrella, which he used as a walking stick.

"Fine," I replied, without breaking stride, "how about yourself?"

"Hey, you speak Spanish really good," he said. "My name's Enrique. Where you from?"

"Canada." I'd made the assumption, wrong as it would turn out, that the average Cuban held a grudge against Americans. Somehow "being Canadian" felt safer.

"Canada? Oh, that's a beautiful country!"

"Ever been there?"

"No, but I've seen pictures. Lots of trees. You looking for a chica?"

"Not right now. I just got here."

"So what are you waiting for? I know some chicas drive you right out of your mind."

"I'm sure you do, but at the moment I'm just looking for a cool place to have a glass of juice."

"Look no further," he said, "there's one right here."

Grabbing my arm, he began to lead me gently but firmly up a flight of stairs. My first thought was to pull free of his grip and flee for my life. But something held me in the young man's sway. He was charismatic and friendly, for one thing. And Pedro had mentioned in Section (2.3) that it might be advisable to contract a "tour-guide" for a few hours, someone who could provide a general orientation, explain locations, going rates, procedures, etc.

And so, balancing in my mind the warning in Section (2.1) with the suggestion in Section (2.3), I allowed Enrique to lead me to a corner booth in what appeared to be a perfectly ordinary Chinese Restaurant. I ordered a juice and he ordered an Island Delight, whatever that was.

"Listen, Enrique," I said, taking immediate control of the situation, "I'll gladly buy you a drink. But that's all I'm buying. And in exchange, I would like a little information. Is that clear?"

Enrique spread his arms wide and gave me his brightest smile. "Clear as day, mi amigo. Havana is my garden. I can show you all the flowers."

"*Excelente.* Just so we understand one another."

"Like a pair of Siamese twins, mi amigo."

"All right, Enrique, here are some of the things I would like to know: Which are the best locations to find chicas? Is there any problem with la *policia*? Is there a certain time of day when…"

"Hey, look who's here!" Enrique exclaimed.

Two young girls (they might have been eighteen) were wobbling atop matching pairs of sky-scraping high heels unsteadily in our direction. They were dressed, if that is the proper word, in bright yellow micro-skirts and red tops which, utilizing a complex system of overlapping strings, made them appear more naked than if they had been wearing nothing at all. Somehow they managed to look completely absurd and highly erotic at the same time: the daughters of a hooker who've just raided their mother's closet.

Before you could say "club sandwich", they'd climbed into my side of the booth, wedging me neatly between them. Enrique suggested I buy the girls a drink, which I did. By the time the drinks arrived (four Island Paradises, replete with miniature umbrellas and plastic palm trees), each girl had slid a hand up and inside my shorts, taking joint possession, as it were, of my genitalia.

"Um, wait a second!"

"You won't find better chicas anywhere," Enrique said in the manner of a car salesman. "Have one, or have them both. For both, you get a special low-season discount. I've reserved a room, conveniently located behind the bar, where you can…"

"But this is only my first day," I said nonsensically.

"What a way to land!"

The girls, meanwhile, had begun to mumble erotic statements, stereophonically, into each of my ears. I can't remember their words now, but I do recall quite vividly the electrifying sensation produced by their small hands grasping me in tandem, as if they were squeezing the handle of a baseball bat. This is not good, I told myself. Or, is it very good? I couldn't decide. On the one hand, I felt like a driver on a winding icy road speeding downhill out of control. On the other hand, it felt…so incredibly good! My will, the desire to control my own destiny, was slipping, slipping, slipping away.

And then I was seized by another kind of feeling, a mounting panic which knew no bounds. This was too much, too far outside my experience, too contrary to the manner in which I had lived my entire life. I was stunned, overwhelmed, like a life-long vegetarian being forced to consume a double cheeseburger.

And the girls, from close up (and we could not have been any closer), looked far too young.

I'm being set up, I decided. The minute my shorts are down, in come the police. And then it's jail, deportation, humiliation. Or worse. Didn't they torture people here? Abruptly, I stood up, spraining teenage hooker number two's wrist in the process.

"The check!" I shouted, trampling teenage hooker number one as I scrambled over her insubstantial corpus and out of the booth.

Enrique looked hurt. "Hey man, what happened?"

"I have to go. No time for chicas now."

"Okay," Enrique said, also exiting the booth. "Then buy this box of cigars. I have a family to feed."

From absolutely nowhere, he produced a box of cigars, opening the lid for my inspection.

"You're joking," I said, throwing some money at the waiter.

"Only twenty dollars," Enrique insisted. "These are genuine Cohibas, stolen directly from the factory. In the tourist stores, this box costs two hundred dollars. Come on, help me out."

"I don't smoke cigars," I said from the top of the stairs.

"Then give them as gifts."

I wanted to tell him that since I was an American I couldn't even admit I'd been to Cuba, let alone bring home a box of cigars. But then I remembered that just minutes earlier I'd proclaimed myself a citizen of Canada. Practiced in the art of deception, I was not.

"All right," I said, handing him a twenty. "I guess I can give them away as tips."

"I'll take one," the waiter called out, but I was already halfway down the stairs, gathering momentum as I descended. Several minutes later I took a seat in the bar of my hotel, ordered a mojito, purported to be Ernest Hemingway's favorite drink, and attempted to calm down.

Everything is fine, I told myself, downing half the minty tasting cocktail in one go. Everything is all right. No thanks to you, of course, I chided myself. Even that sex-lunatic Pedro tells you to take it easy your first day, and what do you do? Within hours of hitting Cuban soil you get yourself pinned in the booth of a Chinese restaurant by a pair of underage hookers. What are you, out of your mind? No, I'm fine, I replied. And tomorrow, I promised myself, I will proceed in a more orderly fashion.

Two mojitos later, I decided to check out of the hotel after all. I'd paid for my room. What business was it of theirs how long I stayed? The hell with their government spies!

Yes, I was drunk.

"Is there a problem, señor?" the earnest young man behind the desk asked with concern.

"The room is far too small," I said without conviction. The room was actually quite spacious.

"We have larger rooms, señor."

"Too dark?"

"We have corner rooms with more windows, señor. The hotel is not crowded. We can change your room at once."

"No, no, what I need is…" Desperately, I struggled to come up with some amenity the young man could not possibly provide. "…I need a bidet with purified water."

"A bidet with purified water, señor?"

"Yes, and a vibrating bed. The kind you put two quarters in."

"Two quarters of what, señor?"

"Never mind. This would never happen in Canada. You take Visa?"

Eustacia was only mildly surprised to see me.

"I hate hotels," I told her, by way of explanation. "They always make me depressed."

"Yes," she agreed, "hotels are so impersonal."

Seriously sloshed, emotionally drained and awash in relief over the fact that as of that moment I had been neither arrested nor deported, I lay down and went immediately to sleep.

TEN

At precisely eight am the following morning, as I was busy moving my bowels (only eighteen hours in the tropics and already they'd begun to loosen), someone commenced to pound urgently on the interior door of my room. The pounding was followed by an amazingly loud screech, like a hoarse parrot shrieking through a bullhorn:

"WHERE ARE YOU?"

"In the bathroom!"

"AT THIS HOUR?"

Several minutes later, poking my head out the door, I found my landlady sitting with her legs crossed on my unmade bed, affording me an excellent view of her left knee, which was swathed like a swollen mummy in several meters of frayed yellowing bandages. On the small square table beside my bed was a tray containing my complimentary coffee and orange juice.

"You look tired," Eustacia screeched—softly, now that we were in the same room. "My late husband also drank too much. That's what killed him."

"I don't normally drink," I said. "First day on vacation and all that. Sorry about your husband."

"No need to be sorry. He was a loyal party-member, until he died. That's how we got this wonderful house. I was talking to my doctor yesterday. She told me that if you're really an orthopedic surgeon, then you must know all about knees."

From death to politics to real estate to medicine? The woman was giving me vertigo. "Yes," I replied warily, "I do have some familiarity with knees."

"Mine is a mess," she snarled. "Maybe, sometime—not now, once you've settled in, like, tomorrow—you could give me an examination. My doctor is very good, but she's young. And very attractive, I might add."

"I would be delighted," I mumbled.

"And single."

"I beg your pardon?"

"The doctor—she's not married. Have a nice day."

The juice was sour and the Cuban coffee so strong it set my teeth on edge. After another visit to the WC, a quick shave and a long shower, I headed out onto the scalding streets of downtown Havana in search of breakfast. Three minutes later, I found myself all but submerged in sweat. Dehydrated and on the verge of passing out, I ducked into the first likely looking place I could find, an indoor-outdoor café on "L" Street.

Some people say it is impossible to ruin breakfast. I say, you haven't been to Havana. The menu was thin. I settled for scrambled eggs, toast and fruit. What I received was a single undercooked egg, a tiny slice of charred bread and a wee chunk of petrified papaya. The sum total of my meal took up so little space in my stomach I was forced to follow the debacle with a tuna fish sandwich.

"Excuse me," I asked the waiter, "is Cuba by any chance experiencing a mayonnaise shortage?" The sandwich was so lacking in moisture it was like eating a dry sponge.

"Mayonnaise?" he repeated in a stunned voice.

While I was "eating", two women took seats at a neighboring table. They weren't exceedingly attractive, but they were young and had a pleasant air about them. When I realized that they were smiling and looking my way on a fairly regular basis, I smiled back. An instant later, as if they'd been teleported by a Sci-fi pimp, they were sitting beside me.

This, I decided, was not such a bad thing. I needed to practice my technique for acquiring a fornication partner, and these two, who did not appeal to me in any great way, would make perfect test-subjects. I bought us all a round of the thick highly potent Cuban coffee. Of the two, Hilda possessed the more provocative personality, and I found myself directing most of my attention at her. The other girl quickly slipped, smiling slyly, from the restaurant.

"Are you staying in a hotel?" Hilda asked, the moment her friend had departed.

"No, I've rented a room in a private house."

"Is it nearby?"

"Four or five blocks."

"Let's go there right now," she suggested. "I want to have sex with you," she added by way of clarification.

"Not so fast," I said. "First, I'd like to get to know you."

"You can get to know me all you want in your room. Let's go."

Were all Cuban girls so direct? It was a little disconcerting.

"Let me be frank," I said. "I have, in fact, come to Cuba to find a chica. But it can't be just any chica. It has to be someone special."

"I'm special," Hilda said.

"Yes, Hilda, I'm certain you are. So tell me, what do you like to do?"

"Whatever you want. Let's go."

"For money, of course."

"That depends."

"On what?"

"On you. If you like me, you can give me something. It's up to you."

"You mean, you're willing to have sex with me on spec?"

"I'm just willing. Period."

"All right. I see. So—don't take this personally, but have you had any venereal diseases lately?"

"I'm a clean girl," Hilda declared with pride. "I get checked once a month."

"Do they give you written results?"

"Yeah, they come in an envelope."

"And would you happen to have them on you?"

"On me? What are you asking?"

"I'm asking if you happen to have your latest test results on your person?"

"No, I don't have them on me. *Que pasa?* Don't you like me?"

I began to explain, albeit awkwardly, that I was not going to jump into bed with the first chica that came along, and that I really did want to get to know the person first, that I had certain requirements, certain standards, etc., etc.

Halfway through this lame discourse, Hilda got up and left the restaurant. "Idiota!" she said on her way out.

I turned around and saw that the cook and the waiter were both staring at me with disapproval. More than likely I had violated some unspoken rule of Sex-Tourism etiquette. But at the moment I was too hungry to care. "Tell me," I asked the waiter, "how many eggs are there in a 'jumbo' omelet?"

ELEVEN

Leaving the restaurant I was accosted at once by a thin young man who asked me for the time. Not wanting to appear rude, I stopped and consulted my watch.

"A little after eleven," I said.

"Where are you from?" he asked.

"Canada." I still couldn't bring myself to admit that I was an American.

"Is this your first time in Havana?"

"Yes. I have to go now. Goodbye."

"I just lost my job at the cigar factory," he said, walking beside me.

"Sorry to hear that."

"I don't know how I'm going to feed my children."

"Surely, the government here provides for the less fortunate."

"The Beard?" He spat the word from his mouth as if it were a dead fly. "He provides for himself, and his friends."

"Are you talking about Castro?"

"Yes, I'm talking about that bastard," he said bitterly. "A lot of people will be happy when he finally drops dead. Maybe then, things will get better. Please, can't you help me out? A couple of dollars..."

We were approaching a busy corner where two well-fed policemen stood, looking surly and self-important. One of them turned our way and frowned. The panhandler vanished.

As I continued to walk in the general direction of *Havana Vieja* (Pedro, in Section 3.6, had recommended that area as a "...happy hunting ground for daytime pussy"), I was accosted again and again by emaciated young men wondering what time it was. What they really wanted, of course, was to find me a chica, or sell me cigars, or "borrow" some money, in that order. I made a brave attempt, for about fifteen minutes, at being civil to these fellows, but eventually I was forced to stow my watch. Then I had to stop making eye contact altogether, walking along with a brisk purposeful step, looking straight ahead, creating about myself a defensive bubble.

I might as well have been back in Manhattan.

In *Plaza de Armas*, a small square in Old Havana surrounded by decrepit colonial buildings clinging by their grimy fingernails to the last remnants of their former charm, I took a seat and in no time at all was well into my second "job interview" of the day. The latest prospect, Alicia, was appetizingly pretty. She was also safely over the legal limit—twenty-two, at least.

The small park, in stark contrast to the surrounding streets, was cheerful, filled with flowers and well-maintained. All of the iron benches, upon one of which I sat with the alluring Alicia close beside me, were freshly painted. *Plaza de Armas* was, I later learned, an Official Tourist Location.

"So tell me," I said, "how is life in Cuba?"

"Bad and getting worse," she said, regarding warily a pair of policemen loitering nearby.

"Are you afraid of the police?"

"Everybody is afraid of the police. If they come this way, hold my hand. You're my boyfriend and we're going to have lunch down the street."

"Okay," I said nervously.

"You have nothing to worry about," Alicia assured me. "They leave tourists alone. Unless you do something really stupid."

"Like go with an underage girl?"

"Yes, that would do it. By the way," she added, looking frankly into my eyes, "would you like to be my boyfriend?"

For a Cuban, Alicia was fairly coy, and I was beginning to warm to her in a serious way. But I wanted a little more background before making a commitment.

"Maybe. Tell me, Alicia, what do you ordinarily do with your time—when you're not, ah, sitting in the park?"

"I'm a school teacher."

"Really? A full-time teacher?"

"A real full-time teacher," she replied with an ironic smile. "Today's Sunday."

"That's right," I said, deeply embarrassed. "I'd forgotten—being on vacation and all. It's not that I didn't believe…"

"*Esta bien*," Alicia said wearily. "Cuba is a crazy country, run by an old lunatic. Nothing makes much sense here."

The interview, as far as I was concerned, was over. Alicia met all the essential requirements, and I was about to tell her so when she sneezed. And sniffled. And sneezed again. "Allergies?" I asked hopefully.

"No, a cold," she said, sniffling some more. "I'm always getting colds."

My mental image of prostitutes had been taken almost entirely from the movies. They stood on nighttime street corners wearing short red skirts and tall white plastic boots. They were all heroin addicts (even the "heart of gold" types), and most of them had AIDS. Among my specifications for an extra-marital sex-partner, good health stood head and ovaries above the rest. Alicia's confessed lack of resistance to viruses placed her, ipso facto, on the damaged goods shelf, and out of contention.

Of course, I was not being entirely fair. As Pedro had explained in Section (3.8), and I was beginning to discover myself from personal experience, many of the readily available young women in Havana were not prostitutes in the true sense of the word. Yes, they were expecting, or hoping, for money in exchange for sex, but it was not for them a true career. Exactly what it was, I could not say, but there seemed to be a certain "innocence" (if I can use that word in this context) involved in these transactions. Nonetheless…

"Certainly, I see you as a potential girlfriend," I said, ill at ease. "But I need to think it over."

"It's my age, isn't it? I'm too old."

"No, no, that's not it at all."

"Yes, it is," she sighed. "I don't blame you. I'm almost twenty-four. How can I possibly compete?"

That was a question for which I had no suitable answer, so I excused myself, got up, and walked away.

TWELVE

Somewhat discouraged by the morning's events, I wandered aimlessly up and down the narrow streets of Old Havana. The streets were lined on either side by narrow crumbling buildings which looked as if at any moment they were going to collapse from sheer exhaustion. The people I passed, none of whom actually appeared to be doing anything, blended seamlessly with their surroundings. They, too, were tall and thin, shabbily dressed and seemingly on the verge of falling over.

I walked on, lacquered in sweat, growing more dispirited with every step, certain that I was about to dissolve into some decaying morass of my own. This is Hell, I thought. What in God's name am I doing here? Then, all at once, I was saved, raised up by the other side of the Cuban coin, the sounds of lively music booming from a corner bar.

Los Viejos Tiempos (The Good Old Days) consisted of one long, high-ceilinged dilapidated room with four large glassless windows. Despite the early hour, it had a decent crowd going, mostly locals. The band, a motley quintet, was playing an up-tempo *son* with an enthusiasm which knew no bounds.

I went inside, took possession of a small round table and ordered a mojito—promising myself the next moment that as soon as I'd "settled in", I would return to my customary state of near-total sobriety. When I ordered my second mojito fifteen minutes later, the waiter, an actual midget named Mario, introduced himself and asked me my name and where I was from. Apparently, no one in Havana could make it through the day without knowing my country of origin.

"Nice to meet you, Mario," I said, extending my hand. "My name is Carlos, and I'm from Canada."

"You're spending a lot of money for a Canadian," Mario said, eying me with suspicion.

"What do you mean?"

"We get plenty of *Canadienses* here, mostly in the winter," the midget explained. "And when they order their mojitos, they always ask for the cheapest rum. You asked for the ten year-old *Añejo*—twice!"

"It tastes better," I said defensively.

Mario the midget flashed a set of bizarrely configured teeth. "And costs five times as much. Are you sure you're Canadian?"

What the hell, I thought, I might as well get this over with. "Actually," I confessed, "I'm American."

"I knew it! I knew it! Let me tell you something, Carlos—that's your real name, right? You don't have to be ashamed of being American. We like Americans. You're way better than Spanish tourists. Or Canadians, or French. Or anybody else."

"*Por que?*"

"You spend money," the uncomplicated little man replied. "Lots of it."

"Oh yes, I suppose we do."

Mario, who I would come to know quite well over the following days, shuffled on his genetically abbreviated legs up to the bar and reported (my "dual" nationality, I suppose) to the bartender, who in turn informed the manager. Now everyone, except the band, knew that I was an American masquerading as a Canadian. I forced myself to take slow sips of my second drink. These minty mojitos were quite delicious, not to mention, refreshing, especially on a hot day. I began to tap my feet in time to the music, my foul mood forgotten.

An hour later Perla entered, stage-left.

She was young (what else was new), light complected by Cuban standards and exceptionally pretty. She was also fresh, clean and glowing with good health. In fact, with her long, straight honey-colored hair and tall slim figure, she could have been a corn-fed co-ed from California.

It did not escape me that on her way across the room she'd favored me with an enticingly timid smile—enticing, because it spoke, to me at least, of a desirable lack of experience.

On the taxi ride back to my room I asked her, for the second or third time, how old she was.

"I already told you. Nineteen. Am I too old for you?" she asked fearfully.

"No, no, not at all. You're, ah...just right."

The driver turned to give me a knowing look. All three of us were sitting in the front seat of what did not in any way resemble a taxi. Perla had flagged the vehicle down outside the bar, assuring me that this was, though technically illegal, a perfectly acceptable thing to do.

"Beautiful car," I told the driver. "What year is it?"

"Nineteen fifty-three," he said proudly.

"My God! How do you keep it running? Where do you get the parts?"

"We make them," the driver said. "When you live in a country as fucked-up as Cuba, you have to be resourceful. So, where are you from?" he asked inevitably. "You don't look Puerto Rican."

As we walked, hand-in-hand like a couple of sweethearts, down the narrow alley beside the house, a louvered window swung open and out popped Eustacia's roller-topped head.

"Buenas tardes," she screeched politely.

"Buenas tardes," I replied.

"I see you have a nice little friend. Dear," she said to Perla, "can I see your ID card, please?"

To my enormous relief, Eustacia, after examining the ID at extremely close range, nodded her head with approval and handed it back. "She looks like a nice clean chica," Eustacia said uncertainly.

"Yes," I said, blushing for all I was worth, "ah...yes."

While Perla demurely removed all of her outer clothing, something akin to a jackhammer began to smash away at the interior of my chest. My episode in the Volvo had been nothing compared to this. I could feel, or imagined I could, my blood alternately boiling and freezing in my veins. The two mojitos I'd consumed earlier were, in all likelihood, all that was keeping me alive.

Men with more experience than myself in the sexual arena may have difficulty comprehending the seemingly exaggerated nature of my response to what was after all merely the sight of a beautiful young woman removing her clothes. Perhaps I had best reiterate (for the last time, I promise), that what I was about to do was without precedent in my life. I might as well have been a virgin. As for the "sex" I'd had with my wife, well…that didn't seem to count.

Perla sat on the bed, dressed in only her bra. "Can I leave my bra on, for now?" she asked timidly.

Bereft of speech, I nodded my head. When I sat beside her, Perla put her hand on my thigh and kissed me on the mouth. "I've only done this a few times," she confessed.

"Es-es-esta b-b-bien," I stuttered like my nephew.

For the next ten minutes we engaged in foreplay. While Perla did her best to feign a passion she obviously did not feel, I went completely out of my mind. Then it was time to consummate. Fully vulcanized and hyperventilating like a lunatic, I knelt between those long cheerleader's legs, those twin intersecting landing strips, and prepared to penetrate. I was, in fact, only centimeters away from crossing the final frontier when something unforeseen occurred: Perla shook her head to flick aside some strands of hair which had fallen over her eye.

So? She shook her head? So what? So, she shook her head exactly the way my daughter did, every fifteen minutes, to flick her long honey-colored hair out of her face. And that was all it took: my heroic erection retracted turtle-like back into its shell, and nothing we said or did during the ensuing sixty minutes would coax the little bastard back out.

Perla was in tears. "I'm too old for you," she moaned.

"Too old? Christ no, Perla! It's just that, I, ah, I must have had too much to drink."

We got dressed and Perla's angst was assuaged somewhat when I handed over her allowance—I mean, her fee—twenty dollars.

"We can try again, another time?" she suggested hopefully.

'Yes, of course," I lied. "We'll try again."

Before she left, she kissed me on the cheek, like Brenda did when I let her borrow the Volvo.

THIRTEEN

By now, I thought glumly, I've probably qualified for the Guinness Book of Records, in the "Most Consecutive Hours In Havana Without Having Sex" category: Twenty-four.

Was there a fine? Or would I be declared persona non grata by the Minister of Tourism? I knew that my late father, a high school chemistry teacher and a great believer in "finishing what you started", would have been bitterly disappointed.

"An 'Incomplete' in Adultery, Karl? You think Harvard will take you with grades like that?"

And my equally late British-born mum, a biology teacher whose pedagogic style was so dry she had once set a record of her own by putting to sleep an entire class of hyper adolescents at nine o'clock in the morning, would have been reduced to droning at me one of her favorite aphorisms: "If at first you don't succeed, Karl, try, try again."

Several hours of unfairly blaming my dead parents (nice folks, for the most part, who did their best to instill in me an unquenchable thirst for mediocrity)—several hours of blaming them for everything I could think of made me even more miserable. I know, I thought with sly masochism, I'll go out and get "something to eat".

Miraculously, at a tiny eatery just around the corner from my room (which for reasons unexplained only opened on odd-numbered days), I was served an entire chicken breast, submerged in a viscous red sauce which tasted not unlike cherry cough syrup. This nearly edible meal succeeded in raising my blood/sugar level to unprecedented heights, but not my spirits. So I shuffled over to the bar of the Hotel Nacional where I consumed my third delicious and refreshing mojito of the day. That didn't help, either.

After refusing the bartender's offer of a chica, ("clean, young and willing") and a box of Montecristos ("smooth, aromatic and recently removed from an official government factory"), I got up and left. It was night outside, but still steaming like an outdoor sauna. Every ten feet someone tried to sell me something: cigars, souvenirs, their cousins, themselves. Sick of the whole sordid circus, I turned down a series of dark side streets, avoiding human contact, thinking my bleak thoughts and struggling to excise from my mind the image of Brenda flicking the hair from her eye, superimposed over Perla's world-class bra-clad body.

I asked myself, as Candace used to when she was eleven, "Dad, are we having fun yet?"

Turning another dark corner, I realized I'd been heading downhill all this time and had wound up at the water. The ocean was "angry", as the locals liked to say. Large swells crashed against the rocks, spraying the boardwalk, which extended endlessly in either direction, disappearing into the melancholy gloom. It was, in fact, unnaturally dark on the *malecon*. Functioning street lights were few and far between, and the sparse vehicular traffic only served to cast the occasional oddly directed shadow, lending the entire scene a sinister spectral air.

I walked across the wide boulevard and stepped up onto the boardwalk, unmindful of the salt spray. With my back to the water I stared across the street at the row of narrow ghostlike apartment buildings, most with unlit windows, going to rack and ruin, missing not only paint, but chunks of mortar, shutters and even the occasional window frame.

This must have been prime real estate in Batista's day, I thought. Now the few patches of pastel color left here and there on the faded facades made the long row of small buildings look like a line of old tattered dresses disintegrating in the wind and the salt spray. The people who occupied these dreary dwellings, who one could glimpse passing to and fro before the windows, had a faded spectral look about them, too: the ghosts of Revolutions past.

This was waterfront Havana. A vacation paradise? Or, Night of the Living Dead?

On my way home I was seized by the urge to punish myself once again with another meal. Veering back onto the main street, *calle San Lazaro*, I found a restaurant falsely advertising "Italian Food". The pizza was appalling. Apparently cheese was hard to come by, as were tomatoes, or anything else resembling a vegetable. But I was hungry, so I ate most of it anyway. Then I paid the bill and began to shuffle home.

In front of the *Havana Libre* a woman who was just about ready for the euthanasia tanks (she must have been nearly twenty-five), stepped boldly into my path and said hello. Needless to say, she was beautiful—never have I even heard of a place with so many attractive women. Her manner was brisk, and her dress flamboyant. Clearly, she was a professional, a bona-fide full-time hooker.

I looked her up and down. Why not, I thought. Standing on the malecon I'd been feeling nearly suicidal. Who cared about verisimilitude? Who cared about disease?

"How much?" I asked.

"Twenty dollars," she said. "Only because I really need the money. I usually charge thirty."

I took her hand in mine and we began to walk. "I have a room nearby," I said.

"How many times have you been to Cuba?" she asked.

"This is my first time."

"Really? And how long have you been here?"

"Thirty hours."

She seemed surprised. "You know the routine pretty well for someone who's only been here one day."

"I have an instruction manual."

We walked past a pair of policemen, and she did not give them a second glance.

"You're not afraid of la *policia*?"

"No, I'm a registered prostitute, perfectly legal," she said with professional pride. "Most of these girls are amateurs.

With them, you don't know what you're getting. I have to be checked at a government clinic twice a month, so you know you're safe with me."

How comforting: AAA Government Inspected Beef. But feeling safe was not what concerned me at that particular moment. What I was thinking was that this woman, with her black skin and her air of professional self-assurance, was in many ways the opposite of Perla, and so, hopefully, would not remind me at the critical moment of my daughter.

And, as fate would have it, she did not.

But when she walked out my door, twenty dollars to the good, all I felt was an enormous disappointment. We had indeed consummated; at least I had got that over with. But her "lovemaking" (what a word!) had been so perfunctory, her manner so cool and efficient, I felt as if I'd been going through the motions with a robot.

For twenty dollars less, I thought, I could have stayed home and had sex with my wife.

FOURTEEN

There she was, at eight o'clock sharp on a parboiled Monday morning, wearing the same ancient housecoat and holding my tray of juice and coffee. I took the tray, and she took a seat at the card table.

"Well, haven't we been the busy bee," she remarked.

Cringing with embarrassment, I nonetheless found the courage to ask, "This is what you meant by total privacy?"

"My doctor's coming over this afternoon," Eustacia croaked. "Will you be home? She is very anxious to meet you."

"Oh, what rotten luck. I have an appointment this afternoon."

"All right," Eustacia sighed with fatigue, "I'll tell her to come tomorrow. Have you noticed any mosquitoes in your room?"

"What? No. Why?"

"The government is running a fumigation campaign against the dengue mosquito," she said matter-of-factly. "We have to tell them which rooms require extra spraying."

"Mine," I volunteered at once. "Mine requires extra spraying."

"But you just said you haven't seen any mosquitoes."

"So far. That doesn't mean the room is not infested. From a breeding standpoint, the environment here is ideal: damp, warm…"

"Warm? Is something wrong with the air conditioner?"

"Well, it wheezes quite a bit. I suspect emphysema. Or it could just be dying of old age."

"Typical of those Russian traitors," Eustacia snarled. "Those cowardly two-faced swine abandoned us in our greatest hour of need." (She was, I later learned, quoting the official Party line.) "Even the Americans are like angels, compared to those filthy, unreliable Russian pigs. I mean," she rushed to add, "I like Americans. I like them very much."

"That's broad minded of you," I said, sipping my coffee.

"The first girl seemed nice," my landlady said, changing gears once again.

"Too nice," I muttered.

"What? What did you say?"

"Yes, extremely nice."

"Well," Eustacia said judiciously, "I'm not sure I'd go quite that far. Now, my doctor, one could say that she is extremely nice. One day some lucky man…"

My landlady, once I was able to get her off the subject of la doctora Eva's extraordinary qualities (both professional and gender-specific), deigned to provide me with the name and location of a restaurant which might be capable of producing a breakfast marginally better than the one I had consumed the day before. It was off-limits to Cubans, she explained bizarrely, and therefore had to maintain higher standards.

Naturally, the superior restaurant was closed, or out of business—in Havana it was often difficult to tell the difference. As I stood on the sidewalk muttering beneath my breath, a 1956 Chevrolet Bel Air (in immaculate condition) pulled to the curb. The driver leaned his head out the window and asked me if I was looking for something.

"A decent breakfast," I replied.

"Get in. I'll take you somewhere. It's not too far, but it's hard to find. Cost you a dollar."

For a dollar, I thought, what do I have to lose?

What I had to lose, it would turn out, was the rest of my life. Or rather, the rest of my life as I had imagined it.

"Where I'm taking you," the driver told me, "is nothing great, but it's the best you're going to do."

"I don't mean to be critical," I said, "but I can't believe how bad the food is here."

"You came to Cuba for the food?"

"Well, no, not exactly."

"I didn't think so. Cuba produces three export-worthy products: cigars, rum and sex, none of which most Cubans can afford. When I die, you know what I want to come back as?"

"What?"

"A tourist in Havana."

When the driver finally dropped me off, it was in front of the same small café where I'd eaten breakfast the previous morning. Resigned by now to the fact that opting to take this trip had probably been a huge mistake, I paid him off and went inside.

"Hey, look who's here," the waiter said, "the world's hungriest man!"

"Buenos dias," I mumbled.

"I'll get you a menu right away," he said eagerly. Now that he knew I was an endangered species (the Blond-Crested Tipping Canadian), he couldn't do enough for me.

"No need," I replied, "I memorized it yesterday. I'll have a jumbo omelet with ham, a ham sandwich, a side-order of ham, and two coffees."

Halfway through the second coffee I looked up and there, déjà-vu all over again, were two young women. One was cute and petit. The other looked like a prize fighter. The pretty one was not what you would call ravishingly beautiful, but there was something about her...

Her companion, the light heavyweight, was gone so fast I never saw her leave. I sipped my coffee, biding my time.

"Hi, my name is Mariela," she said in a throaty voice.

"Buenos dias," I replied. "How old are you?"

How old are you? What was wrong with me? My second day in Cuba and I was already halfway to the Heart of Darkness. I felt like a savage, a brute—no, worse than that: I felt like a German tourist.

On the other hand, she did look frightfully young.

"I'm nineteen," she said. "How old are you?"

"Forty-two," I lied. "You look young for your age."

"So do you," she said, favoring me with an ironic smile.

And then, for whatever reason, I could think of absolutely

nothing to say. A long silence ensued. I grew intensely nervous, but in a strangely enjoyable way. It occurred to me that I had never felt quite like this before. The cause of this unprecedented feeling, this anxious exhilaration, if you will, remained a mystery to me for quite some time. Only now has it become clear: At its deepest, most reptilian level, my mind had divined the fact that, sexually speaking, Mariela was going to be my Perfect Storm.

"So, do you want to go with me?" she asked serenely, as if it were all one to her whether I did or not.

"I don't know," I said truthfully.

Mariela laughed. "You don't know?"

"Well, I want to," I said nervously, "but…"

"Come on," she said, taking possession of my hand, as if I were an uncooperative baby brother. "Let's go."

Obediently, I stood up, threw some money on the table and allowed her to lead me from the restaurant. The waiter and the cook nodded their heads in approval—at my discriminating taste? Or because, especially for a Canadian, I was so good for the economy?

We did not speak on the walk up the hill. It occurred to me that she might be nervous as well. She was awfully young, and though she did seem remarkably self-assured, that might have been an act; certainly there was nothing of the practiced professional in her manner.

Eustacia, normally so congenial, actually scowled at us from her perch astride the windowsill. Peering dubiously down at Mariela, she said, "You're eighteen?"

Mariela handed over her ID card. "Nineteen, señora," she replied politely.

Eustacia handed it back and turned to me. "Is this your appointment?"

"Ah, no, that isn't till later. In the afternoon."

"In the afternoon," Eustacia repeated, shaking her head.

Once inside the room, Mariela undressed—not timidly like Perla, nor briskly like the pro. And not brazenly or seductively, either, like some unaccomplished actress.

Mariela undressed neatly and naturally, like she was getting ready to go to sleep or take a shower. From time to time, as she carefully folded an article of clothing and lay it over the back of a chair, she looked up and favored me with her ironic little Mona Lisa smile. Whether she was amused, curious or anxious, I couldn't tell. Perhaps she was all three.

My feelings at that moment were somewhat less complex, consisting as they did in equal parts of lust and terror. I do not remember actually removing my clothing or laying down beside her on the bed. My next clear recollection is of Mariela saying, "Why are you so nervous? You're shaking like a wet dog."

"I don't know," I replied, kissing her passionately on the mouth.

"Well, calm down," she commanded, "you're making me nervous, too."

"I'll try," I said weakly.

Our first bout of love-making was hurried and awkward, but satisfactory. Satisfactory? Never in my entire life had I been so excited, so supernaturally tumescent. I could have hit a home run with the bloody thing.

When it was over, Mariela asked if she could take a shower. Ten minutes later she emerged from the bathroom, clean, fresh and smoking a cigarette. She began to get dressed.

"No, wait!" I practically screamed.

Mariela carefully replaced her bra on the back of the chair. Then, with her small hands on her narrow hips, she stood staring at me, and I, sitting naked on the bed, stared back.

Mariela was a mulatta, her flawless skin a marvelous shade of copper, her features halfway between African and Latina. Otherwise, she was pure sprite: five foot two, skinny, perfectly proportioned, with small breasts and a lovely rounded little buttocks. Her hair hung in long black braids. Her lips were swollen and pouty. And her eyes, an alluring pale brown, were full of mischief.

We will not consider, at this time, what I may have looked like to her.

Mariela's lips turned up in that enigmatic half-smile. "You want to do it again?" she asked with a laugh, looking unashamedly at my quivering *membrum virile*. I nodded my head. She nodded back, apparently pleased.

"Okay, but you take a shower, too. I'll have another cigarette."

No doubt, I looked particularly ridiculous, as for a second and then a third time I writhed and undulated with a girl less than half my age, and only marginally more than half my size. On the third go-round, Mariela asked me to do her a "special favor", as a result of which she experienced an orgasm. Or so she claimed. In any case, she appeared to be enjoying herself and to me that meant a great deal.

"I have to go," she announced finally, after her third shower. "I'm late for class."

"You go to school?"

"I'm studying to be a veterinarian," she said, slipping on her skirt. "You want to see me again?"

"What do you think?"

"Okay," Mariela said. "Maybe tomorrow."

Maybe? Maybe was not acceptable. "Do you have a phone?" I asked.

"No, but our neighbor does." She gave me the neighbor's number, and I gave her mine. She was totally dressed now, and on her way out the door.

"What about, um, some money?" I asked, ill at ease.

"Sure, why not," she said.

I handed her twenty dollars—the going rate as far as I could tell. She thanked me politely and lit another cigarette. Then, glancing at my crotch, she shook her head, and left.

FIFTEEN

Sometime later, as I lay napping contentedly in the tepid embrace of the asthmatic Russian air conditioner, I was awakened by the sound of the telephone. I picked up the receiver and was plunged at once into an auditory maelstrom, in the midst of which an unrecognizable human voice seemed to be drowning in the background.

"Are you busy?" the voice asked.

"Who is this?"

"Good, I'll be right there. I need to talk to you before the doctor arrives."

"The doctor?"

"She's busy tomorrow, so she's coming today."

"But…"

I just had time to throw on an un-zippered pair of shorts before my landlady lurched into the room, carrying a pitcher of water.

"Sit down," she said. The room possessed little in the way of furniture: the bed, a small card table and two wooden chairs. She sat in one chair, and I, still fumbling with my fly, slid wearily into the other.

"You look all dried out," Eustacia observed.

"Yes, well…"

"Drink some water. In this climate, any strenuous activity is liable to leave a man your age dangerously dehydrated."

"Ah, yes," I concurred. "Four liters of water a day is currently considered the absolute minimum liquid intake for adults living in…"

"Si, si, si," she cut in impatiently. "Now. And don't take this personally. You seem like a decent person. Quite cultured. Supposedly, a man of medicine—a noble profession, in my opinion. And speaking of my opinion, having two girlfriends is perfectly acceptable. I have no objection to that." She paused politely, so that I could interject something, if I so desired.

Although I could not have felt more uncomfortable, I was, paradoxically, exceedingly sleepy, as if I'd taken a sedative.

"Yes, señora?" I said, yawning nervously.

"I understand," the landlady continued sympathetically, "that men come here to meet chicas, and have a good time, and that is perfectly healthy. I look upon it as a cultural exchange."

"I see…" Fatigue was winning the day. My eyelids began to flutter.

"But three!" Eustacia said sharply, jarring me awake. "Three chicas in twenty-four hours! That is too much. That is bordering on…on…prostitution!"

More than likely the word she'd been searching for, but couldn't bring herself to say, was "depravity".

"Yes, I agree," I said feebly. Agree? How could I agree with a statement which made no sense? Wasn't paying one girl to have sex prostitution as well? Why did it require three transactions before it became a matter of professional services rendered?

At the same time, I was a little ashamed of myself, and felt a strong compulsion to justify my seemingly out-of-control behavior:

The first time did not count, your Honor, because at the critical moment I suffered a crise erectus, and so failed to consummate. And on the second occasion, although from a purely technical standpoint coitus did indeed occur, the entire process was so hurried and so devoid of passion, it might as well not have happened at all. As I have stated previously, your Honor, the principle difference between having sex with the hooker and having sex with my wife is that in the first instance the total cost came to twenty dollars, while in the latter case…well, I'd have to consult my accountant to give you a definitive answer, but…

"All I ask for," Eustacia said, interrupting this dopey interior monologue, "is a little self-restraint."

"You have my word," I yawned solemnly. "From this moment forward I will put severe limits on myself."

Eustacia gave me a long speculative look. "Good. I'm glad we understand each other."

"One good chica is plenty for me," I said, thinking of Mariela.

"One or two," my landlady said authoritatively. "The doctor will be here in half an hour, so if you want to try to make yourself presentable, you still have time."

It being a special occasion I was invited into the main part of the house, into the tiny parlor where three uncomfortable chairs were crowded around a coffee table. La doctora Eva stood up to shake my hand. A dark statuesque mulatta, she was in her mid to late twenties, had startling green eyes and was easily the most beautiful woman I had ever seen.

This is almost frightening, I thought sleepily, like a horror movie, but in reverse.

Exquisite she may have been, but la doctora Eva was far too cool and professional for my liking. It seemed improbable, for example, that she was in the habit of having sex for money with foreigners in her spare time. Though on this sweltering madcap island anything was possible.

"Do you have a specialty?" I asked, to be polite.

If she had answered "Fellatio", I would have been surprised, but not shocked. "No, I am a family practitioner," she replied. "And I understand you are an orthopedic surgeon?"

"Yes."

"And do you have a particular specialty within your field?" she inquired crisply. No, I concluded, she was definitely not a hooker on the side. What she was, I would learn, was a rather fine human being.

"The knee," I replied.

Eustacia pounced. "The *knee* is your specialty? Why didn't you say so?"

"What a fortunate coincidence," la doctora said. "I have been treating doña Eustacia's knee, but without much success. Honestly, I have had very little experience with degenerative joints. Most of my patients are children. Perhaps you could examine her. I'm sure I would find your observations instructive."

Yes, she's tall, I told myself, and gorgeous like an Egyptian goddess. But compared to Mariela, she's a walking block of ice.

"Of course," I yawned, "let's have a look."

Eva did the honors, unwrapping the wide bandage from my landlady's knee which, once exposed, showed itself to be swollen like a cantaloupe. Prodding it gently here and there, I asked a few questions, tested for range of motion, etc., and wondered aloud if there was an x-ray lying about someplace.

La doctora said she had several x-rays at the clinic, which was only a few blocks away. She offered to go and retrieve them.

"That would be helpful," I said. "And perhaps you could bring back something I could use to drain the liquid? And some cortisone, and a syringe?"

"Cortisone is very difficult to come by here," la doctora said.

This was my first glimpse into the great dichotomy in Cuban medicine: of qualified doctors, there was an endless supply; what was lacking were the various medications, many of them standard, those skilled physicians required to treat their patients.

"There is no cortisone available at all?"

"Well, there is," she admitted, "but it is excessively expensive."

"How expensive?"

"Fifty dollars a dose."

It would have taken Eva two months to earn fifty dollars. It took me about two minutes. I removed a hundred dollar bill from my wallet and told her to buy two doses, just in case. As she took the money and made to depart, it occurred to me that, motives aside, once again I was placing cash in the hands of a beautiful young woman.

While we waited for Eva to return, I asked Eustacia a few more questions about her knee. Then I fell asleep.

The x-rays were of passable quality and showed a severe deterioration of the joint. Bone on bone. With Eva looking keenly on, I drained the liquid from Eustacia's knee. Then, still too drowsy to drive a car, I located the "hot spot", and injected the cortisone in four tightly clustered locations, provoking from Eustacia an equal number of grunts—rather stoic on her part; the pain accompanying these injections, though of short duration, is intense.

Eustacia's final grunt was followed by a tension filled sixty seconds of silence. And then. "It feels better already!"

"What you need," I told her, "is a full replacement. After that, you'll be as good as slightly used."

This line never failed to raise a laugh from my anxious patients, and it did not let me down now. Once the three of us had gotten over our little chuckle, la doctora looked at me admiringly and said, "I'm impressed."

I have to get out of here, I thought with sudden desperation, before I cross some critical line, beyond which there is only chaos.

"Um, well, yes," I said stupidly.

"Would you be willing to perform the procedure?" Eva asked, "if I can arrange the facilities?"

"Well, I don't know. I mean, I'm on vacation after all, aren't I?"

"So what?" Eustacia said.

"I understand," Eva said. "I am sure you work very hard."

"You have no idea," I yawned. "Excuse me, I have to go lie down."

"Are you all right?"

"He's fine," Eustacia said, rising to my defense. "He's got this jet-lag they're always talking about."

That makes perfect sense, I thought, taking into account the fact that between New York City and Havana there is no time difference whatsoever.

The question of the surgery was left hanging. "You know, I'm in this country illegally," I told la doctora, as I rose and headed back to bed.

"Yes, but you are legal as far as our government is concerned. And I doubt if there is a single surgeon in Cuba who could perform this procedure as well as you. I know, because I looked you up on the Google."

The hospital web site! Why hadn't I thought of that? Pedro was going to murder me. Section (5.4) could not have been more explicit: "Be like the secret agent man. Don't give nobody your real name. You never know when it's gonna come back and bite you in the ass!"

No, I was forced to conclude as my head hit the pillow, becoming embroiled in a surgery in a country I was visiting illegally (as far as my country was concerned) did not seem like a very good idea. Then I passed out. It was three pm. Just like a real jet-lagged tourist, I was done for the day.

SIXTEEN

The woman who owned the small eatery around the corner where they served my favorite Cuban dish (rice and beans) and the almost edible but not easily identifiable parts of a chicken, greeted me effusively upon the occasion of my second visit.

"What's good today?" I asked.

"I am," she replied. Yarelis was a robust warm-hearted soul in her late thirties whose daring repartee was surpassed only by the depth of her Grand Canyon cleavage.

"Oh, I have no doubt," I said. "But I had my heart set on something with wings."

"You mean," she said, brushing her hip against my shoulder, "an angel, like me?"

"Angels are supposed to be innocent," I said, "and you appear to be anything but."

"How right you are. Today's special is chicken."

"Is it really chicken?" I asked hopefully.

"You said you wanted something with wings. The last time I looked, the poor thing had two of them."

"So does a buzzard."

"Please!"

"All right. I'll accept, for the sake of argument, that it was at one time a living chicken. How was it prepared?"

"It died," she replied evasively, "of natural causes."

Later, as I was attempting, half-heartedly, to chew my "chicken breast", Yarelis came over and sat down at my table. "You don't seem very hungry," she remarked. "Are we in love?"

"Hardly," I said, stabbing idly at the rubbery chunk of flesh.

"But you have a girlfriend?"

"Well, not really. I've only been with her once."

It was remarkable how frankly one could speak to a Cuban woman. They seemed, with the exception of la doctora, to have no inhibitions whatsoever.

"Is she very young?" Yarelis asked slyly.

"Well...yes."

"No wonder you have no appetite. Young girls are exciting, but they are not good for a man's health. Especially a man your age. What you need is a mature woman who will arouse you up to a reasonable point. Someone who is healthy for you. A woman who can take care of all your needs."

"I already have one of those."

"And the fire's gone out?"

"Ashes to ashes," I said, swallowing with difficulty.

I ate what I could, mostly the *cristianos y moros* (rice and beans) which accompanied the enigmatic protein. Then I sat sipping on a coke, casting anxious glances at my watch. Mariela had promised to meet me here, and she was already an hour late.

I'd spent most of the previous day painfully immersed in the Cuban telephone system, yet another decaying relic from the days of Russian aid, trying to reach Mariela. The first forty times I dialed the neighbor's number, it failed to ring altogether. Instead, my ear was assaulted by a hideous noise which sounded like an opera singer being tortured underwater. Perhaps, I thought, the lines have crossed and I'm reaching the police station.

When finally someone did answer, the woman (I think it was a woman) spoke with an accent so garbled, slurred and mangled she was impossible to understand. Cubans, I should point out, are notorious for butchering their mother tongue. Many Cubans have difficulty understanding even each other.

"Can I speak to your neighbor, Mariela?" I shouted into the mouthpiece for the third time.

"Marba caba, dona ticumahcuh?" she replied. Or something to that effect.

"I'm sorry," I yelled, "I can't understand you. Is Mariela there?"

"Maruh?"

Praying that she had just said, "Mariela", I said, "Yes!"

Ten minutes of noisy silence ensued, as I held the receiver glued to my ear, listening to what sounded like a space ship landing at a busy airport. Finally, a voice which might have been Mariela's, said, "Halo?"

"Mariela?" With my left hand I turned off the rumbling air conditioner.

"Yes?" her throaty voice said over the noisy line.

"It's me, Carlos."

"Oh, I was wondering when you would call."

"I've been trying to reach you all day."

"What?"

"I've been calling all day!" I shouted.

"What?"

"I'd like to see you today."

"I can't today. I can see you tomorrow."

Disguising my disappointment, I said, "Okay, fine, what time?"

"What?"

"What time?"

"Can we have lunch?" she asked. "I'm going to be hungry."

"Sure. What time?"

"What? I can't hear you with all the noise on the line."

Somehow, eventually, we agreed on the time and the place, or so I hoped.

When Mariela finally walked in the door, eighty-seven minutes late, I experienced a confusing jumble of emotions: relief, excitement, fear and embarrassment. The embarrassment was due to her appearance. My young partner in passion had come directly from her school, the Jose Marti College of Veterinary Medicine. It seemed odd that college students would be required to wear uniforms, but such was the case. Perhaps it had to do with the ideal of

"Communist Equality", or some other such fantasy. In any event, the school uniform, with its short plaid skirt, white knee-socks and white blouse, reduced by several years her apparent age.

Half expecting the tourist police to rush in behind her waving arrest warrants, I felt a strong desire to stand up and shout something in my defense: "She's really nineteen!" for example. Or, "We checked her ID! Ask the landlady!"

Mariela went immediately for the chicken-like Special of the Day which, when it arrived at the table, appeared to have been garnered from something far more tubular than a bird. My guess was reptile. Back in my pre-med days I'd topped the class in Vertebrate Anatomy, and I was fairly certain I still knew the difference between a chicken and a lizard.

Meanwhile, my yummy mulatta schoolgirl sat before me dispatching her generic animal matter with impressive vigor.

"So, Mariela," I asked playfully, "how did you know in advance that you were going to be so hungry today?"

"I'm always hungry," she replied between bites. "And so is everybody else—except for Party members. If you see a Cuban who's not skinny from malnutrition, then you're looking at a bloated Communist pig."

A woman with strong opinions; nothing wrong with that, I thought.

"But I like you skinny," I said.

Mariela gave me a wolfish grin, and took another healthy bite of her whatever.

Back at the room it took my pint-sized paramour two entire *telenovelas* to digest her lunch. The small schizophrenic Russian-made television, while switching strobe-like from black-and-white to color, otherwise performed quite well, which was more than I could say for the actors.

"You really like to watch this garbage?" I asked.

"Shhh!"

After a long shower Mariela declared herself ready for bed. Minus the uniform, she looked closer to sixteen than thirteen, which somehow made me feel marginally better about myself.

All I wish to say about Round Two is that it was even more satisfying, more frenetic, more electrifying than its predecessor. There was even an element of (dare I say it) affection involved. Or was it my imagination?

Lounging post-coitally upon her back, Mariela smoked one of her atrocious Cuban cigarettes, while I played idly with the nipple of her small perfectly formed breast. "You should quit smoking," I told her.

"It's better than being hungry."

"Is that why you smoke, to dull the hunger?"

"It helps. Also, I like the taste."

I made a mental note to visit the Nacional gift shop and buy her a carton of imported cigarettes. Hopefully, they wouldn't make me gag quite so much as the domestic variety.

"I'd like to ask you something," I said.

"Go ahead."

"Are you really having orgasms, or are you just pretending?"

"That's a funny question," she said.

"Yes, well, it's just that, you know, in this type of situation…"

Mariela stubbed out her cigarette and looked me in the eye. "I've been with four men," she said. "Two foreigners like you, and two Cuban boys my own age. All of them were in a big hurry, like the house was on fire and they couldn't wait to get out. I never had time to even get warmed up. So, to answer your question, no, I'm not faking. The other day with you, that was my first one."

"Your first one?"

"With another person," she said, qualifying her statement with disarming directness.

"Mariela, I find that totally, ah, surprising."

Lighting yet another cigarette, she stared up at the ceiling and said, "Yeah, it surprised the hell out of me, too."

SEVENTEEN

When I asked Mariela if she would consider spending the night, she said she'd like to, but couldn't. Her mother, she explained, was a devoutly religious woman who held pronounced and archaically conservative views on the subjects of premarital copulation, dating, staying out late and the use of foul language.

"But you're a grown woman," I said, with something less than total conviction. "You should be free to come and go as you please."

"I should, but I don't want to upset my mother. It's not her fault she thinks that way. She was brainwashed at an early age."

"Aren't we all."

After Mariela left I slept for two hours, only to awake famished, energized and clinically tumescent. This last circumstance even I found improbable, given recent events, and set me to thinking about one of my favorite pet subjects: Behavioral Endocrinology.

I have always suspected that hormones play a far greater role in our lives than we would like to believe. Take, for example, my situation that same seemingly satiated evening. Having wild, prolonged and unrestrained sex with an exotically attractive nineteen-year-old was undoubtedly making me feel younger. But at the same time my body was also acting younger—proof positive that hormones can, given certain stimuli, actually produce physical changes which even science itself is unable to adequately explain.

Stuffing with difficulty that improbably engorged product of the power of hormonal thinking into my most spacious pair of Bermuda shorts, I slipped into an equally roomy Hawaiian shirt and opened the door. And there was

Perla, standing nervously on the stair, looking good enough to swallow whole.

"Here I am," she announced needlessly.

"Oh."

"Can I come in?"

Come in? This being Havana, she might just as well have said, "Can I come in, señor, and drain all of your bodily fluids?"

"I don't know how to tell you this, Perla, but I've, ah, fallen in love."

"With someone else?" she asked in disbelief.

"Well, yes."

"Who is she?" Perla demanded.

"Perla, please, try to understand. I am not in the mood for sex right now."

Perla stared in confusion at the unrelenting bulge below my waist, which even three layers of loose-fitting garments could not disguise. "You look like you're in the mood to me," she said hopefully.

"I was on my way out to dinner. I'm very hungry."

"I'm hungry, too," she said.

Christ! She probably was hungry. As Mariela had pointed out, nearly everyone in Cuba was hungry most of the time. And here I was, the wealthy white man, his pockets stuffed with dollars. "All right, Perla, where would you like to eat?"

Perla had the taxi driver take us (in a cherry red 1957 Desoto) to a sidewalk cafe at the eastern end of the malecon, where a makeshift pier serviced small ferries and tour boats. There were a number of round tables spread around the boardwalk, but all of them were taken. Nonetheless, Cubans being Cubans, we were soon invited to join a friendly young couple sitting by the entrance to the pier.

The young man, fair-skinned and quite handsome, turned out to be an actor, a starring character on soap operas shown every week all over Cuba. The woman, not unattractive herself, welcomed me with a warm smile.

Perla moved her chair possessively close to me, resting her head on my shoulder. Gently, I relocated her honey-haired cranium where it belonged.

"Stop that!" I hissed at her.

"But I love you!" she hissed back.

"The problem," Bruno was telling me, "is that I'm a well-known actor. People recognize me on the street."

"Really?"

"I recognize him," Perla said. "He's on two of my favorite *telenovelas*."

"See what I mean?" Bruno said.

"What's wrong with that?" I asked.

"*Soy famoso*," the actor said mournfully, as if fame were some terrible affliction. "I have an image to maintain."

"I still don't see…"

"It's the Cuban dilemma," his friend Maria said, leaning in my direction. Then, looking soulfully into my eyes, she took my hand in hers and said, "We all suffer, one way or another."

Perla stiffened, glaring at what she imagined to be a serious threat to our imaginary relationship.

"Look at my clothes," the actor announced theatrically. All I could see with any clarity was his shirt, so I stared dutifully at that. "You see?" Bruno said miserably. Not at all certain what I was supposed to be seeing, I nodded my head. "How am I supposed to dress," he whined, "like a successful actor when all they pay me is twenty-five dollars a month? Your shirt—very nice, by the way—would cost me an entire month's salary! At times," he concluded tragically, "I am even ashamed to walk the streets!"

Unsure how to respond, I looked to the two young women for guidance. Maria, during the star's soppy soliloquy, had managed to maneuver her chair right up to mine. Now I was neatly hemmed in on both sides by young and attractive women, while the handsome young actor sat alone and forlorn across the table. Then, in response to Maria's tactical approach, Perla began to climb into my lap.

I shoved her, not gently, back into her own chair.

The actor's friend, meanwhile, encouraged by my apparent indifference to Perla's attentions, once again took my hand in hers and, looking into my eyes with all the sincerity of a water moccasin, said, "You are a very interesting man."

"He's mine!" Perla burst out.

"I am not!"

"But, but we are lovers," Perla emoted.

"How could we be lovers," I said, "when we haven't even made love?"

"That wasn't my fault," Perla pointed out.

"So, you *are* available," Maria said, laying her hand atop my thigh.

"No, I am not available," I said. "I have a *novia*."

"You see?" Perla said, scowling at her rival, as she encircled my waist with her arm.

"I don't suppose," the actor said idly, "you'd want to part with that shirt? I couldn't pay you for it, of course, but I could get you a backstage pass to the filming of my next show."

"You can do better than her," Maria said, inching her hand up my thigh. "A lot better."

"Maria," I said politely, "could you please remove your hand from my zipper? Thank you. By the way," I asked the actor, "what's good to eat here?"

"Good to eat?" the actor repeated in amazement, as if unfamiliar with the concept. "You know, I suppose I could spare five dollars for the shirt. You'd still get the backstage pass, of course."

Perla and I had identical orders of rice and beans and pizza. Bruno and Maria claimed not to be hungry, but were not averse to a drink, so I stood them a round of mojitos.

"You know," the actor said, "Hemingway drank nothing but mojitos. He wouldn't hear of another drink."

"Me, either," I said, finishing my own and ordering another. The drinks, with their refreshing mint flavor, were helping to wash away the taste of my meal.

Three mojitos appeared to be my limit, which is one good reason why I should not have had a fourth.

"I don't," the persistent actor was saying, "expect you to go home shirtless. We could share a cab to your place. I won't have the five dollars until tomorrow, but you can trust me."

"Trust you?" I said drunkenly.

"I am not a homosexual," Bruno announced, "so you needn't have any fears on that account. I know actors have a reputation for unusual behavior, but…"

"Say, where's Maria?" I asked. Suddenly, I was missing her hand in my lap.

"Never mind Maria," Perla said. Then I saw her at a neighboring table, looking deeply into the eyes of another foreigner, a man who undoubtedly earned more than twenty-five dollars a month. "Have another drink," Perla suggested. And I did.

Which had a little to do with why, an hour or so later, I found myself shirtless and shortless, laying in my own bed, with Perla attached to me like a blond band-aid.

Apparently, Bruno had walked off with my shirt after all, while Perla, I could only hope, had taken charge of the shorts.

EIGHTEEN

Without opening my eyes I knew a great many things, few of them of an inspiring nature. I knew that it was the next day: sunlight was pouring through the window and bouncing painfully off my eyelids. I knew that I was suffering an ungodly hangover. I knew that I had committed certain indiscretions in the night, the precise nature of which I was momentarily at a loss to identify. And I knew that my overly sensitive nostrils were being assailed by an alien aroma.

It was this unfamiliar odor which, thick in its complexity, finally forced me, against my better judgment, to open my eyes.

"Good morning!" Perla chirped cheerfully. She was sitting on the edge of the bed, wearing one of my shirts. On her pretty face was a fake expression of loving adoration which made me want to vomit. Actually, it did make me vomit, and I spent the next fifteen minutes crouched over the toilet. After a brief shower, I exited the bathroom naked and sopping wet.

"Oh, what a night!" Perla sighed unconvincingly. She was such a miserable actress she could have starred in her own telenovela; or mine, for that matter.

"Get dressed," I said. "In your own clothes."

"Are we going out?"

"You are," I said. "And you're not coming back."

"But last night," Perla cooed. "The things we did..."

The things we did. Yes, it was coming back to me now, especially the worst part, in vivid and disheartening detail.

Perla lay on her back, feigning eagerness. I crouched over her, ready, willing and able to commit the act. "Wait," Perla said. "What about the condom?"

"The condom?" I repeated dumbly.

"Yes, my love. We don't want me getting pregnant, do we?"

Drunk, irritated, and sick of the entire business, I said, "No, of course not. In fact, why don't you just leave."

Perla begged. I shouted.

"Get out!" I said. "Get out and don't come back!"

"No, no, I'll do anything," Perla cried with desperation. "I don't care. Do whatever you want to me. Whatever you want. Just don't get me pregnant."

"All right," I said, "no getting Perla pregnant." Flipping her roughly onto her stomach, I grabbed my swollen pipinnum and…

In all the years of our marriage, Janice had never allowed me to do what I then proceeded to do to Perla. This "unnatural" act was, according to Janice, both painful and unhygienic. That it was painful, Perla had made abundantly clear. As for the unsanitary part, there was always soap and water.

Putting forty dollars (what the actor made in six and a half weeks) into her not unwilling hand, I said, "Here's double the going rate. That should cover any…any damages. Now get dressed."

"But I thought we would have breakfast, or…"

"Get dressed. Now, Brenda!"

"Who's Brenda?" Perla demanded.

"My oldest daughter," I could have replied, "who bears a passing resemblance to you, and who I am now seeing before my inner eye, naked, lying on her stomach, with my…no, no, no!"

"Get dressed and leave," I whispered.

Forty dollars to the good, Perla, seeing the deranged expression on my face, decided not to take any unnecessary chances. In less than a minute she was dressed. I opened the door, and stood there waiting for her to walk through it, which she did. But then she stopped in the small garden and said with a surreal show of optimism, "So, when will we see each other again?"

"Never!"

"Why are you being so mean to me?" Perla whined.

"Hi there," a female voice said. "I hope you're not busy."

It was the hooker, my first Cuban conquest, standing behind Perla in a low-cut high-hemmed dress, hardly appropriate for the hour of the day, which turned out to be around noon.

"Busy?" I said, listing badly to starboard, still stark naked. "Me? Do I look busy to you?"

"We had such a good time the other night," the hooker said, "I thought maybe you wanted to see me again."

"Who is she?" Perla whimpered. "Don't tell me she's the one you're in love with. She's so…so…old!"

"Amateurs," the hooker sighed. "I try to warn my clients, but they never listen."

The door to my room faced the backyard, so I was unable to actually see my landlady leaning out her window, located as it was just around the corner. But I could hear with perfect clarity her froggy voice croaking the following admonition: "Can you keep it down out there! This is a respectable neighborhood!"

"Look," I said, trying desperately to clear my head, "just leave, both of you. Please."

"You want me to leave?" Perla asked. "After what you did to me last night? You give me a few dollars, and then you want me to leave?"

"She just doesn't get it," the hooker said.

"Neither of you get it. I want both of you to leave. Period. End of story. Goodbye!"

"I'm not leaving till she does," Perla said.

The hooker laughed out loud.

"So what do I do," Mariela said, popping around the corner, "take a number?"

"Oh…shit!" I said, the first words of English I'd spoken since my arrival in Cuba.

Mariela, midgeted by the two taller women, favored me with her ironic smile, which for some reason pierced me to the quick. For several moments I stood transfixed, staring at this insignificant little person, paralyzed with confusion.

Then I grabbed her by the wrist, dragged her inside and slammed the door. Outside, the two women continued to snipe at each other for a while before their steps were heard receding down the alleyway.

Mariela and I sat on opposite ends of the bed. I stared at the floor. Mariela lit a cigarette. After a while, I said with an eloquence I did not know I possessed, "I, ah…Mariela, I'm…I don't know what to say, I…"

I was attempting to apologize, but for what? Paying to have sex with someone other than her? Wasn't this all just a series of business transactions? Loyalty, fidelity—what place could they possibly occupy here?

"You don't have to say anything," Mariela said, regarding me through the smoke of her cigarette with the same faint smile.

"It's just that I don't care for those girls at all," I said, still staring at the floor. "But I do care…"

To my amazement, I suddenly broke down and began to weep. I could not remember the last time I'd cried, it had been so long. But now that the thumb was out of the dike, the tears were cascading down my cheeks unrestrained, endlessly. At some point Mariela sidled over and lay my head in her lap, stroking my hair and murmuring consoling words in my ear.

My little lover's tender ministrations were not without effect. My weeping gradually subsided, as I was suddenly burdened by what may have been the most massive erection of my entire life. Mariela gave it a small tentative squeeze. "I'm sick," I moaned, "depraved, perverted." And then I was sobbing again at full throttle.

"You're not depraved," she said, "you're just healthy. I mean, really, really healthy."

Needless to say, we proceeded to make love at once, but without the fervor of our previous encounters. This time was all tenderness and affection…at least for a while.

Moments after we concluded, a sharp knock sounded on the door.

"Yes?" I responded hoarsely.

"La doctora wants to talk to you," my landlady screeched through the wood. "And, when you're done in there, I want to talk to you, too."

The landlady went away, or so I hoped, and Mariela lit a cigarette. "Can I ask you a couple of questions?" she said.

Warily, I nodded my head.

"You don't have to answer them if you don't want to; it's really none of my business."

"Fire away," I said without enthusiasm.

"Who's la doctora?"

"Oh, no one," I replied. "The landlady's doctor. She wants me to operate on Eustacia's knee. What's the other question?"

"When that girl said, 'what you did to me', what was she talking about?"

"You heard that?"

"I heard the whole thing."

"Oh." For some reason I could not bring myself to discuss the subject of anal intercourse with Mariela. Perhaps it was her young and tender age. "I'll tell you later."

"When?" Mariela poked me playfully in the ribs. She did not as far as I could see appear to be jealous in any way.

"Later."

"When?" Mariela persisted, inserting her tongue in my ear.

"I'll tell you," I said sternly, "when you're grownup."

PART II

ONE

Looking back now with some degree of perspective, I believe it was that ironic smile which finally tipped the scales, which tilted my life irrevocably in the direction of disaster. Into that small upturning of those generous young lips it was possible to read so much: amusement, admiration, self-assurance, affection and, last but far from least, pity.

Naturally, at the moment of my infatuation I was far from perceiving any of this on a conscious level. My intellect, if I may call it that, had taken a seat at the extreme rear of the bus, while my heart, overwhelmed with emotions I had never known, assumed the wheel, which it proceeded to direct towards the closest cliff.

Before she left that day I asked Mariela, "How is it you just showed up here? I thought you were going to call me after school."

In my mind there lurked the suspicion that she had come to check up on me, which in a convoluted sort of way made me rather happy. But her reasonable explanation (reasonable by Cuban standards) dispelled this notion. Classes at her school, she said, had been canceled for the day because a delegation of students from Guatemala had been invited by *The Beard* to attend a round of lectures. This happened all the time, Mariela said, because The Beard was more interested in impressing foreign governments than seeing to the needs of his own people.

As we were kissing good-bye at the door, I attempted to press a twenty dollar bill into her hand, but she refused to take it. "This isn't about money anymore," she said. "Call me."

Shortly after Mariela's departure I was summoned to the tiny parlor for the second time by a dour tight-lipped landlady.

"Sit down," she commanded.

Eustacia, conscientious to a fault, served me the orange juice and coffee I had missed out on that morning.

"Thank you."

"You are welcome," she said icily.

"So," I asked, after a long silence, "how is the knee?"

"Much better, thank you. You are an excellent doctor."

"Thank you."

"You are welcome."

This was going far better than I'd expected, and sipping on my muddy Cuban coffee, I began to relax. "Lovely day today," I remarked.

"No, it's not. It's hotter than hell. I thought we had an understanding."

"Understanding? Oh yes, of course, we did—I mean, we do. I can explain everything. You see, last night when I was on my way out to…"

"Si, si, si," Eustacia said impatiently. "I know what happened. That blond came knocking on your door, and you lacked the moral fiber to turn her away."

Moral fiber? Who was she, who had turned her home into a mini-bordello, to lecture me on the subject of moral fiber?

"Eustacia," I said, struggling to retain a smidgeon of dignity, "I do not pretend to be a pillar of self-restraint, but…"

A snort of derision erupted with such force from my landlady's ancient nose, it sent little waves rippling across the surface of my coffee.

"But," I resumed, "the situation was more complicated than you might think."

"Complicated is the word," Eustacia muttered. "Three women at a time—that's complicated, all right!"

"The girl was hungry. I felt sorry for her, so I took her out to eat. Then I had a little too much to drink, and afterwards she took advantage of…"

"Spare me," Eustacia croaked. "What about the red dress? What was she doing here?"

"She came uninvited, as well. They all did. Please believe me, I had every intention of sticking to the 'two-or-less' rule. The fact is, it was none of my doing."

"None of your doing?"

"Well, I mean…in the beginning, I may have contributed to their, ah, interest in coming here. But then I made it as clear as I possibly could that…"

"Never mind. That little mulatta, you really like her, don't you?"

Squirming in my seat, I drank some more of the dense coffee and said, "Well, she's very nice, but of course I've only known her for a few days, so, I, ah…"

The doorbell rang. Saved by the bell, I thought, but I could not have been more wrong.

"You have company," I said, getting to my feet. "I'll leave you…"

"Sit down," Eustacia ordered. "This concerns both of us."

Eustacia returned several moments later with la doctora.

I stood up to shake her hand and was struck anew by how stunning she was: tall, lithe, fine featured. And those electric green eyes! Strange, I thought, that I should feel no desire for her. But then, though it was only beginning to dawn on me, I had already fallen in love with someone else.

Eustacia and la doctora had entered into a conspiracy. The American knee surgeon, whose glowing reputation had reached, via the internet, all the way to Havana, was going to operate on Eustacia's knee. No one else had his skills, his experience. Only he would do.

After a bit of perfunctory chitchat, Eva informed me that she had acquired the "necessary permission".

"The Jose Marti State Committee for the General Health and Wellbeing of the Free Cuban People is thrilled with the entire arrangement," she enthused.

What arrangement? I had agreed to nothing!

"Everything is all set for next Tuesday," she went on. "It will take place in Cuba's premiere hospital. The State newspaper is going to devote extensive coverage."

"Extensive coverage of what?" I demanded.

"I spoke personally with the editor," Eva announced with pride. "He said…let me see if I can remember his exact words…something like, 'This courageously bold repudiation of imperialistic American foreign policy by one of its most eminent citizens'. Something like that."

"What!"

"I know it is a bit of an exaggeration," Eva admitted. "But you know how these newspaper people are—always looking for the sensational angle."

"Do you have any idea," I said, "what you are doing to me? Do you realize that I can be sent to jail just for being here? If word gets back to my government…"

"Why should it get back to your government? Does your government employ people to read our newspapers?" she asked with a laugh.

"Yes, it probably does."

Finally, the unflappable doctora was flustered. "Oh. Oh, I didn't think of that. Well then," she said, recovering instantly, "we will just have to cancel the newspaper coverage."

"You can do that?"

"I think so."

"You think so?"

"Yes," la doctora said. "So, we are all set then."

"No, we are not all set then."

"What's wrong?" Eustacia croaked from her seat on the sidelines. "What are you afraid of?"

"I am afraid, Eustacia, of losing my career, my freedom, my family, my…"

Once again, like a wily old tigress, my landlady pounced: "You have a family?"

TWO

It was a cool autumn morning, by Havana standards, a brisk eighty-one degrees, so I decided to take a stroll. Wandering aimlessly down Twenty-Third Avenue, my watch stuffed safely inside my pocket, I was pulled up short by the sight of my reflection in the mirrored door of a small hotel. The Panama hat, the dark shades and the tropical outfit I'd purchased at the airport all combined to create the image of a man unfamiliar to me, but not totally so. I'd seen other similar men stalking the streets of Havana since the day I arrived, all of them members of the same sleazy fraternity: Phi Beta Sex-Tourist.

This unsettling thought inevitably led to others, as the interior of my troubled mind transformed itself into a noisy Russian washing machine with a host of unwelcome images churning around and around inside it like so many soiled socks:

Mariela, smiling slyly, playing me for a fool. Eustacia's swollen knee, growing larger and larger until it exploded, taking me along with it. Janice. Sexually transmitted diseases consuming my flesh. Pregnant teenagers. Janice. My liver, collapsing under the weight of a thousand mojitos. The embarrassingly evident bulge in my shorts which, against all odds, refused to subside. False ID's, imprisonment and the unspeakable manner in which Cuban convicts would take their revenge on the Yankee-despoiler of their nation's youth. AIDS. Gonorrhea. Non-Specific Eurethritis. Yeast infections. Genital Lice. Genital Herpes. Assorted, as yet undiscovered, Antibiotic-Resistant Infections of the male urinary tract. Janice…

When I'd had, for the moment, my fill of self-flagellation, I decided to distract myself with a keen and close observation of my surroundings. The local architecture, Neo-Decrepit, held little interest for me, so I turned my attention to the people who crowded the streets. On nearly every corner there stood a pair of imperious unsmiling policemen. Every now and then, and for no apparent reason, they would stop a young man and demand to see his official ID card.

While one policeman interrogated the "suspect", the other whipped out his radiophone and, ID card in hand, called headquarters. This procedure typically took quite some time. Finally, satisfied that their victim had been successfully intimidated, they handed him back his card and sent him rudely on his way. Over the course of my stay in Cuba, I witnessed several dozen of these mini-detentions, and in every instance the detainee's skin had been at the dark end of the racial spectrum.

Growing dizzy in the increasing heat, I stepped inside a café and ordered an iced-coffee. Halfway though my second slurp, a stoop-shouldered shabby individual, who in lower Manhattan would have passed easily for a vagrant, came and stood humbly beside my booth.

"Would you mind if I join you?" he asked.

Something about the man, the bleak but intelligent look in his eyes, perhaps, induced me to say, "Sure, have a seat."

Even before he slipped the flat rectangular box out of the threadbare bag he carried, I knew what was coming—another of Havana's ubiquitous black market cigar salesmen.

"It shames me to ask you this," he said, a note of genuine mortification in his well-educated voice, "but I was wondering if you could see your way to purchasing a cigar from me?"

"No, but I'll buy you a coffee," I said, waving for the waiter.

"That is very kind of you. But I am a little desperate for cash at the moment. It's to feed my family," he said, casting his eyes down at the floor.

"I don't smoke cigars. It wouldn't look right," I added, trying to soften the blow with a bit of humor, "since I'm a doctor."

"I am a doctor, too," he announced.

Though the man seemed sincere, I did not believe his improbable declaration for a second. Annoyed at being lied to and scammed yet again, I said, "Oh, is that right? And what type of doctor might you be?"

"An orthopedic surgeon," he replied at once.

A chill ran down my spine. Could he be telling the truth? Wanting, for some obscure reason, to expose this simpering fraud, I began "talking shop", lacing my remarks with technical terms which only an experienced surgeon would understand. To my amazement, the undernourished cigar salesman proceeded to demonstrate, by his complex and knowledgeable replies, that he had indeed been speaking the truth.

The astonishment must have been visible on my face because, after finishing his coffee, he said, "You didn't believe me, did you?"

"No," I confessed. "But why don't you practice any more?"

"I do," he replied with a weary smile. "I perform four or five operations a week."

"So then, why the cigars?"

"A qualified surgeon in Cuba," he explained, "makes twenty-five dollars a month. The same as the woman who mops the floor at the hospital. The same as bus drivers, the same as everyone else—except for the police; they make three times that. And Party functionaries—no one knows how much they earn, but I can tell you this: none of their children go to bed hungry."

"That…that's unbelievable!"

"That," the doctor said morosely, "is Revolutionary Cuba."

"What's your name?"

"Raoul," he replied, "just like the Beard's baby brother."

"Listen, Raoul, I don't know what to say, I…"

"You don't need to say anything. If you would consider buying a cigar, I would be extremely grateful."

"How much for the whole box?"

After the depressed surgeon had gone his weary way, the waiter approached the booth and asked if I wanted anything else. "Just the check," I said.

"Those are good cigars," he remarked. "But you paid too much. *Romeo and Juliets* usually go for twenty dollars a box."

A box of cigars. A woman. Apparently, in Cuba twenty dollars bought you anything. I'd paid a hundred, and couldn't have cared less. "Here," I said, handing him the box, "here's your tip."

Back on the street, I shuffled around the corner and down a narrow alley, desperate for some shade. What, I wondered, was I doing in this godforsaken place? The heat. The miserable food. The poverty. The repression. Desperate girls selling their bodies. Starving surgeons pedaling cigars! Despite the palm trees and the lively music and the beautiful women, this was no paradise—more like hell on earth, if you asked me.

Then my thoughts turned to Mariela, and a hollow pain assailed me in the pit of my stomach, accompanied by a shuddering wave of anxiety. At first I thought I'd taken ill. But then words I'd read once in a poem (something about "exquisite torture") came floating out of my past, and it hit me like a blow: I was in love.

Mariela was unavailable until the following day; she was going to be busy, she'd explained, shoving her slender arm up bovine rectums well into the evening. Was she really? Or was she with someone else? As the ache in my belly intensified, I ran to the corner and hailed an illegal taxi, a 1956 two-tone Chevrolet Impala. I needed a drink. I needed a diversion. I needed to take my mind off Mariela and the downtrodden surgeon.

"Do you know Los Viejos Tiempos?" I asked the driver.

"Every Cuban over forty," the man replied, "has known better days."

THREE

Mario the midget strutted stiffly on his stubby legs up to my table and said, "Buenas tardes, Carlos, you look like shit. A mojito? Ten year-old Havana Club?"

"You've got a wonderful memory, Mario. Yes, a mojito, please."

"Are you sick?" he asked fearfully.

"I don't think so."

"Are you sure?" The little man seemed genuinely concerned.

"Yes, I'm a doctor, and I'd probably know if I was ill. How about that mojito?"

"Coming right up," Mario said, eyeing me intently. "My first American doctor. No wonder you're such a big spender. I hear doctors up there make tons of money exploiting the misery of the oppressed masses."

"Yes, well, I suppose. The mojito, Mario?"

"Sure, sure." When he returned from the bar, he placed the drink on the table and said, "So, if you're not sick, why the long face? Woman trouble?"

I downed the entire drink at one go, not my usual custom, and said, "Give me another, please."

Mario returned shortly with two drinks. Uninvited, he hauled himself up into a chair.

"Salud!" he piped.

"Salud!" I replied, and we clinked glasses.

"So, he said, "she dump you, or what? You shouldn't take it to heart, you know. There's enough hot chicas in this town to give the whole Chinese army gonorrhea."

"Does psychological counseling come with the drinks," I asked, "or will I be charged extra?"

"No charge, Carlos. So, did she dump you, or not?"

I glanced around the room, hoping that Mario's services might possibly be required elsewhere, but the club was deserted. "No, Mario, as far as I know, she has not 'dumped' me, at least not yet."

"And if she's got half a brain, she never will. So, what's the fucking problem, then?"

"Don't they mind you sitting with the customers?"

"What customers?" he replied, looking around with disgust. "Anyway, my sister owns the place. Her husband's a big muck-a-muck in the Party."

"Is she an *enano*, too?" The alcohol was performing its function admirably, and I was actually beginning to almost enjoy the waiter's company.

"No, she's a goddamn beanpole. I'm the lucky one."

"Lucky?"

"Yeah. I love the chicas, and enanos like me, we get tons of pussy. You look surprised. I don't blame you. Most people expect the opposite, but there's a lot of chicas who go for midgets in a big way. You wanna know why?"

"No, but after another drink I might."

"Ha, ha. I love your sense of humor, Carlos. Hey, Miguel," he yelled over his shoulder at the bartender, "bring my friend here another mojito."

As my drink arrived, the band, which had been setting up, launched into the their first song, a spirited tune entitled, *el Cuarto de Tula* (Tula's Room). The lyrics, like those of most songs, were pretty inane, but I couldn't help but tapping my feet and nodding my head to the lively rhythm.

"You like that song?" the midget asked.

"Yes. The words are kind of silly, but it has a great beat."

"It's an old song—a classic," Mario said with pride. "And the words aren't silly at all. You just have to understand the symbolism, what it's really about."

What the song was about seemed evident to me. A woman named Tula falls asleep in her room with the candle lit. The candle starts a fire. The fire department comes, and after a great deal of trouble, puts the fire out, but not before the whole house has burned down.

When I expressed this opinion to Mario, he said, "No, no, that's not it at all. The song is about sex. All Cuban songs are about sex. You see, she's got this man in her room."

"Man? There's no mention of a man in her room. Say, Mario, how about one of your wonderful pizzas. I need to put something solid in my stomach."

"Ham and cheese?"

"You have cheese?"

"Miguel, bring my friend a ham and cheese pizza. And put some cheese on it. This guy's a good customer."

"Damn straight!" I agreed, nicely sloshed now.

"Putting something in her stomach," the midget said, "that's what Tula, the chica in the song, didn't do. That's why the house burned down."

"Mario, what the hell are you talking about?"

"She was giving the guy a blow-job," the midget explained, "but…"

"She was giving who a blow-job?"

Mario sighed with exasperation. "The guy in her room!"

"But there is absolutely no mention of a guy in her room."

"It's understood. If there's a song about a chica, she has to have a guy in her room. The candle is the guy's dick. That's where the symbolism comes in."

The pizza, with suspicious promptitude, arrived at the table. I took a bite. It was awful, but I was drunk as well as famished, and would have consumed with gusto a microwaved slice of cardboard slathered with catsup, which for all I knew…

"The chica, Tula," the midget resumed, "falls asleep before she gets the job done. So the guy, he's still hot; he's burning up; he's on fire! Get it? 'On fire'. And that's how the house burns down."

"He's so hot," I said, my mouth full of partially masticated who-knew-what, "that the heat from his body makes the house catch fire?"

"Exactly!"

"That's ridiculous."

Mario was growing agitated. "No, it's not!" he shouted. "It makes perfect sense. I'm speaking from experience. Like I was saying before, enanos get a lot of action, and me in particular, I have women after me all the time. You know what some of them like? They like to get head while they're standing up. And who can do that better than a midget? We're the perfect height."

"The perfect height?" I began to laugh.

"Yeah, do the math. Take a chica about average height. Then you measure from her feet to the altitude of my mouth. I'm right there, Johnny-on-the-spot! I don't have to bend, and I don't have to stretch. I just stick out my tongue…"

My laughter became so intense I began to choke. I was in no danger, however, as I'd had the foresight to spit the last mouthful of whatever back onto my plate in the nick of time. Unfortunately, this last circumstance went unobserved by the midget.

"He's choking!" Mario shouted. "He's choking!"

The band stopped playing in mid-song.

The bartender dropped the glass he was wiping.

And Mario the midget, once he'd recovered from the initial shock, went forthwith into action. Vaulting from his chair onto mine, he straddled my back and began to perform his genetically-altered version of the Heimlich Maneuver.

Like many midgets, Mario had short but powerful arms, and though I'd been in no danger up until that point, I was now. Due to the extreme pressure the powerful short-armed waiter was mistakenly applying to my diaphragm, I was suddenly on the verge of actually suffocating.

"No, stop!" I tried to scream, but I was laughing too hard to form any actual words. And then, all at once, I was out of air.

As the entire population of the club surrounded our table, shouting out encouragement, the small but powerful midget continued to crush my diaphragm. Out of desperation, I stood up and attempted, unsuccessfully, to toss Mario, bucking-bronco-style, from my back. The bartender, who must have been a rodeo fan, began to count: "One, two, three, four…" Then, top-heavy and faint from lack of oxygen, I lost my balance and fell (along with the midget) heavily to the floor, upending the table.

"You idiot!" I shouted at the midget, as we sprawled half-entwined on the eroded linoleum floor. "What the hell were you trying to do?"

"I was trying to save your life, you ungrateful bastard!" he piped back.

"By suffocating me?"

"You were choking to death, and I was performing the Heimlich Maneuver."

"No, you weren't."

"Yes, I was!" the offended midget squeaked indignantly.

Mario then went on to explain how the government, several years back, had suddenly decreed that every citizen was morally obligated to learn the Heimlich Maneuver. For three days the country had come to a virtual standstill while the entire adult population of Cuba attended special classes.

"I received an A-plus," Mario declared with pride.

"Well, I said, peeling clumps of congealed cheese from my shorts, "you must have had a rotten teacher, because you got it all wrong."

"That's possible," Mario admitted. "But she was one hot chica. And the perfect height for you know what."

FOUR

Mariela wanted lobster, a protected species.

"Isn't consuming lobster illegal?"

"Of course."

"Well…"

Our taxi driver, an award winning novelist, knew of three places with "special permission" to serve illegal lobster, one of them outside town on the water. "You can see the ruins of the old yacht harbor from there," he enthused, "it's very romantic."

"It sounds expensive," Mariela said. "Let's go to Chinatown."

"No," I said, "money is not an object. Take us to the harbor."

"Si, señor."

It was a long ride to the restaurant and I would have liked to spend it in the backseat snuggling with Mariela. But our taxi (a 1954 red and white Dodge Coronet—in suspect condition) was, naturally, operating illegally, so we were required to sit up front with the driver, where we looked less like fares and more like…what? A teenage hooker sandwiched between her pimp and her john?

The restaurant was, by Cuban standards, first-class, and so, deserted. Only tourists or government officials could afford to eat there. But tourists were hard to come by, and the entire government was attending a "mandatory" baseball game: Cuba vs. *el* Salvador. The next morning I read in the *Granma* that Cuba won the game twenty-seven to two.

We sat outside overlooking the water and ordered lobster. The staff treated us with great nonchalance, as if foreign middle-aged men accompanied by their teenage "dates" dined there all the time. Maybe they did.

The lobster was actually quite good and Mariela consumed hers with a concerted enthusiasm one had to admire.

"Tonight could be the big night," she leered at me between mouthfuls.

"What do you mean?"

"Tonight I may allow you to take my virginity."

"Your what?"

"Tonight, Carlitos, if you are very very lucky, you may get to go where no man has gone before."

"They show Star Trek in Cuba?"

"Star *what*?"

The following day was a Saturday, and with no classes to attend Mariela decided to take me shopping. Our first stop was a small rundown department store in Havana Vieja, sparsely stocked with poor quality goods manufactured in oppressed Asian nations.

"I would love to buy you some really nice clothes," I told her. "Isn't there a place with a better selection?"

"Only the boutiques at the big hotels," Mariela said wistfully, "and they're way too expensive."

Poor kid. She still couldn't get used to the idea that what was hopelessly out of reach for her, was for me barely worth a tax write-off. Not that I was planning to write-off this trip.

Mariela insisted that we head over to the hotel zone in an "Orange" taxi. She'd always wanted a ride in one, she said, but could never afford the one-dollar fare. The idea of riding around the streets of Havana in a large plastic orange did not appeal to me on any level. They looked ridiculous, for one thing, weighed next to nothing and were, judging by how they "quivered" in a light breeze, dangerously unstable.

I made a weak attempt at convincing Mariela to take a conventional taxi, while she insisted on riding in the plastic ball. In short order, I gave in. I'd become, I realized, essentially incapable of saying no to her. She even talked me into paying a street photographer to take our photo while we sat cuddled-up inside the "Orange". One of my more embarrassing moments.

Once we finally got underway, the driver, who sat astride the small motorcycle which powered this death-machine, turned out to be (surprise, surprise) a suicidal maniac. On three separate occasions (two left turns, and one right) I distinctly recall thinking, "This is how I am going to die, my trachea severed by a shard of orange plastic."

In Havana, one always seemed to return to the same places over and over. And so I was not surprised when we ended up back at the Nacional, my old hotel, purported to contain the best woman's clothing store in town.

As I steered my young charge toward the main entrance, she gave my arm an urgent tug. "We can't go in there," she said.

"Why not?"

"Cubans aren't allowed inside hotels. Unless they work there."

Fortunately, the boutique had a separate entrance around the corner. The staff, a pair of bored young women, perked up at once at the sight of my well-fed white face. Mariela, like a big brown hummingbird, proceeded to zig and zag all over the shop, picking up and then discarding this pair of panties, that bra, various skirts, blouses, shorts and shoes.

Meanwhile, I had been offered first a chair, then a mojito and finally a cigar. American shopkeepers could learn a thing or two from these Cubans, I thought, sipping my drink and pretending to puff on the long cigar. When, after half an hour, Mariela still had not selected a single item, I asked her if something was wrong.

"No," she said, "I'm just trying to decide what I need more, a blouse or a skirt."

"Why not both?"

"But the prices…"

"Forget the prices," I said, flicking with aplomb the ash from my cigar. "Buy whatever you want. Let yourself go. Get a whole outfit. Get three whole outfits."

The saleswomen must have heard my words of encouragement, because a moment later they were all over me, freshening my drink, cleaning the ashtray, setting a small ottoman-like object at my feet. The prettier of the two even squeezed my knee.

"How do I look in this?" Mariela showed off a pair of tight shorts.

"Wonderful," I replied. The cigar, much to my amazement, was beginning to taste rather good.

"And how about these?" Mariela asked, parting the dressing room curtain, thus allowing me an unobstructed view of her perfectly plump behind, garnished with a miniscule scrap of lacey cotton.

"Good enough to eat," I said, fighting off an erection.

"Tonight," she said, tossing me a sultry look.

This is nothing like shopping with Janice, I thought.

After that, we had lunch. After lunch, we had sex. And after sex, Mariela taught me how to play dominoes. The first four games she slaughtered me.

"Oh," she cried with delight, "you stink!"

Mariela, I could see, was deriving great satisfaction from beating me. But then, she seemed to derive an inordinate amount of pleasure from nearly everything: eating, sex, shopping, talking, watching soap operas. It was as if she were indeed a child for whom every time was the first time.

"You lose…again!" she chirped, upon winning the tenth consecutive game. "You're pathetic."

"Yes, I suppose I am."

"I'm going to teach you a lesson."

"Please do," I said agreeably.

Mariela ripped off my shorts and began to…well… teach me a lesson. Then in the midst of the lesson, the little brown runt blindsided me, just as I was about to experience my latest hormone-driven epiphany.

Gently expelling me from her full-lipped mouth, she said, "Can I ask you a really big favor?"

FIVE

I seemed to be spending half my time in bed, and the other half in taxis. Not that I was complaining. The cars were wonderful and the drivers no less so. Due to the bizarre shambles which was the Cuban economy, their humble profession attracted all manner of men, most of them vastly overqualified for their illegal jobs.

On the long ride out to my destination—the last place I would have chosen to go, had I still possessed some free-will on this fine asphyxiatingly humid Sunday afternoon—my driver regaled me with one startling statement after another.

He was an older man with an imposing nose, thick glasses and very little hair. "I started out as an attorney," he began in a hoarse voice, puffing on a cheap cigarette. "Then, when the revolution came, my professional knowledge lost all relevance. For motives I have never been able to fathom, I took up the repair of watches. At this I made a modest living, until my eyes began to fail. That is when I took up driving a taxi."

"Wait a minute," I said, "I must have misunderstood you. Did you just say that because of failing eyesight, you were forced to seek employment driving a taxi?"

"That is correct. I do not work at night, however."

"Very prudent. But don't you need good vision to drive even in the daytime?"

"I try to work the off hours, when there isn't too much traffic."

"Still…"

"And, as a matter of caution, I drive as slowly as possible."

"I've noticed."

"Do you mind if I ask you a question?" the driver said.

"Not at all. Maybe it will help to pass the time," I added, as we continued to crawl along.

"The address you gave me—it is in a poor neighborhood on the outskirts of Havana. There could be little of interest there for a man like yourself...unless...she is beautiful?"

"She wants me to meet her family."

"And you agreed?"

"In a moment of weakness."

"As a former attorney, may I be permitted to point out that you still have time to reconsider."

"A mother, a brother and a sister," I said grimly, as if I were naming a trio of diseases.

"No father?"

"I don't think so."

"Be careful."

I regarded the driver closely to see if he was joking. Apparently, he was not.

The neighborhood was indeed a desolate one: unpaved streets, no sidewalks, small one-story houses resembling cement bunkers. As we inched down one downtrodden street after another, we passed half a dozen outdoor domino games, with quartets of not-young men sitting around small square tables. The men, looking dazed and weary, slammed the tiles down in robotic rapid-fire bursts, as if their arms did not belong to them.

Mariela's family lived in a square white-washed jail cell. The door was made of dented sheet metal. I tapped it lightly with my fist. A moment later, it was opened by a tall muscular young man.

"What do you want?" he demanded.

Before I could respond, the scowling fellow was pushed aside by one of the more portly women I'd seen in Cuba—given the average caloric intake, she must have had an awfully slow metabolism (or perhaps a glandular imbalance) to be so fat in such a thin country.

"You must be Carlos, Mariela's friend!" she proclaimed.

"Yes, I…"

"God bless you!" she thundered. "I'm Rosanacelia, Mariela's mother. "But everyone calls me Celia. Come right in. We are so pleased that Mariela has made a new friend, especially a British veterinarian like yourself."

"I'm a British veterinarian?"

"Yes, we know," Celia said, "Mariela has told us all about you."

This, I thought, as I was escorted into the house, may turn out to be even worse than I'd imagined.

The oven-like living room, which doubled, then tripled as dining room and kitchen, was sparsely furnished. It contained, aside from a tiny refrigerator and a suspect stove, a table and four battered wooden chairs (the dining room), three misshapen under-stuffed chairs (the living room) and a peeling coffee table. Mama Celia put me into the "best" chair (it still contained a "working" spring which commenced at once to work its way into my rectum), while she settled into the lower depths of another (down and down she sank, until it looked as if she might disappear altogether). The surly young man (Silvio, Mariela's older brother), sat in the third chair, glaring at me as he cracked and re-cracked the knuckles of his disturbingly large fists.

Mariela had mentioned once that her brother had nearly made the national baseball team, and had yet to get over the disappointment. Looking at his outsized frame, I could easily picture him smashing balls out of the stadium.

"So, ah, where's Mariela?" I asked, fighting down a mounting sense of unreality.

"Oh, she and her sister are taking a bath."

Together? I wondered lasciviously.

"How long you know my sister?" Silvio demanded.

"Do you enjoy being a veterinarian?" Celia asked.

"Well, um, I've been in Cuba for eight days," I said, choosing to avoid both questions.

"God bless you! You speak beautiful Spanish, for a foreigner," Celia said.

"How come you talk like a Puerto Rican?" Silvio demanded.

"Would you like some nice hot tea?" Celia asked.

It must have been close to a hundred degrees in the room. "I'd love some."

"Are you a communist?" Silvio asked.

At that moment, Praise the Lord, Mariela and her older sister entered stage-left. As the two female siblings approached my chair, I stood up to greet them.

Eunice was about thirty-five, and looked nothing like her sister. Where Mariela was young, fresh, lean and vibrant, Eunice was faded with age, stale, sagging and listless. She gave the impression of having already lived the better part of her life, which hadn't been all that good to begin with.

I shook Eunice's hand, as the introductions were made. Then, at something of a loss, I shook Mariela's hand as well. Then a bell rang—it sounded like a cowbell.

"That must be Dr. Flores," Celia said. Eunice shuffled off to let the man in. Dr. Flores, besides being a doctor, was apparently a close friend of the family.

After Silvio was booted out of his chair and replaced by the young physician, Mariela and her sister pulled over a few wooden chairs and we all formed a nice cozy little group sweating to death around the coffee table—except for Silvio, who stood sullenly in the corner glaring at me.

A short but uncomfortable silence ensued. "Carlos," Mariela chirped brightly, "is one of the top veterinarians in England."

She and I exchanged a brief look, hers apologetic, mine murderous.

"How nice," Dr. Flores muttered. "So tell me, Celia, how is your knee doing?"

"Not as good as it might be," she admitted.

"She's in pain all the time," Eunice sighed.

People with bad knees are attracted to me like bees to honey, I thought, no matter what country I'm in. Mom's knee was all bundled up, much like Eustacia's.

"Well, let's have a look," Dr. Flores said, kneeling to unwrap the bandage.

While he was thus occupied, I asked, from force of habit, "How would you describe the pain? Dull? Sharp? Burning? Throbbing? Intermittent? Constant?"

Everyone turned to regard me strangely.

"Sra. Rodriguez," a badly putout Dr. Flores said with ill-humor, "in case you haven't noticed, is a human being, not a pussy cat."

"Yeah," Silvio said.

I looked to Mariela for help; she sat staring at the ground, refusing to meet my eye.

"Our neighbor has a sick dog," Celia offered charitably. "Maybe you could treat him. He can't stop going to the bathroom."

SIX

From that point forward, the afternoon grew increasingly improbable.

Silvio decided that he needed to speak to me alone, man-to-man, out in the "backyard", which turned out to be an infinitesimally small square of bare concrete, surrounded on all sides by more concrete. It's only occupant was a lonely little poinsettia, literally dying for company.

"Since they locked up my father," Silvio informed me without preamble, "I am the head of the family."

"What," I inquired fearfully, "did they lock him up for, if you don't mind me asking?" Nothing violent, I prayed; that sort of behavior was known to run in families.

Silvio ignored my question—an ambiguous sign, at best— and said, "What are your intentions towards my sister?"

"Intentions?" What a question! The honest answer would have been, "To continue pillaging and plundering her wonderful wee body until it's time to return to the bosom of my family." But I opted instead for a show of silent confusion. If only the large young man would step back a foot or two.

"You lay a hand on her," Silvio said with an odd lack of emotion, as if he were reading from a bad script, "I'll smash your face in."

Understandably, I was speechless.

"Did you hear what I said?" Silvio demanded.

"Oh yes, absolutely. You know, Silvio, Mariela and I met only recently. We've barely had an opportunity to get to know one another."

"What do you mean, get to know one another?" Silvio snarled, crowding me with his too-large chest up against the hot wall.

"I assure you, Silvio, my intentions towards your sister are entirely, ah, honorable?"

"I know what you foreigners are like," Silvio said. "You can't fool me. I'll break your face. I'll break your legs. I'll break your hands. You touch my sister, cabron, you'll be giving rabies shots with your mouth!"

Giving rabies shots with my mouth?

"Silvio, please, there's nothing to be concerned about. Calm down."

"Don't tell me to calm down!"

"All right, Silvio, you get just as upset as you want. Let yourself go. Kick the wall a few times. Punch a bus."

"Listen to me!" Silvio ordered, as if I had another option—our faces were so close I could have licked his chin. "You touch her tits just once, you're going to bleed for the rest of your life."

Silvio paused, seemingly confused by his own admonition.

"I understand," I said, casting my eyes skyward. "May God strike me dead," I continued, hoping he took (religiously speaking) after his mother, "if I even brush accidentally against your sister's…"

"Silvio, you *culero*!" It was the voice of salvation, Mariela, grabbing her much much larger brother by the shirt and spinning him around.

"I forbid you to use that kind of language," Silvio informed his baby sister.

"Fuck you!" Mariela replied.

"What…"

"Get your useless black ass back in the house, Silvio. Now!"

For several moments Silvio attempted to stare down his sister, but Mariela's eyes were incandescent with rage and the big dullard never stood a chance. Before going inside, Silvio turned back to me and said in that sinister sociopathic monotone, "Just remember what I said. Or you'll be de-worming dogs with your teeth!"

De-worming dogs with my teeth?

"I'm sorry," Mariela said, when we were alone. It was plain to see that she was ashamed, but at the moment I was too angry to care.

"What's wrong with him?" I demanded. "Is he mentally retarded or something?"

"Probably" Mariela said, staring at the ground.

"And why?" I demanded. "Why, in God's name did you tell them I was a British veterinarian?"

"I had to tell them how I met you," she said. "It seemed like the best thing to say, that we met in school, that you were a visiting teacher."

"I hate all this lying," I said.

"Did you want me to tell them the truth?" Mariela asked, finally raising her gaze to mine. "That you picked me up in a café, screwed my brains out, gave me twenty dollars and sent me on my way."

These last words she spoke matter-of-factly, without a trace of self-pity or bitterness. And with a hint of her trademark smile. In her own way, I realized, she was one of the more remarkable people I'd ever known. My anger turned instantly to shame. "All right," I said, "forget it. I'm sorry. Let's go back inside."

Our return to the depressing living room interrupted an argument.

"But he's older than you are!" Silvio was telling his mother.

"The Lord looks after His own," Celia declared.

"So, doctor," I said affably, "what's the diagnosis?"

"The knee? I am afraid that there is little to be done. There is no arguing with old age."

Mariela's mother, I later learned, was forty-five years old.

"Well, then, I suppose some anti-inflammatory medication…" I began gently.

"Good luck finding them in this country," the doctor said with disgust. "We have a wonderful medical system here in Cuba. The only problem is, we have no medicine."

I picked up my tea, which had downgraded itself to room temperature, and took a sip. It tasted like cinnamon.

"Will you and Mariela be marrying in a Catholic church?" Celia asked. "I don't mean to pry," she said kindly, "but you are Catholic?"

Choking on my tea, I replied, "Not exactly."

"Oh, that's all right," she said, "neither are we. We're Baptists."

Baptists? In Cuba? Suddenly, I felt as if I'd entered some surreal parallel universe which resembled rural Alabama, but where everyone spoke slurred Spanish. "You know, Celia," I said, desperate to change the subject, "I am a little surprised. I was under the impression that religion was frowned upon here in Cuba."

"The Lord works in mysterious ways," she proclaimed, and that was about as good an explanation of the peculiar state of affairs in that country as I was ever likely to get.

The day dragged on.

After the doctor left, at Mariela's and my insistence, Celia allowed me to examine her knee. She was suffering from tendonitis. Like my landlady, she could have used a shot or two of cortisone. But unlike Eustacia, she did not appear to have a serious problem. In fact, what she really needed, once she'd gotten the inflammation under control, was some exercise.

Just before I finally succeeded in making my escape, Mariela's sister asked to speak with me alone. As we walked outside I hoped she was not about to threaten me with violence like her brother had, though she appeared to lack the energy to do any meaningful damage. As it turned out, violence was the farthest thing from her mind. Taking my hands in hers, she looked soulfully up into my eyes and said, "Please, please…you must take my sister away from here."

"Away from here? You mean, Cuba?"

"Yes. Before she's ground into the dirt, like me. She's not like the rest of us. She's finer than we are. She's smart, beautiful. She has a strong spirit. But anyone's spirit can be broken. And hers will be broken, sooner or later, if she stays here."

"Well," I said, embarrassed down to my toes, "Mariela and I hardly know one another. We just…"

"I know all about you two," she cut in. "Mariela tells me everything. She says you are a fine man, and she thinks you are very fond of her. And she adores you."

"Yes, well, I…"

"How old do you think I am?" she asked.

"I don't know," I said. "I'd guess, about thirty?" Gentleman that I was, I'd reduced her apparent age by five years.

"I'm twenty-three," she said. "In four years, Mariela will be just like me. Unless you get her out. You're her only hope. She deserves better than this." She stepped back, allowing me to take her in, so that there could be no mistaking the fact that *by this, she* meant herself.

Mariela and I left together in a neighbor's "taxi". We told her mother we were going to the zoo—for educational purposes.

"God bless you!" mama cried.

SEVEN

Eustacia rented out a second room, just beside my own. Vaguely, I was aware that this other room had been occupied by someone, but so far our paths had yet to cross. A tall hedge separated the two doors, thus insuring the "total privacy" no respectable sex-fiend could do without.

On the morning after the distressing visit with Mariela's family, my neighbor and I finally bumped into each other as we were leaving our respective rooms. I was on my way out to breakfast. He was on an early morning condom run. Stout, middle-aged and homely, and dressed in the loudest tropical outfit I'd ever seen, my neighbor reminded me of a big brown frog on holiday. Like other Mexicans I'd met, he was infinitely friendly and, by coincidence (if such a thing exists, which I doubt), his name was also Carlos.

"Tocayo!" he cried with glee when I told him my name. Then, shaking my hand with great vigor, he explained that in Mexico people who shared the same first name called each other 'Tocayo'.

"Why is that?" I asked.

"I have no idea, Tocayo. You must come in and have a drink," he said, grabbing my arm.

"It's a tad early for alcohol, isn't it," I said, reluctantly allowing myself to be led away.

"Tocayo, a few drops of aged Havana Club on a cool morning never hurt a single soul."

A cool morning? It must, I thought, be awfully hot in Mexico.

"Yes, Carlos, I suppose you're right."

"Tocayo! Call me Tocayo, Tocayo," Carlos insisted.

My neighbor's room was a mirror image of my own. Although, I have to say, mine was a good deal neater.

As he bustled about preparing our drinks, Carlos kept up a non-stop patter, asking and then answering his own questions. "Tocayo, you are from where? You look like a gringo, but you talk like a Puerto Rican who spent too much time in America. You're here on vacation? I am here on business. Well, business and pleasure. I come to Havana twice a year to recruit dancers for my club in Puerto Vallarta."

"Club?"

"A table dance club, Tocayo. A gay table dance club. You don't look like a *maricon*, Tocayo. I take it you are here for the females? Well, you don't look like a homophobe, either. I hope you are not a homophobe, Tocayo. It would be such a shame, us having so much in common."

"I have nothing against anyone. Except for bigots; I don't hold with bigots."

"Good man, Tocayo! So, here is the rum. Just a little, yes? So, have you been finding some nice chicas? Havana has so many. Nice boys, too, of course, but while the boys here are wonderful, the girls are magnificent. Even I can see that, ha, ha. Of course, I avoid the professionals. The amateurs can be molded to one's taste, and are so much more genuine seeming. So, Tocayo, have you found anyone to your liking?"

"Yes, as a matter of fact, I have found someone very much to my liking."

"Good for you, Tocayo! You know what? So have I. But then I always do. And then I always regret it. Enrique!" he shouted at the closed bathroom door. "Enrique, you can come out now! He's so shy, Tocayo. And you'd never know it to look at him. Enrique! Come out. You have to meet my Tocayo. Don't be afraid, Enrique. He's very nice, and he isn't going to bite you...unless you want him to, ha, ha!"

A few seconds later Enrique, who'd been blessed with an excess of body hair, exited the bathroom dressed exclusively in his boxer shorts and a thick gold chain—a gift from my Tocayo, no doubt. The young man, who must have spent half his life at the gym, was short and muscular like a baby bull.

But as my neighbor had pointed out, for all his muscles he was as timid as a butterfly. Bravely, he shook my hand.

"I'm taking Henry (English for Enrique) back to Puerto Vallarta," Carlos announced, eying his barefoot stud with pride.

"You can do that? I thought Cubans had difficulty leaving the country."

"Yes, Tocayo, they do—on their own. It is very expensive, entails a mountain of paperwork, and you must, absolutely must have a foreign sponsor. But it can be done. Enrique here is my eighth 'visiting employee'. My very own little Henry the Eighth," he added, patting Enrique's butt affectionately. "Of course, like all the others, he'll leave me for the first cute young thing to come along. Won't you, Henry?"

Enrique's face took on a look of unbearable pain. "No, no, never! I love you, Carlos. I love you!"

"Yes, yes, yes," Carlos said. "You say that now. They all say that in the beginning. But then, once they're in a free country, someone comes along and…"

"*Te amo!*" Enrique moaned, his dim-as-a-doorknob eyes filling with tears.

"No, you don't," Carlos said, casting me a wicked wink.

"Yes, yes, I do!" Enrique whimpered, falling to his knees. "I love you!" he further enthused, wrapping his arms about his sponsor's fleshy legs.

As I told my Tocayo, I have nothing at all against homosexuals, but even so, this whole scene was beginning to make me ill. Though Enrique could not have been more different than Mariela, there were, nonetheless, similarities in the two relationships I preferred not to dwell upon.

My neighbor, despite his taste for melodrama, was an astute man. He perceived my discomfort at once. "All right, Henry, that's enough. I believe you. Time to get dressed."

Like a dog who has been promised a walk, Enrique leapt to his feet and trotted happily back into the bathroom, presumably to get dressed, whatever that entailed.

"I'm far too fond of that boy," Carlos admitted.

"I know the feeling."

"Maybe you'll want to take your little sweetheart home with you, too?" he suggested.

"Yes, that would be nice," I said, just to be agreeable.

"And where do you live? You never said."

"New York."

"Oh," my Tocayo tut-tutted, "then you have a real problem. In Mexico there are legal means to import 'temporary workers' from Cuba, but in the United States, I believe it would be far more difficult. Acquiring a visa, I understand is almost impossible. You would have to be very determined to pull it off."

"Yes, well, it's something of a moot point, Tocayo. You see, I'm married."

"Ah! In that case, Tocayo, in order to import your young friend, in addition to being determined, you would also have to be insane."

"Yes, well, I'm far from that," I laughed.

"So then, Tocayo," my host proclaimed, "all you need to do is have a good time screwing your brains out."

"That's exactly what I have been doing."

"Good man! Just be sure you don't allow yourself to become emotionally involved."

"Too late for that, I'm afraid."

"Oh," Carlos said gravely, "then you may be in for some large trouble, my friend. I know. I speak from experience."

"Henry the Eighth?"

"And Eduardo the Seventh. And Mario the Sixth. And so on."

At that moment, Enrique burst from the bathroom all decked out in tennis whites: white shorts, white shirt, white everything. In his right hand he held a tennis racquet; in his left, a small red rubber ball which did not look at all suitable for tennis.

Carlos, his eyes illuminated with lust, said, "Well, Tocayo, it's been a real pleasure meeting you. Have a nice day."

"The pleasure is mine," I said, "enjoy your, ah, game."

For several moments I paused outside my neighbor's door, not eavesdropping exactly, just a little curious. "I love you, Carlos, I love you!" I heard Enrique moaning through the door. "No, you don't!" my neighbor begged to differ. Hard upon this declaration there was heard the thwack of a tennis racket, followed at once by a high-pitched and suspiciously theatrical cry of pain.

Yes, I thought, heading for the street, Henry the Eighth should be a big hit in Puerto Vallarta.

EIGHT

Upon my return from breakfast I was bushwhacked by Eustacia from her command post overlooking the narrow alley.

"You've come back alone?" she asked, arching her sparse eyebrows.

"I went to get some breakfast. Is that a problem?"

"I'm just surprised to see you by yourself," she said, glancing skyward for an explanation, as if my not being accompanied by a young female had required an act of divine intervention.

"Mariela has classes all day," I felt compelled to explain. "So I'm on my own till evening."

"That's good," Eustacia said, "because la doctora wants to talk to you about my knee operation. She's here now waiting for you. In your room."

"What is she doing in my room?"

"Are you deaf? Do I have to repeat everything I say? She's waiting for you."

La doctora Eva was sitting primly at the card table, reading a medical journal, when I opened the door.

"I am sorry to be invading your privacy," she said, rising to her feet, "but matters have come to a head and I needed to speak to you without delay."

"All right, sit down and speak."

"You're angry."

"I'm a little putout, yes. Couldn't you have waited for me in the parlor?"

"What I have to tell you, I didn't want to say in front of Eustacia," Eva explained.

"All right, forget it." It's not easy for a man (or at least a man like myself) to remain angry for very long with a woman as beautiful as Eva. "What's on your mind?"

"I've managed to line up everything we need for the day after tomorrow."

"Everything we need for what?"

"For Eustacia's operation. We have the surgical theatre, the anesthesiologist, the prosthesis…"

"Wait a minute! I did not agree to do this operation, and I never will."

"I would like to convince you otherwise," she said coolly.

"Good luck."

"You may," Eva began, "have wondered why I am so adamant on this subject." I shrugged my shoulders. "Eustacia is more to me than just a patient. My mother worked for Eustacia as a maid for many years. When she died I was only five years old, and Eustacia took me in, became my guardian, a second mother. It is difficult for me to see her in so much pain. As we've discussed, the surgery she requires is not routinely performed in Cuba. It is considered an 'unnecessary luxury' for the average Cuban, and any top party official in need of such a procedure typically goes to Toronto. In other words, if her knee is to be replaced, you are her only option. I've called off the press. No one but the head of the hospital and the Director of Public Health will know that an American has performed the surgery, so you need have no fears on that account."

La doctora's little discourse, far from gaining my sympathy, only made me angrier. Of course I was furious over her relentless attempts to pressure me, but there was something else: her tone, her cold, superior aloof tone of voice as she discussed something which according to her was a matter of great emotional significance, made my blood boil.

"Very touching. But the answer is still no."

"Why? What have you got to lose, besides a few hours of your time?"

This was a question for which I had no answer, so, like a good salesman, I answered it with another: "What gives you the right to tell me when, where and upon whom to operate?" La doctora looked away for a moment. I've scored a direct hit, I thought. Chalk one up for the AMA!

But la doctora was far from defeated. In fact, she proceeded to do me one better. "And what gives you the right," she demanded, "to come here and screw all our young women?"

"It's not a matter of rights," I replied, "it's a matter of, of…" Totally flustered, I said something which did not make a great deal of sense. "I'm on vacation."

"I can't offer you money," she said.

"It's not about the money. I don't need the damn money. It's a matter of principle."

"And what principle might that be? Dirty Old Manism?"

"Winning friends and influencing people isn't your strong point, is it, doctora?"

Eva stood there glaring at me for several moments. Then, to my absolute dismay, she began to remove her clothing.

"What the hell are you doing?"

"I can't give you money," she said, dropping her blouse to the floor. "I can't convince you with words," she went on, unsnapping her bra. "So the only argument I have left," she concluded, slipping out of her skirt, "is sex."

"But I don't want to have sex with you."

"Are you sure?"

The sight of la doctora Eva naked was, to say the least, disconcerting. She was not merely beautiful, she was perfect: from her wonderfully proportioned high round breasts, to her barely rounded belly; from her long magnificent thighs, to her narrow hips, if there was a single blemish anywhere on that peerless café au lait body, it would have taken a loupe to discover it.

"Y-yes, I'm s-sure," I managed to stutter.

La doctora took three steps forward, reached out and gave my willfully hard little friend a gentle squeeze. Then she began to slowly slide her hand up and down, up and down…

I was, in a word, flabbergasted. What had happened to the Ice Queen? "No," I said, my voice a hoarse croak, "don't do that."

"Why not?" she asked, placing her other hand on my chest.

"I already have a girlfriend."

"And a wife, too, if I remember correctly."

"Yes, and a wife, too," I said weakly.

For a few moments I remained frozen in place while fidelity and lust battled for control of my decision-making apparatus. I will be faithful to Mariela, I told myself. I will be faithful to Mariela. I will be…alas, by the third 'faithful' my shamelessly erect appendage was already throbbing away inside la doctora's surprisingly expert mouth. I'd lost. In one fell slurp, I'd lost the battle, the war and what little was left of my dignity.

A little while later, Eva freed up her mouth and said, "Fuck me." Like a well-trained beagle, I obeyed at once.

What followed was a true revelation. Beneath that frosty surface, la doctora Eva was white hot molten lava. I've already stated my aversion to describing this sort of thing in graphic detail, so I will only say this: it was the most electrifying, frenzied sex I'd ever experienced. But once it was over, all I felt was depressed, and drained.

It had involved no affection, no generosity, no…love? Like nothing else could have, my session with la doctora brought home to me the fact that I was truly, deeply and irrevocably in love with Mariela.

Oh yes, and in the heat of animal passion, I'd agreed to perform the procedure on Eustacia's knee.

NINE

Why be coy? Even a vole could see the lunatic direction my life was taking. A growing fondness for Mariela, the demoralizing visit to her home, the short but poignant conversation with her sister and my neighbor's casual query ("Maybe you'll want to take your little sweetheart home with you, too?") had all combined to fill my addled cranium with a single notion: get Mariela out of Cuba! And into a studio apartment, conveniently located somewhere within walking distance of a Long Island Railroad stop.

Up until now I have not made a serious attempt (except for the "aloof wife" defense) to justify my less than model behavior. But before proceeding with the rest of this little tragicomedy, allow me to make a lone mitigating point in my favor. I promise to be brief.

Had Mariela's circumstances been different, had her prospects in Cuba been not quite so grim, I don't believe I would have chosen the path I eventually did. When I pictured Mariela living in that concrete oven, hungry, aging with time-lapse speed, working her round little butt off probing the orifices of ailing farm animals for twenty-five dollars a month, while in her spare time pedaling said derriere to the occasional foreigner; when I imagined the miserable hopeless existence which lay before her, I was overcome with an unbearable anguish—a feeling of guilt so all-consuming it completely devoured the last crumbs of my objective faculties.

Well, there you have it, short and to the point: the moral pretext for my immoral behavior.

The realization came upon me suddenly as I walked along the spray-tossed malecon, trying not to think about what had just transpired with Eva. To distract myself, I began to run a fantasy on my interior screen in which I really did, somehow, get Mariela to New York. The daydream began as a joke, on myself, but then…

Then it dawned on me that moving Mariela to America might not only be possible, but desirable (oh, how desirable!) as well. It might even be my ethical duty as a human being. A jolt of electricity ran down my spine. I began to walk faster.

"I could do it!" I said aloud in English, surprising a hooker who'd been shadowing me for the past ten minutes. My heart began to hammer like a carpenter on amphetamine. I continued to walk, faster and faster, arriving eventually at Los Viejos Tiempos. Badly in need of a sedative, I rushed inside.

"Mario, get me a mojito, quick," I called out. "And a Cojiba."

"Hey, look who's here," the wee waiter squeaked, "it's Dr. Pan-America: the Canadian/American/Puerto Rican. The man who's got the whole western hemisphere covered. The man with…"

"A drink, Mario, I need a drink. Please."

"And a cigar, right?"

"The cigar can wait. Just bring me a drink."

"I don't remember you smoking a cigar before," the midget said suspiciously.

"Mario!"

"Get me two mojitos," the miniature man yelled over his shoulder at the bartender—ten year old HC."

"Thank you."

"No problem. So, how you been doing? Getting any?"

"More or less."

"I've been telling everybody about how I saved your life the other day," Mario said proudly.

"Is my drink ready?"

"Is his drink ready?" Mario called over his shoulder.

"Yeah," the bartender shouted back, "why don't you get your little legs in gear and come get it."

"Why don't you stop fucking your mother," Mario replied.

"Why don't you kiss my ass, if you can find a step ladder," the bartender suggested.

"Why don't you get a job," the midget said.

"My drink!" I screamed. "Where's my goddamn drink?"

It was another slow afternoon at Los Viejos Tiempos. Two couples sat around the large airy bar. The band was on a break. Eventually, I was served my mojito, along with a cigar. Mario, who must have had an awfully tolerant sister, climbed into a seat beside me with a drink of his own.

"Here's to you, Doc," he said, raising his glass.

"Salud!"

"You're not mad at me, are you?

"Why should I be mad at you?"

"From the other time."

"What other time?"

"When you were choking on the pizza."

"I wasn't choking. And that wasn't pizza."

"You're still mad."

"No, Mario, I'm not angry with you. I'm upset, but it has nothing to do with you. How about another mojito?"

"Sure, don't mind if I do."

"I meant for me," I said, draining my glass.

"Two more!" Mario shouted at the bartender.

"Go fuck yourself!" the bartender shouted back.

"So, Doc, what are you upset about?"

"Nothing. It's personal." I set fire to my cigar. "How's that drink coming?"

Mario leapt off his chair and went to the bar, returning a few minutes later with two more mojitos. "Gracias," I said, taking a large slug.

"Salud!" Mario said, clinking my glass.

"Salud!"

"What is it, more woman trouble? Come on, you can tell Mario. Get it off your chest."

Why not? I thought. God only knew, I needed to talk to someone. From the moment I'd begun to actually consider exporting Mariela from Cuba, I'd been seized by a massive anxiety attack which showed no signs of abating. Yes, I needed, as Mario said, to 'get it off my chest', and what better audience was I likely to find than a half-sized alcoholic Cuban waiter with an attitude problem?

"Mario, I'm in love," I said, washing down my words with the remainder of my second drink. The rum was delicious, as was the cigar. I hoped I wasn't turning into a smoker.

"You don't seem very happy about it," Mario observed.

"I'm thinking about bringing her back to the United States with me."

"You can get her out?" Mario asked.

"I'm not sure. But the thing is, I'm already married."

"So?"

"So? So I will be condemning myself to a life of lying to the woman I have sworn a solemn oath to love, honor and cherish for all eternity."

"So?"

"If she finds out, it will hurt her deeply. She'll probably divorce me."

"Then you're all set. I don't see where the problem is."

These macho Latin men just don't get it, I thought. "Mario," I asked the midget, "don't you have any respect for women at all?"

"What do you mean?"

"Mario, I love my wife," I declared, fighting the urge to order another drink.

"You're not making any sense," the midget reprimanded me. "First it's respect, then it's love. What does one thing have to do with the other?"

"Everything," I began, "they have…"

"Listen, Doc, just answer me this: Who do you love more, your girlfriend or your wife?"

What should have been a relatively easy question to answer was, I realized, not easy at all. Did I love Mariela? Yes, without a doubt. Did I love Janice just as much? Hmmm. Did I love Janice at all? Certainly, I cared about her well-being enough to torment myself endlessly over the prospect of wounding her, but love…

"The girlfriend," I said finally.

"Well, there you go!" the midget declared happily. "Case closed. Ready for your pizza?"

TEN

We lay in each other's arms as the consumptive Russian air conditioner wheezed on and on, keeping the room nice and lukewarm, like a cup of abandoned tea. Mariela reached for me, but I pushed her hand away.

"What's the matter?" she asked slyly. "Are you finally running out of gas?"

"Nothing's the matter. I just want to hold you for a while."

"All right," she said, laying her cheek against mine. Then, after a minute she said, "Do you want to play dominoes?"

"No."

"You're not getting tired of me, are you?"

"Hardly. I love you to pieces, you little runt."

"And I love you, too, you dirty old dog." Mariela began kissing me about the ears.

I may have been suffering a provisional paucity of bodily fluids due to my encounter with la doctora earlier in the day, but growing tired of Mariela, I most definitely was not. In truth, I'd never felt so much tenderness for her as I did at that moment.

"You're so beautiful," I said.

"There's lots of chicas in Havana prettier than me."

"Maybe," I admitted, "but none of them are you."

"You're getting corny, and I'm getting horny." She began kissing my neck, my chin, my mouth. Five minutes of this was apparently sufficient to refill the tank, and then we were off to the races, but at a slow trot instead of a gallop.

Later, after a post-coital snack, I agreed to be slaughtered once again at dominoes. "Is there some kind of trick to this game?" I asked. "Something I don't get?"

"There's a lot of tricks to dominoes," she giggled, "and you don't get any of them."

"I'm starting to feel like an idiot."

"Don't feel bad. All white people are bad at dominoes. Like you're missing a gene or something. It's called racial inferiority."

After she'd beaten me four times in a row, I sued for peace and we went back to bed. "Mariela, I want to ask you something. It's an important question, no fooling around."

"What's wrong?"

"Nothing's wrong. What I want to ask you is, what do you think about the possibility—it's only a possibility—of leaving Cuba?"

"To be with you?"

"Well, yes."

"Let's go."

"I'm being serious, Mariela."

"So am I."

"I haven't really looked into it yet," I cautioned her. "I don't even know if we can get you out."

"We can try," she said hopefully.

"Yes, we could certainly try," I agreed. "But before we do, you should know a little bit about what your life would be like if we pull it off."

"Tell me," she said eagerly.

"It gets very cold in New York; far colder than you can imagine."

"Then you'd have to buy me all kinds of beautiful warm clothes."

"Yes, I would. And then there's the language. And you won't know anyone there, besides me. You'll miss your family, even your idiot brother. And…"

"And you won't be able to live with me, because of your wife."

"That's right. I can't leave my wife, Mariela. I have an… obligation. Maybe when the kids are out of college. Who knows. I'll have to sneak away to see you. You won't be able to call me at home."

"I don't mind," she said. "I'll have you—whatever part of you I can get. And I'll have a life."

Mariela, for her mother's sake, had to be home by ten pm; any later and the old gal would work herself up into a religious frenzy, pleading with the Lord for the safe return of her baby girl in a booming contralto which set all the neighborhood dogs howling in pain.

"I'll walk you to your taxi," I said. Her safety on the streets of Havana at that hour was not an issue—in a police state, street crime is fairly rare—I just wanted to prolong our time together, even if it was only for a few minutes.

Hand-in-hand we walked to the corner in search of a gypsy cab. But the corner was already occupied by a pair of beefy policemen. None of Havana's unofficial taxis would pick up a fare with those thugs standing around, so we continued on down the street. Mariela tightened her grip on my hand as we passed the policemen. There didn't seem to be a great deal that frightened her, but she was certainly terrified of Havana's Finest. And who could blame her? They scared me, too.

On the next corner we flagged down a 1955 Buick Special. As it came to a slow squeaky halt, I suddenly felt that crippling panic jabbing at my heart again, but for a different reason. My new preoccupation was that it would prove impossible to get Mariela out of Cuba, and that she would be embittered for life by the disappointment. Before she got in the car, I had to warn her, to emphasize that this could all be nothing but a pipe dream.

Reaching across the front seat, the long-armed driver opened the front passenger door—no mean feat; the car was immense. Then, as I was about to speak, Mariela, who hadn't uttered a word since we'd left my room, grabbed my arm and began to whisper urgently in my ear.

"It could all be just a fantasy," she said. "Don't get your hopes up. I don't want to see you disappointed. Just your wanting to try means a lot to me. Whatever happens, happens. At least we're having a good time."

As she climbed into the car, I thought I saw a pair of tears running down her cheeks. I know they were running down mine.

ELEVEN

On the corner with the two policemen I ran into Carlos.

"I have some news for you, Tocayo," he said, shaking my hand with unnecessary vigor. "I was just about to go knocking on your door."

News? Since our last encounter, only twelve hours had passed, though it seemed much longer. What could have happened in only half a day? Had Enrique won Wimbledon?

"Where's Henry the Eighth?"

"He had to go home, Tocayo. His mother worries about him. I put him in a taxi not two minutes ago. And your sweetheart?"

"Ditto," I said. "Worried mother, taxi—the whole nine yards. Tocayo, are we out of our minds?"

Carlos and I regarded each other for a long moment. Then we burst out laughing. We were a pair of absurd, middle-aged sex-tourists, and we knew it.

"Yes," Carlos finally replied, "we are most definitely deranged. But what a wonderful time we are having! You know, Tocayo, I am not the least bit sleepy. Can I invite you out for a drink? I know an interesting place not too far from here."

Why not? I thought. More anxious than drowsy, I was dying for some company. And I liked my neighbor; he was a bright fellow and had a certain sleazy charm I found appealing. I wondered if all gay Mexican pimps were as likeable as Carlos. Perhaps it was a national trait.

"I'd be delighted, Tocayo. What's this news you mentioned?"

"Oh, it is something you may find helpful. Are you sober? Yes? I'll tell you over drinks. It is not a topic best discussed while sober. Let's grab a taxi. I love these old cars. Don't you? Last night we took a ride in a beautiful Flymowth. It must have been from World War II."

"Plymouth," I corrected him.

"Puh-lee-mowth?" he repeated carefully.

"Muth."

"Mouth?"

"Close enough."

The interesting place my neighbor had in mind was a flamboyant nightclub called *el Cordero Rojo* (The Red Lamb). A marquee above the door proclaimed in bold letters: "Boys with Boys! Girls with Girls! Boys with Girls!"

"Something for everyone," Carlos announced, patting me on the back, as I stood on the sidewalk peering dubiously at the sign.

The club was dimly lit and sparsely populated. It was only ten o'clock and Havana nightlife didn't attain escape velocity until after midnight. We sat at a small table near the stage. A pretty young girl dressed in a thong, high heels and a bright yellow wig, approached our table and said, "Good evening, gentlemen. Are we here for the boys or for the girls?"

"Both," my Tocayo said.

"Oh, how interesting!" the girl yawned with enthusiasm; she was trying very hard not to appear bored. "And what will you have to drink?"

"Mojitos, what else," Carlos said. "If they were good enough for Hemingway, they're good enough for us. By the way, you have lovely little nipples, dear," he added, appraising her bare breasts with a professional eye.

"Thank you," she replied.

"You would have made a beautiful boy."

"Thank you again, I guess."

"Make the mojitos with the ten-year-old Havana Club," I told her, before she could teeter away on her six-inch heels.

"Wait a minute, dear," Carlos told the waitress. "Tocayo," he said gravely, "they are going to charge us up the ass for the Black Label. Surely, the five-year-old is good enough. Yes? Young lady, we'll have…"

"It's all right, Carlos; I'll put them on my expense account. Señorita, the ten-year-old, HC, if you please."

"Do you like my nipples, too?" she asked, eying me with respect—few customers, I imagined, were in the habit of so blithely ordering twenty dollar mojitos. "I'm not sure," she continued, "what an expense account is, but you could probably put me on it, too. After the show. All of me."

"Yes, I'm sure."

"Including my nipples."

"Very nice. We'd like our drinks now, please. So, Tocayo, what's this news you have? I'm dying of curiosity."

"Ah yes. The news. Since our conversation this morning, Tocayo, I've been doing some checking around with my contacts. About getting your girlfriend out of Cuba and into the United States. I thought you might be interested. I hope I haven't presumed? No? As I suspected, Tocayo…"

At that moment the drinks arrived, and their manner of presentation momentarily stopped all conversation. Instead of glasses, they were served in mugs. One mug was in the form of a female breast—you drank, naturally, from the nipple. The other was shaped like a full set of male genitalia, with the penis forming the "straw". Our waitress, a seasoned professional, placed the breast in front of me, and the penis in front of Carlos.

"Salud!" he said, clinking my breast with his testicles.

"Salud!"

"The first show is all-girl," Carlos said, sucking briefly on the tip of his mug, "It should start pretty soon."

I took a brief pull on my nipple and said, "Can't wait."

"To the news. Getting your little love-cushion back to America will not be easy. Please allow me to explain."

"Por supuesto."

"First of all, gaining legal permission to leave the island is and is not a problem. Two, maybe three thousand dollars in bribes, a small mountain of forms, and in a few weeks, you're almost good to go. If you're not in a huge hurry, you could probably get it done for fifteen hundred."

"That seems reasonable," I said carefully. Once again we clinked mugs.

"Salud!"

"Salud!"

"Yes, Tocayo, that is the cheap way, but unfortunately, it may not work for you. You see, in order to finalize the exit-permit, you must first have a visa to enter the United States. I had reason to check into this not too long ago. An American client. It's a long story. You don't want to hear it, do you? No? I didn't think so. In any case, the Americans might take years to approve the visa, or they might never approve it at all."

"I can't wait years, Tocayo. For her sake. I've seen what life here does to people."

"Yes, Tocayo, you are absolutely right. The flower wilts before your very eyes. So, I'm sure you see my point: if you cannot get her legally into the United States, then you cannot get her legally out of Cuba. Do you see what I mean? Yes? What do they call that in English? A studio fifty-four?"

"Catch twenty-two."

"Of course. I love the English language. It is so colorful. Well, Tocayo, that leaves us with the expensive way. We don't worry about legalities at all. We hire a professional driver with a good boat, someone experienced and dependable, someone who has done this many times. Salud, Tocayo!"

"Salud!"

Carlos offered me a Monte Cristo, which I accepted without a thought.

For a while the two of us sat there puffing contentedly on our cigars and sucking every now and then on our respective body parts.

"The boat," my *Tocayo* resumed, "would drop her off on a remote beach in Florida. One cannot know the exact location beforehand. The boat might have to take evasive action. Now, once she sets foot on American soil, she's home free, thanks to your government's bizarre *Wet Foot/ Dry Foot* policy."

"What's that?"

"It was enacted a few years, ago, Tocayo, and it makes absolutely no sense. It says that if a Cuban is caught at sea, then he is sent back to Cuba." Carlos paused to take a long pull on the head of his flesh-colored mug. "But if that very same Cuban manages to land on US soil without being caught, then he can stay, apply for a permanent resident visa, and eventually, citizenship. Is that not insane?"

"My country's entire policy towards Cuba is insane, Tocayo. Salud!" I said, raising my ceramic mammary.

"Salud! All right. Now we have the question of how your friend makes it from Point A to Point B without being caught. And the answer is…"

"A fast boat?"

"Correct, Tocayo. A fast expensive boat."

"How expensive?"

"That depends, Tocayo, on a number of factors. How fast is the boat? How big? How new? How many émigrés besides her are going along for the ride? Generally speaking, the bigger, the faster, the less crowded the boat, the more it will cost. The range is huge: from as little as five, all the way up to fifty thousand dollars. Would you be prepared to spend so much?"

"That depends," I said. Suddenly, I was suspicious. What if my seemingly well-intentioned Tocayo was in reality an unscrupulous grifter? All I knew for certain about the man was that he was having some kind of sex with a short Cuban weightlifter.

"On what, Tocayo?"

"Risks. Guarantees. Timing. That sort of thing."

Carlos appeared to be mildly offended, but his tone was all-business. "Tocayo, take this information for what it is worth to you. I only meant to establish whether or not this was a real conversation."

"All right," I said cautiously, "let's say it's real."

"Well then, arrangements for these boats are normally made in Florida by family members of the interested party. They pay…"

"Wait a minute. Pardon my ignorance, Tocayo, but why Florida? Why not make the arrangements here?"

"For two reasons, Tocayo: one, the money is there; and two, so are the boats. Or they are in the Bahamas, or somewhere. No one knows for sure. Obviously, you would also have to arrange the pick-up procedure with someone here in Cuba. It can be quite elaborate, due to the risks involved."

"The boats are not kept in Cuba?"

"Of course not. That would be far too dangerous. Many of them, I understand, are stolen."

"That means," I said, "that first, the boat has to sneak into Cuba, then it has to sneak into the United States?"

"You are forgetting, Tocayo, sneaking away from Cuba. The government occasionally regards these little forays as violations of national sovereignty, and does whatever it can to discourage them. Salud!"

"Salud!"

"And so," Carlos continued, "typically, the family in Florida pays half upfront, and half upon completion. Once the delivery is made, the rest is up to you."

"Please explain to me again, Tocayo, about the price range; it seems awfully wide."

"The more you pay, the better the boat and the less crowded it will be. To maximize their profits, the smugglers usually try to pack in as many people as possible. Overloaded boats can be quite dangerous, especially if the weather is rough. As long as the money is not a problem, it would not be wise to skimp, would it, Tocayo? Of course not. If you love this girl enough to go ahead with your insane plan, then you'll want her delivered to you in good condition, won't you?"

"You make her sound like a package of meat, Tocayo."

"Well," Carlos said, "you have to admit, it is, in some ways, an apt analogy."

I began to get angry, but then all at once it dawned on me how bizarre this scene would appear to my former self—that is to say, the man I had been only seven days ago. Because the man sitting here in this live-sex club in Havana, swilling down his mojitos, puffing on his cigar and listening with rapt attention to his gay Mexican pimp pal lecture him on the subject of how to smuggle one's teenage mistress into the United States—that man could not possibly be me.

All right, so he's not me, I thought. So what? I sucked hard on my mojito. So he looks like me. He sounds like me. And, like Carlos said, he's having a good time. But still: sucking on a ceramic nipple in a live-sex club?

The lights flashed on and off. "Showtime!" Carlos announced in English.

And so it was. A lurid blue spot lit the small stage, revealing the presence of two young women dressed as nurses. They appeared to be just out of high school and were quite attractive, naturally. Nurse A lay down on what looked like a hospital gurney. "Take off your clothes!" Nurse B commanded, "I'm going to give you a complete examination!" Reaching into a black leather bag she removed an apparatus which looked like a stethoscope, except that two long plastic phalluses took the place of the ear pads. The flesh-colored dildos, utilizing the latest in sex-toy technology, began to wink on and off, like the lights of a Christmas tree.

A few minutes later, I passed out. It had been a long day.

TWELVE

The next morning, my second Tuesday in Cuba, I awoke feeling awful. I couldn't recall how many nipple-mugs I'd drained the night before, but it must have been a new personal best. Of how the evening ended, I had little recollection, either. Carlos had gotten me home somehow and tucked me in. I pried my eyes open a millimeter or so and took a painful peek under the too-short sheet: yes, I was there all right, and dressed in the same pair of boxer shorts I'd slid into the previous day. Halleluiah!

Someone was knocking on my door, but the sound was shunted aside at once by a brief but intense attack of panic. What if, I wondered numbly, my boy-smuggling buddy had felt inclined to take advantage of me while I lay there unprotected in a mojito-induced stupor? Carlos seemed like a gentleman...but look what he did for a living!

No, no, I told myself, it was highly unlikely. In the first place, I was far (about thirty years too far) from being his type. And wouldn't I know if something untoward had occurred? Wouldn't I be, if not the first, at least among the first to know?

The knocking was joined by the creaky voice of my landlady encouraging me to get up and face the new day. I glanced at the travel clock; it was well after eleven. "All right," I growled, "leave it by the door."

After those first few blissful days of courtship, when Eustacia had made a point of handing me my breakfast tray with her own two desiccated hands, she had abruptly lost interest. For the past week the orange juice and high-voltage coffee had been deposited on a small table outside my door. But now...

"Open the door," she croaked, "I have extra orange juice. And some cheese and bread. And real eggs!"

Real eggs? What had I been eating all this time: artificial ova left-over from the days of Russian aid? My head throbbed with relentless pain. I prayed to a God I had never managed to believe in to please make my landlady go away. But of course she didn't. She was relentless, too. I threw on a robe, ran my fingers through my hair and opened the door.

Eustacia burst in with a gimpy bustle you had to admire, all but bowling me over as she made for the card table. After placing my tray in front of one chair, she sat down in the other and lit a cigarette.

"I haven't smoked a cigarette in twenty-five years," she declared proudly. She paused, hoping I would ask why she had started again now. I did not. I sat in the vacant chair gritting my teeth, taking shallow breaths and hoping I did not begin to dry heave onto my breakfast.

"I'm nervous," she finally answered her own unspoken question. "I've never been this nervous. Eat your eggs before they get cold."

"I'm afraid I'm not all that hungry. Perhaps I could eat them later?"

"Cold eggs? Who ever heard of eating cold eggs. Come on, chow down. We've got to keep our strength up for the big operation. Those eggs are loaded with real protein. They're not too loose for you, are they? My God!" she exclaimed, her eyes widening in alarm, "you're green!"

"Oh, you've noticed," I said, fighting off the urge to gag. "If it is any consolation to you, Eustacia, I feel far worse than I look."

"That's what's making me nervous! The operation is tomorrow, if you remember. And look at you! More dead than alive! Hold out your hands," she ordered. Reluctantly, I obeyed. "They're shaking! They're shaking!" she shrieked like a featherless parrot. "Do they shake like that when you're operating?"

"No, they only shake when I'm sober."

"You operate while under the influence? I knew it. I knew it. Drink your juice!"

"It was only a joke," I moaned, taking a tentative sip of the coffee.

"You go in there drunk," my landlady conjectured, "you're liable to repair the wrong knee."

"No danger of that," I assured her. "Prior to surgery I always paint a large 'X' on the appropriate limb."

"What color?"

"What color?"

"What color are you going to paint my knee? It's ugly enough as it is. I can't stand mauve. Or orange. Anything but mauve or orange."

"I was joking, Eustacia."

"Joking, always joking. When the scalpel slips and you cut off my artery, will you make a joke out of that, too? Maybe we should call this whole thing off. While I'm still intact."

"Not a bad idea."

"Eat your eggs."

Against my better judgment I inserted a tiny forkful of loosely scrambled egg into my mouth. Moments later, it had the feared effect.

"Excuse me, please," I mumbled, lurching for the bathroom.

Quite a while later, after finally managing to pry myself from the commode, I found Eustacia precisely where I'd left her, staring at my puffy pasty face with an expression of mounting horror.

"I better call la doctora," she announced.

"No, no, please, don't! I'll be fine…by tomorrow."

"I understand," Eustacia said coyly, "you and Eva hit it off pretty well."

"Ah…"

"Even better than with your little playmate. Eh?"

"I wouldn't say that."

"I would," my landlady said, with the smug assurance of someone who has seen (and heard) it all. "I thought the walls were going to come down."

"I happen to be very fond of my little playmate," I said with ill humor.

"But she's so young. Didn't you find Eva more... adept?"

"Well," I said, losing my temper completely, "she gives tremendous head; I'll give her that."

For a moment Eustacia was confused. But she recovered quickly. "That's probably because she's taller," she said knowledgeably.

"What does her height have to do with it?" The conversation was taking a truly fantastic turn.

"Well, it should...I mean...wouldn't that give her some kind of advantage?"

"Yes, it would. If we were playing basketball. But when it comes to oral sex, height is immaterial."

"It is?"

"Yes, most definitely."

"Well," Eustacia said, grudgingly conceding the point, "I suppose you should know."

"What's that supposed to mean?"

"I was just thinking, by now you must have had enough women here to make your own basketball team."

Quickly I counted on my fingers: one...two...three... four. "No," I told my landlady, "I'm still short a center."

Eustacia narrowed her eyes. "You're one of those Christians, aren't you?"

"One of what Christians?" From sex to basketball to Jesus Christ: not even a hummingbird could have followed the erratic flight of my landlady's wildly careening mind. I attempted to change the subject. "Don't you want to know what a center is?" I asked.

"Absolutely not! I happen to be a respectable woman, in case you hadn't noticed."

The next moment she was up and out of the chair "Wait here," she ordered. "I'll be right back."

I sat in my chair, taking small cautious sips of coffee, feeling marginally better with each sip. What I really needed,

I knew, was a mojito—just one, to take the edge off. Briefly I considered throwing on my clothes and taking flight. But before I could even locate a shirt, Eustacia was back.

For a moment she stood there in the doorway, her lined face contorted with revulsion. At arm's length, she held by its flyleaf, as if it were a dead rat, an old moldy copy of the Holy Bible.

Sliding my breakfast tray aside, she placed the musty book before me and said:

"Put your right hand on top of it, and repeat after me." Though I am far from being religious, some buried atavistic instinct made me hesitate. "Go ahead," Eustacia ordered me.

"Are you a Christian?" I asked.

"Of course not. I'm a good Communist, just like my husband was."

"Where did you get the bible?"

"One of my tenants, a religious pervert from Yugoslavia, left it here."

"But you're not a Christian?"

"God forbid!"

"Then why do you want me to swear on a bible?"

"I saw them do it on television."

"So?"

"You are a Capitalist," she said, "and all Capitalists are superstitious."

"I'm a medical doctor, Eustacia, not a witchdoctor."

"Whatever. Just put your hand on the stupid book." When finally I complied, she said, "Now, repeat after me: I swear not to have any alcohol for the next twenty-four hours."

Despite the brutal hangover, I began to giggle. A Communist atheist coercing a Capitalist atheist into swearing on the Holy Bible—even Janice would have appreciated the irony. On the other hand, maybe she wouldn't. Between giggles, I repeated the oath.

"I also promise," she continued, frowning at my small bursts of hilarity, "to go to bed early tonight. By myself."

I repeated this, as well.

"And," Eustacia intoned, "I swear to eat three good meals today. As soon as I can keep them down."

When the bizarre procedure was over, Eustacia gathered everything up, and headed for the hall. "Just remember," she said, pausing in the doorway, "if you break your oaths, you're going straight to Hell, just like on television."

THIRTEEN

By mid-afternoon I was feeling well enough to leave the comfort of my lukewarm room and brave the life-annulling heat outside. The closest place to get a drink was the bar of the nearby *Havana Libre*. To this location I slogged as quickly as I was able. Their mojito, rumored to be the best in town, did not disappoint. And as I'd hoped the alcohol went a long way towards easing my hangover. At the very least, I would go to hell feeling a bit better.

Suddenly, I was hungry. I paid for my drink and walked across the street to the café where I'd met the impoverished surgeon. As I approached the door a tall young man asked me what time it was. Glancing at my watchless wrist, I mumbled, "Quarter past."

"Okay!" he said. "You speak good Spanish. Where you from?"

"Uranus."

"Oh yeah," he said, nodding his head with approval, "one of those European countries."

"Yes, on the border with Yourprickenstein."

Inside the cafe I was greeted by the waiter with an explosive display of friendliness. Apparently, he remembered me, which was understandable; for a tip I'd given him an entire box of cigars—a gesture I now regretted.

"Oh, my friend!" he exclaimed. "It is *so* good to see you! Have you been well? Enjoying yourself? A little too much?" he asked with concern. "Those chicas can really wear a man out. Señor, it is *so* good to see you!"

"I'll have a ham and cheese sandwich," I said sourly.

"No coffee? How about some juice? A plate of spaghetti?"

When I did not respond in any way, he scampered off. A moment later I heard him yelling at the cook: "And make it snappy. This is an important customer. Not some cheap Canadian. Use the real cheese. Come on, get moving!"

"Stick it in your ass," the cook grumbled, echoing the bartender at *Los Viejos Tiempos*. In New York, I recalled, restaurant workers cursed each other with far more vigor. This lack of enthusiasm on the part of the Cuban service sector I attributed to the communist economic model. With no hope of advancement, workers in Havana simply had no incentive to go that extra kilometer.

A mere five minutes later, my sandwich, in all its glory, was laid before me. "I made sure they used this month's ham," the waiter whispered in my ear.

"As opposed to?"

The waiter shrugged his bony shoulders. "Well, señor, you know how it is."

I took a tentative bite. This month's ham was a little on the rubbery side. In fact, it did not feel like ham at all. In my mind's eye I saw a herd of handicapped pigs limping about the Cuban countryside minus most of their chewy body parts: ears, noses, lips, hooves and anuses. No, that didn't sound right. Did the word anus even have a plural form? Annai? 'My proctologist examined three annai today.' No, I concluded, continuing to chew, in all likelihood there is no provision in the English language for contemplating more than one anus at a time.

Halfway through this profile in courage, my cigar-selling doctor friend suddenly appeared like a wraith beside my table, looking shabbier than ever.

"Hello, doctor," I said.

"Good afternoon," he replied formally.

"Raoul, isn't it?"

"Yes. Your memory is better than mine, I'm afraid."

"Carlos," I said, offering my hand. "Have a seat."

"Thank you."

"Hungry or not, Raoul, I'm treating you to a sandwich this time."

"That is very kind of you."

The doctor, with his elongated face, small goatee and pointy ears reminded me of an emaciated Mephistopheles. Was my retribution to be so swift? It had only been a single mojito, after all.

"Have you been ill, Carlos?" he asked with concern.

"No, a hangover."

Sagely, he nodded his head. His sandwich arrived and the two of us chewed in silence. "This is not bad," he announced eventually.

"You think it's good?"

"I did not say that," he replied with precision.

"Do you happen to have another box of cigars on you, Raoul?"

"Yes, by chance…"

"Twenty dollars, right?"

"You want the whole box? Again?"

"Yes, is that a problem?" Perhaps he made more money selling them individually.

"No, not all. It just seems that…well, I hope you have not been smoking to excess."

"No, no," I laughed, "smoking is the very least of my problems. Besides, I don't inhale."

"A wise policy. Nonetheless…"

"Raoul," I said after a while, "you seem like a man one can confide in. Would you mind if I unburdened myself for a few minutes?"

"Of course not, Carlos. I am all ears." And with his comically long auricular add-ons, he was not far from wrong.

"Raoul, tomorrow morning I am going to perform a total knee arthroplasty."

The doctor was surprised. "Here in Havana?"

"Yes."

"Which hospital?"

"I think it's called the Jose Marti Revolutionary Hospital for Corrective Surgery and…something or other. Do you know it?"

"Of course. It is the best hospital in Cuba. Only high party officials or their relatives are admitted there. How in the world…" The doctor trailed off, his haunted intelligent eyes fixed on…something.

Working around my experience with la doctora (Raoul seemed broad minded, but one never knew), I gave him a quick synopsis of the entire situation. The destitute surgeon shook his head a number of times during my little discourse, muttering, "Only in Cuba, only in Cuba."

When I finished speaking, he looked me sternly in the eye and said, "If I may be so bold…why in God's name did you agree to this? Don't you realize…"

Raoul was no fool; he'd gotten to the heart of the matter at once.

"To be perfectly candid, Raoul, I'd rather not say."

"What about the prosthesis? Where is that coming from? The expense…here in Cuba…"

Once again the doctor left his remarks dangling in the air, as if he'd reached the edge of an abyss, and dared go no further.

"I've been told that it's all taken care of. Everything I need will be there waiting for me."

"Your patient must be extremely well-connected. After all…"

"Apparently, her husband was a party member in good standing. Aside from that, I wouldn't know."

"You feel confident?" Raoul asked.

"About what?"

"That you can successfully perform the procedure. I only ask because…" Because I gave every appearance of being a hopeless drunk, was what he was thinking, I am sure. But of course he was too polite to speak the thought aloud.

"I've performed this procedure several hundred times. I could do it in my sleep. And," I added, giving Raoul a small smile, "I'll be well over my hangover when the time comes. I'm not normally a heavy drinker."

"That is good."

"So, Raoul, would you like to assist me?"

"I would be honored, but I don't know how much good I could do. I've never performed this type of surgery before. As far as I know, no one…" Yet again, Raoul stalled in mid-sentence.

"That's not a problem. I'd just like to have another surgeon there. Just in case."

"Of course. I know I'll find it fascinating."

"Good. Now, there is another matter. I'm afraid I've fallen in love."

"With your landlady's beautiful young doctor?"

"No," I laughed. "Close, but no cigar."

Raoul was confused. "You no longer want the cigars?"

"No, no, that's just an expression. I meant that I could have fallen in love with la doctora, but I was already in love with someone else."

"I see. Your wife…"

"No, not my wife. Raoul, this is a little embarrassing."

"Carlos," he said kindly, "please feel free to tell me anything you wish. I promise not to be judgmental, just like a priest."

"Judging people is what priests do," I informed him.

"Oh, well, then…a rabbi?"

"A rabbi? Never mind, it's not important. Raoul, the problem, or the potential problem, is that I'm thinking of taking my girlfriend back to the United States and…"

It was my turn to trail off into verbal nothingness, as I stared down into my own abyss.

"You are married?"

"Yes."

"And the girl, how old is she?"

"Nineteen."

"Won't your wife be upset?"

"She, ah…the plan is…she's not going to know."

"I see."

"Yes?"

"I see," Raoul said neutrally, "a highly intelligent man about to do something…"

"Not so intelligent?"

"Yes, that is an excellent way of putting it."

"You're probably right, but what I wanted to ask you about was the feasibility of getting her out of Cuba."

"Yes. It is…possible…" Raoul's eyes seemed to fog over, like a pair of ships lost at sea.

"How do you know?"

"Most Cubans know these things. It is of personal interest. I myself have family members in Florida."

"So it is possible to smuggle a Cuban into the US?"

"Of course. It happens every day."

"But it's dangerous?"

"There is always the danger of drowning."

"But with a good boat and driver," I asked eagerly, "the risk is greatly reduced?"

"Yes, the risk of drowning. As long as the boat is not too terribly overcrowded."

"And as far as you know, there are good safe boats available?"

"If you have the money. Of course."

"And the drivers—they're reliable?"

"They are reliably greedy. You have to understand, we are talking about criminals being contracted by desperate people to break the laws of two countries. Not exactly an ideal…" The doctor took up his unfocused long-distance vigil again.

As I left the café, a box of *Romeo and Juliets* tucked under my arm, the waiter and the cook were having a bitter argument.

"He left only fifteen per cent!" the waiter hissed.

"So?"

"So, it's your fault; you didn't put enough ham in his sandwich."

"Ham?"

FOURTEEN

After brunch with Raoul I shuffled back to the house, shading my throbbing head from the sun with a discarded newspaper. My recently ingested mystery sandwich notwithstanding, I was still hungry, but like a wounded animal all I wanted to do was crawl into a dark place and go to sleep. Before I could even reach my door, I was intercepted by Eustacia, who had shifted into full fawning mode. Upon her cracked lips there was pasted a big phony smile, but her eyes were wide with suppressed terror.

"I've made you lunch. Come along to the kitchen," she said, patting me affectionately on the arm. "A man like you needs to keep up his strength."

"A man like me?"

The kitchen was small but cozy. At that late afternoon hour the sun shone directly through the window, bathing in a warm golden glow all the incredibly arcane junk Eustacia had pinned to the walls. "That photo over the stove," I said as I sat down, "the one of Che Guevara?"

"Which one?" she asked. Images of Che mottled the Cuban landscape like spots on a leopard.

"The one with the flashing neon tubes around the edges."

"The red, or the pink?"

"Oh, the pink, I suppose."

"What about it?"

"Well, it doesn't look like something made in Cuba. I was wondering where you got it."

"It's imported," Eustacia said proudly. "Made in China. My husband bought it for me. Before he died. You can't find anything like that in Cuba today," she concluded sadly.

"That's too bad."

Eustacia proceeded to serve me an excellent meal, which I devoured as if I hadn't eaten in a week, which in a way was true. The food was fresh, well-seasoned and readily identifiable as to origin—even the protein.

"This seems to be real chicken," I said with awe.

"Nothing but the best for my doctor," Eustacia replied, taking the art of shameless sucking-up to new and Olympian heights, "the most virile, most handsome American surgeon in all Havana!"

As forkful after forkful of fresh recognizable food went skipping merrily down my gullet, Eustacia sat nodding her curler-topped head with approval. When finally I began to tire, she commenced to lavish me with encouragement. "Just take it one bite at a time," she urged. "You can do it. Keep going. You're almost done! That's it. One more…now another…"

Apparently, she was convinced (with Aboriginal logic) that every calorie consumed by the great white doctor would reduce by one mystical unit the odds of him accidentally lopping off a leg, or sewing together a pair of ankles.

"That's it, I'm done!" I said, dropping my napkin onto my plate. "That was wonderful; the best meal I've had in Cuba. Thank you, Eustacia."

"You did a good job," she said judiciously. "Of course, the best meal in Havana—that's not saying much," she added darkly.

"How about some of your delicious coffee to top things off?"

"Not on your life! You're getting a good night's sleep, mister. No coffee for you."

"But it's early—only four o'clock."

"That's late enough."

"But no one needs fifteen hours of sleep."

"You might."

"Come on, Eustacia, just half a cup." Mariela would be turning up before too long and I was hoping to acquire a small boost prior to her arrival.

"We'll let la doctora decide," Eustacia decreed. "She'll be here any minute to give me my pre-operation physical. She wanted you to do it, but I told her I didn't feel comfortable with a man putting his hands all over me."

"What about during the operation?" I teased. "I'll have my hands all over you then."

"I'll be asleep. And there'll be other people around. Just in case."

"In case of what?"

"Well, in case of…what I meant was…in a hospital environment…" Eustacia was saved from further embarrassment by the doorbell. "That must be la doctora," she said with relief.

"Shall I let her in?"

"No, she has her own key. She's the kind of person you can trust."

La doctora Eva looked crisp, efficient and impossibly gorgeous in her medical whites as she strode briskly into the kitchen. For a long time she stood looking first at me, then at Eustacia. Finally, she said, "You look terrible."

"I do?" Eustacia asked in alarm.

"Not you, him," she said, aiming her flawless chin at my heart.

"I'm fine. I just need a nap."

Eva scowled. "Yes, a nap and a transfusion. Did anyone mention that you'll have to be awake for the surgery tomorrow? Go take your nap. I have to examine Eustacia."

My nap lasted for only half an hour. I was awakened by an uncomfortable feeling in the area of my biceps: Eva was taking my blood pressure. When she was finished she said, "Stick out your tongue." I complied, but not graciously. After my tongue, she inspected my eyes and took my pulse.

"You're badly dehydrated," she said. "Alcohol?"

I nodded my head.

"In this heat," she said, "what you need to drink is water, not rum. I ought to put you on an IV."

"How about a few glasses of lemonade? Wouldn't that do just as well?"

"Perhaps. But in the present case, I'd rather not take any chances." La doctora began to rummage about inside an old battered medical bag, withdrawing an IV bag, a syringe, a roll of tape and what looked like a rectal thermometer. Deftly, against my weak protests, she inserted the needle, taped it down and attached it to the IV, which she'd hung from the curtain rod. Then she sat down on the bed.

"You know," she said after a while, shaking the thermometer with quick flicks of her wrist, "I really enjoyed myself yesterday."

Had it only been yesterday?

"Yes, well..."

A long silence ensued, as la doctora peered into my eyes, and I stared uneasily at the blurry thermometer. "Despite your obvious shortcomings," she said finally, "I find myself strongly attracted to you." She removed a tube from her bag and squirted a small dab of something onto the business end of the thermometer.

"Excuse me," I said with difficulty—my throat had begun to constrict—"what's with the thermometer?"

"I'm going to take your temperature."

"But that's a...that's a rectal thermometer."

"I know," she laughed. "It's the only kind I have on me. I mentioned, didn't I, that I mostly treat very young children."

"Yes, you did, but..."

"It won't bite you. Turn over on your side."

"I'm, ah, not sure I want to do that."

"You're shaking," Eva said, regarding me with a superior smile. Men are such children."

Yes, I was shaking, but not from fear. The truth is, the mere possibility of la doctora inserting a thermometer into my rectum as I lay there otherwise naked beneath the thin sheet thrilled me in ways only a disciple of Freud could pretend to understand. And then there was the imminent arrival of Mariela to consider.

"Well," I mumbled, "we may be children, but I fail to see..."

"What's this?" la doctora cried with mock surprise, grabbing my swollen pipinnum through the sheet and giving it a squeeze.

"That?" I choked.

"I didn't realize living human flesh could get that hard," she said with furrowed brow. Then she gave my hip a small shove, pushing me onto my side, and before you could say "Oedipus' mother", she'd guided the thin little missile to its pre-programmed target.

"There, that wasn't so bad, was it?" she said, laying a cool palm atop my left buttock and leaving it there.

"Bad?" I said hoarsely. "No, not bad exactly, but…"

Someone knocked on the door to my room—the exterior door.

"It's open, come in!" Eva called out gaily. Frantically, I reached for the sheet to cover my exposed ass, but the IV line would not permit that arm sufficient latitude, and my other arm was pinned beneath me. La doctora favored me with a faint smile. Then, as I lay there, exposed and writhing helplessly, Perla walked in.

Perla, whose long honey-colored hair was pulled back into a pony tail, stared first at me and then at Eva with an expression of utter confusion. Then she saw the IV. Then, last but not least, her eyes fell upon the thermometer, wagging like a baby possum tail and pointing unmistakably, even as it quivered, in her direction.

"What?" she said. "What?"

"Is that one question, dear, or two?" Eva asked politely.

When Perla had a little time to gather her meager wits, she immediately leapt to the wrong conclusion. "You…you…you pervert!"

I was about to say, "This is not what it looks like," when I remembered who I was talking to. So I said nothing. For a few moments silence reigned. Then Perla buried her face in her hands and began to sob. La doctora shot me an evil look before plucking the thermometer from its launching pad. Then, holding it up to the light, she announced, "Temperature's normal."

"That's the only normal thing about him!" Perla informed la doctora. "He's a sodomist," she added, before rushing from the room.

"Sodomist?" la doctora asked, arching her elegant brows.

"Someone," I muttered, "must have loaned her a library card."

FIFTEEN

Waiting for Mariela had become, for me, something of a pastime, but not one I enjoyed. The later she was, the greater my suffering. But not now—now I found myself praying for a clogged carburetor, a Communist Youth march, an unscheduled vivisection—anything which might further delay her arrival.

She'd already missed (thank God!) the thermometer incident, not to mention Perla's short but sour visit. All I needed now was to make Eva disappear.

No longer at risk of launching the mini-glass submarine into the heart of my personal darkness, I turned onto my back and pulled the sheet defensively up to my chin. La doctora continued to sit beside me on the bed.

"Well," I said, "I guess that about wraps things up. It's been an, ah, interesting, ah, whatever. I'll see you tomorrow morning? At eight sharp?"

"You still have thirty minutes to go on your drip," Eva pointed out.

"Yes, well, I am a qualified physician, Eva, in case you've forgotten. I'm sure I can remove it myself."

La doctora reached out and squeezed my no longer tumescent member. "Gosh," she said, "what happened? Maybe you are ill."

"No, I'm not ill. And, by the way, I don't particularly enjoy being humiliated."

"Really? Somehow I would've thought you were the type."

"Eva," I asked, softening my voice, "would you do me a large favor, please?"

"All right," Eva said, "but if you want to sodomize me, I'll have to sedate myself first."

"I'm being serious."

"So am I."

Firmly but gently I took her hand and returned it to her own lap.

"Listen," I said, taking a deep breath, "obviously, I find you attractive. No, not just attractive. Eva, you are an extraordinarily beautiful woman. Which makes me wonder why you haven't married."

"There are two reasons. First, my work: it hasn't left me a great deal of time for a personal life."

"And?"

"And I've never met anyone who meets my high standards...until now."

"I meet your high standards?"

"Well, you might be a little lacking in the ethics department. But, on the other hand, you're a brilliant surgeon, marvelous in bed and wonderfully handsome."

"Wonderfully handsome?"

"That's another thing I like about you, your lack of vanity. You seem to have no idea how attractive you are. My guess is you did very little fooling around before you came to Cuba. Am I right?"

"Eva," I said with mounting desperation, "we need to postpone this discussion. Any minute now..."

Had I not been attached to the curtain rod, via the IV tube, I would surely have locked the door after Perla's departure; not that it would have mattered. Mariela, in one of her more mischievous moods, tried the knob, called out, "Watch out, here I come!" and bounced happily through the door. She'd come directly from school and was wearing her uniform, in which (as I've already made mention) she looked about fourteen. At best.

To her credit, the first words out of her mouth (after she'd ceased her happy bouncing) were, "Are you all right? What happened?"

"No, I'm fine," I said in a nervous rush of words. "Just a little dehydrated. Too many mojitos last night. My landlady's doctor thought I needed some liquids. She wants me to be in good shape, ha, ha, for the operation tomorrow. You two haven't met, have you? Mariela, this is Eva. Eva, Mariela."

"Hello."

"Hello."

They did not shake hands, but to my increasing discomfort they did begin a staring contest, which I knew, given their respective characters, could go on for all eternity. It occurred to me that both Perla and Mariela had made it past my landlady's lookout without interference. I began to smell a rat.

"La doctora was just leaving," I said, hoping to break the stalemate.

"Yes," Eva said, making no move to get off the bed. "But I should wait for the drip to finish, don't you think; so I can remove the needle and…clean you up."

Mariela frowned. My nerves, largely shot already, were approaching critical mass. I tore the tape from my arm and withdrew the needle. "I'll see you at the hospital tomorrow morning, doctora," I said pointedly. "Thanks for the IV. And have a nice day."

Eva never stopped smiling as she gathered up her things. "Nice to meet you," she said holding out her hand to Mariela.

"Nice to meet you," Mariela said grimly.

"So," Eva asked airily, "have you decided what you're going to do when you finish high school?"

"I have finished high school," Mariela replied, regarding her adversary with murderous intent. "I'm studying veterinary medicine."

Eva frowned. "I'm sorry. Please excuse me. And good luck with your studies."

Mariela managed a half smile and said, "Gracias."

All I could do was lay there and stare in wonder at la doctora Eva; she really was in every respect an admirable woman. Briefly, I wondered what would have happened if I had met her first. Then I noticed Mariela, her brow creased with concern, watching me watch la doctora. Quickly, I shifted my gaze to my feet.

Before she left, as she was picking a cotton swab off the sheet, Eva spoke a single word beneath her breath. The word, inserted into my ear with surgical precision: "Pedophile!"

Mariela sat on the bed occupying (symbolically?) the precise spot lately vacated by Eva. Tentatively, I placed a hand atop her bare knee. "How was school?" I asked, my voice unsteady. Mariela regarded my hand as if it were a poisonous insect.

"She's very beautiful, isn't she?" she said after a while.

"La doctora? Yes, I suppose she's quite attractive, if you happen to favor that type."

"And you don't?"

"Well, any man..." I had sworn a solemn oath to always be honest with Mariela. This honesty, I felt, somehow made everything else I'd done, if not all right, at least not quite so despicable. But the idea of hurting her was intolerable. Honesty on the one hand, and compassion on the other, fought for command of my tongue. "...any man would want her," I admitted, "and, what can I say? I'm a man."

For a long time neither of us said a word. I'd never seen my lover so upset. Clearly, something had changed drastically since her encounter with Perla and the professional prostitute. Back then (had it only been a week ago?) Mariela's reaction to her twin-headed competition had been one of amusement. Now, obviously, she was no longer amused. What had changed in the meantime? Her feelings for me? Perhaps. But there was also the matter of self-confidence: face-to-face with la doctora Eva, what woman would not feel inadequate? What woman would not feel a serious threat to her romantic hegemony?

"How does she look naked?" Mariela asked morosely.

"Well, uh..."

Mariela lifted the sheet and peeked quickly at my nakedness. "Well, what?"

"Mariela, I..."

"Just tell me the truth."

Mariela, thankfully, did not look even close to tears, but she was definitely depressed. Lying, I decided, would probably be counter-productive. "Naked," I said as off-handedly as I could manage, "la doctora looks, ah, pretty good."

"Just pretty good?"

"Well, no," I admitted. "More like, perfect. Too perfect, if you ask me."

"Did you fuck her?"

"You mean, today?"

"I mean, any day."

"Just once." Which was true, in a way. "The other day. She seduced me. I was…weak," I concluded lamely.

Mariela stared up at the ceiling for a minute. She appeared to be thinking something over. Then she said, with an honesty shocking in someone so young, "If I was a man, I probably would have fucked her, too."

"Well," I said, "thank God you're not a man."

Mariela continued to wax philosophical. "No one should look that good. It's not fair. But it figures. Just my rotten luck: the most beautiful woman in Havana, and she has to fall for you. If this is a competition, I lose."

"It's not a competition, and she's not in love with me. Yes, she seems to like me, but…"

"You big idiot! Can't you see? She's crazy about you."

And then she did begin to cry, and my heart shattered like a dropped glass. I wrapped my arms around her. I kissed her face. I kissed her tears. I told her over and over again how much I loved her. After a few minutes she stopped crying. Mariela was a tough kid. Sniffling one last time, she said, "Was she good in bed?"

"Mariela, please…"

"Was she?"

"Yes," I sighed.

This was pure torture.

"Better than me?"

"No, not better, just different."

"How different?"

"Mariela, please, can we talk about something…"

"How is she different?" she insisted.

"Baby, I'm no expert in this…this sort of thing. To me, it's not about scoring points or rating performances. To me, what's significant is how the person makes you feel. You, for example, make me feel like I want to hold you in my arms forever, protect you, make you happy, give you pleasure."

"And her? How does she make you feel?"

To this question I had no ready-made reply. My feelings toward Eva seemed to be in transition, and were confused to say the least. "Well," I said, struggling for a painless but honest answer, "when we were having sex, I felt like…like I…I don't know, baby. It was more like two animals rutting than anything else."

What impression this eloquent explanation had on Mariela, I had no idea. She sat there chewing on her lip for a long time. "I'm skipping my classes tomorrow morning," she finally announced.

"What for?"

"I want to watch you operate."

"I'm not sure they'll allow that. I'll have to ask. You know the government…"

Mariela slid her hand under the sheet, got a good grip on my right testicle, and squeezed. "It's not negotiable," she said.

"All right," I wheezed. "Yes. I'll insist. Okay!"

Someone began pounding with great violence upon the hallway door.

"Time's up!" Eustacia screeched tactfully.

Mariela, stepping still further out of character, gave me an impish grin and called out plaintively, "But we were just getting started."

"None of that!" Eustacia croaked back through the door. "The doctor needs a good night's sleep."

"Don't worry," Mariela said with a wolfish grin, "when I'm done with him, he'll sleep like a lamb."

My landlady resumed her pounding. "You restrain yourself, young lady! Tomorrow's another day!"

SIXTEEN

The hospital was modern, well-equipped and immaculate. I'd slept like a dead man the night before and felt fine—no shaking hands, no headache, no fuzzy vision. The procedure was straightforward and went off without a hitch. Eustacia, I guessed, would get a good ten or fifteen years out of her new knee, if she didn't croak, screech and squawk herself to death first.

Naturally, there had been a bit of tension in the pre-op room, where Eva, the anesthesiologist, Mariela, Raoul, the assisting nurse, myself and several men, among them the Minister of Health, had all gathered to sanitize ourselves.

The Minister, with a fearful eye towards a potentially arthritic future, handed me his card, and requested one of my own. He was, he said, "enormously honored" to meet me.

Eva and Mariela shook hands like two knights about to do battle to the death. And, in fact, until we adjourned to the OR they never stopped jousting for position, each woman alternately inserting herself between me and her opponent. I could not help noticing with a pang of guilt that Mariela was at a distinct disadvantage in this contest. Eva was bigger, stronger and, as the patient's family doctor, had the stronger pretext for being near the action.

Many middle-aged men would have felt flattered to have two young and beautiful women fighting so transparently for their attention. All I felt was acute embarrassment. It occurred to me that as much as I was enjoying my reincarnated sex-life, I would never make a successful gigolo.

At one point Raoul took me aside. He did not look happy. "Do you always," he demanded in a stern whisper, "bring your girlfriends to your surgeries?"

"Only one of them is my girlfriend," I countered lamely.

"And what is the other one, your mother?"

"She is the patient's family physician. By the way," I said, hoping to change the subject, "who are those well-dressed men? They look like buzzards waiting for an easy meal."

"You are not far off," Raoul replied. "They are government officials. Which is the girlfriend—the tall one?"

"The short one."

Raoul frowned. "You tourists. You come here for a few weeks and live like Roman emperors. You did say you've performed this procedure before?" he added doubtfully.

"For this type of procedure," I replied, restraining my anger, "you'd be hard-pressed to find anyone on the planet more competent than I am."

"I certainly hope so," the toothpick-thin doctor said. "Here in Cuba we take our medicine seriously."

"So do I."

"We don't invite our girlfriends to our surgeries, as if it were *una obra de arte*."

"I had no choice."

"All right," Raoul said. "I don't mean to be judgmental. But the tall one—you are certain she is not your *novia*? She might be the most beautiful woman in Havana."

"Raoul, would you like me to fix you up? She seems to have a thing for surgeons."

Raoul shook his head. "I am married."

"So am I."

"I have ethics."

I almost said, "So do I", but under the circumstances…

The moment the procedure was finished I was all but drowned in a Caribbean Sea of adulation. The compliments flowed like beer at a baseball game. Leading the pack, naturally, was the Minister of Health, Sr. Villaseñor. This man, himself a surgeon, shook my hand with such vehemence he nearly dislocated my shoulder. Then he presented me with a bronze plaque commemorating the historic occasion, followed by a box of cigars and a framed photo of Che Guevara.

Raoul, too, was beside himself with enthusiasm. "Whatever your personal shortcomings," he said, shaking my hand, "as a surgeon, you are brilliant. I have never seen better. It has been a privilege observing you work. Thank you. By the way," he added, lowering his voice, "I happen to have a box of Montecristos on me. In case you are running low."

Then it was Eva's turn, "You were magnificent!" she declared with shining eyes. Quickly, I thanked her, excused myself, grabbed Mariela and fled the scene, before any additional blood was spilled.

Back at the room Mariela stripped down to her Brazilian thong and stood on tip-toe at the mirror, twisting this way and that, a performance which she knew drove me to unreasonable extremes. Then she turned, pointed her nose at the ceiling and announced, "*Estuve magnifico!*" Her impression of Eva was dead-on, and I had to laugh.

"*Mag-ni-fico!*" she said again. "That stuck-up bitch. I'll show you magnifico!" And then she proceeded to treat me to a truly remarkable twenty minutes of felatio, all the while raping my rectum with her petit pinkie. When it was over, after trotting back to bed from the bathroom, she touched the tip of my nose with the delinquent digit and said, "Better than a thermometer, huh?"

"No! She didn't!"

"She was trying to discourage me," Mariela said with a superior smile. "But all she did was give me extra ammunition."

"As if you needed it," I sighed.

"Okay," she said, sliding off her thong, "your turn."

SEVENTEEN

Los Viejos Tiempos was uncommonly crowded. Mario the midget attributed the impressive turnout to a "two-for-one" they were running on cheese-less pizza. The five-piece band, with its three-string guitar and scorching trumpet, was a blur of rhythm. People were laughing, dancing, singing along. It was the first truly festive crowd I'd seen since my arrival in Cuba: the Worker's Paradise come to life, at last.

Carlos and I sat at a round table sipping our mojitos and waiting for the smuggler. Complementing the jolly mood, the plump gay pimp had, sartorially speaking, outdone himself, his tropical getup so loud it should have been visible from outer space. I asked Carlos if, out of the several million colors accessible to the human eye, any had been omitted from his shirt.

"You don't like the shirt, Tocayo? I think it goes well with the shorts. You don't? Why not? What do you think would go with the shorts?"

"I don't know, Tocayo. How about some Dramamine?"

As we were firing up our cigars, Mr. Garcia appeared, slipping stealthily into a chair. The smuggler, Carlos' polar opposite, was utterly shady, a two dimensional collection of crooked gray lines. Everything about him—his complexion, his clothes, his voice—was drab, indistinct and devoid of color. His chair, though clearly occupied, somehow seemed empty.

I'd suggested Los Viejos Tiempos for our rendezvous and the smuggler had accepted; apparently, he was on friendly terms with Mario.

"I'll vouch for him one thousand per cent," the midget said six or seven times. "I'd trust him with my only son," he further averred. "If I had a son, which I probably do. Somewhere."

My Tocayo, who'd arranged the meeting, assumed the role of translator, even though we were all speaking the same language.

"Can you give me the exact location you will put her ashore?" I asked the smuggler.

Mr. Garcia looked everywhere but at me. He looked at the ceiling, out all four windows, at the door, at the bar and then at his shoes, fidgeting all the while like a nervous bird. Then he said, "No."

"What he means," my Tocayo explained, "is that they never know exactly where they will land because they often have to take evasive action to avoid the Coast Guard. Do you see what I'm saying? He can tell you, for example, it will probably be somewhere along a forty or fifty or sixty mile stretch of coast, but not the exact spot."

"That doesn't do me much good," I said.

Mr. Garcia aimed his forehead inquisitively at Carlos.

"He wants to be there waiting for her when she lands," he told the smuggler.

Mr. Garcia, staring forlornly at the bar, shook his head.

"It doesn't work that way," Carlos told me.

"Then how does it work?"

"He wants to know," Carlos told Mr. Garcia, "how it works."

Mr. Garcia, apparently mesmerized by the mint leaves meandering about inside his glass, said tonelessly, "You hook up later."

"You see, Tocayo," Carlos interpreted, "normally, the passenger, as soon as he hits land, goes looking for an immigration officer to turn himself in to. Then, once that's over, they usually move in with family or friends in Miami. Simple."

"But Sofia (I'd been advised to use only false names, just in case) has no family or friends in Florida."

"She has no family there," Carlos informed Mr. Garcia.

"Not usual," Mr. Garcia muttered unhappily.

"He said," my Tocayo began, "that this is not…"

"Yes, yes, I heard him, Carlos. I'm not *sordo*."

Mr. Garcia excused himself to go to the bathroom.

"He's going to the bathroom," Carlos felt compelled to explain.

"To make number one, or number two?"

"No need to lose your temper, Tocayo. I'm just trying to help. You see that, don't you? Of course you do."

"Tell me this, Tocayo. Why does he call himself 'Mr.'? What's wrong with 'señor'?"

"Because you're an American. He thought it would help to establish a better rapport. What's so funny, Tocayo?"

The discussion, such as it was, went on for another hour. There were, from my point of view, several serious complications of a logistical nature for which no one seemed to have satisfactory solutions. First and foremost, how did I find Mariela once she landed in Florida?

"Let her find you," Mr. Garcia suggested, as he stared at a large breasted young woman who stood at the bar attempting to corral my attention with a combination of winks, head tilts and the occasional pelvic thrust.

"That's right," Carlos concurred. "You get the name and address of a motel in the area."

"What area?"

"The general area. Florida. It's only one state, Tocayo. You give her the address of the motel and enough money for a taxi. Then all you have to do is wait for her to show up. Simple."

But it was not simple, not as far as I was concerned. A short film entitled, "The Perils of Mariela" began to project itself upon the interior walls of my skull:

Mariela, alone, making the dangerous night run, out of Havana and across the suddenly storm-tossed Straights of Florida.

Mariela, alone in the dark, being pursued by the Coast Guard.

Mariela, still alone in the dark, tossed overboard like an empty oil can.

Mariela, who can't swim, being dismembered, a limb at a time, by great white sharks.

Mariela, being dumped ashore in the dark like a sack of mulatta potatoes.

Mariela, even more alone in the dark, stumbling about, trying to find a road, with no English, no map and no one to guide her.

Mariela, emphatically alone in the ever-darkening night (I'm not certain how or why it was becoming darker, but it was), hopelessly lost, falling into ditches, being mangled beyond recognition by rogue crocodiles...or were they alligators? I'd been given an alligator belt for my birthday once, but the label had read, Made In Taiwan.

And every now and then, a quick cut to the interior of the luxurious hotel suite, where Dr. Karl Sanderson, celebrated surgeon, is lolling safely about in his pajamas, watching the Weather Channel, eating peanuts and drinking tiny bottles of rum from the mini-bar.

"What if I go with her?"

"Fine with me," Mr. Garcia said. "But you pay full price, even if you are an American."

"No, no, no, Tocayo!" Carlos yelped. "Why would you want to do that?"

"Are you out of your goddamn mind?" Mario the midget, who'd been eavesdropping on the conversation, piped with outrage. "You're an American, for fuck's sake, not some cheap Canadian! It's your country. Why do you want to sneak into your own country? And if you're worried about the girl, don't be. I told you, if you can't trust Garcia, you can't trust anybody!"

That's what I'm afraid of, I thought. As much as I liked my Tocayo, I could not bring myself to totally trust his motives. And as for Mr. Garcia, he was far too insubstantial to trust; it would have been like confiding in a cloud.

But the midget did have a point: I was, as my dear departed mum would have said, out of my bleeding mind. They don't call it being madly in love for nothing. And then there was the guilt factor. Why wasn't there an expression, "insane with guilt"? You could die of shame. You could be sick with grief. You could even, if you so wished, become paralyzed with fear. It seems to me that the de-rationalizing power of guilt deserves more consideration.

The odd thing was, I felt no guilt whatsoever where Janice was concerned. Of course, up until now I'd done nothing to injure her. As long as she remained oblivious, my successive acts of disloyal penetration were like trees falling in that solitary forest, with no one around to see or hear them fall.

"I haven't decided anything yet," I told my companions. "Let's discuss payment."

"I still can't believe," Mario the midget exclaimed, "that you want to be smuggled into your own country. It's like sneaking a rat into a sewer. Like a Cuban going on a hunger strike. Like a bartender paying for his drinks. Like…"

I ordered another round for the table. "And bring us a few pizzas, Mario, the one's with cheese."

Mr. Garcia was stunned. "They have cheese?"

EIGHTEEN

After we'd made love, I brought Mariela up to speed on my discussions with Mr. Garcia. When I'd finished, she lay there propped on her elbows watching me with large expectant eyes. "Well," I said, "do you really want to go?"

"Of course."

"No misgivings about leaving your country? Or your family?"

"Nope."

"The thing is, baby, we're running short on time. I have to be in New York in six days. So, if we do this, we need to do it soon. No later than Monday. That's only four days from now and…"

"Okay."

Somewhere between my second and third mojitos at Los Viejos Tiempos I'd made the fateful decision, my faculties clouded by the mortal combination of rum and guilt. Now I was reasonably sober, and sensibly terrified. "But will you have enough time to get ready?"

"I'm ready now."

"But you have to pack and…"

"Pack what? I just have to say good-bye to my family. Which reminds me, I need a small favor."

"Of course. What is it?"

"Ask Mama for my hand in marriage."

"What?"

The next morning I took a meeting in my Tocayo's room with Mr. Garcia, Carlos and Enrique the Eighth. Enrique, though he did not take part in the discussion, made his presence felt nonetheless, lying on the floor half-in and half-out of the bathroom, doing first abdominals, then wrist curls and, finally, pushups. I had to admit, the boy was in remarkable shape. For myself, what with the heat and humidity, it was all I could do to remain conscious.

"Why don't you turn on the air conditioner, Tocayo?" I begged my neighbor.

Carlos pointed with his ample nose at Enrique *el Octavo* folding and unfolding his body with heroic speed, like a windup toy gone mad. "It's for his sake, Tocayo," Carlos said stoically. "He says sweating is good for his muscle-to-fat ratio."

"What about his muscle-to-brain ratio?"

"Well, that…" Carlos smiled, trying to put a happy face on a fatal disease. "In this life, Tocayo, a man must take the chaff with the wheat."

"You're a fatalist, Carlos."

"I am a Mexican, Tocayo. When you spend five centuries getting reamed, eventually you learn to like it."

"Like Mr. Garcia is reaming me? Where is he, anyway?"

"Don't worry. He'll be here. As I told you, Tocayo, the man is thoroughly reliable."

"Yes, he's reliably late. What the hell is his problem?" I was feeling increasingly anxious as this whole strange process continued to unfold, and it was beginning to affect my manners. "Sorry, Tocayo. I didn't mean to snap at you. I'm a little nervous."

"Just a little? If I were you, I would be extremely nervous. Let me tell you something, Tocayo, just this one time. Please indulge me, will you? As your friend? I feel that we are friends."

"So do I, Tocayo," I replied, and oddly enough I really meant it.

"And as a friend, Tocayo, I must say that, first of all, the girl is very nice. Worth taking a chance for? Well, what something is worth—that is a personal question every man must answer for himself. Is that not so, Tocayo?"

"Urumphhh!" This sound, akin to the mating call of a moose, erupted hair-raisingly from the salubriously sweating throat of Henry the Eighth, who continued to flop manically up and down on the floor like a dying fish in boxer shorts.

"What was that about?"

"Enrique," Carlos explained with parental indulgence, "emits that sound every time he completes one hundred repetitions. It helps him to keep count. Where was I, Tocayo? That boy is always distracting me."

"I think we were discussing risk-to-reward ratios," I said, recalling words once spoken to me by a stock broker.

"Yes," Carlos said, "an apt analogy from the world of finance. My point is, Tocayo, there are risks, and then there are unnecessary risks. Just by bringing the chica to the United States, you are running a large risk, but not a mortal one. If, on the other hand, you get on that boat with her, you are, in my opinion, Tocayo, risking too much. You are risking your very life. These crossings are not without danger. Boats have capsized. People have died. Or short of drowning, you could be interdicted by the Cuban Navy. I can't say exactly what would happen then, but at the very least you could expect to be deported; at the worst, jailed. In either case, you can be sure that the government would make a great deal of noise. Nothing would please Castro more than to catch an American committing an illegal act in Cuban waters. He could make you into a political pawn, a propaganda…"

"All right, I get the point."

"Do you, Tocayo? Your fondness for the girl, I understand completely. I have, as they say, been there myself, on multiple occasions. But we must maintain a sense of proportion, Tocayo. Risking some money, or even a broken heart for one of these sweet young things is fine, as long as you have the heart and the money to spare. But risking your life? Tocayo, I urge you to take the plane and wait for her in Florida. These people, the ones who flee the country, are desperate. They have little to lose. Putting their lives on the line is no great thing for them. For us, on the other hand…"

I began to laugh.

"What is so funny, Tocayo?"

"You're reminding me," I said, "of a character in a telenovela we watched on TV the other night. It was about a rich young man who falls for a mulatta slave girl."

"We saw that, too. Pure garbage, Tocayo, don't you think?"

"Yes, it was pretty awful. But if it was so bad, why were you watching it?"

"It is Enrique's favorite program. I can't help myself; I indulge that boy's every whim. But which character did I remind you of—the father? The evil brother? Surely, not the good brother?"

"Actually, Tocayo, it was the mother."

"The mother? You're making fun of me, Tocayo."

"No, not at all. It's just that the distinction you're making between us and our lovers isn't that different from the one the mother was making between the slave girl and real human beings."

"But my Enrique and your Mariela are not slaves. They are making their own decisions and so must be responsible for their own actions."

"They are children, Tocayo."

"Please, Tocayo, call them 'young adults'. We may be pariahs, but we are not criminals."

"Urumphhh!"

"Two-hundred *abdominales*," Carlos announced with satisfaction.

"I need a drink."

"So early, Tocayo?"

"It's never too early," I said, "when you're having a nervous breakdown."

"Would you like a Valium, Tocayo? I always keep some handy, in case I overdo it with the Viagra. After three or four hours an erection can become…"

"*Buenos dias.*" Mr. Garcia, only twenty minutes late, stood in the open doorway, wishing, if the direction of his gaze was any indication, a tepid good morning to a small palm tree.

NINETEEN

"Urumphhh!"

"What was that?" Mr. Garcia cried with alarm. His eyes, unaccustomed to the frail light inside the room, had not yet registered Henry the Eighth's perspiring presence.

"One hundred wrist curls," Carlos replied. "And counting."

After a moment, Mr. Garcia's pupils dilated sufficiently for his eyes to penetrate the gloom. "Why are those barbells painted pink?" he asked.

"Well…" my Tocayo began.

"And who is that man?"

"He is a friend."

"He looks Cuban."

"Havana's finest," Carlos confirmed.

"What's he doing here?"

"Well, right now, he is working on his triceps."

"Biceps," Enrique grunted, his head still inside the bathroom.

"I won't discuss anything in front of him," Mr. Garcia said in a stage-whisper.

"I personally vouch for him," my Tocayo whispered back.

"I don't care. Fellows like that, the police get their hands on them, they sing till their lungs burst."

Carlos took a deep breath. "Mr. Garcia, you are absolutely right. Tocayo, can we use your apartment? I'll bring an extra chair. Yes? *Excelente.* Enrique, stay here and continue to sweat."

Before the smuggler would sit down and discuss business, he insisted upon inspecting every inch of my room. He fell to one knee and searched under the bed. He looked inside the closet. He stalked into the bathroom, inventoried its contents and stalked back out.

"There's a leak under your sink," he informed me.

"I never knew," I said guiltily.

I offered my guests a chair, poured two tall glasses of ice-water (mine I was forced to drink from a cereal bowl—Eustacia only provided her lodgers with two glasses) and took a seat at the card table.

"Salud!" Carlos, ever the gracious Mexican, said, lofting his glass. Mr. Garcia, with a marked lack of enthusiasm, nudged his own glass an inch above the table and I, utilizing both hands, raised my plastic cereal bowl.

"Salud!"

Then, Mr. Garcia, having exhausted his personal reserves of sociability, said, "Do you have the money?"

"Yes," I replied, "but I also have some questions."

The smuggler executed an imperceptible shrug.

"Mr. Garcia," I said, looking him right in the cheek, the chin, the top of his head, "how soon can we leave?"

"That depends."

"What he's saying, Tocayo," Carlos broke in, "is that there are a number of factors which…"

"Carlos, please, be quiet," I beseeched my friend. "Mr. Garcia, I need to leave in three days."

"That will cost you more."

"So, it can be done?"

"Yes, it can be done. Four days would be better."

"And cheaper?" my Tocayo broke in.

Mr. Garcia, his eyes glued gloomily to his glass, said, "Yes."

"Four days," I said. "That means we'd be leaving Monday morning?"

"Yes, the boat usually leaves, if there are no problems, between two and three in the morning."

"Tocayo," Carlos felt compelled to explain, "technically, the boat would be leaving Monday morning, but in reality we are talking about Sunday night. I only mention this, Tocayo, because many people confuse the early morning hours of one day with the late night hours of the previous day."

"Tocayo, are you saying," I asked in tones of astonishment, "that at midnight, it changes from one day to the next?"

"I was only hoping to avoid any potential for confusion," Carlos said in a hurt voice.

"You have the money?" Mr. Garcia asked.

"Urumphhhhhhhhhhhhhh!"

The smuggler leapt from his chair. "What was that?"

"My friend," Carlos replied. "He always grunts with extra vigor when he reaches his three-hundredth push-up. Pretty impressive, don't you think?"

"You should tell him to make less noise," Mr. Garcia said, resuming his seat. "Someone might call the police."

"I wouldn't worry if I were you, Mr. Garcia," I said. "Loud grunting is fairly common around here."

"You can never be too careful. You have the money?"

We had already agreed upon a series of payments. The first, due at once, was a five thousand dollar deposit. Just prior to boarding the boat I was to pay another ten thousand. And finally, after we landed, we were supposed to pay the remainder, an additional fifteen thousand dollars.

The first two installments were not a problem; hitting the various ATM machines around Havana on a more or less continual basis would provide me with the first fifteen. The last payment, however, was proving to be a serious sticking point in the negotiations.

"This is all very irregular," the smuggler complained.

"What he means, Tocayo," Carlos began, and this time I allowed him to continue, "is that arrangements for payment are always made on the other side, with the families of the clients. The negotiations, the contracting of services and the payments are all made over there in Florida. The reason, first of all…"

"I'm already doing you a big favor," Mr. Garcia cut in, "by setting it up here. It's very dangerous. Now, for the last fifteen thousand, you want me to trust you?" Mr. Garcia uttered the word "trust" with complete revulsion, as if I were a leper asking for a kiss.

"You can trust him," Carlos said, leaping to my defense. "He is a respected member of his community."

"Within four days of landing, I promise to wire the money into your bank account."

"Bank account! Do you think we are stupid? We have no stinking bank accounts!"

Despite the gravity of the situation, I began to laugh.

"What is funny?" Mr. Garcia demanded.

"Your reference to the Treasure of the Sierra Madre—it was rather clever."

"Treasure? Sierra Madre? What are you talking about? What the fuck," Mr. Garcia said, turning to Carlos, "is he talking about?"

"I'm not sure," Carlos said with concern.

"You told me this man is reliable."

"Yes, well," Carlos said, "his money is good; I can vouch for that."

"I'm already taking enough chances," Mr. Garcia complained. "I don't need a crazy person to worry about."

"I am not crazy," I said.

"Crazy people never think they are crazy," Mr. Garcia said with impressive logic, "because if they knew they were crazy, then they wouldn't be crazy."

"I was only making reference to a movie…"

"All of a sudden," Mr. Garcia said excitedly, "out of the blue, he starts talking about buried treasure. What am I supposed to think?"

"I never said buried."

"And mountains!" Mr. Garcia ranted on. "Cuba is a flat country. Maybe you don't believe me. Look out the window and tell me if you see any mountains."

Dutifully, I looked out the window. "The only thing I see," I told the agitated smuggler, "is a cement wall and a bougainvillea bush."

"Exactly!"

"All right," Carlos said to Mr. Garcia, "how about this. I will personally take responsibility for the final payment in the event that for some unforeseeable reason my Tocayo fails to come through."

"We know where you live," the smuggler reminded him.

"That is correct. You also know that if worse comes to worse, I will pay the remaining fifteen thousand dollars, because..."

"If you don't, we will remove your intestines and feed them to the rats—while you are still alive."

"I was going to say, because I am a man of my word."

Mr. Garcia shrugged. "Very well. I don't like it, but I will accept this arrangement. As long as," he added darkly, "there is no further talk of mountains or buried treasure."

"It's just the name of a movie, for Christ's sake."

"You have the money?"

TWENTY

Three seconds after receiving the five thousand dollars, Mr. Garcia was out the door. "You will be contacted," he called back over his shoulder. "Be ready. Don't forget the money."

"When? When will you call?" I asked, but he was already gone and the only response to my urgent query was a muffled and prolonged, "Urumphhhhhhhhh!" erupting from my neighbor's room.

Then it was my Tocayo's turn. "I have to go," he said tensely.

"Carlos, I really must thank you for your..."

"Thank me later. I have to get back before he showers."

Before he showers?

Once I was alone it hit me chest-on, like a heart attack. Money has changed hands. This is really happening! Was I, as Carlos the gay pimp and Mario the nosey midget had both implied, out of my frigging mind? Really desperate for a drink now, I ventured forth into the asphyxiating heat, heading for the Havana Libre, where I hoped to obtain from the concierge the name of a topnotch restaurant for my formal "betrothal" dinner that evening with Mariela and her mother.

By the time, two mojitos later, I found the concierge sitting at attention behind his desk in the hotel lobby, I was feeling considerably calmer. The concierge, a prim little mannequin, was wonderfully responsive to my questions.

"The best restaurant in Havana is La Mamba Negra, señor. It is, you should be advised, extremely expensive."

"But the service, the food—they are first-class?"

"You will find no finer dining establishment in all of Cuba than *La Mamba Negra's*, señor."

Despite the concierge's ringing endorsement, I was not entirely convinced. Something was bothering me—perhaps the name. Wasn't the black mamba a large poisonous snake? The name seemed more suitable for a sex-club than a restaurant. For all I knew the concierge might believe I was speaking in code, and instead of looking for the best restaurant, I was really searching for the best strip joint. Waltzing my "future mother-in-law" into a high class sex-club, with naked dancers flopping their bare breasts beneath her puritanical nose, would not make a good impression.

"This restaurant, I imagine it is totally respectable?"

The concierge was confused. "Respectable, señor?"

"What I mean is, this place—it is just a restaurant?"

"What else would it be, señor?"

"I don't know. That's why I'm asking." The concierge gave me a blank look. "Please don't take offense," I said, "but it just seems that here in Havana practically every tourist-oriented enterprise has something to do with sex."

"If you want sex, señor," the concierge said, taking offense anyway, "you will not find it at La Mamba Negra!"

"Yes, of course. I understand. But the waitresses—they are fully clothed?"

"They are waiters, and they wear tuxedos. Despite what some tourists seem to think, señor, Cuba is more than just a tropical bordello."

The fellow must be a communist, I thought. "Yes, well, very good. One last question: will I need to make reservations?"

"No, señor. As I said, it is very expensive. Few Cubans can afford to eat there."

"What about tourists?"

"At this time of year, señor, most of our visitors are, shall we say, on the frugal side?"

"Canadians?"

"Precisely, señor."

For Mariela's sake I wanted the evening to go smoothly. She loved her mother, like a good daughter should, and it was not my intention to cause either of them any distress if I could help it. Unfortunately, things got off to an awkward start.

Mother and daughter were scheduled to arrive at six o'clock. At five minutes after, I was startled out of my latest anxiety attack by the sounds of a commotion coming from the alley. Fearing the worst, I raced outside and around the corner. Mariela and her mother were standing, open-mouthed, beneath Eustacia's lookout post. My landlady, wearing a scowl which could have sent into retreat an entire panzer division, was saying, "This is not acceptable!" Then she saw me and said, "There he is, the sex-maniac surgeon! I'm in terrible pain. What have you done to me?"

For a moment I stood there unable to decide which accusation to answer first. In the end, I opted for the knee; I could, I reasoned, defend my surgical practices far more easily than my personal behavior.

"There is always pain after surgery," I said with professional detachment. "It is perfectly normal. Are you doing your exercises?"

"So now it's two at a time?" she screeched.

"What?"

"There will be no managers-a-trois in my house!" Eustacia croaked.

Celia looked confused.

Mariela was livid. "This is my mother!" she shouted.

"Your mother? Well then…shame on the three of you!"

"Are you out of your mind?" I asked my landlady. "Have some respect, for God's sake!"

"Don't raise your voice to me, young man, or I'll throw you right out of here on your perverted ass!"

"Is that so?" I said.

"Mothers and daughters!" Eustacia snarled. "It's just plain disgusting. You bet I'll throw you out."

"And refund my money?"

"There are no refunds," Eustacia said smugly. "Government policy."

"You know," I remarked, "we were just on our way to dinner,

but if you want, I'll move out right now and you'll never see me again. Of course, in that case I won't be able to give you the critical instructions you'll need for your successful recovery."

"What instructions? I thought you gave la doctora all the instructions."

"No, I left one out," I lied. "It must have slipped my mind."

"Well, you have a wonderful dinner," Eustacia said in honeyed tones. "All three of you."

"Thank you," Celia said in polite confusion.

"And after dinner," Eustacia added, "you do whatever you want. You know we Cubans, unlike you North Americans, are tolerant people, especially where sexual deviation is concerned."

"Have a nice evening, Eustacia. And don't forget," I added with a broad smile, "to do your exercises—no matter how painful they are."

"Is that the critical instruction I was missing?"

"No, afraid not."

I took Celia and Mariela by an arm each, and led them awkwardly out to the street. Between Celia's limp and my Gulliver-like height advantage, walking in lockstep was out of the question. If individual people look like ants from the tops of tall buildings, the three of us must have looked, as we progressed disjointedly up the street, like an injured centipede.

The restaurant was more than ten blocks away, and with Celia fading fast we decided to take a taxi. On the short ride over, Mom felt compelled to ask, "What is wrong with that woman, anyway?"

"Poor thing," I replied at once, "she suffers from a degenerative brain disease which causes her to fade in and out of reality. Just now, for example, she thought she was talking to a knee surgeon. And last night she mistook me for her deceased Weimaraner."

"That's how it is," Celia said, nodding her gray head.

"That's how what is?"

"The Lord," she said with conviction, "He always takes the husbands first."

"Mama," Mariela pointed out, "a Weimaraner is a dog."

"Most men are dogs," Celia sighed. "Present company excepted, of course."

"No, mama, a real dog. A Weimaraner is a real bow-wow kind of dog."

"It is?"

"Yes, mama."

"Lord have mercy!" Celia said, making the sign of the cross.

TWENTY-ONE

La Mamba Negra's blaringly nondescript facade gave no clue as to what lay inside. Behind the windowless white stucco wall and the solid wood door there could have been any number of activities going on. Silently, I prayed that one of them was not sex-by-the-hour.

When I reached for the doorknob, Celia put a restraining hand on my wrist. "Is it all right to just barge right in?" she asked. "Shouldn't we knock first?"

"It's a restaurant, mama," Mariela said, "you don't have to knock."

"Oh," Celia said, "can you imagine that."

I opened the door, allowing the two women to enter, Mariela with her head held high, her mother in breathless trepidation. Once inside, we were met by a blast of cold air and an immaculately attired maitre d' who took a moment to scan our little party with the critical eye of a customs agent. Mariela and I formed a recognizable and acceptable unit: a well-to-do tourist with his date. But Celia? Obviously no man's sex-toy, her black skin and shabby Cuban clothing spoke of an economic standing several geologic strata below La Mamba Negra's customary clientele. "To seat, or not to seat?" the man's conflicted expression seemed to say.

Finally, with an audible sigh and an enormous air of self-importance, he led us to a linen-clad table in a small elegant dining room. The room was lit by a pair of crystal chandeliers and paneled in tropical hardwoods. The floor was variegated onyx. Mariela, though dazzled by this Bourbon display of opulence, managed to maintain her composure, while her mother froze in place like a spot-lit deer.

After a while Celia thawed out and recovered, more or less, her powers of speech. "I never thought...in my whole life...I never expected...like a dream...like Heaven..." As her words trailed off, her astonished eyes locked on to the polished silverware, the gleaming glasses, the sparkling china. "Praise the Lord!" she concluded.

The prices were indeed obscenely high. Even so, we were not the only diners. Across the small room a table of six men sat drinking, eating and smoking with abandon. They were dressed in well-made suits, and looked nothing like tourists.

"Cubans?" I whispered in Mariela's ear.

"Government officials," she whispered back. "They say Raoul owns this place. Only his friends can afford to eat here."

"The Beard's younger brother?"

"Yes," Mariela whispered. "Raoul owns half of Havana."

As we continued to whisper back and forth, Celia regarded us with bliss-soaked eyes. "Ah, young lovers!" she sighed. "Praise Jesus!"

Mariela looked down at the floor, embarrassed by her mother's anachronistic comments. I looked away as well, unnerved at hearing my girlfriend's mother, a woman four years my junior, refer to me as a "young lover".

Moments later we were rescued from our discomfiture by the waiter, a young man who introduced himself as Eriberto, and who asked in the most polite manner imaginable if we would like something to drink.

"Yes, well, ice-water all around for starters," I said, taking command of the situation. "And I suppose you have a wine list?"

"Of course, señor."

"We don't drink alcohol," Celia announced cheerfully. Mariela rolled her eyes.

"For the moment," I told the waiter, "bring me a mojito, with Havana Club Añejo."

"And for the ladies?"

"I'll have a coke," Mariela said unhappily.

"An orange juice, please," her mother said.

After the waiter left Celia turned to me and said, "I don't know much about these things, but this restaurant looks awfully expensive."

"Carlos doesn't have problems with money," Mariela explained.

"Oh…that's nice," Celia said uncertainly.

The menus, encased in Corinthian leather, were entirely in French. I didn't mind French food, and Mariela enjoyed eating everything, but Celia was clearly disoriented by the names of the dishes.

"Bou-ill-a-baie?" she said. "What's that?"

"I have an idea," I said. "I'll do the ordering for everyone. Now I know what Mariela likes, but you, Celia, is there anything you would particularly care to eat?"

"Put it on my plate, I'll eat it," she declared.

"All right. But don't you have a preference for chicken, or meat, or fish? You can have whatever you want."

"I like to eat chicken," Celia admitted.

"Well, there you go," I said, polishing off my mojito. "Mariela, how does *le civet de lièbre* look to you?"

Mariela barely nodded her head, her huge eyes glued to the menu.

"Wonderful! And shall we all begin with some French onion soup?"

My question seemed to send Celia off into orbit somewhere. Mariela smiled bravely and squeezed my knee under the table. I launched my right hand into the air, and within seconds Eriberto was standing beside our table.

"Yes, señor?"

"All right, Eriberto, first off, another mojito. Then we'll all begin with *la potage dóignan*. For her main dish, la señora will have le coq au vin, la señorita will have *le civet de lièbre* and I'll have la *blanquette de veau*."

Eriberto, clearly impressed, complimented me on my command of the French language. I thanked him half-heartedly, and off he marched to deliver our order to the kitchen. In reality, the only French I knew was restaurant

French, and that was due entirely to Janice. Despite her nutritional fads, her vast social conscience and her no-holes-barred battle for justice and equality, my wife was inordinately fond of French cuisine and there was not a single over-priced French restaurant in Manhattan we had not patronized on multiple occasions.

Surprisingly, the food was quite good. Certainly, Mariela enjoyed it. And Celia, too, although she did look askance at her coq au vin for a full fifteen seconds before daring to put a forkful of the strange looking dish into her mouth.

At some point—I believe it was during the soup—my mind wandered off for a few moments, and I found myself back in New York, having dinner with Janice at Chez Philippe.

"How is the duck?" Janice asked.

"A bit dry. Janice, I have a confession to make."

"You had a snack before dinner?"

"No, it's not that."

"You're always stuffing yourself with garbage from that horrible cafeteria," she scolded. "No wonder you're not hungry. Eating all that processed food can give you cancer. Or worse."

There's something worse than cancer? I imagined myself thinking fearfully.

"Yes dear," I said, "but what I wanted to tell you is…I'm in love with another woman."

"Stop making jokes and eat your *Moules á la crème Normande* before they get cold."

"I'm serious, Janice."

Long dramatic pause.

"You're…serious?"

"Yes, I'm afraid I am."

Instead of turning red with fury, Janice turned pinkish, like a block of bloody ice. "Who…is…she?"

"Well, dear, the truth is, she's just someone I met."

"Met where?"

"In Cuba."

"Did you say, Cuba?"

TWENTY-TWO

"Are you all right?" Mariela asked, rousing me from my guilty reverie.

"Ah, yes, yes, I'm fine. Why do you ask?"

"You looked like you were in pain, like you were being stabbed or something."

"Close."

"Huh?"

"Just a little indigestion. This food is a bit on the rich side. Eriberto," I called, "another mojito!"

Celia was concerned, too. "Another drink? Won't that make your tummy worse?"

"No, not at all. The mint leaves have a wonderful calming effect, like herbal tea."

Halfway through the main course, Mariela leaned into my ear and whispered, "What am I eating?"

"Rabbit," I whispered back. "Do you like it?"

She nodded her head. "I was just curious."

"Ah, young lovers," Celia sighed again.

As the table was being cleared, I was suddenly seized by the most uncomfortable feeling. It was as if Janice's frowning face, in the form of an ever-inflating balloon, had been inserted into my cranial cavity, growing larger and larger until it crowded out everything else, including the true purpose of the dinner. Absentmindedly, I raised my hand to signal for the check, and received at once a sharp kick in the shins. In case I had missed her meaning, Mariela, now that she had all of my attention, pointed at the ring finger of her left hand.

Deceit has never come naturally to me. Until recently, I'd always prided myself upon being as honest and straightforward as possible. But Mariela would not be denied. Her mother would be far happier, she'd maintained, believing that we were going to be married, and outside of my reluctance to make a fool of myself, I had little ammunition to counter her argument. And even if I had, like my Tocayo Carlos, I found it all but impossible to refuse my lover's least desire.

And so, I gritted my teeth, swallowed my pride, threw moral rectitude to the wind and said, "Eriberto, another mojito."

The drink poured itself down my throat with such enthusiasm I nearly swallowed the wad of sodden mint leaves along with the rum. Fortunately, at the last moment I was able to choke them back into the glass. Then, having achieved a suitable level of stupefaction, I began.

"Celia," I said, displaying the majority of my teeth, "I think you know how I feel about your daughter. And I believe you know, too, that I am taking her to the United States, where she can have a better life. But first…"

"Don't you mean, England?" Celia cut in.

Too late, I remembered that I was supposed to be from Britain. "Oh, yes. Of course…but first we have to go to America. It's closer, you know."

"God bless you!"

"Thank you. Before our departure, I would like, with all due respect, to have your blessing for…"

"Bless you! Bless you!"

"Yes, ah, thanks a lot. So, I am formally, here and now, with God as my witness, and Jesus as my…as my other witness, I am humbly, respectfully, diligently (diligently?) asking for your daughter's hand in marriage."

I attempted, with little success, to paste a worried smile upon my face, as if I feared she might turn me down.

"Young man," she proclaimed, "you not only have my blessing, you have God's blessing, St. Michael's blessing, St. Peter's blessing and all the saints and angels in Heaven. Bless you a thousand times. Bless you a million times!"

"Celia, I take it that was a yes?" I asked drunkenly.

"No, no, no," she said sternly."

"No?"

"From now on," Celia commanded, "you call me Mom."

"Oh. Of course. Fantastic…Mom."

"This calls for a celebration!" Mariela cried, winking in my direction. Under ordinary circumstances, Mariela rarely drank alcohol. But earlier in the evening she had made it clear that she would like to try a "sophisticated" drink tonight, and naturally I was not about to disappoint her.

"Excellent idea!" I said grandly. "Eriberto! Bring us three *Courvoisers*."

Eriberto's fawning smile grew and grew until it threatened to split open his cheeks. In one fell swoop, I'd doubled the bill, and hopefully his tip. "Si, señor!"

"What is it?" Mariela asked, when the glasses had been set on the table.

"It's Cognac, darling. From France. Well," I said, raising my glass, "here's to…"

"Is this alcohol, son?" Celia asked fearfully.

"Not exactly. It's more like a digestive aid."

"Like Pepto-Bismol?"

"Something like that, Mom," I replied, getting fully into the spirit of the occasion. "So, here's to…"

"But it's not pink, son," she pointed out.

"True," I allowed. "They've removed all the impurities. Those nasty impurities, that's what makes it pink. So. Here's to Mariela, the most wonderful girl in the world!"

"Amen!" Celia cried, and we all took a drink. The cognac was delicious. I sighed with satisfaction. Mariela grinned with pleasure. Mom made an awful face and spit her cognac back into the glass as if it were rat poison.

Eriberto rushed over, his face convulsed with terror. "Is anything wrong?"

"Everything's fine, Eriberto," I reassured the worried waiter. "Just went down the wrong pipe."

"This drink contains alcohol!"

"Don't worry, mama," Mariela said, snatching her mother's glass. "I'll make sure it doesn't go to waste."

"Would the gentleman care for a cigar?" Eriberto inquired.

"You read my mind, Eriberto."

The waiter produced an enormous *Corona Gigante*, expertly cut the tip, passed it to me and set it on fire.

My non-mother-in-law-to-be, smiling bravely at this unbridled display of depravity, said, "Mariela, are you sure you should be drinking that?"

"Aw, mama, how many times does a girl get engaged?"

"Hopefully, only once, child."

"It's all right, Mom," I said, savoring the exquisite blend of flavors, "surely one drink will do her no harm."

"She's having two drinks," Celia pointed out, "hers and mine."

"It's good, mama."

Mom let out an enormous sigh. "Well," she said stoically, "I guess my little girl is growing up."

"I'd say she's all grownup. Mom."

Celia looked pensive, as if she were thinking my declaration over. Then, nodding her head with conviction, she said, "Children, life is not always a bag of papayas."

"I beg your pardon?"

"You never know what to expect. So you got to be prepared for a capitalist invasion. And you got to plan. Once you are married, you will probably start to have…" Celia paused to cross herself. "…relations."

Mariela began to giggle.

"This is no laughing matter, child," Celia advised her daughter.

"Sorry, mama."

"Now, these relations, sooner or later, are going to produce a baby. And babies are good. Babies are the breath of life itself! If you prepared yourself. But if you didn't prepare, they can be an awful trial. That's why you got to take pre-cautions."

"Pre-cautions?" Mariela said, her huge eyes somehow growing even larger.

"That's right, child, pre-cautions! And you got to take them yourself, cause you just can't depend on a man to take those pre-cautions for you. For example…"

"Um, wait a minute, Mom," I broke in, the alcohol getting the better of my tongue. "I think you're forgetting something: I happen to be a doctor, and a doctor knows far more about…"

"Excuse me, son," Celia said politely, "but you are an animal doctor. Now, there is nothing wrong with being an animal doctor; we can't have cows and such dropping dead in the streets. But animals and people ain't exactly the same thing."

"True, Mom," I replied reasonably, "but all mammals do have certain, shall we say, biological functions, in common?"

"Don't talk to me about no biological functions," Celia warned, "not at the dinner table."

"Sorry, Mom, I was just trying to point out…"

"All this talk," Celia vociferated, "about pulling out ahead of time never got no woman nothing but a belly full of babies!"

"Oh mama!" Mariela groaned.

"Or that rhythm method," Celia went on. "The only thing rhythm is good for is dancing; not that I approve of dancing."

"Mama…"

"Let me speak my piece, child. Now, exactly how many children are you planning to have?"

"We're not sure, Mom," I said thoughtfully. "Maybe eight or nine. How many would you suggest?"

"That depends on the Lord, son," she said, seemingly contradicting all of her previous advice. "The main thing is to be prepared. Son, I've heard terrible things about the unreliability of capitalist condoms. Now, if I were you, I'd stock up on some good solid Cuban condoms, while you still can. They're plenty thick and keep accidents to a minimum."

"Mama!"

Poor Celia, she'd been brainwashed by not one, but two of humanity's worst ideas: communism and religion.

"Thanks, Mom," I said with filial respect, "that's good advice. We'll pick up a gross on our way to the boat."

TWENTY THREE

My sojourn in the Worker's Paradise was drawing to a close. In just a few days, if all went well, I'd be back on US soil, ready to begin my new life as a duplicitous husband—if I wasn't arrested, drowned or shredded by sharks first.

I'd spent the better part of two days draining every ATM machine in Havana in order to amass the ten thousand dollars for Mr. Garcia. This awesome feat of cash accumulation would not have been possible without the aid of my "limitless" Platinum card which, at Janice's insistence, was held solely in my name. Janice had her own cards, of course (about eight of them), so that, in her words, "We won't have to squabble over each other's bookkeeping."

And (praise Jesus!) I'd had the foresight to call my bank in advance. "I've just joined Doctors Without Borders," I'd fallaciously informed a friendly female voice, "so don't be surprised if you see charges coming from some unusual locations."

"Yes, sir, we won't be surprised," she chirped.

"Just keep the cash coming," I added, to be sure we understood one another.

"Oh, we will, Dr. Sanderson. Don't worry. And you keep up the good work!"

Mariela, against the wishes of her insane mother and her feeble-minded brother, moved in for good early Friday evening. She brought with her a heartbreakingly small denim bag containing all of her worldly possessions: the clothes I had bought her, a pair of faded shorts, her identity card and a few photographs, one of them of her long absent father.

"Well, here I am," she said, smiling bravely.

"Yes," I agreed, "here you are."

"I still can't believe we're going to do it."

"Neither can I."

"But we are," she said. "Aren't we?"

"No stopping us now," I said, sounding more resigned than elated, like a man sinking inexorably into a pool of quicksand.

After a few moments of strained silence, Mariela burst into tears, throwing herself into my arms. We made love for hours, alternately crying and laughing until we were too exhausted to move. Then, for a long time we lay eye to eye, nose to nose, unwilling to allow more than a centimeter of space to come between us.

"I'm a little scared," she said after a while.

"You needn't be. I'm sufficiently terrified for the both of us."

"We've got to be strong," Mariela said, "for each other."

"I'll be strong," I promised. "Petrified, but strong."

"*Ay, mi arbolito!* Do you love me?"

"I've never loved anyone as much."

"Mama's upset with me. She thinks it's a sin to move in with you before we're married."

"Well…mothers," I said helplessly.

"When my father was put away, that's when she went crazy with the religious stuff."

"It must have been tough, growing up without a father."

"It was tough growing up, period. In Cuba everything is tough."

"But in your case, especially difficult without a father around."

"I guess."

Mariela and I had danced around this subject before. I was naturally curious as to why a young beautiful girl should be attracted to a man so much older than herself. Not that I was complaining, but it didn't seem natural. Yes, there was the money. I may have been insane, but I was not completely naïve. Money alone, however, could not explain the frequency and intensity of Mariela's orgasms. Or could it?

I know that a woman can fake an orgasm during intercourse, but during oral sex it is far more difficult. And without getting into too many lurid details, I will only say that on those frequent occasions when I gave Mariela pleasure in that manner, I'd come close to drowning in the process.

That I was some type of father figure went without saying. But to what extent did that form the basis of the attraction? In the end, it didn't really matter one way or the other, but for some reason I had to know. I decided to finally tackle the issue head-on, asking her outright if she thought I might somehow be filling the vacuum left by the departure of her father.

"I don't have time for all that psychological *Santeria*," she replied, relegating Freud and a good chunk of twentieth century thought to the dust bin, where it probably belonged. "In Cuba you see older men with younger women, and younger men with older women all the time. It makes sense."

"How is that?"

"Okay, you take a couple like us. I'm young, sexy, inexperienced and poor. You're old, experienced, rich and horny. I give you what you need, and you give me what I need. We're a perfect match."

"I'm not that old."

"No," Mariela smiled, "lucky for me! But one day you will be, and I'll still be young. So, after benefiting from your wisdom and experience, when you're really old and feeble, I can take care of you until you die. And then I get part of your money. My comparative zoology professor calls it a symbiotic relationship."

"Your professor calls older foreign tourists going with young Cuban girls a symbiotic relationship?"

"No, stupid, he was talking about birds pecking the bugs off a rhinoceros. But it's the same thing."

"Symbiosis. Who would have thought?"

"In a country like Cuba," Mariela pointed out, "you have to be practical. I see dumb young girls all the time falling for dumb young guys. The young guys come like roosters, in two seconds—not like you," she smiled with proprietary pride—"and out of that, the girl gets what? Not an orgasm, that's for sure. What she gets is pregnant. And then the babies start coming and the three or four or five of them spend the rest of their lives fighting and starving. Does that make sense?"

"I guess not, but…"

"Do we fight?"

"No, never."

"Are we starving?"

"Hardly."

"Do we have great sex?"

"It's certainly great for me."

"Me, too. Time for my show." Mariela reached for the old Russian remote control, upon which all the numbers had vanished long ago, along with the Soviet aid and the glorious, early, hope-filled days of the Cuban Revolution.

TWENTY-FOUR

The following morning I awoke with Mariela lying beside me in bed, and I have to admit it felt a bit strange. The only other woman I'd ever woken up beside was Janice. Beside, I might add, in my wife's case, was a relative term. Janice had never been an avid cuddler, and though we slept in the same king-size bed, it felt more like being berthed on opposite ends of a cruise ship.

Mariela was still asleep. Propped on an elbow I watched her breathe. Then I began to gently stroke her arms, her stomach, her legs. Eventually she woke up, stretching and yawning like a sleepy cat.

"What are you waiting for?" she purred.

Like a starving kitten, I needed no further encouragement. Closing my eyes, I bent to my task at once. The world went away. No bed, no room, no city, no island—just that dank but delicious dimple in the loamy earth, an altar in the jungle. And my mouth, taking small, breathless prayerful sips, the mundane secretions transmuting themselves upon my tongue into golden nectar, Divine Juices, the Source of Everything, the...

KNOCK! KNOCK! KNOCK!

Unbelievably, someone was smashing on my door again, interrupting what could have been my first religious epiphany! I felt Mariela freeze with fear. In Cuba, the line between paranoia and reality was a blurry one. Anything was possible.

"Do you think it's one of your ex-girlfriends?" she asked hopefully. Anything, even an entire chorus line of potential rivals, would have been better than the police.

"I'm—I'm not expecting anyone," I spluttered.

"Mariela? Carlos?" a deep female voice called through the door.

"It's my mother."

"We know you're in there," a man's voice, sounding like an actual policeman, said.

Mariela let out a small moan. "And my brother. I'm sorry, Carlos. I can't believe they would…"

KNOCK! KNOCK! KNOCK!

It had to be the dimwitted outsized brother doing the knocking; of the two, only he possessed the strength required to make an entire room vibrate with the pounding of a single fist. Or had he brought along an old baseball bat?

"Just a minute," I sang out.

Mariela was already out of bed and throwing on her clothes. "I'll kill both of them," she muttered. "Especially my brother."

"If you don't open up, I'll break the door down!" Silvio shouted.

"Give them a chance," I heard Celia tell her son. "They were probably asleep."

"Asleep?" Baby Huey snorted. "They wasn't asleep. They was awake and doin' the dirty…"

"Hush!"

Meanwhile, I'd thrown on a pair of shorts and a Hawaiian shirt, and after a quick glance at Mariela, was about to open the door when my lover reached out and grabbed my wrist.

"Go wash your face," she hissed at me, "you smell like a fish market!"

Realizing she had a point, I dashed to the bathroom and frantically doused my face with water. No, that won't do the job, I thought, so I grabbed the nearest thing to hand, a bottle of aftershave, and splashed the better part of its contents all over my head. Then, still dripping, and smelling like a sardine who has been floating gills-up for several weeks in a vat of cologne, I opened the door as Mariela, fully dressed, primly took a seat at the card table.

Fortunately for everyone concerned, Celia had managed to install herself in the doorway, provisionally separating me from Silvio. The young man in question, wearing a black tank top which highlighted his absurdly large muscles, appeared to be dangerously agitated. Like an enraged Rottweiler standing on its hind legs, he loomed over Celia, straining at an invisible leash—the ancient taboo against trampling to death one's own mother.

Of all the marvelous ways I had envisioned myself being humiliated (in retribution for my ethically suspect behavior), this particular scenario had never quite made it over my mental horizon. I was trapped like an aroused rat in my rented room, and what my captors planned to do with me, I could only guess.

"Well," I said, "what a wonderful surprise!"

"Son," Celia said, sniffing uncertainly, "what is that smell? Have they been fumigating again?"

"Yes," I replied at once, "it's that darn dengue fever. Mom."

"Son," she continued, "I haven't slept for forty-eight hours. I been praying and I been worrying and I been communing with the Lord. And the Lord told me He would not be happy if my baby-girl, the light of my life, the hope of our family, left the island of her birth…"

"I swear," Silvio, who could contain himself no longer, overrode his mother, "if you did the dirty on my sister, you're a dead man. Or worse!"

"Silvio, you hush your mouth! Son," Celia continued, "the Lord would not be pleased if you and my baby daughter departed this island in a state of mortal sin, the island of…"

"Yes, yes, Mom, you said all that. Could we please get to the point?"

"Son," Celia said, "I want you to meet Señor Manuel Robles. Señor Robles is a justice of the peace. "

With a sense of mounting unreality I finally noticed a third party standing in the background, a small nervous man wearing a green sun-visor.

"Mama!" Mariela cried. "Mama, how could you do this to me?"

"It's the Lord's will, child!"

Señor Robles attempted to wedge himself into the congested doorway. When that proved impossible, his hand, after circumnavigating Silvio's Magnalite midsection, managed to finally make land in my vicinity. Awkwardly we shook hands, while Señor Robles raised his eyebrows at me in a suggestive manner, three distinct times—why, I had no idea, unless he was doing a Groucho Marx impersonation which, under the circumstances, did not seem likely.

In the absence of any viable alternative, and in order to get the ordeal over with, I decided to invite everyone inside.

"Gosh," I said, "I am one awful host. Why doesn't everyone come on in. We're all civilized people," I added, stretching the point a little in Silvio's case, "and I'm sure we can work things out to everyone's satisfac…"

Ninety per cent of Señor Robles had retreated back behind Mighty Jose Young's hulking frame, leaving only his visored head exposed. From where I stood, it looked as if Señor Robles' head was growing out of Silvio's bare bulked-up bicep, a disorienting image to say the least. And then, when Señor Robles, looking like a grownup birth defect, began to high-eyebrow me again, I lost my train of thought entirely.

TWENTY-FIVE

The next minute my small room was filled with three people too many. I led Mom and Señor Robles to a seat at the card table. Then I turned to Silvio. "We seem to be out of chairs," I said to the glowering young giant. "Can I offer you a stout branch?"

"A what?"

"Something to drink," I said. "I'm afraid we're a little limited in the beverage department. We have orange soda (Mariela's favorite), some apple juice and, that's about it."

"Mariela," Celia said, "get everybody some soda pop. Son, have a seat, here, next to me. Señor Robles, maybe you could stand up for a minute."

Everyone rushed to obey Mom's orders. Once we were all repositioned with our respective glasses and cereal bowls, Celia ordered her daughter back to the table.

"Sit down, child," she said, "next to your fiancé. Now, as I understand it, the two of you was planning to get married."

"The minute we set foot on British soil, Mom," I assured her. "Right, Mariela?"

"That's right, mama." Mariela, I could tell, did not like lying to her mother.

"Well," Celia said, "I am here to ask you both to do this old woman a small favor."

"Mama," Mariela said, "you're not old. You're only forty-four."

"Well, I feel old. What with the arthritis, and the high blood pressure, and the ethereal scarlosis, and the…"

"Mama!"

"Children," Celia said, taking both our hands, "if, God

forbid, something should happen on that boat, and you were to die at sea, I could not go on living knowing that my daughter—and you too, son—was going to spend all eternity rotting in putrefaction down there in Purgatory someplace. Children," she added, "I know, no matter what, you're too good for that other place."

"Thanks, Mom."

Celia heaved an enormous sigh. "But getting back to the favor I want to ask…"

"Or else!" Silvio exclaimed.

Celia threw her son a murderous look. Mariela stared at me with imploring eyes, mouthing the words, "I'm sorry." I smiled and shook my head.

"The Lord," Celia said brightly, as if the idea had just this minute occurred to her, "would be mighty pleased, and I would sleep a whole lot better—not that I sleep so good anyway—if you two beautiful young people got married right now."

"Right now?" Mariela and I said in unison.

"Yes, children. You know what they say: there's no time like the present tense."

"I happen to have an open slot," Señor Robles chimed in, glancing theatrically at his watch, "but we'll have to hurry. Half of Havana seems to be getting married today. Ha, ha." Once again, he showed me a raised eyebrow and suddenly I knew what he was after: I was a foreigner; we were in Cuba; Señor Robles wanted his gratuity. Just for the hell of it, I arched my eyebrows back at him, a gesture he seemed to interpret with restrained optimism.

Quickly, I considered the situation. Here, crowded into my small room, I had three determined people who seemingly shared the same agenda—an agenda with which I did not sympathize, necessarily, but for which at the same time I felt a certain attraction. Marrying Mariela might not be all that bad an idea. It would, in a way, legitimize our relationship, making her feel more secure, and me feel less like a sex-offender.

As for the legal ramifications, as far as I knew the American and Cuban governments were not in the habit of sharing this type of intimate information, or any kind of information for that matter, so the chances of our Cuban marriage becoming known back home should be all but nil.

Or, at least that is how my hormone-addled brain perceived the matter at that particular moment.

When I looked outward from my inner deliberations, everyone was staring at me. One of those inordinately long and uncomfortable silences ensued. I felt Mariela's embarrassment, her mother's desperation and her brother's animosity all blowing up like balloons about to burst. I took a deep breath. What the hell, I told myself, in for a peso, in for a dollar.

"Well, then, let's get started, shall we," I announced to looks of joy and incredulity. "I don't have a ring on me, though," I said, patting the pockets of my shorts. "I should have a ring, shouldn't I, to put on my *novia's* finger?"

"Of course, you should," Celia said, producing one at once. "My neighbor wanted seventy dollars, but I got her down to twenty-five. It's genuine ten carat gold. I said I'd pay her tomorrow."

"A bargain," I said, reaching for my wallet.

Mariela grabbed me by the arm and dragged me towards the bathroom. "We'll be right back," she told the others.

"Are you sure you want to do this?" she asked, once the door was closed. "You don't have to; not for me. Isn't it illegal? To marry two people at the same time?"

"Technically, yes," I admitted. "But as long as I'm only married to you here in Cuba, baby, I don't see what the problem is. Unless you'd rather not?"

"No," Mariela said, her eyes aglow, "I have no problem."

"Good. That settles it."

We sealed the deal with a long passionate kiss, then went back to the room, where the tension was so thick you could have cut it with a dull machete. I took my time, looking each person in the eye. I put my hand on Mariela's shoulder. I cleared my throat and said, "Okay, where do I sign?"

TWENTY-SIX

Señor Robles was a blur as he shot from his chair. He had no bodies to impede his progress now, and was at my side straight away, reaching eagerly for my hand.

"*Felizidades!*" he cried, frantically pumping my arm. "Yes, I have the official register right here. Of course, we don't sign until after the ceremony. And we cannot perform the ceremony until we have dealt with a minor formality, the small fee, which I am certain you will find quite reasonable."

"How much?" I asked, reaching once again for my wallet.

"Let me see," he said, putting forefinger to chin. "First, we have the 'Standard Ordinary License' fee. Then, there's the special one-time 'Permission for Foreigners to Co-matrimonialize' tax. Plus, the 'Home Delivery' fee. And, finally, the 'Express-Service' surcharge. Which brings us," he concluded, showing me all twelve of his teeth, "to a grand total of only five-hundred dollars."

If they ever decided to do a Cuban version of the Amos 'N Andy TV show, Señor Robles would have made a wonderful Calhoun. The man was so transparently corrupt, it was laughable. But he had me in an awkward spot: I was breaking one law that I knew of, and perhaps there were others. As I began to extract the bills from my wallet, Mariela launched herself at the rapacious justice, stopping just short of his throat.

"Five-hundred dollars! What kind of fools do you take us for? I'm reporting you to the anti-corruption police!"

"D-d-did I say f-f-five-hundred?" the little man stuttered. "I meant, fifty, of course. What was I thinking? Are you certain I said five-hundred? Perhaps you misunderstood. As you know, we Cubans are famous for our misapprehensions, due to our profound accentual diversifications, which often render intrapersonal communications…"

"Nineteen dollars," Mariela ordained. "Not a centavo more."

(The potentially symbolic significance of that amount did not escape me. Later in the day Mariela confirmed my suspicion. "That bureaucratic pig," she said with disgust, "no way he's worth as much as a Havana chica. Even an ugly one.")

"Nineteen?" Señor Robles feigned first shock, then resignation. "Very well," he said. "But I'm afraid I have no change for a twenty."

"I have change," Mariela said.

Once that had been settled, I suggested we adjourn to the garden where we wouldn't be so crowded. It was still early, not yet nine. It wouldn't become unbearably hot outside for another fifteen minutes. Everyone was amenable and we all headed for the door, even Silvio, who, as he brushed by me on his way out, said, "I scared you, didn't I? That's why you're marrying my sister."

"Silvio," I told my soon to be bogus brother-in-law, "you could scare a Columbian death-squad."

Silvio seemed to grow even larger as he puffed up with pride and said, "Maybe you're not so bad after all."

The garden really wasn't a great deal larger than my room, but it felt nice to be outside where, if I had to run for my life, I would at least have a pair of viable options.

Mariela and I lined up in front of the justice of the peace, holding hands and grinning like idiots. Mom and Lurch stood just behind us. Señor Robles appeared troubled. "What's that smell?" he asked, twitching his nose.

"Dying day-blooming jasmine," I promptly replied. "The garden's full of it."

"But I smelled it in the house, too."

"It's pungent scent permeates the entire neighborhood," I claimed. "Can we get on with the ceremony, please?"

"Yes, of course." Señor Robles proceeded to fumble with a dog-eared book for a moment, searching I assumed for the section on civil marriages.

"It's in here someplace," he muttered, "right after the official births section, and just before the official deaths section. Don't want to mix things up, here, ha, ha. Let me see."

"Yes, you be careful, Señor Robles," Celia said severely. "We want to be declaring these young people man and wife, not dead on arrival."

"Tocayo!" a voice called out. "What in God's name are you doing?"

Carlos and Henry the Eighth, dressed so garishly they made even the bougainvillea droop with envy, were standing directly behind us. Apparently, they were on their way out, to do a guest appearance on Liberace's Live From My Lanai show.

"Who are those men?" Celia asked.

"Yeah, who are they?" Silvio growled.

"Everyone, this is Carlos and Enrique, my, ah, neighbors."

"Nice to meet you," Celia said uncertainly.

"So?" Carlos said.

"I, ah, seem to be getting married, Tocayo."

At this news my Tocayo's brow furrowed like a field of recently planted beets, while Enrique, clasping his hands over his heart, began to bounce stiffly up and down like a human pogo stick.

"Tocayo," Carlos said, "can I speak to you a moment? In private?"

"Of course, Tocayo. Everyone? Please excuse us for just a minute."

Carlos and I adjoined to my room while Silvio was saying, "What's a Tocayo?"

"Watch your mouth!" Celia told him.

Carlos, once we were alone, put a hand on each of my shoulders, looked me in the eye and said, "Tocayo, I already knew that you were insane, but what I need to know now is, are you out of your fucking mind?"

"I know what you're thinking, Tocayo. But I'll only be married in Cuba. Once I'm back in the US, it'll be as if I'd never been married at all."

"Except to your wife," he reminded me.

"Yes, well, there is that."

"In Mexico, Tocayo, we have laws against this—not that anyone pays them much attention. But in America, I have heard that they take their laws quite seriously, isn't that so, Tocayo? Being married to more than one person at a time? Bigamy, I believe, is the name of the crime? Tocayo, forgive me for saying this, but you appear to have lost all sense of proportion."

"Tocayo, you may be entirely correct. And I appreciate your concern, but it's too late to back out now. Why don't you join us for the ceremony?"

My neighbor bowed his head. "All right, Tocayo, I can see that your case is hopeless. We will be honored to attend. Enrique loves weddings. Don't ask me why."

Back in the garden, Silvio and Enrique were admiring each other's muscles, exchanging weight-lifting tips and, seemingly, making friends. Silvio, as far as I knew, was not gay, but the two young men did make an interesting couple: combining their two bodies, you could have made one hell of an offensive lineman; just as, by combining their IQ's, you could have come close to creating a genius.

As I rejoined Mariela, Silvio was asking Henry the Eighth what a "Tocayo" was. "I'm not sure," Enrique replied helplessly. "I think it has something to do with Mexico."

"Well," Señor Robles said with a hint of irritation, "I hope we can get started now." Once again, he made a point of looking at his watch which, I noticed, appeared to have stopped several years ago.

"What time do you have?" I asked the justice of the peace, just to be friendly.

"It's, uh, just after, um, let us begin!"

"Praise the Lord!"

"What do you bench press?" Silvio asked Enrique.

"One fifty-five."

"One sixty-five," Silvio said.

"Well, you're certainly a healthy looking specimen,"

Carlos said to Silvio as he stepped between the two young men. "But, hands-off. He's already taken."

"Huh?"

"Today," Señor Robles began his spiel, "we are gathered here to celebrate the union of two…"

"What is going on back there?" a voice, sounding like a rooster on its deathbed, crowed at us from an undisclosed location nearby. "I demand to know! This is my house!"

"What was that?" Señor Robles asked fearfully.

"I'll have the bunch of you thrown in jail!" Eustacia's disembodied voice bounced off the garden wall. The painkillers, I thought, must be affecting her mind, not that it needed much affecting.

"Jail?" Señor Robles was truly alarmed now, on his toes, poised for flight.

"It's only my landlady. She's a bit…"

"She's crazier than a bedbug!" Celia broke in. "Poor woman."

TWENTY-SEVEN

"She never got over the tragic death of her husband," I explained. "A fisherman. Mutilated by a small shark. Took him forever to die. Her mind hasn't been the same since, but she's really quite harmless."

"She doesn't sound harmless to me," Señor Robles, craning his neck in a futile attempt to see around the corner of the house, begged to differ. "What if she calls the police?"

"Hopefully," I said, "by the time they arrive, you will be long gone."

"We," he resumed reading at breakneck speed, "are gathered here today to celebrate the union of two young—of two comrades who have chosen to make a joint lifetime commitment to the Cuban Revolution."

I turned my head just enough to make eye-contact with Carlos. He looked at me with sorrowful eyes, shaking his head, like a man watching a friend throw himself off a bridge.

"No matter how dire," Señor Robles sped on, "the threat from the Imperialist Bully to the north; no matter the hardships, the struggles, the pain…"

"I know what you perverts are doing!" the disembodied voice of my landlady screeched. "Men with girls. Men with boys! Men with men! Filth! Slime! Foreigners!"

Señor Robles was, once again, stopped dead in his trachea. I took advantage of the pause to ask him who had written the marriage manual. "Somehow," I said, "it doesn't sound like your style."

"It was written," he replied distractedly, by "*el Comandante* himself."

"That would explain it."

"Explain what."

"Never mind."

"The Revolution must go on!" Señor Robles continued. "They may steal our Olympic gold medals in boxing. They may blockade our island fortress. They may take the food from our mouths and the medicine from our veins. They may try to steal our best left-handed pitchers, our shortstops and our catchers. But they will never…"

Someone was sobbing. I turned around and there was Henry the Eighth bawling his eyes out. Carlos shrugged apologetically. "I'm sorry, Tocayo. Weddings always affect him like this. It's a good sign, though, don't you think? Shows sensitivity?"

"…but they can't take away our revolutionary zeal!" Señor Robles resumed. "They can't take away our…"

What stopped him this time was not Enrique's sobbing, which continued unabated, nor Eustacia's insane outbursts, which hadn't been heard for several minutes. What brought Señor Robles to a crashing halt on this occasion was a vision. You could see it in his awe-filled eyes and his gaping mouth. Everyone turned around, as if on command, to stare at la doctora Eva, standing bolt-upright like an avenging goddess at the mouth of the alleyway.

"What in the world is going on here?" she demanded.

"Who is that?" Celia asked, the flood waters of her confusion about to crest.

"Eustacia is practically hysterical," Eva said, glaring at me.

"Practically?" Señor Robles muttered.

"It's my landlady's psychiatrist," I told my soon to be mother-in-law in a low voice. "Thank God she's here! Hopefully, she brought along some thorazine."

Celia made the sign of the cross.

"Doctora Eva," I said glumly," so glad you could make it."

"Do you want to tell me what's going on here, doctor?"

"It's just a wedding. Nothing for your patient to get upset about."

"Who's getting married?"

"Well, I am."

"You?" Eva said. "Didn't you tell me you were already married?"

"Already married?" Señor Robles and Celia said in unison.

Carlos and Enrique, I noticed, were holding hands now, as Enrique continued to weep with abandon. Silvio, comprehension finally seeping through the leach-field of his mind, shouted, "Mama, mama, these men are homosexuals!"

And just like that, Celia was hors de combat, fainted dead away on the small patch of lawn. For a moment everyone froze. Then two fumigation men arrived, wearing gas masks and army fatigues, and carrying what looked like giant bazookas left over from WW II, but which were in fact "insecticide rifles" manufactured decades ago in the Soviet Union.

The fumigation men attempted to ascertain if anyone had seen any mosquitoes lately, especially ones with black and white stripes on their abdomens. Naturally, everyone ignored them, except for Silvio, who wanted to know if their weapons could "kill an actual person".

Eva was already at Celia's side, taking her pulse. I knelt beside her, feeling a little dazed myself. "Is she all right?"

"Her pulse is steady," Eva said. "What do you think? Should we call an ambulance?"

"What are you asking him for?" Silvio said. "He's just a cow doctor."

"A cow doctor?"

"Ignore him," I told Eva. "Brain-damaged at birth. Hopeless case."

"We're going in," the fumigation men announced.

Fortunately, Celia was unconscious only a short time. When she came around, however, she began to speak in tongues, which made a strong impression on everyone but her two children. "We're used to it," Mariela told me. "It happens all the time."

Soon we had Celia back on her feet, where she gave every appearance of having returned to quasi-rationality. "Children, stop fussing," she said. "Let's go on with the ceremony."

Everyone resumed their former positions facing Señor Robles, who was looking a little stunned. "Where was I?" he asked himself.

"Eva! Eva! What are they doing?" Eustacia screeched from her perch around the corner. "Is there perversion going on? We must stop the perversion!"

"Now I remember," Señor Robles answered himself, "I'm in Hell."

"Everything is fine, Eustacia," Eva called out. "They're getting married."

"Who's getting married?"

"Your tenant and his…companion."

"He's marrying that hairy boy?"

"No, no," Eva said, "your other tenant, the doctor. He's marrying his girlfriend."

"Which one?" Eustacia screeched.

"Which one?" Celia repeated numbly.

"The animal doctor!" Silvio called out helpfully.

"Poor woman," I told Celia. "She's having one of her medically themed hallucinations. Right now she thinks she's running a boarding house for doctors."

"She does?"

"Of course she does. Just ask her psychiatrist. Doctora Eva, please confirm for us your diagnosis…"

But la doctora Eva was already stomping off to pacify her apoplectic patient. Before disappearing around the corner, she turned her head and blasted us with those improbable green eyes. It was a brief but devastating look, a fire-and-ice glare that could have melted marble, and then congealed it again. It affected everyone, especially Mom.

"She's not staying for the cake?"

TWENTY-EIGHT

The call came on Saturday night.

"Do you know who this is?" a mangled voice asked in my ear.

"I think so."

"It's me," he confirmed.

"Yes?"

"You have the rest of the car parts?"

"Car parts?"

For a moment I wondered if this could be a wrong number. The voice was unrecognizable, but that didn't mean a great deal. Cuban phone lines made everyone sound as if they were talking through voice distorters.

I spent a moment worrying over the man's strange choice of words. Car parts? Something smells wrong here. What if all this time they've been setting me up? For now, I decided, I'll only admit to having the car parts. How serious a crime could that be? Certainly, no worse than bigamy.

"Uh…yes."

"You have them?" the voice insisted.

"Yes, of course," I said with more conviction.

There was a long pause. "Tomorrow night," the fractured voice gurgled. "Don't go out after nine. Be ready. I'll call."

No, it was not a wrong number.

"That was Mr. Garcia," I told Mariela. "It's on for tomorrow."

"Good."

"I'm having a little rum," I said, reaching anxiously for the bottle. "Orange soda for you?"

As I busied myself preparing the drinks, Mariela fixed her eyes upon me in a most discomfiting way. "You really are crazy," she said after a while. "Risking your life, when you could be taking the plane. I'm Cuban. I have no choice. I'm desperate."

"Well," I said with a nervous laugh, "I'm desperate, too. Desperately in love."

Our nerves were stretched tight, like the skin of a conga drum. We hadn't spoken a word in over an hour.

"What time is it?"

"Just after midnight."

"I guess they could be calling any time."

"Anytime."

Another hour passed. We were dressed, packed and as ready as we were going to get.

"That lobster was pretty good," Mariela said, just to say something.

Earlier, we'd gone over to Chinatown to celebrate our impending departure with an illegal lobster dinner: our Last Supper?

"Yes," I agreed, "they don't have illegal lobster like that back home."

Another hour passed.

"Maybe we should turn on the TV," Mariela suggested. "There's not much on, but it's better than just…"

The telephone rang, so loud it seemed it would wake the whole neighborhood. I picked it up. "Go out to the street," Mr. Garcia's distorted voice said. "Turn left and start walking. Act natural." The line went dead. Had Mr. Garcia hung up? Or had the call been cut off, leaving unsaid potentially critical instructions? We waited two minutes. No one called back.

"Let's go." We grabbed our small bags and slipped quietly out the door. Eustacia, for whom I'd left a short apologetic note, was safely sedated with pain killers and did not pounce upon us from her window aerie. I felt a little guilty about not saying good-bye, but only a little; she'd been an absolute beast since her surgery and I was happy to see the last of her.

We turned left and began to walk. The streets were deserted. I'd never been out at this hour and the absence of activity felt strange and menacing.

We walked, holding hands, for two blocks. Nothing happened.

"Are we acting natural?" I asked.

"I'm not sure."

On the next block a car passed, but didn't stop. I'd given the car what I hoped was a "natural" glance; it contained a single driver, a man I'd never seen before.

"I hope something happens soon," Mariela said. "If we run into the police, we could have problems. It's too late to be just walking around."

The police. In my small bag, aside from my passport, wallet and several other essentials, was ten thousand dollars in cash. I tried to maintain an outward appearance of calm, which was not easy; I felt like I was tumbling off of a tall building.

Mariela, Carlos, Mario and Raoul (Was I forgetting anyone?) had got it right: I was insane. We'd turn around, go back to the room and reschedule—a solo passage this time. The hell with the guilt and the gallantry! Paying her way was enough of a gesture. There was no need to share the danger.

A car, the same car (a pre-Hispanic Chrysler, I believe), pulled to the curb. The rear door was thrown open. "Mr. Garcia sends his regards," the driver said. We jumped in. "Lay down on the seat," the man instructed, and off we went.

We lay like that, entwined in each other's arms atop the lumpy foul smelling backseat, for a long time, as the car conveyed us to our unknown destination. Every now and then we took turns murmuring reassuring words into each other's ears. We were both frightened, me perhaps more than her, but alongside the fear (in my case—I will be frank—abject terror) I could feel a new deeper intimacy growing between us which had nothing to do with sex. This was in fact the first time I had been in such close contact with Mariela for more than twenty minutes without achieving an erection.

I attempted, once, to communicate with our driver. "Will it be much longer?" I asked. He did not reply.

In the event, it was a good deal longer, and although I could not actually see anything from my prone position, I had the uncomfortable feeling that we were the only vehicle on the road, painfully exposed and vulnerable.

An hour passed, though it seemed much longer. We hadn't stopped for a traffic light, or even slowed down at an intersection for a long time. Clearly, we had left the city behind. Then our driver braked, bringing us to an abrupt halt.

"Are we here?" I asked.

"Quiet!"

Someone with a flashlight approached the driver's open window. Craning my neck, I was just able to make out the figure of a man wearing a uniform. The man leaned in the driver's window, training his light on the backseat.

"Who's that?" he asked.

"Nobody," our driver replied.

"There's two of them," the man said.

"Yes."

I heard the sound of paper rustling. Then, miraculously, the flashlight was withdrawn and we were on our way again.

A few minutes later we pulled onto an unpaved road where we bumped along for another thirty minutes. The road was atrocious, deeply rutted and full of potholes. On two occasions we were nearly bounced off the seat. Then we stopped.

"This is it, get out," our driver said.

We climbed out and stood beside the car, which turned around and sped away, leaving in its wake a cloud of salty dust. It was too dark to see the dust, but we could feel it on our skin and taste it in our mouths. The ground beneath our feet felt soft and sandy. I could hear what sounded like a gentle surf lapping the shore not far away.

"Now what?"

"Someone should be here," I said, "to..." To what? To lead us to a boat? To rob us of the substantial amount of cash I was carrying? To stick knives in our ribs and throw our bodies in the water?

"I'm sure you're right," Mariela whispered. She was really frightened now. For the first time I could hear it in her voice.

"They'll be coming any minute," I said, my own voice hoarse and quavering.

It was cloudy, moonless and black—a perfect night for smuggling human beings into a new and better life across the water. I did not, however, find the lack of light reassuring. An attack, which I expected imminently, could come from any direction and we would have no warning.

Several minutes passed.

"Where the hell are they?" I hissed. The knife, the one which would be slipped at any moment between my ribs, would be long and thin, I decided.

"They'll be here," Mariela said. "Don't worry."

"You know, baby," I said, squeezing her hand, "this really isn't as much fun as I thought it would be."

Mariela forced out a laugh, and squeezed back. "Yeah, fun."

Someone or something prodded my shoulder. Certain it was a gun, I threw my hands in the air and yelped, "Don't shoot! It's yours! Take it all!" I was hoping, I suppose, that if I made the robbery an easy one our assailant might not feel compelled to kill us. "We can't see you," I pointed out. "We can't see anything!"

"What the hell," a man's voice growled in my ear, "are you talking about?" The man, whoever he was, seemed to be in a bad mood. "You're late!" he snarled, flicking on a dim light. "Everyone's waiting."

"Oh," I said, putting my hands down. "We've been waiting, too, you know. If there's such a…"

"Quiet! You have the money?"

"Yes."

"Show it to me."

"I was told…"

"Just show it to me!"

Reluctantly, I opened the bag. Our grumpy friend shone his light on its contents, grunted and said, "Follow me. Hurry up. You're late."

TWENTY NINE

The speedboat was obscenely long, a potent fiberglass phallus capable, overloaded as it was, of outrunning the Cuban Navy and the US Coastguard combined. Or so they said. Though it was not cold, I began to shiver. Mariela squeezed my hand and told me not to worry.

"That's right," a woman nearby said angrily, "don't worry. The worst that can happen is the navy blows us up and we all die."

"Well, if that's the worst…"

"Better than dying little by little on that damn island," she said. Several people in our immediate vicinity grunted their agreement. "And better than getting eaten by sharks," she added gloomily, "if a big wave hits us the wrong way."

"It seems pretty calm now," I remarked.

"This time of year," she said, "the storms come out of nowhere. Or we could hit a log, or other floating debris. Or a rock. The engine could die."

"Yes, that's nice to know. Thank you very much."

Mariela and I were sitting on a bench in the precise center of the boat. We'd been the last to board, and wedging us into this choice spot had not been easy. The cigarette boat was packed solid with refugees. The crew consisted of the captain, who stood at his wheel just behind us, and his mate, who seemed to be in charge of maintaining maritime harmony. It was this wiry young man who had coaxed us over around and through a nearly solid wall of uncomplaining humanity to our present location.

According to Mr. Garcia, Mariela and I were the only passengers whose fare had not been pre-paid by friends or relatives in Florida. That kind of cash did not exist in Cuba, not outside the Presidential Palace. The boat and crew had come from the United States, as well: a form of foreign aid: Give us your tired, your poor, your huddled masses...or better yet, sneak them over in a cigarette boat.

No doubt, the fact that we were the only refugees carrying so much cash was the reason for our preferred treatment, seat-wise. In this way the captain could keep an eye on us and, more importantly, our money was less likely to be washed overboard.

The boat began to slip slowly away from shore, the powerful engines gurgling discreetly. It was just the least bit lighter out on the water and I was able for the first time to examine our closest neighbors, who were more or less sitting in our laps.

They seemed to be typical Cubans: undernourished scarecrows badly in need of some decent food, some decent clothes and several bars of soap. In the midst of this amorphous bony mound of humanity, Mariela and I (freshly bathed and dressed for a Sunday afternoon at the beach) would, in the light of day, have stuck out like snow flakes on a briquette. But the light of this particular day, if ever we came to see it, was a long way off. And hopefully, by the time it deigned to shine upon our well-groomed selves, we and our shipmates would have long since gone our separate ways.

We were doing about twenty knots, still creeping along by cigarette boat standards, still well within sight of shore, when the searchlight of a patrol boat snapped on, its beam gliding like a giant white finger across the water in our direction.

"Uh-oh," Mariela said. My lover had a real gift for understatement, and more balls than a matador.

The beam caught us a minute later. Everyone began to shout at once. Someone said to duck. Someone suggested we should all jump overboard. And several people opined that we should surrender forthwith. Then all the voices were blotted out by an enormous roar.

We've been hit by a mortar! was my first thought. But no, we were still intact. What had felt like an explosion was merely the result of our mammoth motors being engaged to their full capacity. The captain, apparently, was not about to surrender.

The forward thrust was truly impressive. Had there been any space between bodies, everyone would have fallen over backwards. Instead, we merely shifted back and forth, like an elongated bowl of lumpy Jell-O. Briefly, I wondered if the refugees in the very last row were still with us.

The boat's nose, in true phallus fashion, rose eagerly into the air as we took off, faster, then faster still, spray flying, hull thumping, people screaming. Soon it became apparent that the patrol boat, its searchlight stuck to us like a leech, had little hope of catching up. But it must have a radio, I thought, and if there are other boats ahead of us, blocking our path…

"We can still make it!" Mariela shouted into my ear. "If we're lucky!"

Lucky? Wasn't it glaringly obvious that lucky was precisely what we were not! At best, we were getting off to a really poor start.

Confirming my worst fears, two additional lights suddenly appeared in front of us on the water. Two more boats. It was impossible to judge in the featureless gloom their size or distance, but I had the impression that they were smaller and more agile than the first boat. They were also coming directly towards us from different angles, a pair of pincers. Together with our original pursuer, the three boats formed a rough triangle, with us in its center, not a promising configuration.

Our captain, hopeful or not, proceeded to take evasive action at once. Still gaining speed, he veered sickeningly to the left, and then to the right, and then back to the left again, eluding in this manner the three sweeping beams. Wee bursts of yellow light began to flicker on the decks of our pursuers. It took a moment to sink in. They were machine guns. Machine guns were shooting at me!

This was beyond belief, beyond my worst imaginings—beyond anything! If, up until this point, I'd thought I'd known what fear was, I'd only been kidding myself. My thought processes ceased altogether. It was all physical now—one long, shuddering wave of numbing terror.

Then, in a remarkable show of solidarity, nearly all the passengers, including myself, began to throw up.

Between spasms, hunkered down in our death-bound juggernaut, vast quantities of spray soaking my clothes, I realized suddenly that we had ceased to zig and zag. Looking up, I saw that our intrepid captain was attempting to make a long looping curve around the two bullet-spitting speedboats, who in turn were doing their level best to cut us off, to pin us against the coast.

It was going to be excruciatingly close. We, on the one hand, had the faster boat. Our enemies, on the other, had the angle, the guns and the home field advantage. And now that we were back on a predictable path, making a flat-out run for our lives, the searchlights had little problem finding us again, nailing us in the cross-hairs of their beams, lighting us up for the guns. The land was coming up fast. If we could just get clear before we ran out of water, our chances were good. Unless we capsized. Or hit a rock. Or were blasted into oblivion.

Done vomiting for the moment, I chanced a look behind us. Everyone but the captain was hunkered down as low as they could get. He, whether foolish or fearless (of course he could have been both), stood perfectly erect, gripping the wheel. His defiant posture somehow reassured me, along with the sight of the original slower boat falling further and further behind.

When I turned to face front again, the prospect was not so cheering. As we and our pursuers raced for the same spot of water, the invisible finish line beyond which we could at least aspire to the possibility of safety, we were drawing closer and closer together. And as we did, the angle between us grew wider, until it had attained a perfect (perfect for them) ninety degrees: the optimum angle of fire. Broadside. Straight on. I imagined flying bullets smacking into the water all around us, smashing through the hull and thudding dully into human flesh. I imagined a high speed collision, complete with cinematic fireball. I imagined, as we neared the coast, our hull being ripped out by hidden rocks. Clearly, we were not going to make it.

At the last possible moment, just when it appeared that at least one of my nightmare scenarios was sure to come true, our wily captain suddenly "slammed on the brakes". The two small patrol boats, along with their nasty bullets, went shooting harmlessly across our bow, before they were forced to brake themselves in order to avoid running aground. Then, while our enemies were busy getting their noses turned around and pointed in the right direction, we leapt back into high gear and sped away.

The navy tried to follow, naturally, but their hearts were no longer in it. Their lights slowly faded from view, as did the coast. Soon we were out on the open waters of the Florida Straights. We had won. We were still a little numb with fear, soaked to the bone and lightly speckled with communal vomit, but we were safe! We were alive! At least for the moment.

THIRTY

The need for stealth forgotten we pressed on at full throttle, flying insanely across the narrow band of water separating Cuba from the coast of Florida. Mariela and I held each other tight, giggling with relief, shivering, telling each other over and over that we'd made it, that everything was going to be all right.

And then, out of the murky nothingness, suddenly, miraculously, there was Florida! And not a Coast Guard cutter in sight! The first mate, or whatever he was, came climbing over our seatmates and asked us for the cash, which I gleefully handed over. He stuffed it into a dirty canvas bag and said, "Don't forget, you still owe us."

"Yes, yes," I said. "Don't worry. You'll have it in a week."

"We'd better."

In darkness the boat slid quietly towards shore. Then it stopped. "We're here," a voice said. "Everyone out." A mad scramble ensued. Soon, clutching our two small bags, we were over the side, standing waist deep in water. The bottom was sandy, and after a few minutes of sloshing forward we were out of the water, standing on the beach.

Our shipmates gathered together, shouting, screaming and jumping for joy. Then, as if on cue, they all began to chant. "*Mi-gra! Mi-gra! Mi-gra!*" They couldn't wait to turn themselves in to the friendly forces of US Immigration, since as of now they were in terra firma possession of the Cuban immigrant's Holy Grail: Dry Foot status. The sooner they found the immigration authorities, the sooner they could be processed, united with their families and begin their new lives in the land of Milk, Freedom Fries and Honey.

We stood off to one side, basking in the generalized glow of joy. Eventually, in New York City, she too would turn herself in. But right now, the last thing I wanted to bump into was an Immigration Officer. Or an alligator. "Let's get out of here," I said. Holding hands, we turned our backs to the water and headed inland, in search of a road. For better, for worse, for whatever, our new lives were about to begin.

Mariela, like her liberated compatriots, was ecstatic, full of hope and excitement. As we trudged across the sand, she kept stopping to hug and kiss me. "We did it! We did it!" she cried. I felt enormously happy for her. And I was happy, too, in a way—happy and frightened out of my mind. Yes, you did it, I told myself, you really did it. But what, in Fidel's name, have you done?

PART III

ONE

The sun was just coming up when we finally stumbled, zombie-like with exhaustion, into the empty parking lot of the Seaview Motel. The Seaview looked abandoned—peeling paint, overgrown garden, opaque slime-green pool: a total dive.

"Hide behind that palm tree," I told Mariela. "I'll be right back."

"Why do I have to hide? You said I wouldn't have to worry about the police here."

"You don't," I assured her. "But I do. You look underage, and it's just as illegal here as it is in Cuba for a man to go with an underage girl."

"But I'm not underage, and I can prove it."

"Yes, with your Cuban identity card. But I'm not ready to deal with that yet. Just be patient, baby. Once we get to New York and get your papers straightened out, you'll be free as a bird."

The motel manager, a crackle-skinned old reptile with enormous amounts of nose-hair, sat slumped behind the reception counter in a plastic beach chair. He appeared to be asleep, although in the dim light it was hard to tell. He might have been dead. I banged the small bell three times with increasing violence before he began to stir.

"I need a room," I said.

"Yeah, yeah, take it easy." When he was more or less standing up, he proceeded to lurch in my direction until his stomach came to rest against the battered counter. Listing badly to port, he yawned, grimaced and fluttered his lids for a while. He was, I supposed, waking up. Or going back to sleep.

"I didn't hear a car," he said finally. "I always hear the car. I may be old, but I've still got my sensations intact."

I was glad I'd made Mariela wait outside. This would have been her first contact with a real American in his native habitat, and who knew what disheartening conclusions she might have drawn.

"You didn't hear the taxi?"

"You came in a taxi?"

"Yes, my car broke down. I had to leave it back in town." Silently, I prayed that he wouldn't ask me which town, as I had only the most approximate idea where we were. "It won't be fixed until this evening."

"It's kind of early, ain't it?" he said, narrowing his eyes.

"Early for what?"

"Early to be here."

"Here?"

"Checking in."

I looked at my watch. "It's seven-thirty."

"Why didn't you stay in town?"

"I wanted to be near the beach."

"Town is near the beach."

"Not near enough," I said, taking out my wallet.

The old man began to sniff the air, like an old Labrador on its last legs. "Smells like puke in here," he frowned.

"I've been driving all night," I said. "I'm tired. I'd like to get some sleep."

"An unusual time to be going to sleep, if you ask me," the clerk said, still sniffing noisily at the air.

I removed a hundred dollar bill from the wallet and placed it on the counter. "How much for the room?"

"You paying cash?"

"No, I'm paying with food stamps."

"Don't go wise-cracking on me, young man. Your clothes are wet."

Mister, I thought, if your wife's dead—and for her sake, I hope she is—I've got the ideal mate waiting for you down in Havana, Cuba.

"I'm not used to the heat," I said, wiping my damp brow.

"That must be where the puke smell is coming from," he said, screwing up his face in disgust. "You from up north, then?"

"Yes I am. So how much for the room?"

"Don't get many northerners this time of year. If I were you, I'd take myself a shower, pronto."

I took the bill and held it up two inches from the old man's face.

"One night is exactly one-hundred dollars," he said, snatching it out of my hand. "Number six," he yawned, throwing down a key. "All the way at the end. Closest room to the beach. If it wasn't for that damn sewage treatment plant, you could almost see the water."

"Thanks," I said, picking up the key.

"I know there's towels. I'm not sure about the toilet paper."

"That's fine. I wasn't planning on going to the bathroom anyway."

"Still smells like puke, if you ask me."

A short while later Mariela and I were lying on the lumpy bed in the dusty threadbare room, freshly showered and too tired to move.

"This room is really nice," she yawned.

"Goodnight, baby," I said, kissing her on the nose. "And welcome to America."

When I awoke some hours later, I was seized at once with another in what was becoming an unending string of anxiety attacks. The focus of my disquiet this time were two words written large in my mind's eye: Now what?

I'm in a motel, I told myself, somewhere in the south of Florida, lying beside a quasi-legal Dry-Footed Cuban alien for whom I am now totally responsible. Even though I already have a family. Even though…no, wait! I've thought this all through. I have a plan. I even have a schedule.

The plan was to rent a car and drive to New York City. The schedule called for me to arrive no later than the day after tomorrow at four-fifteen pm. At that precise hour Irving and Burt would be picking me up at Kennedy Airport, where I would be arriving on American Airlines flight number 235 from San Juan, Puerto Rico. That I would in fact be arriving in a rented car from somewhere in Florida was beside the point. The important thing was not to miss the deadline. Missing the deadline would not be good.

I picked up the phone. After nine rings my friend from the front desk picked up and said, "Yeah?"

"This is room number six…" I began.

"I know what room it is," he said impatiently. "You're the only ones here. It's low season."

"Right. Could you please call me a taxi?"

"A taxi?"

"Yes. I have to pick up my car."

"On a Monday? Did you know it's Monday?"

"Don't the taxis run on Monday?"

"Of course they do. This ain't Alabama, buster."

"I'm delighted to hear that. The taxi?"

"'Bout twenty minutes. By the way, you were entitled to a complementary 'Good Morning Coffee and Doughnuts'. Free of charge."

"Great. I'm famished."

"But it's too late, now. We put everything away at ten o'clock."

"Of course."

"You can get some food in town. The Happy Crab's pretty good, but I don't think they'll have breakfast, either. Not at this hour."

"Twenty minutes? For the taxi?"

"More or less. It's Monday. In case you didn't know."

Mariela slept like the dead. It took a while to get her in motion. Shortly thereafter the taxi arrived.

"I need to rent a car," I told the driver. "Where's the nearest agency?"

The driver, a small young man with rat-like features who could not take his eyes off Mariela, said, "In St. Helena. That's about forty miles. Not gonna be cheap."

"How much?"

"Two-hundred bucks."

"That seems a little steep."

"That your daughter?" the driver asked. "She doesn't talk much, does she?"

"One-fifty."

The driver nodded his head and put the car in gear. "Cute kid," he said, leering into the rearview mirror.

"Yes, she takes after her mother."

TWO

Irving and Burt stood shoulder-to-shoulder scanning the stream of passengers pouring out of customs. Burt held a bag containing my grubby "camping clothes", into which I would soon be changing in the airport bathroom. It was something of a tradition with us, to return to the bosoms of our respective families looking like the hillbilly sodomites in *Deliverance*. After more than two weeks of roughing it in the wilds of Upstate New York, our loved ones expected no less.

"I love Karl like my own brother," Burt was saying, "but he's a total wimp where women are concerned. I'll bet you fifty bucks he chickened out and spent the whole trip at the San Juan Hilton—dying of guilt and reading back issues of Orthopedics Today."

"I will not take that bet," Irving said. "Our amigo Karl, though his fine and exceptional qualities are an inspiration to us all, is at heart a conventional man incapable of straying to any significant degree from the straight and narrow. Plus, as you say, he's a complete wimp."

I tapped first Irving and then Burt on the shoulder.

"Well, look who's here!" Irving said.

Both men regarded me with sadistic smiles. If I hadn't ruined their vacation, I had at least put a damper on it, and now they were going to have their "good natured" revenge.

"So, the prodigal pussy hound re…" Burt began to choke, literally, on his own words. Irving's jowled lower jaw went into free-fall.

Mariela, with a dazzling smile, held out her hand and said in charmingly accented English, "My nem eez Mariela. How do jew do?"

As we snuggled in the backseat of Irving's car, Mariela said to me, "Why are your friends so fat?"

"They eat too much."

"They eat too much?"

"Karl," Irving announced for the fifth time, "you're out of your fucking mind."

Burt, in a voice tinged with awe, said, "I'll say one thing, Karl. She's totally, totally—I'm getting a hard-on just sitting in the same car with her."

In the past I'd found Burt's vulgarities mildly amusing. But this time he'd hit a sore spot. "Though she can't understand you, Burt, I would appreciate it if you would show a little respect. Like you would in the presence of any woman."

"Oh, ex-cuse me."

"Speaking of respect," Irving said, "in so far as women are concerned? What are you planning to tell your wife when we drop you off: 'I found this Cuban nymphet wandering around the Adirondacks and decided to adopt her?'"

"She is not a nymphet, Irving. She's nineteen-years-old. And we are not going to my house, not directly. We have to make a stop in the City first."

"Nineteen?"

"A stop in the City?"

I explained that we were going to check Mariela into a small hotel in lower Manhattan, one with a colorful and checkered history and known for its tolerant policies vis-à-vis guests, visitors and eccentric behavior in general. The Times had once referred to it as a "Rock 'N Roll Rest Home".

"And then what?" Irving demanded.

"Then you take me home and your part—for which I am truly grateful—in this, ah, situation, is over and done."

"Let us hope so," Irving said glumly.

The lanky individual standing behind the desk of the Westchester Hotel regarded us with a lazy smile. With his long grey ponytail, bushy moustache, leather vest and faded work shirt, he looked like an aging musician, which is exactly what he turned out to be: the ex-bass player for a band that had enjoyed a brief but stellar success in the late sixties.

"What can I do you folks for?" he said serenely. His eyes were slightly glazed, and his breath smelled of marijuana. I liked him right away.

"I want to rent a room," I said, "for at least a week. Can I pay cash in advance?"

"Abso-fucking-lutely. Your lady friend will be, like, staying with you?"

"Well, actually, she's doing the staying. I'll just be, you know, popping in and out."

"In and out," he repeated with a knowing smile. "She over the age of consent?"

"Abso-fucking-lutely," I said, attempting to bond with the aging hippy. "By the way, my name is Karl."

"Leonard. Pleasure to meet you. You know, I hate to say this, man, but I need to see some ID. Personally, I could care less. 'Judge not, lest ye be fucking-judged yourself.' That's our official motto here at the Westchester. But we do have to cover our asses, man, if you know what I mean."

"I know exactly what you mean." I passed him Mariela's Cuban ID. "You read Spanish, Leonard?"

"*Yo hablo un poquito,*" he said, perusing the document. "Cuban, huh? This her only ID?"

"Yes, Leonard, I'm afraid it is. You see, she's a very recent arrival—a political refugee. Tomorrow, first thing, she's reporting to the local Immigration office, but for the time being…"

"No problema," Leonard said. "Far as I can see, what you got here, man, is a nineteen-year-old, dry-footed political dissident—not our first, I might add. The Westchester's collective ass is now officially covered."

"Great! Terrific!" I handed him a wad of bills.

Leonard looked confused. "You said a week, right?"

"Yes?"

"This is…about two hundred bucks over and above, man."

"That's for you, Leonard. This girl is near and dear to my heart. I'd appreciate it if you could make a special effort to help her out. Get her taxis. Tell her where to eat. Direct her to someplace in the neighborhood she can buy some warm clothes."

"Not to worry, man," Leonard assured me.

"Thanks, man."

"No problema. Like I said, she's not our first refugee. Though she might be the cutest. And we've had some lookers, man. There was this chick Mick brought in once, South American, I think."

"Leonard, you're a prince."

"Count on me, dude."

"I'll call you tomorrow," I told Mariela. "Don't worry. Everything is fine."

"I love you."

"I love you, too."

"True romance," Leonard sighed, looking on wistfully as Mariela and I kissed good-bye. "Takes me back to '69. Me and Little Morning Star. Déjà-vu all over again, man."

THREE

Improbably, Janice was at home. All of the NGO's in the Greater Metropolitan Area must have shut down for the day. She met me in the hallway. I dropped my bags and opened my arms for the traditional welcome home hug.

The hug was perfunctory, as was the quick peck on the lips.

"Ouch!" Janice said. "When was the last time you shaved? And those clothes! It's off to the showers for you, young man."

Our reunions had, over the years, become highly ritualized, involving a certain amount of light-hearted banter, followed by a rare session of somewhat animated coupling. I was not looking forward to the "sex". As for the banter, I seemed to have forgotten my lines.

"Off to the showers," I said.

Janice gave me a quizzical look. That was not the standard response. I was supposed to say something about her not appreciating my manly odor, or my virile beard, or something of that nature. But I couldn't get the tone or the words right. I felt disoriented, out of place, as if, instead of returning home, I had crossed over into a parallel universe where everything seemed both familiar and strange at the same time.

"You got far too much sun, again," Janice scolded. "You're so lazy about putting on sun block. You know what happened to your father. Aren't you afraid of getting melanoma? I swear, sometimes, you're worse than a child."

I had in fact gone through enough sun block to protect a platoon of albinos, in an attempt (successful I am happy to say) to keep my exposed legs and arms nice and pale, like a flounder's belly.

"Tough woodsmen like me don't have to worry about skin cancer," I said, remembering my lines at last. "Ultra violet rays just bounce off us."

"Okay, Mr. Tough Woodsman," Janice said, stretching painfully for that teasing tone, "time for a shave and a shower. And maybe then, if you get lucky…"

"Yes, mam," I said, dutifully marching up the stairs. "How are the girls?"

"Brenda's fine. She calls once a week. And Candace is… Candace. I wish you could talk some sense into her. I'm not getting through at all."

"She home from school?" I asked hopefully. If she was home there might be a way to postpone our appointment in the bedroom. Somehow, I just didn't feel up to it.

"No, she's…I'm not sure where she is. But she'll be home for dinner. So, hurry and get in the shower," she added, attempting a lewd smile.

As I stood in the shower, supposedly washing off multiple layers of dirt and grime, I began to grow increasingly nervous about my imminent performance (or lack thereof) on the mattress. Everything had to appear perfectly normal. There could be no atypical behavior that might arouse suspicion. Already, I had flubbed badly with the banter business. Now I feared that when the moment came, I would fall short in the lust department as well.

Generally speaking our infrequent couplings were lackluster, to say the least. Once upon a time, however, the "torrid sessions" (as Janice referred to them) which followed on the heels of my annual return from the mountains had in fact been, if not torrid, at least pleasantly warm. Then, over the last ten years they had cooled down all the way to room temperature. Even so, I had never, in twenty-something years, ever failed to perform.

"You can do it," I told myself in the shower. "You're a regular stud. Remember Havana!"

Janice lay atop the covers wearing her only negligee, one I had given her in college and which she had taken out of deep storage especially for the occasion. The negligee, smelling faintly of moth balls, still fit her. In fact, for a woman her age she looked quite well in it. At another time, or to another man, she might even have appeared alluring.

My wife, who had no trouble remembering her lines, though her delivery, as always, left something to be desired, said, "Come and get it, big stuff."

In the light of my new alien vision, Janice, lying there "eagerly" on the bed, looked perfectly pathetic. I fought off a sudden urge to weep.

"Here I come, you hot mama," I said, remembering (thank God!) the correct timeworn response.

As we embraced, Janice said, "Did you miss me?"

"Of course. Terribly."

Then we proceeded to have at it.

Kiss her the way you normally do, I reminded myself. No lip-sucking. No biting. And keep your fingers...

"What's wrong?" Janice asked ten minutes later when, despite our best efforts at feigning a passion neither one of us felt, I remained as flaccid as a spoiled banana.

Think! I commanded myself. You need an excuse. Something plausible. You failed to rise to the occasion once, but you must not fail again!

"I'm worried," I said. Which was true enough.

"About what?"

Hmmmm...

"My...ah...colon."

"What's wrong?" Janice was up on one elbow, all thoughts of love-making banished, her brow furrowed with concern.

"I've been experiencing some...troubling symptoms."

"What kind of symptoms?"

"Ah..."

You idiot! I cursed myself. Couldn't you think of something a little less drastic?

"You know, dear, ah, black tarry stools, that sort of thing."

"Black tarry stools? Are you certain?"

"Well, yes, I think so. Although," I added quickly, "they might have been very dark brown. You know those outhouses up there—it's, ah, quite a drop from the seat to the, ah…I mean, even if you leave the door open, it's not that easy to, you know, accurately classify one's, ah, fecal characteristics."

"I'm sure it's just your imagination," Janice said bravely. "You're such a worrywart where your health is concerned. But I think you should get a colonoscopy anyway. For your peace of mind, if nothing else. You've put it off long enough."

"Yes," I agreed eagerly, "a colonoscopy. I'll call Hal first thing in the morning." Hal was our family physician.

"No, I'll call Hal. Right now."

Efficient, cool under fire, my wife discarded the negligee, put on a robe and reached for the phone. As she chatted with Hal's receptionist I lay back wondering how low I would eventually have to sink in order to protect my dirty little secret. Janice, despite her minor faults, was a good woman, and so, for that matter, was Mariela. Lying louse that I was, I deserved neither of them. What I did deserve was some particularly cruel form of medieval torture.

"You're on for Friday," Janice informed me. "Hal's office is faxing you the pre-procedure instructions."

"Wonderful."

Now I had something to really look forward to: three days of progressively starving myself, followed by one day of forcing down four quarts of liquefied scum while concurrently defecating my brains out and, capping off the entire extravaganza, being sodomized by a stainless steel tube.

Not quite boiled in oil, but a good start.

FOUR

The following morning over breakfast Janice said to me, "I wish you hadn't flushed so hastily."

"Sorry, dear. Force of habit. But I did get a pretty good look on the way down."

"And was it black?"

"Possibly. If not black, then very dark brown."

"And tarry?" she asked, her slice of dry seventeen-grain toast hovering breathlessly in the air.

"Well, that's hard to say, dear. It did seem to be unnaturally dense. But I wouldn't necessarily call it tarry."

A dark cloud passed over my wife's eyes. "You've lost weight, haven't you?"

"A pound or two (I'd lost eight). But I wouldn't read too much into it. I always lose weight on my fishing trips."

"Still," Janice said, "I would have liked to have a look at your stool."

"Yeah," Candace said, bounding into the kitchen, "and what about me? When do I get to get to see one?"

"Candace!"

"I read somewhere," Candace continued, pouring herself a glass of juice, "that's all old people talk about— going to the bathroom."

"We're not that old," I said.

"That's what worries me. You're not even senile, and you're talking bowel movements over breakfast."

"Yes, well…"

"By the way, Dad, you look great. Like, ten years younger. You should go on these stupid fishing trips more often."

Janice forced out a stoic smile. "Yes, doesn't your father look marvelous!"

It felt good to be back at work where my role in life was clearly defined and where I was far too busy to indulge in the guilt I'd been lacerating myself with all morning. On the train ride into Manhattan I'd been besieged by a pair of appalling images I could not get out of my mind: my wife's panic-stricken face on the one hand, and the shamefully normal light-brown bowel movement I had stealthily flushed down the toilet, on the other.

Also, I was a little anxious about Mariela. I'd called her from the train station and she'd sounded uncharacteristically shaky. She was about to leave for the Immigration office to turn herself in.

"Will they lock me up?" she asked.

"I don't know, baby. They might, for a day or two. Or they might not. But you won't be mistreated. This is the United States, not Cuba. There's nothing to be afraid of. Just follow the script and everything will be fine. Trust me."

"Goo-bye," she said in English.

I spent the majority of the morning rebuilding a torn anterior cruciate ligament on an overpaid wide-receiver, and pruning the frayed meniscus of an overpaid power-forward. The basketball player was good to go, and would surely live to rebound another day, but the football player was another story. If he was a racehorse, I would have shot the lame fellow on the spot. My advice to him, once he was sufficiently conscious? Put your savings in municipal bonds, get a library card and hope for a career in broadcasting.

Everyone was overjoyed to see me back, especially Dulce Mendez.

"Welcome back, Dr. Sanderson," she said, eying me frankly, "you look great."

In my pre-Cuban past I would have thanked her politely and continued on my way. But my response to frank looks on the part of pretty young women had apparently been reconditioned in Havana. Automatically, I returned her admiring look with one of my own. Breaking out into a large lascivious grin, she said, "Dr. Sanderson, I love your tan."

"And I love your beautiful ass; let's go to my room," I was about to say, when I remembered what country I was in.

"Ah, thank you," I said. "Have you seen Pedro?"

"No. Dr. Sanderson, can I ask you a personal question?"

The way she said the word "personal" set off some kind of chain-reaction in my refurbished autonomic nervous system and I became instantly aroused. Dulce noticed the bulge in my trousers, took a step closer and fixed upon me what could only be described as a smoldering gaze. Like a mouse hypnotized by a snake, I stared back into her eyes for a long moment. Christ, I thought, Pedro and Burt were right: she's mine for the asking.

"See you later," I said abruptly, as I turned and fled the scene.

"See you later," she called after me.

I finally ran into Pedro just after noon outside the hospital pharmacy.

"Hey, Doc!" Pedro said, "Welcome back. What a tan! You looking for some antibiotics? You get the clap down there? Syphilis? How about something for a yeast infection?"

The pharmacist, an elderly fellow just two months shy of retirement, gave us a curious look.

"Let's take lunch," I told Pedro, grabbing his arm. "My treat."

"Sure, Doc. So tell me all about those hot Latin…"

"Not here," I hissed, squeezing his arm as hard as I could.

In the taxi on the way downtown Pedro was expiring with curiosity. "Okay, Doc. We're out of the hospital. Now you can tell me. How'd it go? What happened? You get your rocks off, or what?"

"Not here," I said.

"Huh? Now what are you afraid of—hidden microphones?"

"No," I said, aiming my chin at the turbaned driver.

"Him? You think he speaks Spanish? Or maybe he plays bridge with your wife. You ever think of that?"

The worst Japanese restaurant in New York City was, thankfully, still in business. The first thing I did was down two Sakis in rapid succession.

"It still smells like shit in here," Pedro complained. "Why couldn't we eat someplace decent?"

"People dine here for the atmosphere, Pedro, not the food."

"Atmosphere? What atmosphere? I've been in Jamaican men's rooms with more atmosphere. Okay, Doc, so what happened? Come on. How'd it go?"

"Well, Pedro, the weather was awful, hot and humid. And the food wasn't much better—except for the illegal lobster, which was excellent. My accommodations were acceptable, though the air conditioner could have been…"

"Cut the crap, Doc. Did you get laid or not?"

"Pedro, getting laid does not begin to describe it."

Pedro grinned with paternal pride. "Congratulations!"

"Thanks, Pedro, I never could have done it without you."

"Glad to be of help. So, I guess you followed my instructions, then? In the manual?"

"All but one, Pedro."

"Which one was that?"

"The bit about not becoming emotionally involved with a chica."

"Ha!" Pedro was enormously pleased. "So you fell for a chica, huh?"

"I'm afraid so."

"And now you miss her something awful," Pedro moaned. "She's so far away, and you can't wait to go back to Cuba. Am I right?"

"Actually, no."

"Oh, so it's love 'em and leave 'em. Is that it?"

"Well, yes and no. I loved, but I didn't leave."

"What? Oh, I get it. Cuba's not so far away. You just get on a plane, and you're back in business. But you know what they say, Doc. So near, and yet…so far!"

"Forty blocks."

"What?"

"That doesn't seem very far, Pedro, no matter what they say."

"What's forty blocks?"

"She is."

"Who is?"

"The chica."

"What chica?"

"The one I brought home with me."

"From Cuba?"

"Where else."

"What the fuck are you talking about?"

"In direct violation of Section (10.1), Pedro, I fell in love and smuggled the object of my affection home with me. I've got her stashed down at the Westchester."

"The Westchester Hotel?"

"Yes."

"On Twenty-third street?"

"Yes."

Pedro took a deep breath, and burst out laughing. "Oh, you are good, Doc, really good. I almost believed you."

"She's nineteen-years-old," I told the orderly. "A mulatta. Very pretty. But more than pretty, she emanates…something. I can't put it into words. The thing is, Pedro, I need to ask you a favor. She's going to the Immigration office today to turn herself in. Since she's a Dry Foot, she'll have no problem getting permission to stay. But they always ask for a friend or family reference, someone who can take responsibility for her. And I'm afraid she's going to tell them that you're her uncle. I hope you don't mind. I know you're not Cuban, but I thought, well, at least you're in the ballpark. I doubt if they'll ask you any trick questions, like, what province is Cien Fuegos in, or what's the population of Santiago…"

"Wait! Wait! Stop!" Pedro cried, holding up both his hands, as if I were an automobile about to run him over. "You're serious? You really brought one back?"

"Afraid so."

"But, but, but, how?"

In a hundred words or less I told my friend about Mr. Garcia, the cigarette boat, our near escape, etcetera, etcetera. When I was finished, Pedro sat there speechless, his mouth agape, his eyes wide with shock. The waiter brought another round of the cheap tepid Saki.

"Well, salud!" I said, downing the small cup in a single gulp.

Pedro took an absentminded sip of his own drink and said, *"Estas tomandome el pelo, cabron!"* (You're pulling my leg, you bastard!)

"Her name's Mariela, and I really love her, Pedro. I know she's too young for me. In fact, you look at her and think, she can't be a day over sixteen. But she's wise beyond her years."

Pedro, who was not a religious man, crossed himself and said, *"Dios te ayuda!"*

FIVE

Performing a partial knee replacement only an hour after tossing back four Sakis was, for me, an unprecedented act of unprofessionalism. Fortunately, the effects of the alcohol were largely mitigated by the hearty lunch of soggy tempura I'd consumed, and my digital dexterity was not impaired to any significant degree.

Done for the day, I called Janice and told her that an infected post-op joint had fallen into my lap. "I'll be home a little on the late side, dear."

"Did you get the fax from Hal?"

"Sure did," I replied gaily. "Can't wait to dig my spoon into that first big bowl of Jell-O."

"No cherry," Janice warned. "You can't have anything red."

"Yes, I saw that."

"Good. I bought your laxative packets."

"Oh, thank you, dear."

"The fridge or the stove?" Janice asked, meaning, would I be a little late, or very late.

"I think the fridge, dear."

Over lunch, I'd persuaded an increasingly agitated Pedro to accompany me to the Immigration office where he would play the role of Mariela's uncle. On the ride downtown he was several shades shy of his usual friendly self.

"Fucking *idiota! Estupido! Baboso!* Did I tell you to bring one back with you? Was that part of my instructions? Did you even read sections (10.2) thru (10.6)?"

The person in charge of "New Arrivals" at the Immigration office, a busty black woman who bore an unnerving resemblance to the late dictator Idi Amin, replied to our ingratiatingly polite hellos with a fierce glare. Pedro and I had agreed beforehand that, come what may, he would speak only English and be on his best, most charming behavior. "Don't worry," he told me in English, "I deal with government morons all my life. I wrap them around my little toe."

Pedro, smiling flirtatiously down at the seated woman, said, "I'm a uncle of a Cuban girl who come in this morning."

"And are you an American citizen?"

"One hundred percent," Pedro said. "Where you from, Jamaica?"

"The Bronx. You have proof of citizenship?"

Pedro, whether out of a sense of pride or just plain paranoia, always went about with his American passport on his person. With a flourish he whipped the pristine document (protected by a Zip-lock bag) from his inside jacket pocket and laid it gently atop the dented steel desk.

The woman (Mrs. Banks, according to the nameplate) regarded the immaculate Zip-locked document with distaste. "Could you please remove it from the plastic bag, sir?"

"Of course," Pedro said, forcing a smile. "You know, thas a genuine Zip-lock bag, not a regular plastic. I like to keep my citizenship protected. For, you know, respect."

"They're also good," Mrs. Banks commented dryly, "for keeping sweet potatoes."

"Sweet potatoes, huh?" Pedro removed the passport and handed it to Mrs. Banks, who proceeded to spend an entire minute comparing the photo with Pedro's actual face. Finally, she nodded her head and put the document down.

"And who might you be?" she asked, turning to me.

"I'm a character witness."

"For the girl?"

"No, for him."

"Why would he need a character witness?"

"We thought it might help expedite matters. I'm a surgeon, you see, at the hospital where Pedro…"

"Mister," Mrs. Banks cut in, "you could be Jesus Christ on the Cross, nails and all, and it wouldn't make a bit of difference. The young woman—I assume you're talking about the one who came in this morning, on her own recognition—Mariela Gomez Rodriguez?"

"Thas her," Pedro beamed, "my darling niece. She's a good girl. I swore to her mother, before she died, her daughter would have big opportunity…"

"Mr. Lerma…"

"She's smart, too, smart as a whippet. In school? Her grades? Fahgettaboutit!" (Pedro worshipped Al Pacino.) "This girl, I wanna tell you, could be president of the United…"

"Señor Lerma! Could you please shut up," Mrs. Banks said in butchered but comprehensible Spanish.

"I'm Mr. Lerma," Pedro muttered, not señor. I live in Brooklyn, not the Bahamas on some island somewhere. Like some people I could mention."

"Congratulations," Mrs. Banks said.

"Thank you. And let me tell you, Mrs. Banks, that niece of mine? She was first in the class at the Cuban Girls Academy. She even had to give a speech."

"Yes, Mr. Lerma, I agree; that girl is sharp as a tack. But even if she was dumber than a dill pickle, it wouldn't matter. And, by the way, Mr. Lerma, a whippet is a dog."

"So? Aren't dogs suppose to be intelligent?"

"Can they fill out forms?"

"You mean, racing forms? I don think so, but…"

"But I bet you can," Mrs. Banks said with sadistic glee, whipping out a whole bundle of official, numbered governmental forms. "Print clearly."

There were twelve two-sided pages to be completed, a daunting task for most people, but a cakewalk for me. I was almost as good at forms as I was at knees. A task which might well have taken Pedro several days to perform took me only half an hour.

Mrs. Banks greeted our premature return to her cubicle with a pleasant smile. "Need help with something?"

"No, we all done," Pedro said, plopping down the pages, which landed with an audible slap on the desk.

Mrs. Banks regarded the pile of forms with undiluted skepticism. Then, still smiling, she put on her serious glasses, picked up the papers and began to peruse. Ten minutes later she looked up in wonderment and said, "Very good."

"Thank you," Pedro said politely.

"In fact, this might be a record."

"Yeah, well, jus one of these things. Runs in the family. My grandfather…"

Abruptly, Mrs. Banks turned into a zombie. "It is now my duty," she said in a disorienting monotone, "to inform you that you have just signed an official document making you legally responsible for Miss Gomez for a period not to exceed six months, or until her permanent resident permit is approved."

Pedro shot me a brief, intensely hostile glare. "I did?"

"Among other things," Mrs. Banks droned on, "until she has received permanent resident status, you have agreed to be financially responsible for the young woman until she can properly acclimatize herself to her new surroundings and acquire gainful self-sustaining employment."

"Financially is no problem," Pedro said. "But I like to know what this acclimatize means, because it sounds like I have to get her weather-proofed or something."

"Adjusted, Mr. Lerma. It means adjusted."

"You sure?"

"By signing these documents, Mr. Lerma, you are also assuming responsibility for any crime Miss Gomez might commit, any debts she may incur, any…"

"Wait a minute!" Pedro said. "Thas not fair. Thas not right. Thas not American!"

"Probably not," Mrs. Banks agreed, "but if your niece is the paragon of rectaltude you say she is, you should have no cause for concern. Also, if she disappears or, for any reason, does not show up for a scheduled appointment with this office, you may be subject to fine and/or arrest."

"Arrest? Like, you mean, in jail?"

"Yes, Mr. Lerma, that is usually where they put arrested individuals."

SIX

In the elevator Pedro said, "I'm going to kill you."

"Pedro," I assured my friend, "trust me. Mariela is not going to engage in any criminal activity."

"How do you know? You been with her what, three weeks? Wasn't she already a criminal in Cuba?"

"No," I laughed, "hardly a criminal."

"Okay, then, a prostitute," Pedro insisted. "Even in Cuba, a prostitute is practically a criminal."

"She wasn't a prostitute."

"No? She never took money from you?"

The elevator door chose this opportune moment to open. We had arrived at our destination, Sub-Basement Level Three. Mrs. Banks, once she had finished frightening Pedro to her complete satisfaction, informed us that Mariela would be released forthwith into his personal "precognition", and to that end we were to proceed to the "above-mentioned below-ground location forthwith".

"She's a dry-footed Cuban with a responsible local relative," Mrs. Banks had explained. "That makes her acceptance automatic. We have no reason to hold her here, and even if we did, there's no room."

Pedro handed a stamped document to the uniformed official standing behind the counter. "I'm here to pick up my niece," he said without enthusiasm. When the man disappeared into another room, Pedro turned to me and whined the following:

"You had no right to put me in this position. Not for some chica. Now I'm going to jail. And for what? You could've had the Mendez sisters. Both of them! But no, not you. You decide to ruin my life, instead. What if she takes off? Did you ever think of that? No, you never thought of that. You just thought about yourself.

And you're supposed to be a doctor? Even a Jamaican…"

If only I'd had a camera I could have captured for all time Pedro's radical transformation (from bitter resentment to religious awe) when Mariela was led out into the room.

"Holy mother of God!" Pedro gasped. "Is that her?"

"Uncle Pedro," she said demurely, "am I really free?"

When Uncle Pedro, his mouth agape, failed to respond, Mariela turned to me. I nodded my head and she leapt into my arms. "I'm free! I'm free!" she cried.

The official was understandably confused. Shaking his head, he handed Pedro another handful of forms to sign and said, "Here's her temporary resident permit. She's got an appointment back here in thirty days. Make sure she makes it."

"Okay," Pedro said, signing the forms.

"That's it then," the official said. "She's all yours."

"I wish," Pedro muttered beneath his breath.

My old friend Leonard, the former bass player for Mark and the Mandalas, sat in a state of partially suspended animation behind the reception desk in the small dainty lobby of the Westchester Hotel. His eyes were red, half-closed and fixed apparently on a location somewhere over Maui. Smiling benignly, and dressed in the latest sixties chic, Leonard said, "What it is."

Naturally, I had no idea what he was talking about. "Leonard," I said, "my sentiments exactly."

"You two look happy."

"Couldn't be happier."

"Joy to the world," Leonard declared, pushing Mariela's key across the desk.

"You seem pretty happy yourself today, Leonard."

"What can I say," Leonard grinned, "life is good."

Upstairs, Mariela and I tore each other's clothes off and made love for two hours.

"Oh, baby!" she cried during her first orgasm. She was, I was pleased to see, making rapid progress with her English.

When we were done, we made plans to meet for lunch the next day. Then, after scrubbing myself raw in the shower, I got dressed and headed for Penn Station and the train ride home.

"You look tired," Janice said.

"Long day," I muttered, shoveling down the reheated vegetarian lasagna. I preferred my pasta with meat, but Janice had been attempting to wean me off that particular "artery-clogger" forever.

"You shouldn't push yourself so hard," Janice said with concern.

Oddly enough, Mariela, just a short while earlier, had told me the same thing. She'd been afraid I was going to have a heart attack and suggested that I let her get on top for a while. I'd told Mariela to be my guest. To Janice I said, "You're right, dear. But what can I do? You can't just tell someone with an infected joint to come back next week."

"I know," Janice said. "I'll feel a lot better when you have those test results."

"Me, too. I'm really looking forward to that colonoscopy."

"Was it your patient?"

"No, Webber's," I lied smoothly. "He's out of town."

"Is something wrong with your lip?" Janice asked. "It looks bruised."

"My lip? Oh, right. A self-inflicted wound, dear. Worst pothole I've ever seen. You'd think these taxi drivers would look where they're going."

Yes, the lies were leaping from my lips now with depressing ease, like fleas off a soapy dog.

"I know," Janice said, "it's criminal how they drive. By the way, don't forget, tomorrow is Day One of your diet. I've stocked up on gelatin and clear liquids."

"Thank you, dear."

"Tomorrow isn't too bad. You can have all the boiled chicken you want."

"Wonderful."

"But no fiber."

"Wouldn't think of it."

And so began my new life of duplicity and lust—with a fiber-free diet.

SEVEN

Brian Westin, in all his six foot-four inch glory, was standing outside my office signing autographs for a gaggle of employees when I arrived at the hospital the following morning. Among his hyperventilating admirers was Dulce Mendez. The god of Hubris favored the sexy nurse with an appreciative look, causing Dulce to melt before our eyes into a puddle of molten adulation. *That chica's in heat!* I marveled. *Too bad I'm already taken.*

Brian wrapped a proprietary arm around my shoulder and led me into my office. "Have a seat," he said graciously.

"Brian," I yawned, "what a surprise. Are you here to make an appointment?"

Irony wasn't merely lost on Brian Westin, it was buried irretrievably beneath geologic strata of vanity and self-absorption.

"Did you see me destroy St. Louis on Sunday?"

"I don't think so. Is the arch still standing?"

"I went twenty-five for twenty-seven."

"Is that good?"

"Hah! You're putting me on."

"Not now."

"It happens to be a team record. And speaking of records," the handsome egomaniac continued, "no one's beat us yet, and an undefeated season is a definite possibility. Only Miami's done it, and back then they only played fourteen games."

"What about the Third Reich? Didn't they go fifteen-and-0 one year?"

"The third what?"

"How's the knee?"

"It seems all right."

"Then what are you doing in my office, Brian? At eight o'clock in the morning. Without an appointment. I've got four procedures to perform today."

Brian was impressed. "Is that a hospital record?"

"No, it's not a record, Brian."

"A personal best?"

"Afraid not."

"What's the most operations you've done in one week?"

Brian, of course, could have cared less about how many operations I performed. He was, in his own limited way, attempting to make conversation.

"In one week, Brian? I guess that would be the time I went twenty-six for twenty-seven."

Brian was confused. "Twenty-six for twenty-seven?"

"That's right. And I would have been perfect, but on my last cut of the week, a nurse dropped the scalpel."

Brian digested this for a full five seconds before saying, "Ha! That's a good one, Doc." Then he began to remove his pants.

"Brian, what are you doing?"

"I've got this red spot, Doc, just below the knee cap. I want you to check it out."

"Does it hurt?"

"Not yet."

"Is it hot to the touch?"

"No, but it doesn't look natural."

Brian climbed bare-legged onto my desk in order to afford me a better view of the imperiled joint.

"What do you think?" he asked anxiously.

"I think it's a freckle, Brian."

"Is that normal? I mean, on the knee?"

In fact I only had two procedures to perform that day, one in the morning and one in the afternoon, leaving me a solid two hour block of free time, which I intended to employ efficiently. Like a battlefield commander I'd laid out my plan: meet Mariela at the Westchester; have an hour of sex; go shopping; and then, if time permitted, grab a quick lunch.

The Westchester guests, many of them month-to-month residents, were an eclectic bunch. On my way up to Mariela's room I passed two transvestites clutching to their padded bosoms a pair of teacup poodles, a man dressed entirely in what appeared to be black vinyl, and an overly thin pale young woman sitting on the stairs writing poetry. She was wearing corduroy trousers and as I passed her she looked up at me and said, "Pain."

"Are you in pain?" I asked.

"The Earth groans," she replied.

Mariela opened the door dressed in a G-string bikini bottom and stiletto heels.

"Today, you are my sex-slave!" she announced theatrically.

"I am?"

I soon learned that she had gotten her hands on some questionable reading material, the Spanish language version of a "woman's magazine" filled with tips on how to keep one's husband or boyfriend eternally tumescent.

Mariela slithered up to me, grimacing lustfully. I began to laugh.

"What's so funny?" she demanded.

"I thought you were going to buy clothes which make you look older."

"I don't look older in my new clothes?" she asked, doing a pirouette so I could get a good gander at her thonged-behind.

"Not exactly."

An hour later we prepared to go shopping in Greenwich Village. "This time," I told her, "you're going to buy clothes you wear on the outside, where other people can see them."

"Okay, Carlitos, whatever you say."

The first shop (Nights in White Satin), was manned by a slim severely dressed lesbian. "May I help you?" she asked in a frosty voice.

"Yes," I said, "we're looking for three or four entire outfits. And we're after what I suppose you would call a 'mature' look."

"For her?"

"Well, they aren't for me."

"All right," the woman said, "define mature."

"We were hoping—that is, we were sort of shooting, more or less, for the age of consent. Around eighteen?"

"Shame on you," the woman said.

"No, no, you don't understand. She's actually nineteen. We have the paperwork to prove it. But she looks so much younger than her actual..."

"You pig! Leave right now or I'm calling the police. Miss," she added, eying Mariela tenderly, "is this man mistreating you?"

Back on the sidewalk, Mariela demanded to know why we'd left the store so abruptly. "That woman didn't seem very nice. What did she say to you?"

"She said that she...didn't have anything in your size. She suggested some shops up the street that cater to, ah, younger people."

We came upon another shop half a block later. This one was called Pandora's Box.

"Let's go in here," Mariela said.

"I don't know, baby. It looks like a lingerie store, and you already have plenty of that."

"Maybe they have other stuff, too," she said hopefully.

"I doubt it."

"What does that mean?" she asked, pointing to the sign.

"It means," I explained carefully, "The Vagina of a Character out of Greek Mythology."

"They named the store after an imaginary vagina?"

"Well, yes, more or less."

"Okay. Let's go someplace else."

On the next street we finally encountered what appeared to be a suitable shop (Glad All Over), and into its colorful depths I steered my little lover. "Maybe they'll carry my size in this one," she said.

We were approached by a young woman, unmistakably Latin and wearing a broad smile.

"Hello, I'm Carmen," she announced.

"Hello," I said. "We're looking for some outfits for my, ah…friend."

"What's your favorite color?" she asked Mariela.

"She doesn't speak English," I told Carmen, "so, I suppose I'll have to act as translator."

Carmen smiled and repeated her question in Spanish. Mariela's eyes lit up like a pair of sun lamps. As the two young women began to chatter happily back and forth, I felt a substantial layer of guilt peel off and fall from what was left of my conscience.

No matter how much "better" life would be for Mariela here in the United States, there remained the fact that I had removed her from her family, her friends, her home and everything which had made up her personal universe. I knew this separation had to be difficult for her, and that I alone could not make up for everything she'd lost. The two young women seemed to take a genuine liking to each other. Could Mariela have found a friend? I prayed that it was so.

"The problem," Mariela was telling Carmen, "is that I look too young."

"That's not usually a problem, chica," Carmen said sagely.

"Yeah," Mariela said, "I know. It doesn't bother me. But it bothers him. He feels like everyone thinks he's some kind of pervert. If we were the same color, maybe we could pass for father and daughter. But I'm not getting any lighter, and he's not getting any darker."

"He looks like he'd be a nice *papi* to have," Carmen said, assaying me with a practiced eye.

"He is, and he's mine," Mariela said.

"Hey, I got a boyfriend," Carmen said. "Don't worry about me. What's he do?"

"I'm a doctor," I told her in Spanish, before she could embarrass herself further.

"Whoa! Jackpot!" Carmen said. Apparently, she did not embarrass easily.

Mariela suggested that I take a walk while she and Carmen sorted out the wardrobe situation. That was fine with me. I decided to go look for someplace to sit down and have a coffee. Before I left, I said to Mariela, "Remember, older on the outside."

"His Spanish is perfect!" I heard Carmen saying as I walked out the door. "How is he in bed? Does he hate his wife?"

Around the corner I found a nice Bohemian-looking bistro and went inside. As I sat down, I was suddenly seized with my first anxiety attack of the day. Shopping with Mariela in Greenwich Village? What was I thinking? This was just the type of trendy street one of Janice's friends, or even Janice herself, might choose to go grazing on. The fear of exposure gripped my heart. I began to tremble.

"It's kind of early, mister, but you look like you could use a drink." It was the waiter, standing pad in hand at my table.

"A drink? No, I've got a ruptured—something to do later."

"Too bad," the waiter said, "we're having a special on Cuban mojitos today. Ever have one? Hemingway's favorite drink."

My trembling became more violent as I realized how close to the edge of the abyss I was teetering. "Ernest Hemingway?" I mumbled. "The writer?"

"Yeah, the guy who shot himself," the waiter said pleasantly.

Back at Glad All Over (God only knows where they come up with those names!) the two young women had managed to accumulate a small mountain of clothing: blouses, skirts, sweaters, jackets, dresses and even a pair of calf-length boots. Mariela was frothy with excitement. "We're doing great," she said. "I'll have enough clothes to last me till I'm thirty!"

"That's wonderful, baby. Listen, I've got to get back to work. We'll have to skip lunch. Do you have a sub-total?" I asked Carmen.

"Sure do. As of now, we're up to twelve hundred and sixty-five dollars."

"Terrific," I said, handing her my credit card, "let's pay for this now, and if she picks out anything else, we can collect it tomorrow."

Carmen favored me with a brilliant smile. "You don't have a twin brother somewhere, do you?"

On the way to the hospital I went through an entire packet of breath mints hoping it would disguise the smell of the two mojitos the waiter had forced upon me down in the Village. Having consumed nothing but Mariela since breakfast, the mojitos had hit me more strongly than I'd expected. Could I still operate? Of course I could! Was I not the best knee man on the East Coast, sober or not?

As luck would have it the attending nurse for my afternoon surgery was Dulce Mendez. For a few minutes we found ourselves alone in the scrub-room. I smiled at her. She smiled back. And the next thing I knew we were passionately making out by the sterile sink. When I came to my senses, I pushed her away and said, "No, we can't."

"You're right," she agreed, "someone might come in. I'm free tonight."

"Uh-huh," I said, wondering if I should cancel the surgery. I was about to operate on the star point guard for the New Jersey Nets. Even allowing for depreciation, his knee had to be worth upwards of forty million dollars, and repairing a ruptured tendon is no walk in the park. I could fake taking ill, I thought. A sudden case of food poisoning.

"Go find the anesthesiologist," I told Dulce, and she wriggled reluctantly from the room. The moment I was alone, I held my hands out to see if they were steady. They were. I closed my eyes and mentally went through the entire operation step by step. I'm fine, I told myself.

Fine. Just what the drunk driver tells himself as he's about to take out the utility pole.

EIGHT

I took off early from work so that I could spend the late afternoon and evening poisoning myself in the comfort of my own home. Janice was out, of course, fighting the good fight against Global Sunburn, or Childhood Pudginess, or Homogenized Trash Disposal. But Candace was home, sitting across the kitchen table picking out Robert Johnson tunes on her acoustic guitar and providing me with her version of moral support.

"You've got one quart down, Dad," she said, "only three more to go."

The first quart of the slimy foul-tasting colon cleanser had already made me nauseous. I couldn't even imagine drinking three more.

"Yes."

"So," Candace asked, bending the G string of her guitar a full one and a half steps, "when do you start shitting your brains out?"

"Pretty soon, I would imagine. How's school?"

"Boring. You know, Dad, you seem different since you got back from your fishing trip."

"Different? How so?"

"I don't know. More laid back, I guess. And younger. You've got this sexy swagger I never noticed before."

"Sexy swagger? Don't make me laugh."

"I'm serious. You're like one of those alpha male baboons on Animal Planet."

"It's all in your mind."

"I don't think so. You know my friend Karen?"

"That little brunette? Who goes around half-naked?"

"Yeah. She told me she thought you were a real hunk.

You better watch out, Dad—before you know it, some hot young thing is going to be jumping all over you. What would mom say?"

Suddenly I felt my bowels loosen. Was it fear? Or was the poison finally taking effect?

"Very funny," I said, running for the bathroom.

When I returned to the kitchen, Candace was singing in a soft voice the lyrics to a song she'd been playing on the guitar. She didn't like the sound of her own voice, but I found it soothing. "A woman is like a dresser," she sang, "some man always running through its drawers…"

"Don't let your mother hear you sing that," I said, eyeing the second quart of Liquid Plumber with trepidation.

"How'd it go, Dad?"

"What?"

"In the bathroom?"

"Oh. Pretty much the way you'd expect."

My anus had erupted like the nozzle of a fire hose, but I was not about to share this datum with my daughter.

Candace began picking away at another song, *Love In Vain*. "You're looking a little gray around the gills," she remarked.

"This stuff is making me ill. I don't know what I'm going to do next, shit or puke."

Candace stopping playing. "That's what I'm talking about! You never said stuff like that before. You've changed, Dad! Was it an epiphany? Did you see God on your fishing trip?"

"I never used to talk that way in front of you," I corrected her. "But now that you're older…well…you're older. So I can talk to you like an adult."

"Shit and puke? That's adult talk, Dad?"

"Candace," I said, picking up the second quart, "please, do not patronize me."

"Hey, don't get me wrong, Dad. I like the new you. Even if it's only one of those mid-life crises they talk about, like a, you know, phase you have to go through?"

Shuddering inwardly, I thought, not for the first time, that my hyper-intelligent daughter with her frightening spot-on insights, more resembled some highly evolved visitor from outer space than my own flesh and blood. I took several large gulps of laxative in rapid succession, praying it would make it all the way down before I realized what had hit me.

"Good one, Dad!"

"I'm nauseous," I whimpered, "really nauseous."

"Hold on, Dad, I'll be right back." Candace scampered from the room.

Somehow I managed not to throw up, but a moment later I was forced, once again, to retreat to the bathroom. When I came out, Candace was sitting at the kitchen table smoking a thin lumpy cigarette. "Here, take a hit," she said. "This is the best anti-nausea agent known to mankind. And don't worry, one joint won't give you lung cancer."

I'd last smoked marijuana in my sophomore year of college. I hadn't liked it then, and I liked even less seeing my seventeen-year-old daughter openly smoking it in front of me. In my own kitchen!

On the other hand, I knew that Candace was right, that cannabis was an excellent anti-nausual, and I was desperate. In my mind, anything was better than throwing up the laxative. Hal had been quite clear: get all four quarts down in the allotted time, or put yourself through the entire torture all over again tomorrow.

"All right," I said, "but if you tell your mother, I'll kill you."

Shaking her head, she handed me the lumpy cigarette. Then she began to play something baroque and soothing on the guitar. "This will help your stomach, too. I transposed it myself."

"Vivaldi?"

"Bach."

Smoking the marijuana, which entailed a good deal of coughing and choking, did indeed eliminate the nausea. In fact, it actually made me hungry. But I was banned from eating until after my procedure, so I took a few more gulps of laxative instead. Surprisingly, it didn't taste half-bad. I swallowed some more.

Candace, meanwhile, was observing me carefully as she continued to play her transposed Bach. "How we doing, Dad?"

"Terrific," I said, polishing off the second quart.

"I told you. From now on, it's all downhill."

"Be right back."

Sitting on the toilet voiding my colon, I became introspective. Why was it, I wondered, that the two people whose company I enjoyed the most were teenage girls? Was I sick? Should I seek professional help? Of course, neither was what you could call an actual teenager. They were young women. Very young women, certainly, but each in their own way, far beyond their years. Candace was a match, intellectually and emotionally, for any mature woman I'd ever known. And Mariela…well, Mariela was another story.

I wondered if Candace was having sex yet. Which, in turn, led me to wonder if I was being a responsible parent. Smoking marijuana with one's daughter certainly didn't seem responsible. And what about keeping a nineteen-year-old Cuban mistress in a residential hotel occupied by deviates and drug addicts? And performing delicate procedures (successfully, thank God!) while half in the bag? Or terrifying my wife with make-believe tales of tarry stools? Was this 'Pillar of the Community' type behavior?

But, I concluded on an optimistic note, at least I'm not throwing up. I flushed the toilet and floated back to the kitchen.

"How you feeling now, Dad?"

"Groovy."

Candace laughed. "They don't say that anymore."

"No? What do they say?"

"Excellent."

"Excellent? Are you sure?"

Suddenly the sound of Janice's Volvo pulling into the driveway intruded upon my fuzzy consciousness. "Shit," I said, "your mother's home! Put that stuff away. And, and, and what do we do about the smell?"

"Isn't there some *Glade* in the bathroom?" Candace asked calmly.

"Right, right," I said frantically. "The Glade! In the bathroom!"

"Well," Candace said when I remained motionless in my chair, "aren't you going to go get it?"

"Get what?"

Candace rolled her eyes at the ceiling. "The Glade, Dad."

"Right!" I said, shooting from my seat, "the Glade!"

As Janice walked in the door I was chug-a-lugging Quart Number Three. "Hi, honey," I said, putting down the extra-tall glass of diluted snot, "I'm almost done with the laxative."

"I've been providing him with moral support," Candace said.

"What's that smell?" Janice demanded, wrinkling her nose.

"That's Glade, Mom," Candace said.

"Glade? Yes, that's what it is," Janice said, "but who sprayed it all over the kitchen?"

"Dad did."

Janice turned to me. "Why on earth, dear, have you been spraying bathroom deodorant in the kitchen? It smells like...like a bathroom in here."

Sometimes my wife was somewhat lacking in imagination.

"Well, dear, you know, what with all the, ah, evacuating I've been doing, the bathroom couldn't contain one hundred per cent of the malodorous, ah, emanations, so I thought it would be, ah..."

"He must have emptied half the can in here, Mom," Candace complained. "Maybe we should open a window before we all get green lung disease."

"Yes, maybe we should," Janice said distractedly. "How are you feeling, dear?"

"Not bad, not bad. I became a little nauseated there for a minute, but now...oops. Gotta go."

"Here," Candace said, tossing me the aerosol can, "you better take this with you."

Once I was safely ensconced inside the half-bath I found myself reluctant to leave. Would Janice be able to tell that I was high on marijuana? Hopefully, no. She would not approve. Unlike Mariela, I thought, who would not care very much one way or the other. I began to visualize Mariela slowing removing her lingerie while I lay in bed watching.

At once, my hormone-hood began to wedge itself uncomfortably against the inner lip of the toilet bowl. With difficulty, I managed to extract it from its cold porcelain prison whereupon it began to nod its head up and down with gratitude. For some time, I sat watching it, fascinated, marveling at how the long tubular appendage seemed to possess a life of its own. I had, I realized, never taken a really good look at my penis before. It was absurd-looking, to be sure, but in an otherworldly way, as if it existed in its own mystical dimension, totem-like, imbued with primordial significance…

"Karl," Janice called out from the other side of the door, "are you all right?"

"All right?"

"You've been in there an awfully long time."

"I know, dear, but it just keeps going and going, like a faucet I can't turn off."

Janice was clearly concerned. "Are you sure you're all right? Can't you come out for just a minute."

Leaving the half-bathroom at that moment was, of course, out of the question. My supernatural Category Five erection showed no signs of abating. Even beneath my various layers of clothing it would have been visible to a blind man.

"I'm fine, dear. I'll be out as soon as I can."

"All right, dear. I'll be in the kitchen."

"Down, boy! Down! Down!" I hissed at the stubborn appendage.

"What? What did you say, darling?" Janice asked through the door.

I flushed the toilet, said, "Yes, dear, it's going down now," and hoped for the best.

NINE

It was time to make my balloon payment to the smugglers. I called the number provided by Mr. Garcia and was instructed by a man who spoke limited English to bring the cash to an Albanian delicatessen in Brooklyn at ten pm the following evening. Mr. Bazhunaishvili (a rough approximation) told me to look for a fat man wearing a green suit.

Mr. Bazhunaishvili, the only human being in the establishment, was indeed perfectly round and enclosed in a lime-green suit, like a giant green tomato. He sat beaming in the corner, waving frantically in my direction.

"So nice," he said, violently shaking my hand, "make business respectable peoples. Want glass Dhallë? I treat."

"Glass what?"

"Albanian buttermilk. Nectar from gods!"

"Ah, no thanks. Don't you want to count the money?"

"So hard watch waistline," he replied, patting his enormous belly, "when cousin own best Albanian food place in Brooklyn."

"There's more than one?"

"One what? Let me buy for you big plate Harapash."

"Harapash?"

"Intestinal lamb. Very much good. Melt all over mouth!"

Prior to the big payoff I'd been forced to undergo another ordeal, the final act of the "tarry stool" fiasco.

Even though the whole affair had been nothing but a smokescreen, even though my flawless turds appeared to have been sculpted by the Auguste Rodin of bowel movements, when it came time to obtain the results of the exam, I was suddenly a jumble of nerves. I would not, I thought anxiously, be the first man to die under such infinitely ironic circumstances. The lack of symptoms meant nothing. Didn't they call colon cancer the silent killer? Or was that hypertension? Fatal conditions, which generally speaking do not involve the knee, have never been my forte.

In the end, I passed my colon inspection polyplessly, which is to say, with flying shades of healthy pink.

"You have the colon of a teenager," Hal told me in his office.

"You should see my prostate."

"Ha, ha. You know, Karl," Hal said, turning serious, "middle-aged men like ourselves, in the latter years of a long-term marriage? We have a tendency to, shall we say, 'under-use' a certain organ?"

"You mean, we stop having sex with our wives."

"Exactly. It's only natural. My point is, Karl, you might consider masturbating every now and then, say, once a week? Just to keep the old wheel greased, as it were."

"All right, Hal," I said with a straight face, "I'll pick up a copy of Playboy and see if I can't go a few rounds in the shower now and then."

"Karl," Hal said, "at our age Playboy can be, how shall I put it, a little on the tame side? Stimulation-wise? If I were you I'd go with Teenage Slut Monthly. They carry it in the better sex shops."

I began to laugh. Hal cut me off.

"This is no joke, Karl. The prostate is like the engine of your car. If it remains idle for too long, it tends to malfunction. Karl, would you please stop laughing and listen to me?"

Once that charade was over and I'd met my financial obligations to the Miami mafia, I entered upon a period of blurred beaver-like activity. First, I enrolled Mariela in an intensive ESL class which met for one hour five nights a week at Manhattan Community College. Then I aided and abetted her "mature makeover", performed twenty-seven procedures, had five consignments and, last but not least, purchased one-hundred dollars worth of high-grade marijuana from Leonard, my main man at the Westchester Hotel.

"Tell me, Leonard," I said, stuffing the small zip-lock bag into my pocket, "back in your salad days with the band, were you Mark, or were you one of the Mandalas?"

"I was a only a Mandala, man. Mark Schlablotsky—the singer? He was the front-man. You want to rent a bong, Dr. Sanderson?"

"You rent bongs?"

"Yeah, only ten dollars a month. It's, like, you know, a public service. And they're one hundred per cent sterilized between bongees."

"Sure, Leonard, rent me a bong."

"My man!"

Leonard and I exchanged an enormously complicated hand-shake which we'd been building up to for weeks.

"What is that?" Mariela asked, when she saw the bright purple tube in my hand.

"It's, ah, you know…" It occurred to me that Mariela might not approve of me smoking marijuana. "…one of those sex toys."

"It looks kind of big," she said, eying the colorful cylinder with a frown. Then she smiled, did a small pirouette and said, "How do I look?"

This was it, I realized, the culmination of the entire "Mature Makeover" process. With her new best friend Carmen leading the way and yours truly footing the bill, Mariela had been all over Manhattan: to another dozen clothing stores, a hair salon and two Licensed Beauticians, both of them gay and criminally overpriced.

Knowing how important this was to her, I took my time, studying Mariela's new look with the kind of intense scrutiny I normally reserved for an inconclusive MRI. On her small shapely feet she now wore a pair of three-inch heels, thereby mitigating somewhat her childlike stature.

Her new pants were composed of an extraordinarily flexible bright yellow material, which flared nicely below the knee, but which hugged her buttocks so tightly it made me jealous. Her long-sleeved blouse was conservatively cut, bright red (to go with the yellow pants?) and definitely "mature". Her hair had been straightened, and then braided into long cornrows. And she was wearing makeup.

"So?"

"You definitely look older," I said cautiously.

She looked, in fact, like a cross between a very young receptionist and a very young hooker, on their day off.

"Carmen says I could easily be taken for twenty, or even twenty-one."

"I'll take you any way I can get you," I said, taking her in my arms.

"But I do look older, don't I?"

"Sure, baby, you look almost old enough to…ah…join the army."

"I liked these pants so much I got five pairs of them in different colors."

"Thank God."

"What?"

"Highway-yellow isn't exactly my favorite color. You and Carmen pick out a few earth tones by any chance?"

Once we were in bed I had no choice but to reveal to Mariela the true function of the bong.

"Marijuana?" she said in dismay. "Doesn't that make you crazy?"

"We're about to find out," I said, flicking the lighter, which Leonard had provided at no additional cost.

"Well, I'm not having any."

Once I'd finished coughing and choking, I turned to Mariela for a kiss. "I hope you're not turning into a dope fiend," she said.

"No, baby, just a sex fiend."

When we were done, Mariela looked at me wonderingly, shook her newly corn-rowed head, and said, "Wow! If your tongue was a paintbrush, you'd be the new Antonio Contreras!"

Antonio Contreras was the "Rembrandt of the Cuban Revolution". Mostly, he painted forty-foot-tall portraits of Che Guevera's head. The giant murals, which covered half the windowless walls in downtown Havana, were eye-grabbing to be sure, but Antonio's palette was rather limited, consisting almost entirely of cherry-red, burnt-toast black and olive green.

Food. Why was everything suddenly reminding me of food? For a very good reason, I realized. I was hungry, more hungry than I had ever been in my life!

"Baby, you wouldn't happen to have a Hershey's Bar lying around here someplace, would you?"

"A Herpes Bar?"

"Ah…maybe we should put you in a different English class."

TEN

Ninety minutes later I found myself sitting in our brontosaurian breakfast nook, drooling with anticipation as I waited for my dinner to be re-convected back up to an acceptable temperature.

"Your eyes are red," Janice said. "I hope you're not coming down with a cold."

"Me, too. Janice, don't you think it's been in there long enough? I'm wasting away here."

Janice frowned. "Wasting away?" The little bell went off. Janice removed the steaming food and set it on the table. "Now that we know your colon is all right, maybe we should have your brain examined. I swear, you've been..."

Janice was stopped in mid-grumble by my unprecedented eye-popping display of speed-eating. One minute the plate was full, and the next it was wiped clean. I'd even polished off four slices of seventeen-grain whole wheat bread, something which I ordinarily shunned, since it reminded me of baked dirt.

"De-licious! Any more where that came from?"

"Seriously, dear, I think you've been working far too hard. Maybe you should cut back a bit. I know the kind of demands they put on you, but at a certain point you have to draw the line. You deserve to have a life, too, don't you? Apart from your work?"

"If anyone deserves to have a life, Janice, I'm fairly certain that it's me. Now, I know you've got more of that mercury-free parmesan and pistachio-crusted sea-bass hiding around here somewhere. Just one more taste, Janice, and I'll die a happy man."

"You're still hungry?"

"I'm making up for the deprivations of that miserable colonoscopy diet. My very cells, darling, are crying out for sustenance."

Janice peered down at me for a long moment. "There's no more fish, but if you're still hungry, there's some apple pie in the fridge."

"Apple pie? Perfecto! What about the ice-cream? We got vanilla?"

"I have work to do," Janice said. "If the pie doesn't fill you up, you can always order out for pizza."

Pizza? Not a bad idea. Then I realized that my wife was being sarcastic, which was odd. Janice was always so literal. Not for one moment did I, in my altered state, consider the possibility that her unusual behavior might be a reaction to my own.

Once I'd maxed-out on the pie, I went to look for Candace. She was in her room, picking away as usual on her guitar. "Hey, kiddo, what's up?"

"Listen to this," Candace said, "I've been working on it all week."

I made myself comfortable in a chair while Candace, sitting perfectly erect on the edge of her bed, played a strange haunting little thing in some kind of really odd time.

"Excellent," I said when she was done. "Totally excellent."

Candace gave me a searching look. "Dad, are you stoned?"

"Young lady…keep your voice down."

We began to giggle like a pair of lunatics.

"I can't believe it, Dad. You're actually turning into…"

"A pothead?"

"No, a human being."

"A human being? What was I before, Candace, a fucking civet?"

"Well, Dad, you've always been kind of, you know, detached. And prudish. What they call, anal-retentive. Uptight. Stiff."

"All right, all right, I get the idea."

"A classic workaholic," my seventeen-year-old daughter concluded her critique. "Don't get me wrong. I've always loved you, Dad, for all your good qualities. But the truth is, you've always been kind of wimpy and boring. I mean, when did you ever have any fun? But now... I wonder if mom suspects."

"Suspects what?" I nearly screamed.

"That you're stoned," Candace said. "What else?"

"Well, she did mention something about my eyes being red."

"She always notices the eyes. What you need, Dad, is a plausible excuse. I blame mine on my bogus allergies."

"Bogus? Your bogus allergies?"

Candace began to strum some chords. "How about a Beatles tune, Dad? Something nostalgic from your late adolescence."

"What about all those visits to Dr. Finkel?"

"Oh, Dr. Finkel." Candace rolled her eyes. "A total idiot. Or a quack. He still gives me lollipops. Can you believe it?"

"You have no allergies?"

Candace began to sing:

"Something in the way she moves

Attracts me like no other lover.

Something in the way she..."

"But the pills—you've been taking them for two years. I've seen you taking them."

Candace regarded me with a sad indulgent smile, like a mother who must finally inform her child that there is in fact no Santa Claus. "Placebos, Dad. I throw the real ones away."

"You're joking."

"Nope."

She wasn't joking. Apparently, my daughter, since the age of fifteen, had been: a) smoking marijuana; and, b) playing her parents—Mr. and Mrs. Howdy Doody—like a pair of mentally impoverished puppets. Under different circumstances I would have been furious. Under the influence of the cannabis, I was more startled than angry. Reality, it turned out, wasn't real, after all.

"You mean, you've never had an allergy?"

"No, Dad. Isn't it great? I'm allergy-free!"

ELEVEN

Thanksgiving rolled around, time for yet another tribal get-together. Didn't we just do this? I thought bitterly. To make matters worse (much worse), it was Charles' turn to play host at his immense co-op apartment overlooking the East River. This Bourbon behemoth, with its eighteen rooms, parquet floors, Himalayan ceilings and over-priced works of post-modern art, was a fitting monument to my brother-in-law's limitless ego. It was also, just behind Kim Il-Sung's basement, the next to last place I would have chosen to spend my holiday.

At my home, despite what could be regarded as evidence to the contrary, Charles was generally on his best behavior—that is, he made some small effort to put a damper on his more toxic tendencies. But presiding over his own fiefdom, Charles gave new meaning to the term, insufferable prick. I wished no man ill, but were Charles' death to come prematurely, the only tears I believe I might shed would be those of relief.

Thanksgiving Day dawned cold, gray and dreary, a perfect match for my mood. We rarely drove into Manhattan. The twin terrors of traffic and parking were more than our fragile family could normally bear. But today, being a holiday, traffic would be thin; and with Charles owning two extra parking slots in the basement of his building, berthing the Volvo would not present a problem, either.

I wondered, as I steered my family down the Long Island Expressway at an unbelievable sixty-five miles per hour, if Brenda, home from college, could really have grown even more aloof in only three months. Our nineteen (going on fifty-five) year-old daughter had voiced grave doubts about attending the dinner, pointing out correctly that Thanksgiving is not Christmas; and, incorrectly, that "no one" goes home for Thanksgiving.

"You do," Janice said, ending the discussion.

Charles' building was one of those grand old limestone affairs, built to house the obscenely wealthy. Polished bronze, plaster cherubs, exquisite oriental carpets, Tiffany lamps and immaculately overdressed doormen littered the imposing lobby. The co-op fees were, as one might imagine, astronomical. A single monthly payment could (but never would) feed an extended family of Afghani offal collectors for their entire lives.

Charles was on the fourth floor. His door, one of only two, was unmarred by numbers or any other identifying scars. It was located by seeking the "door on the left". The door on the right belonged to the CEO of Time/Warner.

Dinner began with Charles' version of Grace; a very personal version in which he enumerated at length all of his reasons for feeling grateful, but somehow managed to omit everyone else's. Perhaps, we didn't have any. After all, who could possibly feel grateful for not being Charles?

"I am so grateful," Charles said, "to be surrounded on this special day by my entire extended family…" And so on.

As muted classical music eased itself into the outsized formal dining room with its priceless view of the river, the staff of three went to work serving the first of what would be a veritable chorus line of dishes. It must have cost a fortune to get three people to work on Thanksgiving, but, as Charles would later inform us several times, no expense had been spared to make this our best Thanksgiving dinner ever.

The food, though not on a par with Janice's, was more expensive, more abundant and more elaborately prepared. The turtle soup, for example, which in its fabrication had apparently involved the slaughter of half the world's endangered species, was a little on the salty side. And the lobster stuffing, though original, did not seem to blend harmoniously with the thirty pound bird into whose cavity it had been crammed. But this meal was not really about the food. It was not about giving thanks, either. It was all about one man (my admittedly neurotic obsession), brother Charles.

"So tell us, Brenda," he said, utilizing the royal We, "how are you finding college life? Any particular courses grabbing your attention?"

Brenda, sitting ramrod straight, the proverbial Ice Queen, replied respectfully, "Yes, Uncle Charles, I am particularly enjoying my Zoology and Comparative Anatomy course."

"You are?" I asked in surprise. I had been forced to suffer through the same course myself. It was a prerequisite for all pre-med students. And it was not a course one generally "enjoyed".

"Yes, I find it fascinating, particularly the anatomy. So far we've dissected a turtle, a snake and a pigeon. I can't wait until we get to the mammals."

"Yes, I loved the mammals, too," I said. "I think my favorite part was cutting the laboratory cat's head in half with a hacksaw."

"Karl!" Janice gasped.

"Yes, Karl," her brother sneered down his mile-long nose, "we are at dinner."

Everyone regarded me oddly, except for Candace, and Steven, the strange stuttering son. Candace was unusually subdued today—on her period I'd been told. Nonetheless, she nodded her head and favored me with an approving smile. Steven, forever fearful of his overbearing father's short-fused fury, bit down hard on his wrist to suppress his laughter.

When he deemed that the interval of painful silence had gone on long enough, Charles, in a fit of noblesse oblige, offered to personally fix everyone a drink. This gracious offer allowed him to kill two birds with one swivel stick: show off his legendary bartending skills, while humiliating yours truly in the process.

"First the adults," Charles announced grandly. "I am now ready to take your orders."

Janice and Ann opted for very dry martinis (Charles' preferred drink). "And you, Brenda," Charles continued. "I believe you now qualify for adulthood. What would you like?"

"I'll have a mineral water, please."

"And you, Karl," he said, inserting me ambiguously after the last adult, but before the first minor, "can I interest you in something for a change? After all, you are an adult, too."

Aside from his myriad other claims to fame, Charles maintained that there was not a single civilized drink which he could not prepare from the comfort of his own supernaturally equipped bar. He'd been tried, he'd been tested, but never stumped. Remembering this now provided me with the inspiration to say the following:

"You know what, Charles, I think I will have something, for a change. Make me a mojito."

"A mojito?"

"Yes, Charles, you know how it's made, I'm sure."

"Of course."

"A mojito, dear?" Janice, finally overcoming her shock, said. "Where in the world did you get that from?"

"From the Hemingway bio in the Sunday Times," I lied smoothly. "The author claimed that the mojito was Hemingway's favorite drink. Isn't that right, Charles?"

"Of course. It's a Cuban concoction," he said without a trace of smugness, and I knew I had him. That Charles was capable of fabricating a mojito, I did not doubt. The fresh mint leaves, however, were unlikely to be lying around his house. And without the mint, there was no mojito.

"Karl, tell me," Charles asked, "what made you decide to have a drink all of a sudden? It's quite out of character."

Charles, I realized, wanted to talk me out of the mojito. In his mind anything was preferable to admitting defeat. Allegedly, he'd smashed dozens of tennis rackets over the years in the course of losing matches.

Then something odd occurred. Suddenly, I really did want a drink. I wanted a drink immediately. It would be the perfect antidote to Charles. Quickly, before he could expand upon his "out of character" theme, I sent a searing forehand down his throat, ending the match.

"What, no fresh mint leaves in the fridge, Charles?" I asked with good humor.

Charles turned to glare at poor mousey Ann. "You did remember to buy the mint leaves? Remember, I told you last week that we'd run out."

Candace and I exchanged knowing glances.

"That's all right, Charles," I said, alarmed at the look of animal fear glazing Ann's eyes, "just give me a shot of some decent rum and I'll be fine."

"You want a shot of rum?" Janice asked, beside herself with astonishment.

"Just to be sociable, dear."

Still scowling at his wife, Charles said, "I happen to have some superb rum," and strode from the table.

"You'd better mix it with something to water it down," Janice said with wifely concern.

"You're right, dear. Charles," I called out—Charles was already down at the far end of the immense dining room—"while you're up, throw some coke and a few cubes of ice in there, will you, please?"

Back at the table, tray in hand, Charles snorted with disgust. (Due to the unnatural length of his nose, his snorts were extra loud and disconcerting.) "You can't be serious," he said, once again secure in his superiority over me and everyone else on the planet. "This is twenty-year-old Gillington's. One takes this rum neat. One does not adulterate it with coca-cola."

"Charles," I said, the horror seeping from my voice, "don't tell me you're out of coca-cola, too?"

TWELVE

In the end, to placate Charles I had my Gillington's straight, with a coca cola chaser.

"Charles," I said, "I'm no judge of alcohol, as you know, but this rum is absolutely delicious."

"You'll never have better," Charles said. "One hundred and seventy dollars a bottle, and worth every penny."

Ann and Steven winced. Brenda briefly closed her eyes. And Candace made one of her "I'm going to throw up" faces. Only Janice, blinded by sisterly devotion, failed to register her brother's radical display of vulgarity.

"I'll drink to that," I said, downing the remainder of my glass in one fell gulp.

"Karl," Janice said *sotto vocce*, so as not to alarm the children, "please take it easy. Don't forget, one of us has to drive home."

"I can drive," sharp-eared Brenda said.

"There you have it," I declared. "We've raised a chaufferette. Charles, do you suppose you could pour me another measure of that superlative rum?"

Charles may have despised me, but he was far from immune to flattery, no matter what the source. "With pleasure."

"You know, Charles," I said, beginning to feel the welcome effects of the alcohol, "you were absolutely right."

"About what?"

"It would have been felonious to defile this sublime nectar with a bunch of dirty leaves. What could I have been thinking?"

"That reminds me," Charles said, apropos of nothing, "I hear your quarterback is having quite the year." Charles, who had no interest in football, was desperate to distance the conversation from the mojito debacle.

"So he tells me."

"So he tells you?" Charles snorted, and I could have sworn I heard the windows rattle. "Haven't you seen the covers of Time and Newsweek?"

"GQ, too," Mousey Ann said in a small voice, finally daring to enter the conversation.

"And W-w-w-w-w-w-omen's W-w-w-w-ear D-d-d-d-d-d-d-d…" Steven attempted to add.

What, I wondered briefly, was Steven doing with a copy of Women's Wear Daily?

"Yeah, Dad," Candace yawned, "what's it like being so chummy with a big celebrity?"

I took another sip of my rum. It really was unbelievably good. "Brian Westin is a world class pain in the ass. A poster boy for himself. The second largest egotist I've ever known. If I could pawn him off on another surgeon, I'd do it in a heartbeat."

Charles was delighted. We were firmly off the subject of missing mint leaves, and quotes or misquotes from the above would make wonderful conversational tidbits when he was trying to impress his friends:

"My brother-in-law may be a bit on the dull side, but no denying he's a crackerjack surgeon. And you should hear him on the subject of his famous patient. 'Brian Westin is a world-class pain in the ass,' he told me. Etcetera, etcetera."

"Who's the first, Dad?" Candace asked.

"The first what?"

"The first largest egotist."

"Sorry, sweetie, that's, ah, privileged, confidential doctor/patient type information. Right, Charles?" Well on my way to being sloshed now, I threw him a sly wink. He did not wink back.

"Give us a hint, Dad. Is it another celebrity?"

"Yes, he is famous, in a manner of speaking, but that's all I'm going to say."

"Dear, you never told me you had another famous patient," Janice said unhelpfully.

"He's only famous for being an ass-hole, dear, so I never thought it worth mentioning."

"Karl!"

After dinner the entire clan adjourned to the Versailles-sized living room, sorting itself out by age and/or gender. The women collapsed into over-stuffed chairs in the vast room's geophysical center. Charles and I took up positions at the north end, beside Bar Number II. And the kids collapsed onto couches at the south end—off in the distant haze.

"Some port?" Charles suggested.

"You know, Charles, I'd love some port, but I think I'll stick with the Gillington's for now."

"You can't go wrong with Gillington's," Charles said agreeably.

In twenty odd years the two of us had never gotten along so well. A Maori tribesman observing us interact for the first time might even have used the word "cordial" (or its Maori equivalent: "greased spears that rub together silently") to describe our relations. This millennial thaw in our life-long feud was of course, like many traffic accidents, alcohol-induced. The Gillington's had, after all the years of torment, effectively vaccinated me against Charles' rabid behavior.

As for the psycho shrink himself, he had won a great personal victory. After two arduous decades of attempting to browbeat me into consuming his booze, he had finally achieved his objective. So why not be affable for a change?

I must have been on my third Gillington's when Charles, certain I'd refuse, offered me a cigar. It was, Charles said confidentially, a Cuban cigar. "Not easy to come by," he added.

I found the idea of a Cuban cigar nostalgic in the extreme. Janice would not be pleased, but what could she say? I'd be puffing shoulder-to-shoulder with her beatific brother, Dr. Perfect.

"I'd love a good cigar, Charles. Montecristo?"

"No, Cohiba."

"Even better."

I'd never seen Charles more surprised, or more pleased, as he extracted the cigars from their humidor, cut the tips with a titanium clipper, and lit us up. For several minutes we stood leaning against the bar, drinking and smoking in comradely harmony, content to merely stare out over the steppes of Charles' living room.

"There's something I want to show you," my brother-in-law said after a while.

From a drawer beside the bar he extracted a computer printout and held it up for my perusal. "I got this from my realtor," he said in an oddly loud voice. I glanced down the length of the room and saw that Charles had drawn everyone's attention, even the kids, from their distant couches out there on the horizon.

"These are comparables," Charles explained. "Properties roughly equivalent to mine which have sold over the past year. As you can see, nothing moved for under eleven mil. With my two extra parking places I should be pushing fifteen."

Charles paused so that I might express my admiration.

"That's wonderful, Charles," I said, slapping him on the back.

"Say!" Charles said a moment later, as if he'd just been struck by a sudden thought. "How much do you suppose your ranch out in the burbs is worth now?"

"No idea."

"Two million," Charles said with a frown. "At best."

I let out a long sigh. "That's, ah, very interesting, Charles."

"If you'd listened to me," he went on, "and moved to the City when I did, you'd be sitting on a small gold mine by now, instead of being stuck in that sluggishly appreciating house of yours."

"Charles," I said, looking him directly in the nose, "what can I say? I've been a fool. But no longer. I swear that from now on I will swallow whole your wise, unerringly prophetic counsels, as if they were globules of saliva dripping from the lips of the Almighty Himself."

"You're being sarcastic."

I shrugged.

"You think you're being noble," Charles said, "with your supposed indifference to wealth. But what you're really being is selfish."

"Selfish?"

"You amass wealth," Charles enlightened me, "for your children's sake." He paused, awaiting my response. Still staring him squarely in the nose, I produced an elaborate yawn. "For your children's sake," he said again. "Karl, you may believe that you've put away enough for your future needs, but what about your children? And their children? What about their future?"

"Gosh, Charles, I'm afraid they'll just have to manage with what they can earn. That, plus the five or six million they'll inherit when Janice and I drop dead."

"Karl," Janice called down the room, "don't talk like that!"

"Sorry, dear!" I called back, cupping my hands around my mouth to boost the volume.

"Is that your entire net worth?" Charles demanded in mock amazement. "Mine is pushing fifty." When I did not respond, he added grimly, "You know, Karl, your family deserves better."

I believe it was at this point that I began to lose my temper.

"Well, I couldn't be more pleased for you, Charles," I said, my tone mild and friendly. "So, what shall we talk about next: your miraculously performing stock portfolio vs. my meager mutual fund holdings? Your dazzling tennis game vs. my plebian jogging? Your degree from hallowed Harvard vs. my lowly diploma from humble Johns Hopkins?"

"Really, Karl," Charles said, chuckling with pleasure, "no need to take it like that. I was merely attempting to point out…"

"Or," I interrupted, "should we just cut to the chase: whip out our cocks and see whose is bigger?"

I hadn't meant to shout this last bit, but the rum had gotten the best of me. Everyone heard, even the kids, all the way out in the cheap seats.

"All right, Karl," Charles said in his no-nonsense Dr. Doom voice, "let's take it easy, shall we."

"Why? What are you afraid of, Charles? You got a teeny weenie?"

"Aren't we," Charles asked soberly, "supposed to be setting an example for our children?"

"That's the point, Charles. That's why I want to settle this once and for all. For the children's sake. Quien es mas macho? Karl or Charles? Ladies and gentlemen," I said, addressing our respective families, "you be the judge. Who is more macho, me or Charles?"

"Now I see why you don't drink," Charles sneered. "It's obvious you can't handle your liquor."

"The only thing I can't handle is you, Charles. You sleazy, pompous, self-serving, hypocritical prick!"

An audible gasp was heard, stage-right. Janice, on her feet, pale and trembling, stood staring at me in slack-jawed astonishment. Beside her, Ann had risen to her feet as well, her eyes shining with a mixture of disbelief and gratitude.

"Take that back!" Charles commanded.

"You bully your family," I continued in a calm voice. "You take advantage of your patients. You cheat on your taxes. You cheat at tennis. You cheat on your…"

"Enough!" Charles roared, crowding me against the bar (nipple-to-nipple, so to speak) before I could finish my damning statement. "I will not allow you to defile my home, on this day of all days, with your venomous envy, your adolescent feelings of inadequacy. No, sir! Not in my home. I demand an apology. At once!"

The possibility of violence was implicit in Charles' tone and posture. But I knew it to be a hollow threat. Actually coming to blows in his own home, with his own family, on Thanksgiving? No, it was not going to happen. Nonetheless, Charles continued to press forward, his leviathan nose so close to me I could have licked it with my tongue. But I wasn't drunk enough for that, so I merely pursed my lips and blew some air up his nostrils.

Charles let out a low growl. "Apologize now, or…"

"Or what, Charles?" If he laid a hand on me I was prepared to give him the thrashing he deserved. And he knew it.

"Or, or, leave my home at once!"

"Charles, please!" It was Janice, rushing to insert herself between us. "Chuck," she implored her brother, "he never drinks. He's not used to alcohol. It's just the rum talking."

"You're right," Charles said, glad for an excuse to back off, "he's drunk."

"He's drunk," Janice said.

"He's d-d-d-d-d-runk," Steven added.

Smiling broadly, I held out my hand. "What do you say, Charles? Call it a draw? Water under the bridge? Bygones be bygones?"

When the psycho psychoanalyst refused to shake my hand, I gave him a coy look and said, "Come on, Charles, let's kiss and make up. For the children's sake."

Then I threw up, copiously and spontaneously, all over my brother-in-law's blazer.

THIRTEEN

The fallout from the Thanksgiving Day Massacre (as Candace called it) was extensive. Janice pronounced herself "completely humiliated", then proceeded to proffer me the proverbial cold shoulder for precisely seventy-two hours. Charles expressed his discontent by refusing to hear my name uttered in his presence "ever again". And Brenda, before rushing back to college, told me to my face that I had "behaved like a boor".

On the other hand, I had with my drunken outburst brought bright smiles to the faces of Ann, Steven and Candace. Three in favor. Three opposed. Bernie (my accountant) would have called it a "wash".

Of far greater concern were the dubious glances Janice continued to cast my way long after my sentence of silent punishment had been commuted. Janice was nothing if not a straightforward person, and after twenty years of marriage I could read her face like an open book of tofu recipes.

"What's gotten into him?" she was thinking. "Drinking rum? Smoking cigars? Working insane hours? Wolfing his dinner down like a starving dog? And giggling! Karl never giggles!"

Soon, I'd entered into a state of perpetual paranoia. At any moment, I was certain, my wife would pick up a copy of Vogue (or some other piece of glossy garbage) and come across one of those boilerplate bits, entitled: The Seven Signs Your Husband Is Cheating On You! And that would be that.

I'd read one these bush-league essays personally, in a Spanish language version of Cosmopolitan, while busying myself in Mariela's bathroom. When I asked my lover why she was reading this trash, she replied (God help me!): "I'm learning how to be an American."

Needless to say, my original plan (to maintain an outward appearance of humdrum normality while discretely screwing my brains out) had gone horribly awry. Where, I asked myself, did I go wrong? The answer was, unfortunately, everywhere.

But I didn't feel wrong. That was the problem. I felt—how can I say this without resorting to a string of clichés? I can't. I felt liberated, thirty years younger, bursting with energy, excited about life. And, of course, I was desperately in love. Being in love, they say, can make a person behave irrationally. That is perfectly true, but misses the larger point, that being in love is irrational, something along the lines of functional schizophrenia.

This has to stop, I told myself. Somehow, I must regain enough self-control to present to the outside world (Janice) at least some semblance of my former predictable self. I can and I will, I swore. Too much is at stake.

Fifteen minutes later, in the vice-grips of Mariela's rigid thighs, I was slowly suffocating. But what did I care? Everyone has to die under one circumstance or another, and what circumstance could be better than this? Drooling to death in a managed care facility with Wolfe Blitzer babbling in the background? No thank you.

Meanwhile, Mariela lay on her back moaning in her rapidly improving English: "Yes, yes, oh baby, yes! Eat me, baby, eat me!"

Mariela was still attending her intensive language class five days a week. The course was entitled, Practical English as a Second Language. After our shower, I said, "So, that's what they're teaching you—how to say, 'Eat me baby, eat me!'"

"Yes," she replied with a demure smile, "that's why they call it practical."

A while later, back at the ranch, Janice and I were sitting in the kitchen having our own meal.

"Eat your broccoli," she urged me.

Determined to be on my most normal behavior, I'd refrained from ingesting any cannabis at Mariela's, and now my appetite was back to its lackluster self.

"I'm not that hungry, dear," I said, snaring a small bit of the rubbery vegetable with my fork.

Janice shook her head. "I don't understand you anymore. Some nights you come home totally ravenous, devouring everything in sight. And other nights, you hardly eat a thing. And this new taste you've acquired for rum—it's not like you."

"I find the rum relaxing, dear. A little Gillington's in the evenings to help me wind down from a stressful day—I don't think that's going to kill me anytime soon."

"That's not the point. I wasn't saying you were drinking to excess. What worries me is that you're drinking at all. It's almost as if you're turning into another person. Someone I don't recognize," she concluded with a catch in her voice.

My wife's stifled sob pained me like a scalpel to the heart. Oh how I yearned (schizophrenically) not to wound the woman I had vowed to honor and protect.

"Well, it's still the same old me," I said.

Janice stared deeply into my eyes. "Do you still love me?" she asked.

"Of course," I said, and it would have been nice if I'd meant it. As it was, I couldn't say for sure one way or the other. This would have been the ideal moment (from a tactical standpoint) to throw down my fork, drag her up to the bedroom and demonstrate just how much I still wanted her. But I didn't have it in me, and I knew it. And she knew it, too.

In fact, by now all the elements of the equation had to be neatly aligned in my wife's orderly mind, requiring only one simple calculation to arrive at the value of X:

7 signs x Karl = X = Cheating Husband.

For the next few days I came home promptly after work, did my best to act dull and tired, laid off the cannabis, cut back on the rum and, one night, after popping a double dose of Viagra, actually had sex with my wife. The Viagra performed as advertised, but it was if a stranger's inflexible phallus had been grafted on to my indifferent groin. I went through all the motions, feeling absolutely nothing. As for Janice, she may have been reassured by my unexpected display of faux ardor, but not in any great way.

My sense of impending doom continued to mount like a…like a…whatever.

And then the Jets, Nets and Knicks all began a run of wounded knees—a veritable massacre. "Getting away for lunch" became impossible. I was reduced to calling Mariela twice a day from the payphone in the employee cafeteria. I explained to her about the terrible demands being put on my time. She said she understood. We practiced a little phone-sex in English and we made plans to spend the coming Saturday together. Janice had a twelve hour symposium to attend: The Benefits of Organic Fertilizer—Fact or Fiction?

It seemed highly implausible to me that anyone could spend an entire day discussing the potential virtues of manure. But God bless them, I thought, never one to look a gift horse in the anus.

SIXTEEN

Friday was an evil day, the culmination of an entire week *sans* Mariela. I felt her absence like a painful void in the pit of my—oh, screw the similes!

At the hospital I was visibly distracted. Everyone noticed, especially Burt, who felt compelled to lecture me on the dangers of "overdosing on teenage nookie".

"You look all desiccated," he told me, "like a human prune. Maybe you should try to conserve your bodily fluids for a few days. You know, Karl, too much of a bad thing isn't necessarily good."

"No, Burt, it's just the opposite. I haven't seen her for a week, and it's driving me crazy."

"A week, huh? You poor bastard."

In the afternoon, as I sat in my office attempting to eat a soggy tuna salad sandwich, Brian Westin burst in, accompanied by a small man carrying an armload of equipment.

"Don't worry, Doc, this is only going to take a second," the quarterback said.

It took several moments to rid my mouth of the wad of sandwich I'd been working on. In the meantime Brian's friend buzzed about my office like a crazed wasp, plugging in cables, propping screens against walls and knocking over my carton of reconstituted orange juice. From his neck there dangled three cameras, leading me to deduce that he was probably a photographer.

"What," I finally managed to blurt out, "is only going to take a second?"

"It's for the Team," Brian said. "A little publicity. They just need one photo—the quarterback with his trusted doctor. Somebody thought it was a good angle," he added vaguely.

"A good angle for what?"

"For the Team," Brian uttered piously. "Everything I do is for the Team. You, of all people, should know that, Doc."

"I should? Brian, what the fuck are you talking about?"

"Whoa, Doc," the overpaid narcissist said. "Never heard that kind of language coming out of your mouth before. Phil, are you good to go? The doctor's a busy man."

"Just about," Phil said, unscrewing a lens cap.

Brian put an arm around my shoulder and told me to smile.

"He's not smiling," Phil announced, his eye glued to the viewfinder.

"Smile, Doc," Brian said, squeezing my shoulder.

Wincing with pain, I turned towards Brian, who continued to squeeze my shoulder with his outsized hand. Phil, his camera on full-automatic, took an entire clip of photos, nodded to Brian, and began to gather up his gear.

"So, this is for what, the team magazine?"

"Gotta run," Brian said. "Don't forget to watch the game Sunday. Cleveland's secondary sucks. I might set another record."

Over the course of the day I continued to deteriorate. Everyone in the OR could feel the strain. At one point Dulce Mendez put her hand on my arm and stared up at me with concern oozing from her pretty brown eyes.

"Are you all right?" she asked.

"Of course," I snapped. "Why wouldn't I be?"

"I don't know," she said. "Maybe you're lonely. What are you doing after work?"

"Going home to the bosom of my frigging family. All right," I snarled, turning to my team, "let's cut this bastard open."

SEVENTEEN

My foul mood was not improved to any great extent when, upon arriving home, I learned from Candace that Janice had been called away to an emergency meeting of SPEW, the Sands Point Ecological Watchdogs.

"Something about leaky faucets," Candace said.

"Leaky faucets?"

"If you're hungry, mom left an organic arugula and tomato salad and some…"

"Fuck the arugula salad!" I shouted, throwing my briefcase against the wall.

After a respectful pause my daughter said, "You seem kind of tense, Dad."

What a fool I was! Rushing home to play the role of the standardized husband, only to discover that my abnormal wife was off at a leaky faucet meeting. What about my leaky faucet? Why, I berated myself, hadn't I faked another evening emergency at the hospital? At this very moment I could be wrapped in Mariela's slender arms, kissing her outsized lips, caressing her wonderfully firm round little…

"Yes, I might be feeling a little tense," I admitted.

"You should get high, Dad. You need to chill."

"No, sweetheart, I think I'll just have a drink or two. That should take the edge off."

"Alcohol's for losers. I've got some great new stuff— Mendocino Mindwipe. Two hits, Dad, and you won't even remember what an edge is."

Candace was correct. The Mindwipe was, at least in my inexperienced opinion, wonderfully great "stuff". We sat in her room passing the joint, clouds of intensely odiferous smoke floating about our heads. After a minute or two I did indeed feel myself "chilling out". Candace turned the volume way up on her guitar and began to play *Foxy Lady*. Even in my far off youth, I'd never been a fan of Jimi Hendrix. His music had always sounded disjointed and abrasive. But under the influence of the Mendocino Mindwipe, I found myself rather enjoying it.

Dun-dun, dah! Dun-dun, dah! Dun-dun…

Until I was seized by a sudden spasm of parental paranoia.

"By the way," I said, grabbing her wrist, "where do you get all this great stuff? Isn't it expensive?"

"People give it to me."

"People?"

"Guys."

"Guys?"

"Yeah, they like me, so they give me pot."

"Just because they like you?" I asked darkly.

Candace laughed. "What do you think, Dad, I'm trading sexual favors for drugs?"

Blushing intensely, I rushed to say, "Of course not. Such a thing would never cross my mind. What I meant was…"

"To tell you the truth, Dad, I don't even like guys."

She doesn't like guys? I thought, my pot-induced panic veering wildly in another direction.

"What do you mean, you don't even like guys?"

"I'm not sure," Candace said, "but I think I might be a lesbian. Don't tell mom. It might upset her."

Candace resumed playing *Foxy Lady* through the cranked-up amplifier.

"It might upset her?" I repeated numbly.

A moment later the door to Candace's room opened, and there stood Janice, looking in my altered state like an invader from outer space.

The emergency meeting of SPEW had been interrupted, and then cancelled entirely when the president was called away to attend to a different sort of emergency—her teenage son, after consuming an entire six pack of beer, had ridden his mountain bike into a parked car.

This last datum, naturally, was not made available to me until much later. For the moment the significant fact was that my wife was standing in the doorway staring with the world's widest eyes at her husband and teenage daughter sharing a marijuana cigarette.

I could see that Janice was confused, momentarily unable to process the visual and olfactory stimuli (the fog of pungent smoke, the smoldering joint in my hand) being transmitted to her brain. But when in short order her neurons were able to sort it all out, it was as if she'd stuck her finger in a wall socket, causing her entire body to go rigid with shock.

"Busted," Candace muttered.

"Karl, I need to speak to you," Janice said in a frightening voice. "Alone. You, young lady, I will deal with later."

As I rose and followed my wife out the door, Candace, ever the fountain of filial support, whispered, "You better leave your balls here, Dad—they'll be safe with me."

EIGHTEEN

I followed my wife's narrow unnaturally erect frame down the stairs and into the kitchen where I was told to take a seat. Janice chose to remain standing, or rather, pacing. For some time she continued to walk slowly and stiffly back and forth, stabbing me with the occasional stupefied glare, resembling in her rigid repetitive movements a malfunctioning android who at any moment was going to say: "For English, press one. For Spanish, press two."

Janice was not one to raise her voice. When she finally came to an abrupt halt in the vicinity of the dishwasher, she spoke with an *Invasion of the Body Snatchers* controlled arctic calm. "Now," she said, "I understand everything."

My heart, already pounding uncomfortably, began to fillibrate with complete abandon. She's made that last calculation, I thought grimly.

"You're in the midst of one of those trite mid-life crises they're always writing about," she said, one thumb still stuck in the dike.

I'm a dead man, I thought.

"This explains all your strange behavior," she continued.

"I'm sorry, Janice…" I began.

"Risking our livelihood," she ground relentlessly on, "wasn't bad enough, was it?"

"Janice…"

"Poisoning your mind and body with drugs—apparently, that wasn't sufficient, either."

"Oh, Christ," I moaned.

"No. Not for the renowned surgeon, Karl Sanderson. He had to take it one step further. He had to involve his impressionable young daughter in his sick illegal activities. Are you listening to me, Karl?"

"Yes, dear." Suddenly, I sensed a wee glimmer of hope.

"Is what I'm saying penetrating your…your dope fog!"

"Ah, I…uh…"

"Your own daughter!" she shrieked, finally, irrevocably losing control.

Heaven help me! She doesn't think…

"Sharing drugs with your own adolescent child! What in God's name were you thinking?"

Knowing this was a rhetorical question, I nonetheless finally felt the courage to say something in my defense. "Janice, I'm not going to attempt to justify my behavior."

"You'd better not."

"I would, however, like to, ah, put matters into perspective."

Janice was incredulous. "Into perspective?"

"Well, ah, clarify a few things. About Candace. First of all, our daughter is not a child. And she is not impressionable. In fact, she was the one who corrupted me—if you want to look at it that way."

"Candace is seventeen-years-old! And she is your daughter!" Janice screeched.

Those were facts with which I could not argue, so I attempted another tack. "Candace is not a typical teenager," I said, in a tsunami of understatement. "She is both wise and mature far beyond her years. If I were you, I wouldn't…"

"Don't tell me what you would do if you were me!" Janice snarled. "You are in no position, or condition, to give advice to anyone! Charles was right. You need help. Professional help."

"You think I need to see a shrink?"

"A psychiatrist," Janice corrected me. "Yes, I do."

At this point, Leonard (my favorite receptionist) would have said to himself, "Far fucking out!"—a sentiment I shared wholeheartedly. Talk about dodging a bullet! Being busted smoking pot with my daughter seemed to be paying a marvelous and unexpected dividend. Apparently, Janice was prepared to attribute all of my odd behavior to an acute but generic mid-life crisis involving the consumption of cannabis, a little rum and, hopefully, nothing else.

"You know, dear," I said, feeling more empowered by the minute, "I think you need to consider the possibility that you may be over-reacting just a little bit…"

"Overreacting!"

"Please, Janice, hear me out," I said patiently.

Janice folded her arms, stood even more stiffly, if that was possible, and glared at me with icy menace. "Go ahead."

"First of all…" I began, but was momentarily unable to continue due to an extreme dryness of the mouth brought about by the extra-potent marijuana. "Excuse me," I mumbled, getting up to pour myself a glass of water. Drinking it down in one great gulp I resumed my inferior seated position and continued. "Janice, there are two issues here, and I wish we could consider them separately. First, there is the issue of me and my, ah, distorted frame of mind."

"Distorted is right."

"That colon cancer scare," I said, aiming low, "it set something off. An awareness of my mortality, I think. I don't know. Call it a mid-life crisis if you want, but that's just jargon. It doesn't begin to describe the sense of impending doom I began to feel. It was as if I suddenly found myself standing at the edge of a precipice and…"

"Get to the point!"

"Yes, dear. You see, I couldn't escape this feeling of impending catastrophe, imminent disaster, looming annihilation. The marijuana seemed to help. And the alcohol. And working so hard I had no time or energy left to contemplate my approaching end. The utter finality. The…"

"For God's sake!" Janice cut me off. "You're not even fifty!"

"I know, I know. It's all irrational. I see that now. I do need help. And I will seek it," I concluded bravely.

Biweekly imaginary visits to an imaginary shrink, it had occurred to me, would provide an excellent cover for additional visits to you know who. What a turnaround: From Damnation to Ejaculation in only sixty seconds!

"Good," Janice said, mildly mollified.

"I'll start looking for someone tomorrow," I promised.

"I'll call Charles and ask him for a referral."

"No!" I said emphatically. "Not Charles. I happen to be a physician myself, Janice, and I'm sure I can find a qualified person on my own."

"That's another issue you need to discuss with your psychiatrist," Janice declared, "your adolescent resentment of my brother."

Under other circumstances I would not have allowed this to pass, but arguing the point now would have been counterproductive to my overall strategy: sacrificing the odd platoon in order to save the battalion.

"All right," I winced. "Before proceeding to point number two, dear, I want to apologize to you for any distress or inconvenience my erratic behavior may have caused you."

Janice dipped her chin ever so slightly in acknowledgement.

"Now," I resumed, "as for Candace. First of all, I realize it was wrong to smoke marijuana with her."

"Wrong? That's putting it mildly."

"All right, it was inexcusable."

Again, Janice dipped her chin with approval.

"Inexcusable," I said again, since Janice had liked the sound of it so much the first time. "And it will never happen again. I promise you that. On the other hand, I don't think you really understand Candace. She's...different."

"Nonsense. She's extraordinarily bright, and a bit of a rebel, but aside from that, she's perfectly normal."

"Normal?" I said, playing my trump card. "Well, I suppose in these enlightened times being a lesbian could be considered normal, but..."

"What? What are you saying?" Janice's eyes went wide with horror, and I felt like a total heel (on two counts), but

I was fighting for my life, in a manner of speaking, and I had little room in which to maneuver.

"I'm saying, Janice," I said with brutal candor, "that Candace is a lesbian."

"No, I don't believe it!" Janice ran to the foot of the stairs and began to shout her daughter's name. In short order the two of them were standing before me in the kitchen—Janice, on the verge of hysteria, Candace, as mellow as a Mahayana monk.

"All right," Janice said. "I want to ask you something, Candace, and all I want from you is an honest answer."

"Sure, Mom."

"Are you...are you a lesbian?"

Candace favored me with a disappointed look. "Dad, you promised not to tell."

"Oh, my God!" Janice moaned.

"Mom," Candace said gently, "it's not like I've got leprosy or something. And I'm only seventeen. It's probably just a phase I'm going through. You'll see. In a few years I'll be screwing every guy I can get my hands on."

NINETEEN

Saturday finally rolled around, as did we, from ten until noon.

For the first time since Havana we had an entire day together, and I intended to make it a memorable one. We taxied deep into the bowels of Greenwich Village where, in an obscure deserted trattoria, I asked for a table in the rear.

The young waiter, a real Italian, would not hear of it.

"Itsa sucha beautifula day!" he said comically. "You and youra bella…uh…friend shoulda sit ina the window."

Mariela pressed against me, narrowed her eyes and said in English, "We likea the dark." The young waiter, flustered beyond repair, dropped the menus, picked them up and broke into unintelligible Italian, while guiding us to the most remote corner of the restaurant.

Mariela, as was her custom, ate like a famished wolf. Where it all went, God only knew. She might have added a few pounds since her hungry Cuban days, but the wee bit of extra flesh, like a smart bomb, had directed itself to precisely the right location.

After lunch, we rode the subway up to Spanish Harlem where we took in a movie. Improbably, there was a theatre showing *Casablanca* (my all-time favorite) with Spanish subtitles.

"This is an old movie," Mariela complained.

"Yes, but it's a wonderful film, and it will be good for your English."

As it turned out, she loved Casablanca. She even cried at the end. "He should have stayed with the girl," she said when the lights came on. "You would have stayed with her, wouldn't you?"

"Probably. But then, I'm no hero. And I would have spoiled the ending."

"You're my hero," she said, hugging my arm.

From the theatre we taxied up to the zoo. Along the way, as we drove through the desolate ruins of the South Bronx, Mariela, shocked to see such decrepitude in the land of plenty, turned to me and said, "This looks like Havana Vieja, only worse!"

"Yes, it's a lot worse," I agreed.

The zoo was a total success. As we went from exotic birds, to primates to big cats and beyond, Mariela grew extraordinarily animated, hopping up and down, giggling and shouting. This was my bite-sized lover at her most appealing: the young innocent with a savage appetite for everything.

"I still want to be a veterinarian," she told me, as we watched a pair of otters horsing around in their miniature lake.

"You should," I said, feeling uncomfortably paternal. "In this country, veterinary medicine is a good career."

"Would I get to treat otters and polar bears?"

"Not likely." Mariela frowned. "But you never know," I added quickly. "This is America, where anything is possible."

From the zoo we went to an early dinner at an upscale French restaurant on Seventh Avenue. I knew I was taking a bit of a risk here, in that it was the type of place where we might encounter someone I knew. But the hour was unfashionably early and this was New York City, a vast anonymous place where you rarely ran into acquaintances.

As it turned out, the place was nearly deserted, but we did experience an uncomfortable moment when the maître d', an officious little amphibian, indicated a certain reluctance to seat us.

"We have reservations," I informed him.

"Yes, that may be," he replied in his condescending French accent, "but I am not certain this is an appropriate place for a…couple such as yourself to be dining."

What he meant of course was that we looked like a teenage hooker and her john. Mariela did not quite understand what the man was saying, but she was, I feared, catching his patronizing tone. Desperate not to have what had been a perfect day up to this point spoiled by this toad in a tuxedo, I leaned into his ear and said, "Do you know who I am?"

"No, monsieur, I do not," he replied stiffly.

"Do you have a family?" I said with gentle menace.

"A family?"

"Yes, a wife and children—children you would like to see grow up with all of their limbs intact."

I can't say that I've ever been much of an actor, but so inspired (deranged) was I by my all-consuming desire to please Mariela that I must have momentarily unearthed some deeply buried talent. Or perhaps it was the fact that a man with the nerve to bring someone like Mariela to a restaurant like this had to be, in the maître d's mind, a potentially dangerous individual. Whatever it was that convinced him, after a moment's shocked hesitation, he bowed formally and escorted us to our seats.

Throughout the long romantic meal, the conflicted waiters, their faces frozen with fear, tripped all over themselves in a frantic effort to provide us with faultless service, while at the same time straining not to stare at Mariela. She of course was oblivious to everything but the food. Watching the utter pleasure with which she devoured her meal filled me with intense joy. I left a lavish tip, paying with cash. It would probably not, I decided, be prudent to pay with my credit card, after threatening to break the arms and legs of the maitre d's children. He might decide to complain to the authorities, and that would be the end of my Platinum Privileges™.

At the door of the Westchester Mariela said, "This has been the best day of my life."

"Mine, too, baby."

I was so happy I nearly began to cry. Then we kissed goodnight. It was growing late and I had to get home before Janice returned from the manure symposium.

TWENTY

It took two weeks to locate a suitable psychiatrist. In the course of this un-therapeutic interlude I repaired eighteen knees, kept my wife more or less at bay with repeated promises of imminent psychic reformation and still managed to see Mariela on five happy occasions.

On three of the dates, instead of screwing ourselves silly, we went out for lunch. Going out was Mariela's idea and, perversely, I was pleased. The fact that she wanted to spend time with me outside of bed made me feel as if our relationship was turning into something more than just a sexual marathon.

At one of the lunches Mariela complained, albeit wryly, about the strangeness of her fellow lodgers at the Westchester. "Am I the only normal person in that whole hotel?" she asked.

"Probably," I said, munching on my cheeseburger. "They do seem to attract an eccentric crowd."

"Eccentric? Most of the men go around dressed like women, and the women, if that's what they are, are always French-kissing each other in the hallway."

"Well, it's, a, you know, bohemian sort of hotel."

"Perverted is what I'd call it."

"In America, baby, tolerance is our greatest virtue. Or at least it used to be."

"Oh, I'm tolerant. I just wish I didn't have to live surrounded by a bunch of weirdoes."

"It's only temporary," I assured her. "As soon as I have time I'll find you an apartment."

"The sooner the better. I like Upper-Broadway."

She liked Upper Broadway. I had to laugh. My little

ingénue was growing up. And her English was improving at breakneck speed. I was enormously pleased. That her customary ardor in the sack seemed to be waning somewhat did not trouble me at all. My own embers had also cooled. We had, after all, been at it long and hard for some time now and a slight slackening of the pulse was to be expected.

TWENTY-ONE

Dr. Harold Rosenbaum was an intense bespectacled young man with a sparse goatee who could have been auditioning for the role of young Sigmund Freud—if young Sigmund Freud had been born in New Jersey. Fresh out of Witchdoctor School, he had only just begun to establish a practice. He was desperate for my trade and so, perfect for my nefarious purposes.

"I don't understand," he said, as we sat in his tiny office, incidentally located just two short blocks from the Westchester Hotel. "You want to see me once a week, but pretend you're seeing me three times a week?"

"That is correct, Dr. Rosenbaum. And I'll gladly pay for the other two sessions."

"But why?"

"Dr. Rosenbaum, if I may speak frankly?"

"With your therapist? That is the idea, Mr. Sanderson."

"It's Dr. Sanderson, Dr. Rosenbaum."

"Are you a medical doctor?"

"I'm an orthopedic surgeon."

"I see. That could explain some of your symptoms. Surgery is a stressful business."

"But I have no symptoms, Dr. Rosenbaum. Please allow me to explain."

"Excuse me," he interrupted, "*are you the Dr. Karl Sanderson?* The knee surgeon?"

"Goodness me, *I'm not the anything.* But yes, the knee is my specialty."

"Well!" the shrink chirped. "Living up to a reputation like yours can be a serious burden. It could well explain your symptoms."

"I don't have any symptoms," I said for the second time.

"No symptoms?" he said with disappointment. "But then, why are you here?"

"That's what I'd like to explain. You see, I'm doing this for my wife. To make her happy. This is her idea. That's why I want to see you only once a week, but present the appearance of seeing you three times a week."

Rosenbaum was now entirely confused. "I beg your pardon?"

"My wife believes that I am in need of intensive therapy," I said with a laugh. "In order to placate her, I'm willing to submit myself to one session a week, but not three."

"Why does your wife think you need intensive therapy? What does she think is wrong with you?"

"Doctor Rosenbaum," I said, smiling conspiratorially, "I am having an affair."

"And does your wife know?"

"Of course not."

"Does she suspect?"

"Well, she was on the verge of suspecting, I think, due to what I have to admit was some atypical behavior on my part, when…"

"What kind of atypical behavior?"

This intense nosey young man with his thick glasses and fuzzy beard was beginning to get on my nerves. Even worse, he was beginning to remind me of my brother-in-law. "Let's see," I said with reluctance, "working abnormally long hours, having the unaccustomed drink or two. Losing my temper. Things like that."

"And that's all? That made her think you were in need of intensive psychotherapy?"

"Well, no. Then she caught me smoking marijuana with our teenage daughter. That's what really set her off."

Dr. Rosenbaum's expression turned dour. "You smoked marijuana with your teenage daughter?"

"Didn't I just say that?" Christ, the man was annoying!

"And you don't find that…" Rosenbaum struggled for a

moment to locate the adequate phrase. "…you think that is normal, healthy, acceptable behavior?"

"I'm no expert on normal, healthy or acceptable, Dr. Rosenbaum, but I will say this: it's a lot of fun. My daughter is a real kick in the pants."

"Kick in the pants?" he repeated suspiciously.

"Is there an echo in this room?"

"An interesting choice of words."

"If you say so."

"Dr. Sanderson, surely you must realize that encouraging your teenage daughter to break the law is not…"

"Oh no, Dr. Rosenbaum, it was she who encouraged me. I'd only tried cannabis once, way back in college. Mr. Straight Arrow, that's me. Or at least, it used to be," I laughed.

"Nonetheless. By smoking an illegal mind-altering substance with your daughter, you were giving your tacit approval to her behavior."

"So?"

"So?"

"Dr. Rosenbaum, do you have a hearing problem?"

"Are you being hostile, Dr. Sanderson?"

"Of course not, Dr. Rosenbaum. Are you?"

The therapy session was beginning to take on a Vaudevillian tone, like a scene from *A Day at the Races*.

"Me? Don't be ridiculous, Dr. Sanderson. I'm the psychiatrist, and you're the patient."

"I knew that, Dr. Hackenbush."

"Hackenbush?"

"Sorry. Slip of the tongue."

Suddenly, against all odds, I was beginning to enjoy myself. By tormenting Dr. Rosenbaum, I was, in an indirect sort of way, getting back at my brother-in-law. And being able to speak openly to a total stranger was rather refreshing. Perhaps, I thought, this therapy business isn't a total waste of time, after all.

"So," Rosenbaum persisted, "you don't see anything wrong with sharing an illegal mind-altering substance with your under-age daughter?"

"Dr. Rosenbaum, what's the big deal? We're talking about pot, for Christ's sake, not heroin or LSD. And Candace, that's my daughter, is the most self-assured, level-headed person I've ever known. Even if she does think she might be a lesbian," I added.

This set Dr. Rosenbaum to tugging at his patchy beard for a while. Then he decided to change course. "Tell me about your lover," he commanded.

"Well, she's Cuban," I began, "quite attractive, a little on the petite side and…"

"No, no, I mean, what kind of person is she? What does she do for a living? Is she married, too?"

"She doesn't do anything for a living. Right now, she's studying English. She wants to be a veterinarian."

"She's a student?"

"Yes, and a good one, too. She's only been in this country a short time and already she's made amazing progress with her English."

"How old is she?"

"Nineteen."

"Nineteen?"

"Nineteen!" I said in a loud voice. "Can you hear me now, Dr. Rosenbaum?"

"Has it occurred to you, Dr. Sanderson," the shrink said after a moment's thought, "that the fact that you are smoking marijuana with your teenage daughter, and that you are having a sexual relationship with a girl about her same age— has it occurred to you that the two could be related?"

"A Cuban mulatta and an American WASP? Not likely, Dr. Rosenbaum."

"I was referring to their ages," the frustrated shrink snapped, "not their genetic makeup."

"What are you trying to say, Dr. Rosenbaum?"

"What I'm trying to say," he replied with a repressed snarl, "is that you chose someone close to your daughter's age to have an affair with because unconsciously you are symbolically having sex with your daughter, Dr. Sanderson."

"Dr. Rosenbaum, are you by any chance of the Freudian school?"

"Yes, I have been trained in the Freudian school. But that is beside the point. Getting back to the ages of..."

"No, no, Dr. Rosenbaum, please, wait one minute. I don't believe it's beside the point at all. You know, I've always preferred Jungians to Freudians. You Freudians, it seems to me, take rather a limited view of things. Everything with you is neurotic sex. A man loves a younger woman, he's really screwing his daughter. A man loves an older woman, he's screwing his mother. Why does sex always have to be fraught with symbolism? Why can't a man just go out and enjoy a good fuck once in a while? You Freudians, if you ask me, Dr. Rosenbaum, are a bunch of party poopers."

"You must admit," the repressed analyst replied, "it is unusual for a man your age to be carrying on with a nineteen–year-old."

"Yes," I agreed, "it is unusual, and perfectly wonderful. Who would have thought a man my age could achieve three orgasms in two hours? And I'm talking about multiple occasions, Dr. Rosenbaum. As for my daughter, even if I did want to have sex with her, I've already told you that she thinks she's a lesbian, so what would be the point?"

At this Dr. Rosenbaum's jaw fell open, as for several moments the know-it-all shaman was actually rendered speechless. Leaping into the breach, I glanced at my watch and said, "Whoops, where did the time go. I've got to run."

"But you still have twenty minutes left."

"Yes, but I've got an arthroplasty scheduled in half an hour. So, our next 'appointment' is in two days, but I'll really be seeing you next week." I stood up, and so did Rosenbaum.

"I'm not certain, from an ethical standpoint, I can go along with this phantom appointment arrangement you have proposed," he said uncertainly.

"Sorry, doctor, it's that or nothing."

"I feel that..."

"Let me ask you something, Dr. Rosenbaum. Based upon what you have seen and heard here today, do you believe that I am a deeply troubled man?"

"Yes. Yes, I do," he said with conviction.

"Well then, like any physician, since you have taken the Hippocratic Oath, you are ethically bound to help a sick individual like myself. As long as he pays, of course. Is a check all right?"

"Yes, a check is fine, but…"

"I can't tell you how grateful I am, doctor," I said, as I wrote out a check for three sessions and handed it over.

"Well, all right. I'll see you next week then."

"You certainly will. You know something?"

"What?" he asked warily.

"I feel better already."

TWENTY-TWO

Candace stood in the hallway wearing an ironic smile. "Guess what, Dad. You're famous."

"Of course I am," I said, giving her an un-incestuous peck on the cheek. Where's your mother?"

"She's upstairs on the phone. No, really, Dad, you're seriously famous. All the morons at school are going to want your autograph."

"That's nice. Maybe you can trade the autographs for more of that Mindwipe. What's for dinner?"

"Dad, will you listen to me!"

A moment later Janice came rushing down the stairs, clutching a magazine, an enormous freeze-dried smile on her face. Apparently, she had not heard (Praise Allah!) my remark about the Mindwipe. Since I'd begun my "intensive" course of psychotherapy, pretended to stop drinking and feigned a newfound admiration for her brother, Janice had been as happy as a Little Neck clam.

"Darling, you're a celebrity!" she cried with controlled glee, waving the magazine in my face. "It came by special courier, compliments of Brian Westin himself. He wrote you a short note. Apparently, the issue won't be hitting the stands until tomorrow. Why didn't you tell us?"

With a sinking feeling I took the magazine from her hand. It was the latest issue of *Sports Illustrated*, and there on the cover was a full page photo of Brian Westin with his apelike arm draped around my unwilling shoulder. The bold headline read: THE LEGEND AND THE SURGEON. Beneath that, in much smaller type, was the following: Brian Westin And His Doctor, Karl Sanderson, The Man Who Saved the Quarterback's Career—Twice!

(The New York Giants, I should point out, were at this moment in mid-December, 13-0, seemingly on their way to an undefeated season, and the heavy favorites to become the first Super Bowl Champions in history to win nineteen consecutive games. To the millions of people who unaccountably cared about such things, this was a very large deal, indeed.)

"I didn't tell you," I told Janice, "because I didn't know." Briefly, I recounted for them the photographic blitzkrieg on my office and Brian's vague inference that it all had something to do with "team" publicity.

"But this is wonderful!" Janice exclaimed. I'd rarely seen her so excited. Like most wives, like most human beings for that matter, Janice craved recognition. She would certainly be recognized now, albeit vicariously. But more to the point, so would I. My mind began to race with visions of disaster. That maître 'd at the French restaurant, for example; what if he saw the photo? He would know the name, the profession and place of employment of the man who had threatened to cripple his children!

"Has anyone actually read the article?" I asked, as calmly as I could.

"Of course," Candace replied. "It doesn't really say much about you. It's mostly about Brian, and what a wonderful, modest regular kind of guy he is."

"Yes," Janice agreed. "But they do make the point that Brian is so humble because he attributes most of his success to you."

"And Jesus Christ. Don't leave out Jesus, Mom."

"Yes, dear," Janice said uneasily. "The writer also mentions, in passing, that you are the top knee surgeon in the world."

In the world? This was not good.

"I bet Charles is going to be jealous," Janice said with a mischievous smile.

"That, Mom," Candace said, "is the understatement of all time."

Janice shot her daughter a warning look, and then rested her glowing gaze on me. It was obvious that despite everything Janice was enormously proud of me, which made me feel like an enormous louse.

"So, is the world's greatest knee surgeon ready for dinner? We're having wild salmon, organic fingerlings and organic arugula, tomato and walnut salad with a champagne vinaigrette."

"Of course," I replied distractedly, "that's wonderful, dear. I'm so hungry I could eat a...a..."

If I'm lucky, I was thinking, the maitre d' is not a sports fan. Or, if he is, his game is probably soccer. French people, I'd once heard, were crazy about soccer.

"How about a cow, Dad?" Candace offered helpfully.

"A what?"

TWENTY-THREE

By Monday morning it was all over the hospital.

"You stinking little rat!" Pedro enthused, smashing me on the back in the employee cafeteria with one hand, while waving his personal copy of the magazine in the other. "A fucking celebrity. We got a fucking celebrity, here!" he shouted. "Breakfast is on me today."

"Gosh, Pedro, thanks."

In the course of the afternoon, both Mendez sisters insisted upon giving me inappropriately prolonged congratulatory hugs. Dulce, ever the more bold of the two, even allowed her hand to wander down to my ass.

Edna, the hospital administrator, an unpleasant woman with whom I had never gotten along, called me into her office to offer her personal congratulations. Though she did not go so far as to grab my ass, she did briskly shake my hand and tell me how fortunate the hospital was to have a surgeon of my stature. She then held out the carrot of a larger office, an unexpected offer to say the least. Prior to this, she had on multiple occasions complained to me about how selfish I was to take up valuable hospital space with my "personal outsized office". Other surgeons, she'd pointed out, had to "share", or else were confined to "spaces no larger than a phone booth".

And on and on it went for an entire week. The whole world wanted to shake my hand and tell me what a credit I was to the hospital. Candace's remark about autographs proved to be prophetic. Everywhere I went magazine covers and pens were shoved under my nose, by surgeons, orderlies, technicians, nurses, janitors and, unbelievably, an accident victim being wheeled by on a gurney!

I looked like a movie star, I was told. Even standing side-by-photogenic side with the handsome and charismatic Brian Westin, my good looks shone through with the brilliance of…God only knew what! The possibility of an acting career, to my acute embarrassment, was mentioned more than once by giddy nurses of either gender.

Even Dr. Rosenbaum, who only with a supreme effort was able to disguise his distaste for my person, got into the act. Smiling awkwardly, he asked if I would sign a magazine cover for his son, who, he confided, worshipped the very artificial turf Brian Westin trod upon.

"I've never had a celebrity patient before," the over-educated twerp said snidely.

"You've barely had a patient before, period," I'd wanted to reply. But instead, I smiled deprecatingly; I had, after all, to stay at least marginally within the Houngan's good graces.

"My fifteen minutes of fame," I mumbled humbly.

On the occasion of my seventh phantom psychiatric session, Mariela produced a copy of the now famous Sports Illustrated cover—the issue, unfortunately, had been an immense hit, especially with the lobotomy set. Oddly, she did not seem pleased by my newfound notoriety.

"You never told me you were famous," she pouted.

"But I'm not famous," I said with a laugh.

"Then what are you doing on the cover of this magazine?"

"It was an accident."

"Carmen says that only famous people get to be on the cover of such big-time magazines."

"Carmen?"

"My friend from the boutique. You remember—that time we went shopping?"

"Oh, yes, I didn't know you two were still seeing each other."

"She's my best friend."

"That's nice. Let's make love."

Mariela was on her period and not in the best of moods. She had, she said, no desire to "get both of us full of blood".

Once we'd exhausted the topic of my celebrity, she began to complain again about the perverts at the Westchester, and wondered aloud if people didn't think that we were perverts, too, due to the vast difference in our ages.

"I don't feel like a pervert," I said lightheartedly, "do you?"

"I'm no pervert."

Though she would not, due to her menstrual cycle, have intercourse, I did, after a brief struggle, manage to persuade her to put on one of her sexy outfits and favor me with an uninspired blow job. If only Dr. Rosenbaum could see me now, I thought.

When I was about to leave, Mariela planted herself in my path, but not for a good-bye kiss. Hands on hips, she glared up at me and said in a tone of voice I'd last heard her use on her brain-dead brother, "You should have told me you were famous."

"But I'm not famous."

"Yes, you are!"

"No, I'm not!"

PART IV

ONE

For the world's greatest knee surgeon, as well as everyone else on the planet who hadn't expired in the interim, life went on.

At the hospital I continued to average fifteen procedures a week while fending off the advances of Dulce Mendez, as well as several new devotees, including a male nurse who asked me if I was related to Rock Hudson.

At home, Candace and I, exercising extreme caution, shared the occasional hit of Mindwipe. At my insistence we'd dedicated a corner of her closet to the tools of teenage subterfuge: a six pack of Visine™, a case of breath mints and an economy size can of Nature's Blessing Unscented Room Deodorant. Candace had lobbied strenuously against the Nature's Blessing, and in favor of sandalwood incense.

"Are you insane?" I told her. "A parent smells incense, the first thing they think is marijuana."

"These room deodorants," she fired back, "have been known to cause cancer in laboratory rats."

"Sweetie, if we have to choose between rat-cancer and getting busted by your mom, we'll take our chances with the rats."

As for Janice, now that her famous husband's psyche was in the process of being professionally refurbished, she was back to bouncing merrily from NGO to NGO, secure in the knowledge that Karl was "on the road to complete recovery". She'd even admitted in a moment of euphoric relief that her brother could at times be, "a little on the domineering side".

At the Westchester, Mariela, albeit with diminishing enthusiasm, continued to rut regularly with yours truly twice a week, while down the street and around the corner, I made myself at home once a week on the rookie shrink's secondhand couch, confessing my most shameful sins and inventing for the doctor's edification suggestive dreams featuring circumcised totem poles, parted pomegranates, blond Indian maidens (who looked, I volunteered, nothing like my daughter) and, just for good measure, rivers of blood. The neurotic quack was, needless to say, in Freudian heaven, especially on the several occasions when I "accidently" referred to him as Dr. Rosenprick.

In short, my life had in its own bizarre way slipped into something of a routine, which was fine with me. It was a wonderful routine, as long as I could continue to get away with it, which, as it turned out, would not be very long.

When the time came for my next actual therapy session, I ran into a bit of luck. Rosenbaum had come down with the flu. "We'll have to cancel," he informed me nasally over the phone. "We can re-schedule a real session for one of the timeslots set aside for an imaginary session."

"Sounds great," I told the wheezing shrink. "But don't be in too much of a hurry to get back to work. These bugs can get nasty if you don't take care of them."

"Yes, I know. I am a physician, too (sneeze). As you might recall (cough)."

"And a fantastic one at that," I agreed. "Nonetheless, you'd better take some codeine for that cock, Rosenbaum."

"Codeine for my cock?"

"Cough. I said, cough. And watch out for dehydration, Rosenbloom. They don't call it the silent killer for nothing."

"Rosenbaum! (Sneeze, Cough). And it's hypertension they call the silent killer, not dehydration."

"Whatever. Just make sure you drink plenty of daughter."

"What? What did you say? Hello? Hello?"

After hanging up on Rosenbaum in mid-sneeze, and before you could say, "Bearded Snake Oil Salesman", I was back on the phone, to Mariela of course, who sounded a little nasal herself, but who nonetheless was amenable to a short visit later in the day.

Arriving at the Westchester four hours later, I found my main man Leonard looking atypically grim. I wondered if he, too, had come down with the flu. Or were his forty odd years of smoking marijuana finally catching up with him? Even his bushy gray moustache seemed to be drooping today, like a neglected houseplant.

"Leonard," I said, extending my hand for our customary soul-brother handshake. "How's it hanging?"

"All right."

"You don't look so good, Leonard. Don't have the flu, do you? It's going around."

"No, I'm fine, man," he said, staring down at his desk. But he didn't look fine. In fact, he appeared to be in pain.

"Listen, Leonard, if you need a prescription—nothing too exotic, of course—I'd be happy to fix you up."

Leonard nodded his head and returned his gaze to the desk.

On my way up the stairs I passed two couples furiously making out, a pair of men, and a pair of women. Why, I wondered, are they always carrying on like this in public? Was it a Westchester tradition? Well, I thought benignly, they're not hurting anyone. And they're young. And life, or death, will catch up with them soon enough. So let them have their fun while they still can.

Alerted by Leonard to my imminent arrival, Mariela had, as usual, left the door unlocked. Stiff with anticipation, I turned the knob and (just like General Custer at Wounded Knee) marched blithely into the greatest debacle of my life—up to that point. Of course Custer had been on a horse, while I was on foot. And no discernible blood would be shed at the Westchester—yet. But it was, in its own way, a massacre nonetheless.

The young man was of medium height, muscular and far too handsome for anyone's good, especially mine. He stood with his arms folded aggressively across his chest, as if he were standing guard over Mariela, who sat behind him on the bed, staring down at the rumpled sheets. He appeared to be of Latin extraction, but did not look Cuban.

Even so, I remember hoping, in those few moments when hope was still an option, that he might be some long lost relative, a distant cousin, perhaps.

Ricardo (later I would learn the little shit's name) glared at me, one end of his mouth twisted upward in a churlish smile. I stared back, open-mouthed and confused.

When he finally spoke, his voice was well-modulated and pleasing to the ear. His English was excellent, tainted by only the trace of a Spanish accent. "Hello there, Mr. Famous Doctor."

"Mariela," I asked, looking past Ricardo, "who is this?"

My lover continued to stare at the sheets, refusing to meet my eye.

"It must be great," Ricardo said, holding up a copy of Sports Illustrated, "to be rich and famous. Especially rich. I always wanted to be rich."

"Good for you. Mariela, what is going on?"

"She's done talking to you, Mr. Rich Famous Doctor. She's done with you, period. Mariela and me are getting married."

It took some time, but finally I managed to eke out a few words. "Mariela. He just said that you and I are through. That the two of you are going to be married. Is this true?"

Still avoiding my gaze, she nodded her head.

The young man, smiling with malicious glee, said, "Hey, your Spanish is pretty good."

Gradually the shock receded, as pain, pure and simple, took its place.

So, it's happened, I thought, just as, somewhere deep in my hormone-saturated psyche, I'd always known it would. I wasn't, after all, a complete fool. Even back in Havana, at the height of my infatuation, I'd not been totally deaf and dumb. I remembered Carlos, my amiable neighbor, repeatedly scolding Henry The Eighth: "As soon as we're settled in Puerto Vallarta, Enrique, you'll leave me for the first cute young thing that comes along."

Of course I'd known the risks, but I was so besotted I hadn't cared. In my mind I'd only wanted the best for

Mariela, no matter what the emotional costs to me. Fine sentiments—how pleasant and appealing they are in the abstract. In the concrete world of my personal catastrophe I was as miserable as I could be. Or not quite. As the mad King Lear discovered, just when you think you have touched bottom, that things could not possibly get any worse, that is precisely when the trapdoor opens beneath your feet, permitting you to plummet even further.

Up to this point in our little morality play (Dr. Sanderson Gets Dumped), I could still intuit, within the storm clouds of my despair, a kind of aluminum lining. For alongside the pain, I found myself feeling a profound sense of relief. The whole sordid business which had become my day-to-day existence, with the lies, the guilt and the stress of leading a double-life, had come abruptly to an end, as all along I'd known it would.

I'd even gone over the scene, heartrending but tender, several times in my mind. It opened with Mariela gently breaking the news that she'd fallen in love with a younger man. But, she added kindly, she would always think fondly of me, and hoped that somehow we could remain friends. It was a bittersweet scene, filled with tenderness and hope for the future. I saw Capra directing.

In real life, my trashy little melodrama had no place for an upbeat ending. That aluminum lining (already downgraded from silver) was about to be demoted still further. To lead. Every cloud has a lead lining? Leer would have thought so.

Ricardo smiled with sadistic pleasure at the sight of the tears dripping down my cheeks. "Here, take a look at this," he said. "Keep it, if you want, as a souvenir. It's only a copy."

He handed me a photograph. It was of two lovers sitting in one of those ridiculous globe-shaped orange taxis that circulate around Havana. They were wrapped in each other's arms and grinning at the camera like a pair of fools. Mariela was wearing her school uniform and looked about thirteen. I looked…like a leering pervert.

As I studied the photo I experienced the predictable gamut of emotions: shame, heartache, guilt, remorse, anger.

And also fear. Why was he showing me this particular photo? The answer was obvious, but not to me.

"We want two million dollars," Ricardo announced. "In hundred dollar bills. We'll give you a week. If you don't come through, your wife gets a nice little package."

Something, something vital, was not adding up. The Mariela I knew could not possibly be a willing partner to this. Falling in love with someone else—that was merely being human. But this…this!

I made a quick grab for the proverbial straw. "Mariela, are you really going along with this? Blackmailing me? If this thug has forced you into it, just tell me. I'll kill him right now with my bare hands!"

Ricardo laughed out loud. Mariela said nothing.

"Mariela, I need to know. Are you doing this willingly? Are you really blackmailing me?"

"Tell him," Ricardo said.

Mariela looked at him, her eyes shining with undiluted adulation. She'd never looked at me that way, and I knew then that all was lost.

"You can afford it," she muttered.

"I can afford it?"

"One week," Ricardo said.

Being in love, as I may have mentioned, is an inherently irrational state, which can make one act in ways seemingly antithetical to one's nature. Certainly it had had that effect upon me. And now it had turned my honest, straightforward little lover into a scheming criminal.

"You'll get nothing from me!" I cried. "Go to hell—the both of you!"

Before I broke down completely, I turned and left the room.

Downstairs, as I rushed past Leonard, he said, "Sorry, man. You know, like, I would have said something, but, hotel policy, man—it's like, don't get involved. You know, with the guests?"

TWO

Alternately choking with rage and sobbing with grief, I commenced to move without purpose west on Twenty-Second Street. New Yorkers, not known for their curiosity, cast vaguely troubled looks my way, wondering, Who is this handsome, well-dressed middle-aged man bawling his eyes out as he staggers zombie-like down the sidewalk?

Violence has always abhorred me. In all my life I'd never struck another human being, or even a pet. As for suicide I was, as they say, not the type. But at the moment, I was utterly out of my mind and capable of anything. Which explains, I suppose, how I finally wound up stumbling into a gay bar on Bleeker Street.

"Give me some ten-year-old Havana Club," I told the pinup boy behind the bar.

"That's a Cuban rum, sir."

"I know it's a Cuban rum. Make it a double."

"We can't serve Cuban rum, sir. It's against the law."

"That's right. Gillington's then. Give me a double Gillington's!"

"That's thirty bucks a shot, sir," the pretty young man said warily.

"So?"

"A double would be sixty dollars."

"Fine!" I yelled. "Just give me the fucking drink!"

"No need to be abusive, sir."

Once he'd served me, he stood there, staring pointedly at my glass.

"What is it now?" I growled.

"Sixty dollars, sir."

"Oh, so it's pay as you go, is it?" I withdrew my wallet

and slapped three credit cards down on the bar, two platinum and one gold. "Go ahead. Take your fucking pick."

Because I had developed an instant and unjustified dislike for the poor fellow, I perversely tipped him thirty dollars.

"Thanks," he said, acutely confused.

It took nearly sixty seconds for me to finish my double Gillington's and order another. I sipped my second drink, instead of gulping it. Charles would have been pleased.

"You ever been in here before?" the barman asked after a while.

"I doubt it."

"I'm only asking because you look familiar, like…wait a minute! You're that doctor. Brian Westin's personal surgeon. You were on the cover of Sports Illustrated."

I grimaced and said, "Aren't you gay?"

"As a sunny day in June. You think they'd have a straight bartender in a place like this?" His eyes swept the room, the walls of which were lined with posters of Marilyn Monroe, Judy Garland, Joan Crawford and Mikhail Baryshnikov.

"I didn't think gay men were big football fans," I said morosely.

"Oh, I'm no sports fan. But I am a Brian Westin fan. That guy is the hunk to end all hunks."

"That he is," I agreed. In the mirror behind the bar I caught a glimpse of my face. My eyes looked like Baron Frankenstein's, as he's about to throw the switch. "And he gives great head, too."

"Brian Westin is gay?"

"You didn't know?"

"Are you sure? He doesn't seem like the type."

"Yes, I'm sure. I speak from personal experience."

"Personal experience?"

"Yes. Every office visit, he sucks my cock, in lieu of a co-payment."

"Are you serious?"

"Completely. Brian craves semen. He's like a camel at an oasis. You want me to set you up?"

"Set me up with Brian Westin?"

"Sure. Fix me another double, and I'll give you his unlisted phone number." And I did. It would serve the self-promoting son-of-a-bitch right.

"But, but what do I say?"

"What's your name?"

"Lance."

"Okay, Lance, just say this: 'Brian, I've been told by a reliable source at the *Post* that you give the best head in the NFL. How about sucking my dick?'"

"The New York Post?"

THREE

Sitting in my seat on the Long Island Railroad, a thousand breath mints fighting for position in my overloaded mouth, I wished I'd had more time to sober up before going home. But a longer delay, I'd decided, might have made Janice suspicious.

Suspicious? This, I thought with drunken desperation, has gone far beyond suspicious!

"Dr. Sanderson, how are you, tonight?" the friendly conductor, a man I'd known for years, inquired.

"Not dead, yet," I mumbled, "but getting there."

The conductor was confused. "A little medical humor, Dr. Sanderson?"

I entered the house attempting to imitate to the best of my ability Rosenbaum's flulike symptoms. In this manner I hoped to accomplish two goals: cover the fact that I was still seriously drunk, and justify an immediate retreat to the bedroom, where I could avoid my wife and reduce to an absolute minimum the need for human interaction.

Hearing my strangulating respirations, Janice bound like an arthritic deer from the kitchen to the foyer.

"Don't get too close," I warned, as I choked and gasped for air—so assiduously had I rehearsed my symptoms on the drive home from the station that I seemed to have actually done real damage to my larynx. "It's the flu."

"Oh, darling, you look awful," Janice sighed, scanning my red eyes and haggard face. Then, with a spasm of maternal instinct, she took two additional steps in my direction.

"Don't," I croaked convincingly. "Contagious."

Janice had a keen sense of smell, and she was more than capable of sniffing out the merest hint of alcohol, buried though it might be beneath a dozen layers of breath-altering carcinogenic chemicals. In any case, I wasn't going to take any chances.

"Going to bed," I added, heading for the stairs.

"What about dinner?"

"Not hungry."

"I'll make you chicken soup. I have a free-range chicken in the fridge."

"No," I said, dragging myself up the stairs. "Can't eat."

"Some Echinacea then. And rosehips tea. It's loaded with Vitamin C. They say the combination gives an enormous boost to one's immune system."

"Superstition," I wheezed over my shoulder. "Call the hospital. Cancel everything."

"Oh dear," my wife said from the foot of the stairs. "Shall I call a doctor?"

"Janice," I groaned, "I am a doctor."

No, no, I thought, stumbling up the stairs, I'm turning into Rosenbaum!

FOUR

Desperately in need of someone with whom to share my pain, I considered calling Irving or Burt. I knew I could count on their discretion, but beyond that, what? Sympathy and understanding? Hardly. I decided to call Pedro, instead. The orderly agreed to meet me during his lunch break, but only if we "went Italian". He suggested Ray's Pizza on Third Avenue.

"No more Japanese," he insisted.

"Fine."

"You got to be sick in the head to eat that shit."

"It's an acquired taste, Pedro."

"Acquire a taste for shit? I don't think so."

Janice, bless her guilt-ridden soul, had already left for the day. She'd felt badly leaving me on my own, but there were three urgent committee meetings to attend, with the very survival of the biosphere apparently dangling in the balance. Hoping to cure me by remote control, she'd prepared the free-range chicken soup after all, and left it in the fridge, along with a note urging me to take thirty drops of Echinacea every four hours, along with one thousand milligrams of Vitamin C. She'd be home by five.

Before leaving the house I pocketed twenty vitamin C tablets, dripped half the small bottle of Echinacea down the drain and flushed two large bowls of free-range chicken soup down the toilet. In this manner I hoped to provide Janice with a credible explanation for the miraculous manner in which I was going to dispatch my imaginary virus.

Pedro said nothing but was far from silent, chewing noisily on three successive slices of grease-soaked pepperoni pizza, as I explained to him the horrific turn of events my life had taken.

"Well," I concluded, "what do you think?"

Pedro emitted a thunderous belch, shook his head and said, "Doc, you're fucked."

"Yes, I know that, Pedro. I was hoping…"

"Unless."

"Unless?" I took a small hopeful swallow of beer. Beer, I'd been told, was the best cure for a hangover, and it did seem to be helping the headache, but not the nausea. If only the orderly would consume his pizza with a tad less gusto.

"You," Pedro said, "have options."

"Options?"

Pedro narrowed his eyes and lowered his voice to a conspiratorial growl. "I know a guy, who knows a guy, who knows a guy. If you know what I mean."

"Not really."

"Okay. Let's start at the beginning. First of all, you can't pay them off."

"Why not?"

"Because," Pedro explained, "blackmail is like a cow's pussy. Hey, one more slice!" he called out. "And don't be so cheap with the pepperoni!"

"A cow's…"

"And make it crunchy! I want something soggy, I'll eat your shorts!"

"A cow's vagina, Pedro?"

"Exactly. There's no end to it. Once you start paying, it'll never stop. They'll bleed you dry, like ticks on a dog. That's how this blackmail racket works. You ever watch the Nature Channel?"

"What?"

"The Nature Channel. One time, they showed a pack of jackals. Or maybe it was hyenas. Eating an antelope when it was still alive. Talk about disgusting! I mean, they're tearing that poor animal to shreds and it's snorting and screaming and wiggling all over the place." Pedro paused to pop a stray chunk of crust into his mouth. "Blackmailers are like leeches," he said, dumping the jackals. "Leeches dig into your body, hang on your flesh, gorge on your blood…hey, where you going?"

When I returned from the men's room, Pedro resumed where he'd left off. "That's blackmailers, for you, Doc: vicious animals with great big appetites. That's why you can't pay them off. It's like throwing a piece of meat to a starving…"

"Yes, yes, I get the idea. I can't pay them off. You said I had options. What did you mean?"

"Okay, Doc," Pedro said, lowering his voice again, "like I said, I know a guy, who knows a guy, who knows…"

"Pedro," I whimpered, "please, get to the point."

"The point," Pedro whispered, "is to get rid of 'em."

"Get rid…you don't mean?"

"Make 'em disappear," Pedro said in his best gangster voice. "Permanently."

"You're talking about having them killed?"

Pedro nodded.

"You're serious?"

"It'd cost you ten, maybe twenty grand at most," Pedro said with chilling nonchalance. "Compared to what they're asking, that's dog food money. One payoff, you're done. None of this slow bleeding business."

"No, Pedro. I couldn't even consider such a thing. I'm a doctor, not some Mafioso."

"You don't have to be in the mafia to have someone whacked," Pedro pointed out. "It happens all the time."

"Forget it."

"Okay," he said brightly, "how about a little warning then. What do they call it, a…a…" Pedro switched momentarily to English. "…a detergent?"

"Deterrent."

"Yeah," Pedro grinned, "break a couple of legs. Smash a few kneecaps. Or slice off a finger. 'There goes your pinky, slimeball. Next, it's your thumb. Then your dick. Then…'"

"Jesus Christ, Pedro! I told you, no violence. I couldn't live with myself."

"Well, then, Doc, I guess we're back where we started."

"Where's that?"

"You're fucked."

He was right. I began to cry. Pedro put a comforting hand on my shoulder. "Don't take it so hard, Doc. And remember, no matter how you feel now, you do have options. Hey, I gotta go. Let me know if you change your mind about, you know, messing 'em up. Should I get the tip?"

Around three o'clock Candace came home from school, peeked in on me and said, "Hey, Dad, I heard you have the flu."

"No, it's just a cold."

"Whatever it is, you look like shit."

"Thanks, sweetie."

Just after five, Janice returned. "How do you feel?" she asked.

"A little better."

"Did you have any soup?"

"Two bowls."

"And the Echinacea?"

"Half the bottle."

"Half the bottle?"

"And twenty thousand milligrams of Vitamin C."

"Are you serious?"

"I always thought it was a bunch of voodoo, dear, but I think it may be working."

"That bottle of Echinacea contained a hundred doses!"

"Well, it seemed like the thing to do. I believe I'm ready for some more chicken soup."

"You sound better," Janice said with an approving nod. "I'll heat up the soup."

"Thanks, dear. I know my taste buds aren't up to snuff, but the soup was really good. It must be that free-range chicken you make it with."

"It's the lack of hormones," Janice explained, as she headed out the door. "The hormones they feed the chickens rob the meat of its natural flavor. And hormones," she added, although she'd already informed me of this fact a hundred times, "can cause all kinds of problems."

Yes, I thought miserably, they certainly can.

FIVE

The following morning I pronounced myself organically cured.

"That Echinacea and Vitamin C will do it every time," Janice said.

"And don't forget the free-range chicken, dear. I think I'll drop a note to the AMA."

At the hospital everyone was all agog over the Giants. On the golden arm of Brian Westin "Our Boys" had indeed marched undefeated into the playoffs where they'd made chopped liver of their first round opponent, a "wildcard" (whatever that was) from Arizona, or Alabama. Somehow I could never get a handle on team geography.

"Your man, Brian, was brilliant," I was informed repeatedly.

My man, Brian. If it wasn't for him and that magazine cover, I wouldn't be in this mess! If only he'd injured his shoulder, instead of his knee. Or broken his neck, or ruptured his spleen. Or how about a series of concussions? I imagined Brian Westin's skull being repeatedly smashed by the helmeted head of a three hundred pound Samoan.

"Hey," a cardiologist I barely knew accosted me, "heard you were sick. Glad to see it wasn't anything serious."

"Thanks."

"Man," he exclaimed, "your boy's rating was off the charts on Sunday!"

"His rating?"

"His quarterback rating."

"I didn't know they gave them ratings."

"Right, Sanderson, very funny. Anyway, congratulations!"

As the fellow walked away I wondered distractedly what he'd been talking about. I knew they rated municipal bonds and corporate debt, but…quarterbacks?

I had four procedures scheduled that day, plus a gaggle of post-op patients, which was a blessing, keeping as it did my mind off the axe hovering over my outstretched neck. When I passed Pedro in the hall he shot me a dark inquiring look. I shook my head, and he shook his.

As the day wore on and I went about my daily routine, the entire blackmail business began to feel less and less real. What if I did nothing? Perhaps, they would simply lose interest and go away. If I didn't pay them, and they carried out their threat and told Janice, there would then be nothing further to hold over me. They would have shot their wad, so to speak, and to no purpose. On the other hand, as long as the threat of exposure remained so, too, would the hope of successfully extorting me.

And aside from telling Janice, what else could they do which would cause me any real harm? Tell the hospital administrator? So what? It was an unspoken rule—the personal lives of doctors were none of the hospital's business. They could inform the police. But, inform them of what? I'd committed no offense; unless, in the State of New York adultery was considered a crime, which I rather doubted. More likely it was encouraged, like car-pooling. The police would laugh in their faces. Maybe this whole mess would just evaporate by itself. I'd get over my loss, and life would pick up where it had left off before the trip to Cuba.

For the first time since the scene in Mariela's room, I began to feel a little better about my immediate future.

SIX

By the morning of Day Five, the relief I'd felt on the afternoon of Day Two had vanished like a puff of steam. I could no longer sleep, no matter how many milligrams of Valium I consumed. My entire alimentary canal was hors de combat, a sonata of gurgles, gasps and groans, like a walking toilet on its last legs. If I wasn't boiling with rage, I was steeping in self-pity, sautéing in shame or deep-frying in fear: an overcooked chunk of human tempura.

Pedro, over breakfast in the hospital cafeteria, summed it up rather well in his infrequent but colorfully creative English. "Doc," he said, shoveling a large lump of saturated fat into his mouth, "you are a basket case waiting to happen. You gonna eat those eggs?"

"No, help yourself," I muttered, sliding my plate across the table.

"Thanks. Listen, Doc, I have an idea."

"Does it involve amputation?"

"I been talking," Pedro whispered, "to that friend of a friend of a friend."

"You mean, the hit man?"

"Not so loud!"

"Sorry."

"This guy, he thinks we can get these bloodsuckers off your back without actually killing or maiming 'em."

"That would be nice. How do we do that?"

"We scare the shit out of them!"

"Go on."

"Two guys show up at the hotel room," Pedro said, his eyes gleaming with excitement. "They grab the punk and shove the barrel of a .357 magnum up his ass. Then…"

"Ah, how about, down his throat, Pedro? Somehow that seems less intrusive."

"Either way. Then they tell him, lay off the doctor or you're dead meat. Then they whack him a few times—nothing serious," Pedro rushed to add, "and that's that."

"It could work. If they're sufficiently convincing."

"Oh, these guys are convincing," Pedro assured me. "And they'll do it for five grand. Unless the punk is carrying; then they want ten."

"Carrying?"

"A gun."

"You think he carries a gun?"

"Nah. Blackmailers are like Jamaican security guards: big badges, small balls."

"I wouldn't want any real violence," I said, warming to the idea.

"Course not. That'd cost extra."

"And they don't lay a hand on…the girl."

"No, they don't touch the girl—if that's the way you want it."

"That's the way I want it."

"You still in love with that double-dealing bitch?"

"I don't know."

"Okay, then. I give 'em the go-ahead, they can do it tomorrow night. Just give me the room number."

I gave him the room number.

"And they'll want cash."

"They don't take Visa?"

"No, these guys operate strictly on a cash basis."

"I was joking, Pedro."

"Joking? Hey, that's a good sign, Doc."

"No violence. No one gets hurt."

"Don't worry, Doc. The only thing these guys are gonna hurt is that little rat-punk-bastard's feelings."

"All right, let's do it."

"Congratulations, Doc!" Pedro said, pumping my hand like a used-car salesman.

SEVEN

That night I prescribed myself a double dose of sleeping pills, which along with a covert shot of Gillington's should have put me down for the count. But every time I was about to drift off, yet another worst-case scenario would pop into my head, sending my supposedly sedated heart breaking from the starting gate like a doped-up whippet:

The kid does have a gun. Shots are exchanged. Mariela is killed in the cross-fire, blood everywhere.

The kid has no gun, but no brains, either. He spits defiantly in his assailants' faces. They overreact, beating him senseless and raping Mariela. Then they decide, what the hell, let's finish the job, no extra charge.

They have no intention of hurting him, but they forget to leave the safety on. The kid sneezes and the gun goes off, blowing his brains out. Now they can't leave any witnesses, so they kill Mariela, too. Then, thorough to a fault, they shoot Leonard, once, between the eyes, on their way out the door.

Everything goes wrong. It's a total bloodbath. Half the hotel is massacred: Mariela, Ricardo, Leonard, two tacky transvestites humping in the hall, a quartet of lesbians playing mahjong in the lobby. All dead, blown away, their bullet riddled bodies…

In the morning I was in no condition to drive myself to the train station, let alone wield a scalpel. I called the hospital. The bug is back, I told my secretary. Cancel everything. Five minutes later the administrator called. She wanted to know how I felt. She said she was concerned. Of course she was concerned, about the hospital cash-flow.

"It's that damned bug, Edna. I thought I had it licked."

"I wish you could have given us a little more notice," she said in her gravelly voice. "I hate to see those OR's sitting empty. And two of your patients are already here."

"I felt all right last night, Edna, but I woke up this morning with my head spinning. There's no way I can operate today."

"Of course not. Murray can do the meniscus. But the other one—that prima donna with the Knicks, the one with the tattoo on his forehead? You know how they are; it's Sanderson or nobody."

"He can keep," I assured her. "He's out for the season anyway."

"Out of his mind, too, if you ask me."

"Edna, you'll have to excuse me. I think I'm going to throw up again."

Waiting for Pedro's call was undiluted agony. I spent the entire day dozing fitfully in front of the television. Oddly enough, I'd never actually experienced daytime TV before. It was quite a shock: fifty million brain-dead Americans were watching this crap; no wonder we were falling behind the Chinese.

Janice was, to say the least, alarmed. "I know you are a doctor, dear," she said, eying me with concern from the foot of the bed, "but you know as well as I do that physicians are not supposed to treat themselves. It's a matter of objectivity."

"You're right, of course, dear. I just don't think my condition is that serious."

"But you've been a mess all week, a nervous wreck. I've never seen you so distracted. Is something wrong, dear? Something you haven't told me?"

Janice's question caught me off-guard. What should I say? There was no denying the precarious state of my nerves. Even a simpleton could see that I was badly preoccupied. And Janice was no fool. I had to invent a plausible explanation. But what? I'd already played the fear of cancer card. And since I'd been "fine" for three or four days now, I could not blame my altered mental state on the flu, which left me with…what?

"Janice," I said, inspired by what seemed like a good idea, "there is something bothering me. It has to do with my therapy."

"Your therapy?"

Now what?

"Yes, my therapy. The other day Dr. Rosenbaum and I had what they call a breakthrough."

"Isn't that good, dear?"

"Well, yes and no. You see, Dr. Rosenbaum really doesn't want me talking about this with outsiders yet. Not until we've achieved a…resolution."

"But I'm your wife," Janice pointed out, "not some stranger. Surely, you can discuss it with me."

"I don't know, dear," I said uncomfortably, "Dr. Rosenbaum…"

"But you must tell me. I can help."

Desperately, I scanned my brain for a potential neurosis, something dire which could explain my abrupt transformation into a mental case.

"Apparently, Janice," I said, stalling for time, "we've unearthed, Dr. Rosenbaum and I, something deep. Really, really deep. Something that's been buried in my unconscious for a long time."

But what? What's been buried? A bone? A treasure? A body? A three point basket?

"Go on, dear."

"It's, ah, not for certain, dear. Dr. Rosenbaum isn't certain. It's just a possibility."

Janice was sitting beside me on the bed now. She'd taken my hand in hers and was watching me carefully, the supportive wife at her loyal caring best. "Go on, dear, you can tell me."

"It's, ah, the doctor thinks, I might, ah, have, what they call… repressed homosexual tendencies."

Christ, I thought, did I really say that?

Janice was understandably confused. "What? That's absurd, dear. How long have we been married? Surely, if you were a…I would have noticed something."

"You know what they say, Janice, the wife is always the last to know. But," I added hastily, "it's not definitive. At this point, it's only a supposition."

"A supposition based on what? There must be some evidence, some reason to support such an outrageous idea."

"Yes, well," I mumbled, "there were several, ah, dreams. You know how these head...psychiatrists place so much emphasis on dreams."

"Of course. Charles has always maintained that dream analysis is the most potent weapon in the analyst's arsenal. What kind of dreams?"

The pompous plagiarizing prick! What textbook did he steal that one from? "Well, dear, it's actually one dream, what they call a recurring dream."

By limiting myself to only one dream I hoped to avoid any further strain on my overtaxed imagination, which was already crumbling like a slice of poorly baked cake.

"Recurring dreams," Janice proclaimed, "are supposed to be especially significant."

"Yes, well, so they say. In my dream I'm an Indian. And I'm wearing all this, ah, paint on my face."

"You mean, an Indian from India?"

"No, an American Indian. Like a Navaho."

"You mean, a Native American, dear."

Incredibly, with her husband's psychic walls collapsing all around her, Janice could not allow even one bit of political incorrectness to pass uncensured.

"Yes, a Native American, dear. And I'm involved in some kind of ceremony. There are totem poles everywhere. And the tops of the totem poles are...this is very difficult for me, Janice."

"I understand, dear. Please, go on. You know, come what may, you can always count on my full support. 'For better or for worse. In sickness as in health'. I've always taken that vow very seriously, Karl. You know that."

"Of course, dear."

Christ help me!

"Go on. The tops of the totem poles?"

"The tops of the totem poles," I floundered on, "are shaped like, like uncircumcised penises, and…they seem to be quivering."

"And the ceremony, dear?"

"The ceremony? Oh yes, the ceremony. There are several young men. Ah…naked. On their hands and knees. And when it comes time for my part in the ceremony, I undo my, ah, what do they call those things, my, ah…"

"Breechcloth?" Janice suggested.

"Yes, that's it, my breechcloth. And I stand over them, and I'm…erect, Janice. Shamefully erect!"

"And then?"

"And then? Ah…I wake up."

"That's it? That's the entire dream, dear?"

"Isn't it enough?"

"Well, I admit," she said, sounding exactly like her brother, "it is somewhat suggestive. But surely Dr. Rosenbaum can't be basing his entire diagnosis on that one dream. No qualified psychiatrist would rely on a single dream, no matter how evocative, to draw such a drastic conclusion. There must be more to it."

More? She wanted more?

"I'm afraid there is," I admitted with a tremor in my voice. Now that I'd gone this far I couldn't leave Janice thinking that Rosenbaum was incompetent. She might insist that I see someone else, someone referred by Charles.

"Well?"

"There was an incident," I said, with what I hoped was a convincing shudder.

"An incident, dear?"

"A patient of mine. Lance. A young bartender in the Village. He was quite friendly. A nice young man. Very cultured. On his last post-op visit he suggested we get together for lunch."

"And you agreed?" Janice was finally beginning (God help me!) to take this seriously.

"Yes, I don't know why. I never socialize with patients. But there was something appealing about him—I don't mean sexually. He was just an interesting person to talk to."

"All right," Janice said, really alarmed now. "What happened?"

"Nothing. Nothing happened. Nothing concrete," I said defensively. "We went out for lunch and he, how do they say it, came on to me."

"And what did you do?"

"I turned him down, of course."

"And that was the end of it?"

"Yes, except…"

"Except what?"

"I don't know how to say this, Janice, but when he propositioned me, I felt certain…sensations."

"Sensations?"

"Excuse me," I said, rushing for the bathroom, "I think I have to throw up again."

EIGHT

The phone finally rang at two in the morning. Wide awake, I snatched it up at once.

"Hello?"

"It's me," Pedro said."

"What do you want?" I demanded.

"What do I want? What the fuck are you—oh, I get it—the wife. You're in bed, right?"

"Do you have any idea what time it is?"

"Okay, Doc," Pedro sighed into the phone. "Bad news."

My pulse, already flying, went into orbit.

"They're gone," Pedro said.

"What do you mean?"

But I knew what he meant. Something had gone horribly wrong. They were dead, both of them. And it was my fault. At once, the guilt began, like acid, to etch...

"They moved out yesterday," Pedro said. "No forwarding address. They asked the old hippy at the desk. Nada. We're out of luck."

"Who is it?" Janice asked sleepily.

"Listen, Lance," I shouted into the phone, "I already told you, I'm not interested! Do not call me again!"

"Who the fuck is Lance?" Pedro asked.

"Yes," I said, "that's the way I want it. Good-bye!"

"Whatever," Pedro said.

"The bartender?" Janice asked.

"Afraid so. Poor fellow, says he can't get me out of his mind."

NINE

I shuddered awake late on the morning of Day Seven rigid with anxiety. Fortunately, Janice was already gone, to a benefit to save the world's smallest mammal, the Bumble Bee Bat. For once I approved. In my present state I could sympathize, even identify, with the blind little endangered bastard all too easily.

Pedro's timing was excellent. His call came just as I'd finished throwing up breakfast. An ulcer was definitely blooming in my duodenum. I could feel it. Taking a vertically integrated approach, I swallowed a Pepsid, a Valium and a Percocet, praying they all stayed down long enough to make their way into my blood stream.

"There's no time to lose," Pedro said with an air of command. "I called in sick. We have to meet. Plan the next step."

"The next step?"

The only next step I could imagine was off of a tall building.

"Right," Pedro said, "Plan B."

I chose Flushing for the meeting. "I know a good Cambodian place," I told the orderly, "just a block from the subway."

"Cambodian? Are you kidding me? They eat dogs in Cambodia. Man's best friends!"

"Somehow I don't think Dog will be on the menu, Pedro."

"How do you know? You read Cambodianese? I got news for you, Doc, they'll eat anything over there: dogs, cats, rats, bats, snakes…"

"All right, all right! How about Italian? There's a nice little pizza place, Gino's, two blocks from the station."

"That's more like it. I know Gino's. I used to do this broad just around the corner. Great tits on that bitch. Maybe I'll look her up after our meeting. Open two cocos with one machete."

"Can you be there in an hour?"

"Sure. I'll grab a couple of condoms—just in case—and I'm out the door."

Pedro was in an adventurous mood, opting for the veal scaloppini instead of his customary pizza, while I opted for a Seven-Up. It was the lunch hour and Gino's was packed. The sex-crazed orderly would talk of nothing but the "broad around the corner", until our food arrived.

"What about the new plan, Pedro?"

"Okay, Doc," he said, his mouth full of scaloppini. "Today's D-Day, right? The big deadline. Fork over the dough or else?"

"Yes."

"So, sometime today, you should be getting a phone call. Here's what you do. You listening?"

I was, in fact, at that precise instant having difficulty focusing all of my attention on Pedro's words. The veal, squishing around in his mouth as he spoke, was making me extremely nauseous. Though my stomach was empty of everything but acid, I nonetheless found it necessary to take slow deep breaths in order to maintain a semblance of alimentary equilibrium.

"Pedro," I said, "could you do me an enormous favor and not speak with your mouth full?"

"What, at a time like this," Pedro asked, his mouth jammed with scaloppini, "you're worried about table manners?"

I took two careful sips of my soda and said, "Pedro, you're making me nauseous."

"Well, excuse me! Okay, Doc, here's the deal. You get the phone call. Maybe it's today. Maybe it's tomorrow. You tell him you can't come up with two mill. The mortgage. The college tuition. The malpractice insurance. Blah, blah, blah. You tell him you got three hundred grand, and that's it. Take it or leave it."

"But I thought you said I shouldn't pay them anything. That it would never end, that they'd bleed me dry."

"That's right. And that's exactly what that little rat-bastard-punk is gonna think: I take the three-hundred now, and in a couple of months I hit him up for more."

"So now you want me to pay him?"

"No, you don't give the Cuban slimeball a goddamn cent!"

"Then…what are you saying?"

"What I'm saying is, no matter what he says, you stick to your story. You got the money right now sitting in a briefcase. He can take it, or he can go ream his mother. He's gonna take it, I guarantee you. Then, he's gonna name a place to make the exchange. Wherever it is, you agree."

Pedro resumed eating, washing down the veal with large swigs of beer. "There, is that better? First I talk, and then I eat. You okay with that?"

"But then what?"

Pedro made a great show of chewing and swallowing his food, and then dabbing his mouth with a napkin before replying. "Then you call me, give me the time and place, and I pass it on to our friends. You show up with the briefcase, our friends grab the cucaracha, and we go back to Plan A."

"You mean, they put the gun in his mouth and tell him to leave me alone?"

"*Exactamente.*"

"But what if he picks a public place?"

"We don't think he will. But if he does, they follow him home and take care of it later."

"What about the cash? It would take me weeks to get my hands on that much money."

Pedro looked skyward in mock despair. "Look, you go to the bank. You get a big wad of one-dollar bills, forty C-notes and some rubber bands. You make up some bundles, putting the C-notes on the outside and the ones on the inside. After our friends are done scaring the punk to death, they walk off with the briefcase. Your problems are over. Simple as that. Just make sure you count good. These guys don't like getting shorted."

"I don't know, Pedro, it seems like an awful lot could go wrong."

"Don't worry, Doc. This kid's an amateur and our guys are pros. And what do you got to lose, anyway? Five grand. Is that gonna kill you? It's worth a shot, Doc. Trust me."

Scare the punk to death. Kill you. Worth a shot. I wished Pedro had chosen his words differently.

"All right, Pedro. We'll give it a try. Like you say, at this point, what have I got to lose?"

"That's the ticket, Doc," Pedro beamed. "Nothing to lose!"

TEN

Upon our arrival in New York I'd given Mariela my home phone number, with instructions to call only in the event of a dire emergency. It had been a foolish thing to do, but I'd felt badly leaving her by herself in the middle of a vast city, in a strange country. She'll feel so lonely, I remember thinking.

After I'd finished my banking, as I was stashing the cash in my study, I noticed that the light on the answering machine was blinking. I hit the playback button. There'd been three calls, all of them hang-ups. No messages.

Suddenly, my stomach was crying out for sustenance. I went to the kitchen and fixed myself a slice of toast and a cup of chamomile tea. I wasn't hungry, exactly. It was more a gnawing feeling, as if in the absence of food my stomach was feeding on itself.

The slice of toast, cut from a loaf of multi-grain preservative-free bread, went down well enough, as did the tea. I decided to press my luck and try another slice, this one coated with Auntie Rachel's One Hundred Per Cent Natural Low Calorie Organic Strawberry Preserves. This too went down well, and I was about to gamble on a third slice when the phone rang.

"Dr. Sanderson?"

"Yes."

"I was worried about you," Ricardo said. "We called the hospital and they told us you were home sick. I hope you're feeling better. You have what we asked for?"

The remainder of the conversation went exactly as Pedro had predicted. With seeming reluctance, after much give and take, Ricardo agreed to accept only three hundred thousand dollars. He told me I was getting off cheap. Then he insisted that we meet that very night to make the exchange.

I said, "All right, let's get this over with."

"You know that dog statue by the zoo in Central Park?" he asked.

"Balto the Dog. Yes, I know it."

"Midnight. Come alone. And make sure it's all there."

"I'd rather meet someplace more public," I said slyly. "Central Park, at that hour? It's too dangerous. What if I get mugged?"

"That's your problem. Don't be late."

I couldn't believe my luck. The young fool had chosen the ideal time and place for an ambush! He must have been awfully sure of himself, or rather, of me—the rich law-abiding doctor—the perfect mark. From me, he obviously had nothing to fear. It was the law that worried Ricardo, the presence of a witness who could testify in court. It never occurred to him, apparently, that I might have a friend, who had a friend, who had a friend…ad nauseum.

I called Pedro and gave him the good news.

The orderly was elated. "Perfecto! Perfecto! Okay, Doc, you know what to do. Don't be nervous. In a few hours this will all seem like a bad dream."

"But that's what it feels like now, Pedro."

ELEVEN

When Janice came home late that afternoon, she found a refurbished man. I was eating, doing paperwork and generally making a great show of having "recovered from my crisis".

"You know, dear," I told my wife, "our little talk did me a world of good. I realized that you are absolutely right. Rosenbaum was way off-base. Although, to be fair," I added, so as not to put the shrink's abilities too much in doubt, "he did say that it was a very preliminary diagnosis."

"Preliminary and misguided. A wife knows."

"Yes."

Several hours later we were sitting in the kitchen snacking on sprouts when the phone rang. I picked it up with the hope that this call would represent the last farce, the last lie, the last time I would have to deceive my wife.

"Everything is set," Pedro said. "Now go ahead and say whatever crap you want. Just don't call me Lance."

"How bad? Yes, I am feeling better. But can't it wait until tomorrow...I see. All right, I'll be there as fast as I can."

"The hospital, dear?"

"Yes," I said with feigned exasperation. "An infected arthroplasty. His GP just admitted him to emergency. The idiot had a root canal and..."

"He didn't tell the dentist about his knee?" Janice helpfully finished my lie.

Had it been real, this would not have been the first such complication of my career. There was always the possibility of infection after a knee replacement, and once every year or two some absentminded individual would forget to take the necessary precautions, no matter how many times he or she had been warned beforehand of the potential risk.

"Apparently, it's pretty bad."

"Are you sure you're up to it, dear? Going to the hospital?"

"Yes, I'll be fine."

"There's no one else?"

"Janice, you know how it is. Malpractice."

The dreaded word worked like a Santeria charm. Janice nodded her head. "Just take it easy, dear. You still seem a little shaky."

"Don't worry. I'll just be doing some damage control. If there's to be a redo, it won't be tonight."

"When's the next train? They don't run very often at this hour. Should I get out the schedule?"

"No, I'll drive. There won't be much traffic, and I can't waste time waiting for the train."

"Drive safely, dear."

I parked the Volvo in an all-night garage on Fifty-Third Street, removed the briefcase from the trunk and began to walk. It was bitterly cold outside and before I reached the corner, I'd begun to shiver. Am I cold, I wondered, or just terrified? Probably, both.

I proceeded up Fifth Avenue walking as fast as I could, trying to get warm, stealing glances at my watch, forcing myself not to break into a trot. At my current pace I would be almost exactly on time.

At Sixty-Second Street I turned left into the park. On this late winter night Central Park, with its bare trees and deep shadows, had a bleak and sinister air. Not a soul was in sight. I felt, despite the "soundness" of Pedro's plan, a sharp sense of foreboding.

Wouldn't it, I thought, be the height of irony if I did indeed get mugged on my way to the rendezvous? But it was too cold out, even for muggers. Only renowned white surgeons, Puerto Rican blackmailers and hit-men of unknown ethnic origins would be braving the park on a night like this.

Ricardo was leaning against Balto the dog's giant bronze behind, striking a relaxed pose: the man with the upper-hand, confident, superior, in control. How confident, I wondered, will he look five minutes from now?

I walked straight up to the statue and handed him the briefcase. He opened it and looked inside. "Is it all here?" he demanded. "If it's not, you'll be sorry."

I smiled, nodded my head.

Ricardo looked putout. He'd expected some serious groveling along with the cash, a little dessert to go with the main course. "Well, Mr. Rich Famous Doctor," he smirked, "I hope you've learned your lesson. Next time you want to get your rocks off, pick on someone your own age, some old bag, like your wife."

When all I did was stand there and smile, he said, "Okay, get lost. Have a nice life."

People were always telling me that I looked like Clint Eastwood. In his movies, I recalled, Clint would never allow the villain to have the last word.

"You, too," I said, "what's left of it."

I'd not taken ten steps before the sounds of a scuffle reached my ears. I continued to walk, but craned my neck briefly around in time to see two burly figures dragging Ricardo off the path and into the bushes. The sight, like violence always did, disgusted me. I prayed that the friends did not accidentally kill him, or do him any serious bodily harm.

On the other hand, if in the course of putting the fear of Mr. Magnum into Ricardo, they happened to break a couple of teeth…well, like Brian Westin liked to say, "Win a few, lose a few."

TWELVE

Whether Plan B/Plan A had succeeded or not I had no way of knowing. That was the problem. I did receive, over breakfast in the hospital cafeteria, a promising report from Pedro.

"According to the boys, Doc, everything went great. It looks like you're in the clear."

"I'm glad everything went well, Pedro. But how in the world can they be sure that I'm 'in the clear'?"

"You're right, Doc," Pedro said philosophically, "nothing's for certain. I mean, you could've been certain, but you didn't want to go that way. What I'm saying is, there were *señales positivos*."

"Positive signs?"

"Yeah. For example, the little Cuban culero peed his pants. That shows…"

"I believe the ass-hole, as you call him, is Puerto Rican," I felt, for some perverse reason, compelled to point out.

"Are you sure? Well, whatever. Anyway, that shows what a coward he is. Also, he shit himself. I guess you could say they scared him shitless!" Pedro began to roar with laughter at his own miserable joke.

"I'm not sure," I said, when Pedro had gotten a grip on himself, "the pissing and such means all that much. Anyone, even tough customers like your friends, under the circumstances, might have…"

"Nah," Pedro said with conviction. "If he was tough, really tough, he would have maintained control of his bodily functions. Also, by the time they left him, he was crying like a little baby. He's definitely *puto* material, and I'm pretty sure you got nothing to worry about."

"Let's hope so. Pedro, I want to thank you for helping me out like this. You know, if there's anything I can ever do for you."

"Fuhgettaboutit, Doc." Pedro had learned a fair amount of his English from watching gangster films. "That's what friends are for. Oh, by the way, there are a few *detailles*."

"Like what?"

"Number one," Pedro said, counting off on his forefinger, "did you know that you put five hundred too much in the briefcase?"

"Yes. That was intentional. I meant it as, well, as a tip for a job well done."

"Okay, I'll pass it along. They were worried you made a mistake. These guys are scrupulous professionals, like I told you. Honest as the day is long. They wouldn't want to take advantage of a client, if he made a mistake or something."

Honest, scrupulous killers?

"That's very nice of them, Pedro. Was there something else?"

"Yeah," Pedro said, a pained expression on his face. "There is one other thing I'm afraid you might not like so much."

"What? What is it?" I asked, imagining some unspeakable atrocity.

"Well, as far as the gun in the orifice part is concerned?" Pedro said, lowering his voice.

"Yes?"

"The Cuban punk—say what you want, Doc, I still don't believe that wimp's a Puerto Rican—the punk, he was doing a lot of wiggling around, and the guys accidentally knocked out a couple of his teeth. Front ones. On top. I'm sorry, Doc. I know how you feel about that kind of thing. But it couldn't be helped. If you want that extra money back?"

"That's it? That was the total damage?"

"That's it, Doc."

"Well, that's all right," I smiled, giddy with relief. "I understand completely. Accidents will happen. In a perfect world, and all that kind of thing. Thanks again, Pedro. And don't forget to tell your friends about the tip."

THIRTEEN

The Giants were going, just as everyone (with the exception of their opponents' mothers) had predicted, to the Super Bowl. There, in some Super-Duper Dome, they would face their only serious obstacle to achieving the first-ever undefeated nineteen-game season, namely, the champions of the other half of the Association, a bunch of defensive brutes from Florida, a gang of mean, joint-crunching savages misappropriately named after the world's nicest mammal. It was being billed, I believe, as the "All-time Greatest Offense vs. the All-time Greatest Defense". Or they might have been calling it, "Civil War II".

As I've said, I wasn't enormously interested.

Two weeks had passed since the night in the park, and not even a low growl had been heard from the blackmailers. I found it hard to believe I'd gotten off so cheaply, that for only a five-thousand dollar fee (plus a miserly ten per cent tip) I'd escaped forever from the clutches of my treacherous lover and her larcenous fiancée.

Forever—that was the inoperative word, the fly in my stay of execution. I was relieved, but only up to a point. I should have been happy, but I was, in fact, intensely depressed. Denial. Anger. Depression. I was right on schedule. Acceptance? Who knew if or when that would come?

Sitting in my comfy study on a snowy Saturday, I went over in my mind for the hundredth time all the reasons I should, at this juncture in the proceedings, be feeling "safe".

Ricardo, after his midnight mauling in Central Park, would be convinced that, for him, I was never going to be a viable source of income. He should also have excellent reason to believe that any type of purely vindictive action taken against me could well result in his personal demise. In other words, by exposing my affair with Mariela he had nothing to gain and everything to lose. His wisest course of action would be to chalk the whole thing up to experience, get himself a bridge and move on to the next scam.

If he'd had some suicidal, overwhelming and visceral need for revenge, surely he would have acted on it by now, while the wound was still fresh. But Ricardo, it seemed to me, was mainly the practical type; he would go wherever his self-interest pointed him. And right now his self-interest should be taking him at a fair trot as far away from me as he could get.

And so, I should be, and probably was, out of the woods. Janice would never be made to suffer the pain and humiliation, nor I the shame and guilt, the disclosure of my affair with Mariela would have brought down upon us both. But I could never be totally certain, and that was the burden I would have to bear for…how long? Months? Years? The rest of my life?

Burt, after hearing the entire story, was of the opinion that I was the luckiest moron who'd ever lived, and that I should be turning cartwheels, not pining away over "some two-timing teenaged Cuban slut".

"You had a great run, Karl," he told me, "with a girl so hot I'd give my left testicle for just one night. Then you did something incredibly stupid, and you got away with it. Don't worry, be happy, you lucky bastard!"

"I guess I'm still in love with her, Burt."

"You'll get over it," the anesthesiologist assured me. "Life goes on. Until it doesn't. And then you're dead, at which point, who gives a shit?"

Janice knocked once and opened the door. "Dear, are you busy?"

Yes, I am. I'm busy sitting in my favorite chair and watching the snow fall outside my favorite window, as I brood over a nineteen-year-old whore.

"No, just relaxing. It's been a rough week. I've been thinking, maybe I should slow down a bit."

"Maybe you should," Janice agreed. "I know you're in tremendous demand, but you will be turning fifty soon."

"Yes, next month. We should go to *Au Claire's*."

"But that's my favorite restaurant. We should do something you want to do. A man only turns fifty once."

"Thank God. But I don't have a favorite restaurant."

"That's your problem," Janice said, "all work and no play."

"Hmmm."

"Darling, about tomorrow. Don't you think we should at least watch the game?"

For the past week Janice had been promoting the concept of a small Super Bowl party. Brenda was home for a three-day weekend, not that I'd caught more than a glimpse of her; apparently, she had a boyfriend. She and Candace, Janice pointed out, could each invite a friend. Then there was Burt and his wife. And a few of Janice's cohorts from SPEW, along with their spouses. "We could have barbecued tofu burgers," Janice enthused, "organic coleslaw, and all the typical Super Bowl trimmings. I think it would be fun, dear."

I'd nixed the idea of course, explaining repeatedly that I found all the attention over my "relationship" with Brian to be personally embarrassing.

"Well," I said, "I don't see why the family can't sit down and watch the game together." Unlike me, Janice was truly enjoying our vicarious moment in the sun, and I felt that I owed her this small indulgence. I owed her, obviously, a great deal more. "But just the four of us."

"Oh, thank you, dear. I'll whip up the tofu and coleslaw in the morning. I wonder if they make organic barbecue sauce? Oh, there's my phone again. Someone else wishing us luck, no doubt. They've been calling all morning." Before rushing off, Janice felt compelled to emit a cheer, but it came out more like a question: "Go Giants?"

Yes, Burt, life went on.

The following afternoon found the five of us spread around the living room eating pseudo barbecue, watching

Super Bowl MCLXXXXXXX and otherwise impersonating, rather ineptly, an average American family.

Steven had joined us at the last minute, which was fine with me. I liked Steven, and he'd left his father at home, stewing no doubt over what everyone within his hearing was calling, "your brother-in-law's Super Bowl". I knew who Charles would be rooting for, and it was not the New York Giants. He'd be shocked if he knew that my sympathies, the few that I had, rested with their opponents as well. I still hadn't forgiven Brian for the magazine business, and would have enjoyed seeing him go down in defeat for a change.

Brenda, after a semester at Vassar, had become even more aloof, if that was possible. Apparently, in her first five months at college she'd mostly learned to act bored and superior. Hopefully, it was just a stage.

"Football is such a brutal, senseless game," she opined during the scoreless first quarter.

"It's s-s-s-s-s-stupid," Steven agreed.

"Some of the players have pretty cute butts," Candace pointed out.

"I think it's exciting," Janice said. "What about you, dear?"

"I'm with the kids on this one," I said, swallowing (with difficulty) a vulcanized chunk of charred tofu burger. Janice was not what one would call an avid barbecuer.

"Hey, Dad," Candace said, "maybe Brian will get his knee broken."

Strangely enough, I'd been thinking the same thing, not that I needed the work. It would, however, allow me to give him a good dressing down while I had him at my mercy.

"Candace, how can you say such a thing!" Janice chided her daughter. "Oh, oh, was that a touchdown?"

"Y-y-y-yes!" Steven, being a boy (albeit an odd one) naturally knew more about football than the rest of us. "G-g-g-giants s-s-six, D-d-d-d…"

By the time my poor nephew could finish his sentence, the Giant kicker had already scored the extra point.

"Seven to zero, our favor!" Janice made another brave attempt at cheering.

Brenda yawned. Steven belched. Candace, who'd confessed to me the previous week that she was beginning to think she was probably bi-sexual, remarked off-handedly that if the cheerleaders showed any more cleavage, they'd have to give the game a "PG" rating.

At one point in the low-scoring contest the Dolphins actually took a six-point lead, maintaining it well into the fourth quarter. Janice was aghast. "Darling," she said, "do you think we might actually lose?"

"It's possible, dear."

But Brian, with the game on the line, marched his team down the field for the winning score with only seconds remaining. And that was that.

"Rah! Rah!" Janice said.

Candace and Steven rushed upstairs to smoke a little Mindwipe and play their weird music. They were in the process, they said, of forming a band. Brenda, borrowing my Volvo, went off to see her boyfriend, an anemic World Lit. major at Colombia.

Janice and I were left by ourselves, staring at the blank TV screen.

"We should celebrate, dear," Janice declared. "Don't you think?"

"All right." There was something truly pathetic about my wife's attempts to "enjoy" life, as if she were reading from a script she did not quite understand. Suddenly, I felt terribly sorry—for the both of us. "What's on in the City?"

"There's a modern ballet at Lincoln Center," Janice suggested. "*Autumn Anger*, I think it's called. I read in the *Times* that it was going to be poorly attended, due to the Super Bowl. If we hurry, we could get there by intermission."

I loathed modern ballet. "Wonderful. Let's do it. After, we could go to Au Claire's."

"That would be marvelous, dear. But do you think we could get in on such short notice? To Au Claire's, I mean."

"Janice, do you think on this night of all nights, they would turn away the wife of the man who saved Brian Westin's career—twice?"

"Oh, darling, I'll call them right away!" And off she flew.

Yes, I thought, as I sat alone in the living room staring at the blank TV screen, life does indeed go on.

FOURTEEN

The Monday following the Stupid Bowl extravaganza was a normal working day, except that I was mobbed everywhere I went, as if it had been me who'd pulled off the last-minute heroics, and not our modern day Sir Lancelot, the man The Post was calling, "Sergeant New York".

Everyone was convinced that the quarterback and I had some kind of special father-son type relationship. I attempted to refute this scurrilous charge, but no one, thanks to the SI cover story, would take my denials seriously. Hadn't Brian officially elevated me right up there beside the Lord Almighty? According to Brian, was it not God Himself who had created the Perfect Quarterback, and Dr. Karl Sanderson who had, paradoxically, repaired him?

The unending round of congratulations, brownnosing and backslapping reached its crescendo just as I was getting ready to go home. Alone in my office, stuffing this and that into my briefcase, I was cornered by Dulce Mendez, who'd been stalking me all day.

"I'm so happy for you!" she trilled, launching herself at me like a surface-to-surface missile. As she wrapped her smooth slender arms around me in a tight suggestive hug, I was left, from a practical standpoint, with only two alternatives: make a pretense of hugging her back, or reject her embrace outright, letting her hang there until she got tired and let go. The latter choice seemed a little cruel. She was a sweet kid, and a quick hug, I felt, could do no harm. Or perhaps my feelings were more complex than that. I was badly in need of some female solace. And I'd always found Dulce dangerously desirable.

Her extreme proximity (like wallpaper on a wall) quickly produced in me an enthusiastic erection, which she was quick to note. A groan escaped her throat, as she pressed against me, gently gyrating her hips. My hands, taking orders directly from General Groin, slid down to her rounded bottom.

"Oh, Karl!" she moaned, tilting her head back for a kiss.

I wanted at that moment with every molecule of my blackguardly being to tear her clothes off and have at it right there on my desk! But something, God knows what, held me back. Maybe it was simply too trite, assuaging my bruised ego with this all-too-easy office conquest. Or, having just escaped one abyss, perhaps I was reluctant to plunge, penis-first, into another.

Whatever the reason, instead of kissing her, I drew back, gently but firmly removing her to a safe distance.

"Dulce," I said, breathing with difficulty, "I can't tell you how much I would like to make love to you. And I can't put into words the reasons that I cannot. Maybe someday we can…but not now."

I gave her a quick not altogether fraternal peck on the lips, grabbed my briefcase, which I was forced to hold at an awkward angle so as to cover the bulge in my pants, and ran for my life.

On the train ride home I could not stop thinking about Dulce. That was a close one, I told myself. For a minute there, it had nearly been out of the frying pan, into the double boiler. Mentally, I gave myself a small pat on the back. I'd shown admirable restraint, hadn't I? Maybe I would come away from all this with something positive after all. Perhaps I've learned something, matured, in a manner of speaking. But it had been a near thing with Dulce—especially when I'd had my hands on her ass.

My erection, right there on the Long Island Railroad, was coming back faster than a speeding bullet, along with the memory of Dulce's angelic upturned face, her silky young skin, her…no, Sanderson! Hold it right there! You are a happily married man. Happily? Well, happy is a relative term. Who's to say what happiness is. I had my home, which I loved, and my daughters, who I adored, though every father has his favorite. And my wife, who I also loved, just not in the way I'd loved Mariela, or could potentially love someone like Dulce Mendez. That ass! Did any woman on the entire island of Manhattan (with the exception of her sister) have a softer, tighter, rounder, more Divinely inspired bottom?

Quickly, I grabbed my briefcase off the floor and put it in my lap before anyone noted the miniature anaconda attempting to levitate itself up and out of my pants. I had ten minutes before the train arrived at the station, ten minutes to rid myself of this beast. I searched for a mental image which would take my mind off Dulce and the entire idea of sex. There, I had it! Closing my eyes, I visualized a charred tofu-burger. I took a bite, and as it broke up into small, black rubbery chunklets, my hyper-swollen *membrum virile* shrank and shriveled until it all but disappeared.

FIFTEEN

Still struggling not to think about my brief but disturbing encounter with Dulce, I opened the door of my home-sweet-home, stepped inside and removed my coat. Although it was still bitterly cold outside, the house felt far too warm. I'd have to remind Candace once again to keep her hands off the thermostat. She was, at least in this one respect, a typical teenager: too lazy to put on a sweater, she'd rather burn through entire tankers of heating oil.

And then there she was, as if I'd materialized her with my thoughts, standing in the doorway to the living room. Distracted though I was, I noticed at once that Candace was upset. It was not easy to upset my unflappable daughter, and I wondered what had happened.

"Hi, sweetie," I said, "is something wrong?"

"You could say that, Dad." For a long moment she stood there regarding me forlornly, as if I were an old family pet in failing health about to be put down.

"You bastard! You monster! You...son-of-a-bitch!"

Janice had appeared in the opposite doorway, the one which gave on to the dining room. "Upset" did not even begin to describe her demeanor, which more resembled that of someone condemned, unfairly and without warning, to the fiery pits of Hell: a soul in torment, howling in anguish, waving in the sulfurous air a copy of the *National Enquirer*.

My heart fell through the walnut floor, the finished basement and the Earth's crust, embedding itself finally in the burning magma at the planet's core: Incredibly, for the second time in eight weeks, I'd made the cover of a magazine!

As she continued to shriek in pain, Janice flung the tabloid in my general direction. Largely intact, it hit me square in the face and fell to the floor. I picked it up and took a good look at the half-page photo of the mismatched lovers wrapped in each other's arms sitting inside the absurd spherical taxi. They'd done, unfortunately, a marvelous job of enlarging and transferring the photograph to newsprint. My face was sharp, clear and easily identifiable. Mariela, all aglow in her little uniform, looked as if she'd just graduated Underage Hooker School.

There were also some rather large words on the front page, among them, "FAMOUS SURGEON", "CHILD PROSTITUTE" and "CUBA", but that was about all I was able to take in before a hand, my wife's, slapped the side of my face with a loud resounding thwack.

"How," she screamed, "could you do this to me?"

For a moment, I thought of denying everything. In fact, the words "doctored photo" were on the tip of my tongue when Janice screeched the following: "A fishing trip? The Westchester Hotel? You liar! You bastard!"

Apparently, the cat was all the way out of the bag, and denial was no longer a viable option. Numb with shame, my eyes glued to the floor, I stood there, waiting. Janice slapped me again. And again, even harder. I did not attempt to defend myself. I wished she would hit me with something heavier and harder than her hand, something which would make me bleed.

Then she turned and fled to her sewing room, in which she never sewed, and slammed the door. From thirty feet away and through the dense wood, I could hear with perfect clarity the sound of her heart wrenching sobs.

"Oh, Dad," Candace moaned, fleeing upstairs to her room.

For a long time I stood in the hallway, paralyzed, staring off into space. Knowing there was nothing I could say or do, I still felt compelled to try, to say or do something. Like a condemned killer, I shuffled to the door of the sewing room, where I found Brenda standing guard, rigid and implacable, a slender block of blond ice.

"I'd like to try to talk to her…" I began.

"You leave her alone," Brenda commanded me, her voice oozing contempt. "You've humiliated us in front of the whole world. I can never go back to school. I couldn't face my friends. My life is over."

"Brenda, your life is not…"

"You sick, pathetic monster," my daughter, my flesh and blood, declared.

"I'd like to try to talk to my wife."

"Stay away from her. She's not your wife. Not anymore. And I'm not your daughter."

From behind the door, Janice sobbed and sobbed.

Arguing with Brenda was pointless. "Janice," I called out, "I'm sorry. Please, open…"

"Get out!" Janice shrieked. "Get out of my house!"

Her house. Legally, it was still my house, too, at least for the time being. But morally, I had not a leg to stand on. So I did what I was told. I packed a small bag and left.

SIXTEEN

I did not get very far. It was only by some miracle that I did not run someone down, or career into another vehicle. Pulling over on a quiet street, I turned on the overhead light and picked up the newspaper. The story ran two pages and was, for that absurd tabloid with its tales of alien abductions and polychephalitic sheep, unusually detailed and accurate—except for Mariela's age, which "sources" estimated to be "between thirteen and fourteen-years-old".

Dates, names and places (Mariela had an excellent memory) littered the article, conferring upon it a frightful credibility. Even the surgery I'd "illegally" performed on Eustacia's knee was mentioned. Everything I'd done in Cuba, the article averred, had been illegal, since my very presence there ran contrary to US law.

The last two paragraphs were the worst of all, discussing at some length my alleged "relations with a number of other Havana prostitutes", "many" of them also of "questionable age".

I damned Mariela. I damned Ricardo. And most of all I damned myself.

I began to weep, but not with self-pity—that was almost a sweet feeling compared to the sulfuric acid of self-loathing eating at me now. On the night of Mariela's betrayal I had toyed with the idea of taking my own life, like a boy playing with plastic soldiers. Now, sitting behind the wheel of the Volvo, bouncing about the walls of this jagged abyss, contemplating suicide felt, not like a game, but more and more like the inescapable conclusion to a life gone hopelessly wrong.

My prescription pad: where, I wondered, had I left it last? More than likely it was locked in the desk in my office. I could drive there now and…

Someone was tapping on the window. A policeman. The same one, it turned out, who had come upon me in similar circumstances the day I'd made my arrangement with Irving and Burt.

Life has a way of spinning us around in unlikely circles. I'd parked, apparently, on the same street, on very nearly the same spot as before. Rosenbaum would have called it an unconscious cry for help, or a sign that I wanted to have sex with my grandmother.

I rolled down the window and the polite, friendly young policeman, observing my distraught state, said with concern, "Sir, are you all right?"

Unable to control my weeping, I nodded my head.

"Sir," he said, "aren't you the person, I, uh, spoke to several months ago? On this same street?"

My eyes were too blurred with tears to recognize anyone. I shrugged my shoulders and continued to cry.

"Sir, can you tell me what's wrong?" he asked.

"So much…so much…is wrong."

"Have you been drinking, sir?" he asked, not unkindly.

He was a nice enough young man, but like most policemen, somewhat lacking in imagination.

I shook my head. Then I did something foolish. I handed him the newspaper. He flashed his light on the front page, examined it for a minute, then put the light on me.

"Is this you?"

I nodded my head.

"Please step out of the car," he said, his tone no longer polite.

Still blubbering away, I was submitted to a breathalyzer test and made to walk back and forth in a straight line. After proving my "sobriety", I sat down on the curb and continued to cry.

"Are you on drugs?" the policeman demanded. When I shook my head, he ordered me in a disgusted voice to get back in the car.

"She—she's really nineteen," I said, just managing to choke out the words.

The policeman scowled. "Sure she is. Don't go anywhere. I'll be right back…sir."

He stalked over to his vehicle to see, I imagine, if there were any outstanding warrants for my arrest. When he returned a few minutes later, he let me go, with a warning: "I'd give this area a wide berth, if I were you. Here in Manhasset Estates we don't take kindly to perverts."

Eventually, I'm not certain how, I found myself parked in an all-night lot around the corner from the Westchester. Once again I was circling back to familiar places, like a guilt-ridden homing pigeon.

Leonard was more than a little surprised to see me. He'd been reading (re-reading, actually) the offending article in the offensive tabloid when I walked in the door. Dropping it like an over-heated bong, he said, "Dr. Sanderson?"

"Yes, it's me, Leonard. I think I need a room. Three-Twenty-Two. And a short length of rope."

Leonard was just about to end his shift. His replacement, an exceedingly pale young man, showed up as I was filling out the check-in card.

"You sure you want that room?" Leonard asked, eying me fearfully.

I nodded my head.

"Take over, Bobby," Leonard told the unhealthy looking youth. "I'll escort Dr. Sanderson to his room." Leonard picked up my suitcase.

"That's not necessary, Leonard."

"No problem, man."

Being back inside Mariela's old room was gratifyingly painful. I shot a fleeting glance at the small Victorian chandelier, wondering if it would support my weight. Leonard put my suitcase down, but made no move to leave.

"Are you all right?" he asked.

"Yes, thank you, Leonard, I'm fine." I attempted to hand him some money, but he waved me off.

"When you asked about the rope…" he began, looking pointedly up at the ceiling fixture.

"Just a sick little joke. Please forget it."

"You didn't sound like you were joking, man."

I sat down heavily on the bed and stared blankly at the floor.

"Can I get you something?" Leonard asked.

"No, I'd…I'd just like to be alone."

"Is that a good idea, Dr. Sanderson? Under the circumstances?"

"I don't know, Leonard. I haven't had a good idea for quite some time."

"Promise me you won't do anything stupid."

"Don't worry. I haven't got the guts to kill myself."

"I'm not so sure. You had the guts to, like, get on that cigarette boat. You know, you're getting a real raw deal, if you ask me, man. That stuff about her being underage and…"

"Goodnight, Leonard."

Finally, reluctantly, with one last worried glance at the chandelier, Leonard left the room.

That night was easily the worst of my life. I could have drunk myself into oblivion, but I didn't want to dull my senses. I wanted to suffer, as I'd made Janice suffer, as she was suffering at this very minute. I stayed awake all night, seeing her face, deformed with pain, hearing her sobs.

How, I tore at myself over and over, could I have been so foolish, so cruel? The one thing I had wanted to avoid at any cost, hurting my wife, I had made all but inevitable with my insanely stupid behavior. There were no mitigating circumstances I could plead before my inner judge. I'd created this debacle with my own two hands. I might as well have picked up a paring knife and buried it in her chest.

Why hadn't I left Mariela in Cuba? I could have assuaged my guilt by sending her money, providing her with a decent life. I could have satisfied my lustful cravings with the occasional visit. Instead, I had brought her to New York. To within twenty miles of my home! What in God's name had I been thinking?

I thought about Mariela and her betrayal. It was nothing, I realized, compared to my own betrayal of Janice. Mariela was a very young and impoverished woman being kept by an older man. She was not my wife of twenty-five years, the person with whom I had spent the better part of my adult life, the woman who had sacrificed her own hopes of a career to put me through medical school. The mother of my children.

And on and on I went until, like Saint Sebastian, I was bleeding from a hundred wounds.

Around three am the telephone rang. In all the time I'd spent in this room the phone had never rung before. It had to be a wrong number, some strung-out junkie trying to reach his connection. I picked up anyway, grateful for the distraction.

"Is this Dr. Sanderson?" a nasal voice inquired.

"Yes?"

"My name is Howie, Dr. Sanderson, and I'm with the Suicide Prevention Hotline?"

I held the phone out in front of my face and stared at it for a moment. This was beyond surreal. I had to be dreaming. "Hotline?" I repeated numbly.

"That's right," Howie said brightly, "with the emphasis on prevention. Ha, ha. I guess this must seem a little odd to you."

"Odd?"

"Yes. Usually, we wait for people to call us. Ha, ha." When I failed to respond, Howie said, "I mean, that's what a hotline is for, receiving calls from people in need? But Leonard gave me your room number and suggested I initiate contact. Believe it or not, we get calls from the Westchester all the time. They've even had four or five actual suicides—no one I talked to, thank God. That's how I know Leonard. But it still feels kind of strange—me calling you, I mean."

I stood there for some time, holding the phone to my ear, staring at the chandelier.

"So," Howie said finally, "how's it going? Dr. Sanderson?"

SEVENTEEN

For the next four hours I sat crumpled on the floor (the bed was too good for me) practicing the fine art of self-laceration. First I imagined Mariela emitting syncopated moans of pleasure in time to the young athletic pelvic thrusts of her delinquent boyfriend. Then, when that image began to lose its edge, I turned to thoughts of my shredded reputation and the damage, perhaps irrevocable, I had done to my career. From there it was just a short jagged hop to Janice. Janice sobbing, her face contorted with pain. Janice shrieking, her world destroyed. Janice crushed by the weight of her humiliation. Janice…

Around eight o'clock Leonard, like a graying raven, came knocking at my hotel door.

"Dr. Sanderson, it's Leonard. Are you all right, man? You need anything?"

"Yes, Leonard. I could use a bottle of rum."

"How about some food?"

"No food."

With a heroic effort I spent the following twenty-three hours, first in a drunken stupor, and then passed out entirely. Though the contents of this lost day largely failed to imprint themselves upon my memory, I do recall staring wistfully at the chandelier for long periods of time, cursing myself out loud and wishing I had the courage to wrap something long and pliable around my neck, thereby sparing everyone the nuisance of dealing with the afterbirth of the disaster I had so expertly spawned.

Just before going out for the count, I received another call from Howie.

"Good evening, Dr. Sanderson," he said with nasal exuberance, "this is Howie. From the Suicide Prevention Hotline? How are we holding up today?"

"Howie, please," I moaned into the phone, "go fuck yourself."

"Good, Dr. Sanderson," Howie said with approval, "you're getting the anger out. Holding in one's anger is often counter-productive and can lead to…"

Amazingly, the phone, upon impacting the bathroom door, remained almost entirely intact.

The next morning I was dragged from my alcohol induced coma by the ex-bass player from Mark and the Mandalas.

"Dr Sanderson? It's Leonard. Are you still, like, alive in there?"

I opened the door and Leonard walked in carrying, with difficultly, a thermos of coffee, two mugs, a newspaper, a box of doughnuts and a purple bong.

"You made the Post, man," he announced, setting his load atop the bureau.

"The Post?"

"Yeah, page two. They ought to shoot those pigs. Get any sleep?"

"More or less."

Leonard handed me a jelly doughnut and a cup of coffee. "Chow down. You need to maintain your stamina." Dutifully, I bit off a chunk of doughnut and washed it down with some coffee. "Howie call again?" Leonard asked.

"Yes. He sounded like he had a cold."

"No man, that's his normal voice. Howie's kind of a nerd, but he does good work."

"He does?"

"Yeah, well, you didn't kill yourself, did you? That makes you, like, you know, living proof. Want another doughnut?"

"Sure, why not?"

"I've got some pretty good bud, here, but I thought you should get some nourishment first."

"Thank you, Leonard, you're… an excellent dude."

We sat there for a while eating our doughnuts and drinking our coffee, the suicidal surgeon and the aging hippy with a heart of gold. The man really cares about me, I thought, and all at once my eyes filled with tears—I was, as the saying goes, skating on thin ice.

"Dr. Sanderson, get a grip, man," Leonard advised me. "I go on duty in an hour and we've got work to do. While you were out of commission, some nasty shit's been going down. I'm telling you, man, you don't get on top of this pronto, you're gonna be, like, royally fucked."

"I'm gonna be? What am I now?"

"Listen to me, man," Leonard said, holding my glassy gaze. "I've been running this place for twenty years. We've had Joplin, Morrison, Sid Vicious, Ultra Violet, Keith Moon. Twenty-two guests have expired prematurely right here at the Westchester on my personal watch. Not all of those big names I just mentioned, but some pretty righteous dudes. Five suicides, fifteen OD's and two heart attacks. What I'm getting at, Dr. Sanderson, is, there are, like, degrees of being fucked."

"Degrees of being fucked, Leonard?"

"Degrees of being fucked. You better believe it, man. I know you're hurting. I know you're down. But you have to, like, start fighting back, man, and the sooner the better."

"Fighting back? Against who? Against what?"

"Whoever it is who's out to get you. This fucking source, man…" Leonard picked up the Post and began to read out loud, "'A source close to the family…'"

"Leonard, spare me, please. My head's about to explode as it is."

"Okay, man. You can read it later. But there's something else." Leonard paused for dramatic effect. "I've been *contacted.*"

Contacted? By whom? Aliens from outer space? Just what I needed in my hour of despair, a UFO nut! To disguise my dismay I urged down half a French cruller and the remainder of my coffee.

"*The Times, the Post, Sports Illustrated,* a couple of those tabloid TV shows, even *People Magazine*—they've all been calling me," Leonard declared, clarifying (thank God!) the contacted issue.

"At first," he went on, "I told them all to go to hell. But then I realized something. Everybody thinks your girl—your ex-girlfriend is like, thirteen-years-old, man, which practically makes you a child molester. But I know otherwise, and I've got the proof, man. I've got the fucking proof!"

"The proof," I mumbled.

"Okay, man," Leonard said, "I can see you're dazed and confused, you know, like the song. Led Zeppelin? We had them here, too. And they were into some weird shit, man, let me tell you. Whips, chains, aerosol cans, the whole nine fucking yards. And the groupies? Those were some serious sluts. But right now we need to get on top of this thing, man, like, ASAP. Are you listening to me, Dr. Sanderson?"

Aerosol cans? "I'm listening, Leonard."

"Remember," he resumed. "when you first checked her in? I asked for ID, and she gave me that Cuban Identity card."

"Yes, Leonard, I remember."

"Well, guess what? I made a photocopy—hotel policy—and I still have it. That's the proof! That she's not underage!"

"Oh, I see."

But what difference does it make, I wondered. Will Janice feel any better knowing that I was not, technically speaking, a child molester, that I had in fact been screwing a nineteen-year-old who just happened to look like she was passing through puberty?

"These reporters who've been calling me, Dr. Sanderson? I think I should give them copies of her ID. But I wanted to ask your permission first. The owner says I should do it—to, you know, like, defend the honor of the hotel? But I wanted to get the green light from you first."

"Sure, Leonard, go ahead. If it'll please your boss."

Leonard shook his ponytail with disappointment. "You don't even care, do you, man? You don't care what happens to you."

"No, not really."

"Do you have a lawyer?"

"A lawyer? Yes, I suppose, ah, Irving. Irving Waxman. He's a lawyer."

"What's his number?" Leonard demanded, picking up the phone.

"Irving," I sighed, "is going to kill me."

"What are you talking about? Your lawyer's job is to defend you, not attack you. What's his number, man?"

"Okay, Leonard, we'll call Irving. But first, let's fire up that bong."

EIGHTEEN

My chunky attorney and close-friend Irving Waxman sat behind his improbably cluttered desk, one bushy brow raised in disbelief, the other rumpled with disapproval—a trick he'd developed over the years to disconcert hostile witnesses.

I sat before him, slouched so low in the client's chair only my head poked above the choppy oceanic surface of his desk. The coffee, the doughnuts and the several hits of bud I'd inhaled had helped to revive my shriveled spirits, but not much.

"Do you feel," Irving began, with what I thought was a certain lack of tact, "like a loser?"

"Irving…"

"Because, from where I'm sitting, that is exactly what you look like. A total loser. I've seen winos passed out on the street who made a better impression. Tell me, Karl, did you sleep in those clothes? Or has your dry cleaner come down with Parkinson's?"

Irving was referring to the impressively wrinkled suit I'd put on, at Leonard's insistence. "I left the house in kind of a hurry, Irving. And since then…"

"How did this happen?" Irving intoned. "How did a brilliant physician, a decent man, a respected citizen, sink so low so fast?"

Irving did not expect an answer and I did not give him one. My head hurt. My heart hurt. My conscience hurt. I was, as I slouched lower and lower in the leather chair, one big bean bag of pain. "Thanks, Irving," I mumbled, "for the moral support."

"Moral support? Moral support? Karl, I'm no hypocrite. I do not pretend to be a saint. I have, as you know, wandered from the herd from time to time myself. But always in an ethically discrete and responsible manner. But this, this calamity you have brought down upon yourself and your loved ones. This galactic shithole into which you have dug yourself. This humiliation and pain you have dumped upon your family. This is beyond the pale, Karl. And as Janice and the girls twist slowly in the wind, you sit here in my office, comfortably drunk from what I can see, and ask me for moral…"

"I'm not drunk, Irving, and I'm not all that comfortable, either," I groaned. And then, to my acute embarrassment, I began to cry. I stood up. "Good-bye, Irving."

"Good-bye, Irving? You poor miserable schmuck," he said, taking a somewhat softer tone. "Sit down. We have work to do. Unless you would rather just kill yourself, in which case why waste my valuable…"

Something, the bleak look in my eyes, perhaps, stopped Irving cold in mid-rant. His gruff demeanor gave way to something resembling fear. "Sit down, Karl. Please?"

I sat down.

"All right," he said, eying me warily, "let's play lawyer. First, there is the divorce. Unless Janice has a sudden change of heart, it is going to be ugly, brutal. A real demolition derby. No point kidding ourselves."

"Wait a minute. How do you know she…"

"They've already filed."

"What? So fast? It's only…"

"Karl, just let me talk for a minute. Okay? I received a call first thing this morning from her attorney, Herman Bormann, the Hannibal the Cannibal of divorce lawyers. A total vampire. 'Amicable' is not a word he even understands. You hire Herman Bormann, not to divorce your spouse, but to dismember, to eviscerate, to bleed the victim dry. Are you getting the picture?"

"I can't believe Janice would hire such a person. It's not like her, no matter how angry she is."

"She didn't hire him, Karl. Your brother-in-law, the sleazy shrink—he hired Bormann. From what I understand, Janice is officially hors de combat, under sedation, out of the picture—leaving brother Charles to personally take charge of the carnage. And Charles has set his sights high, or low, depending on your point of view. Crucifixion or bust. Did you see the Post?"

"I saw the headline. I didn't have the—I haven't actually read it yet."

"They quote a source, a 'close to the family' source. It has to be Charles. Scruples? We already know he was born without them. And he has a pathological hatred of you. You told me so yourself. It has to be him."

"It's him," I agreed.

"A pathological shrink. Just what the world needs. The article is a total hatchet job. The unnamed close-to-the-family source strongly implies that you have a history of child molestation! The lying son-of-a-bitch! This is very bad, Karl. Everyone is assuming the girl is underage, and she's disappeared, so we have no way of proving otherwise. There is a lot of other crap we have to deal with, but as of now, that is the tip of the dagger. That...what?"

I'd raised my hand, like a pupil asking permission to speak. From out of my wrinkled jacket pocket, I pulled a copy of Mariela's ID card and handed it across the desk to Irving. Leonard had run off a dozen copies and given one to me. "I have proof," I said without enthusiasm.

Snatching it from my hand, Irving looked it over and grunted with approval. "This is good," he said. "This is very good, as long as it is genuine."

"It was good enough for the *INS*."

"It's on-record, then, official. Excellent! That takes one thorn out of your crown." Irving picked up the phone. "Debbie, call that guy at the Times. Tell him we are prepared to make a statement... yeah, just tell him to call me." Irving replaced the receiver. "That is a big one. A touchdown, plus two extra points."

"Rah, rah."

"Don't be a schlemiel, Karl. This is of vital importance. Now you can present yourself to the courts as a run-of-the-mill lying cheating husband; instead of a lying cheating child-molesting pervert. It may not help you hold on to a lot of assets, but it should keep you out of jail."

"Jail? For adultery?"

Irving laughed. "Jail, for adultery? Hardly. No, I am talking about a bona fide felony: Human Smuggling. A federal offense."

"Human Smuggling? But, but…"

"Take it easy, Karl. It would be tough to make it stick. Human Smuggling is defined as an illegal enterprise, and in your case there is no monetary payoff. Unless you want to count free-sex. On the other hand, if the US Attorney was really out for your blood, he might decide to give it a shot. I don't know, I'm no expert. I'll have to ask another attorney, just in case. I can handle the divorce, not that there is much to handle. We haven't got a testicle to stand on."

"But I didn't smuggle her into the country, Irving. I…"

"No? What would you call it? Like I said, it may or may not be a problem. Let us go on to the next thing."

"The next thing?"

"In these cases, Karl, there is always a next thing. For example, the small matter of keeping your license to practice medicine in the State of New York. I cannot deal with that, either. So that is another attorney you'll need."

"Jesus," I moaned, "I've really dug myself a nice hole, haven't I?"

"That is what I have been trying to tell you, Karl. But look on the bright side. Now that we can prove she is not under-age, they cannot go after you for Crossing State Lines for the Purposes of Corrupting a Minor. For that type of charge you would definitely need a specialized criminal attorney, which would make three blood-suckers all together. Present company included."

Good old Irving. He never lost his sense of humor—no matter how dire the circumstances his clients happened to find themselves in.

Before allowing me to flee his reassuring presence, Irving insisted, even though I wasn't hungry, on taking me out and force-feeding me lunch. He was, he said, concerned about my health.

"Mental or physical?" I asked.

"Both."

Over pastrami sandwiches at a nearby deli, where Irving was on a first name basis with the entire staff, my attorney asked for the address and phone number of my hotel.

"The Westchester? Isn't that where you put up the girl, where you had your romantic trysts?"

"Yes."

"Wait, let me guess. You're staying in her old room. Am I right?" Sheepishly, I nodded my head. "You really are a sponge for punishment, Karl. Well, masochism aside," Irving said, daintily wiping some mustard from his mouth, "I don't know if that is such a good idea, PR-wise. Revisiting the scene of the crimes. Not exactly showing remorse for our sinful behavior, are we?"

"Where do you think I should stay, Irving, the YMCA? Would that be showing sufficient remorse? We could claim that I'd rejected the idea of sex with women altogether."

"Don't get cute." Irving took a large bite of his sandwich, chewing it slowly, his jowls rigid with concentration. "Actually, the Westchester might be good," he said finally.

"What?"

"I am formulating a strategy. Okay. How's this: He did it for love. It wasn't just about the sex. He was really in love with the girl—I mean, the young woman. He rescued her from a terrible fate on that Communist Devil's Island. Risked his life bringing her to the land of liberty. Then, whore that she was all along, she betrays him, dumps him for a pimp her own age. But he still loves her. In fact, he still loves her so much that he moves into her old room, despite the painful memories, in the pathetically vain hope that she might return. True love. Yes," Irving said, nodding his head, "that could be our best approach. How does it sound to you?"

"Like the truth," I said sadly.

"Truth?" My attorney scowled. "What's truth got to do with it? You know, Karl, I'm thinking, maybe we should finish up with a little cheesecake."

NINETEEN

Leonard, buzzed out of his brain behind the front desk, told me that I was looking better.

"I am?"

"Yeah. Well, kind of. Anyway, things are looking up, man. I've been faxing copies of Mariela's ID to everybody but the Pope. The Times, the Post and Sports Illustrated already called back. They all want interviews. The trend is, like, copacetic, man, so don't worry."

"Worry?" My stomach began turning somersaults at the thought of my name being plastered across the pages of every publication (with the possible exception of *Guns 'N Ammo*) in America. "Why should I worry, Leonard? You didn't tell anyone I'm staying here, did you?"

"Of course not. At the Westchester protecting the privacy of our guests is, like, our number one priority."

Back in my room I attempted to ignore the half-bottle of rum sitting on the dresser, and the chandelier hanging from the ceiling, at least for the time being. There were some calls I had to make, no matter how unpleasant; not that they would accomplish anything, but I had to try.

"Karl." The hospital administrator pronounced my name as if it were a disease.

"Edna," I said, returning the favor.

"We've been wondering when we might hear from you."

"Yes, well, I've been, ah, indisposed."

"I can imagine. Just tell me, Karl, is what I've been reading in the papers true? We need to know."

"More or less," I said, choking on the words, "except for the girl's age. She's actually nineteen."

"Really? She certainly doesn't look it."

"Trust me, Edna, she's nineteen."

Sadly, this was my only defense, that the waiflike Cuban hooker I'd been banging was legally an adult.

"Well, that's wonderful," Edna said. "Then they won't be arresting you any time soon, I imagine?"

"I may have behaved...badly, Edna, but I have not committed any crimes."

"Maybe not, but you have generated mountains of negative publicity for this hospital. I'm afraid, for now, Karl, it would best for everyone if you took a leave of absence."

"What about my patients?"

"They've already been reassigned—at least the ones who'd accept substitutes here at our humble institution. A few have decided to search elsewhere, for someone of your caliber."

"I see. So, this leave of absence—how long?"

"Until this unfortunate business blows over. If it blows over. Is there a number at which we can reach you? I understand you are no longer living at home."

That was a low blow, though of course I was in no position to complain. I gave her Irving's number and we parted telephonic company, coolly but politely. With my affairs still in a state of flux, neither of us could afford to totally antagonize the other. Although, I did wonder as the line went dead if they'd already divvied up my office, among surgeons of lesser renown but of greater moral turpitude.

After that uplifting conversation I tried to call my home. No matter how poor the odds, I had to make an attempt at reconciliation. But after steeling myself for the worst, all I got was Charles' voice on the answering machine. He'd erased my message, the bastard, and replaced it with his own. Charles the Usurper: an Elizabethan villain for the Ages.

I continued to call the house every half hour, only to be treated to the sound of my brother-in-law's condescending voice. Then, on the sixth or seventh try, Candace answered. She sounded depressed.

"Hi, sweetie."

"Hi, Dad. Are you all right?"

"More or less. Mostly less. How are you?"

"I'm okay, I guess," she said, and my already crackled heart proceeded to fracture further. "It's kind of weird around here. Uncle Charles has moved in. He's taken over the house. He's got mom sedated. I'm not supposed to answer the…"

The sounds of a small scuffle reached my ear. Then Charles' imperious voice: "I told you not to answer the phone. Go to your room."

"Go to my room?" I heard Candace say. "Are you joking? I don't answer to you, and I never will. You want to play bully, go home and do it in your own house." (Good girl! I thought, the tears streaming down my face.) "I love you, Daddy!" she shouted. "I don't care what you did."

Unable to remove Candace from the proximity of the phone, Charles must have walked away from her. I heard steps and then a door slamming. If I knew Charles, it was the door to my study. Then I heard what sounded like the air being squeezed out of my favorite chair by his oversized ass.

"Are you still there?"

"Yes, I'm here."

"You have a lot of nerve calling this house. You've destroyed her. Utterly. You know that, don't you?"

"I'd like…I'd like to speak with my wife."

"Over my dead body, you shameless son-of-a-bitch."

Charles, I could tell, was really enjoying himself. But he could have used a ghost writer. The man was an encyclopedia of clichés. His delivery needed some work as well. His tone was gloating, when it should have been outraged.

"I just want to speak to her, Charles."

"She doesn't want to speak to you. Not now. Not ever. Your marriage is finished. And so is your career. I intend to see to that personally. You're a fraud, Sanderson, a liar and a hypocrite. A miserable excuse for a human being. I've always known it, and now the whole world will know it, too."

Talk about projection!

"Charles, please, listen to me, I just want to…"

"No one cares what you want. When Bormann finishes with you, you'll wish you'd never been born. And that's only the beginning. You pathetic pervert. A child, fornicating with a mere…"

I hung up the phone. Humbling myself before Charles was pointless. The man was berserk with hatred. I decided to give up for the day on trying to reach my wife, on salvaging what was left of my reputation—on everything. My eyes running like a pair of faulty toilets, I reached for the rum.

TWENTY

A week crawled by, a week in which events moved rapidly, and I moved not at all. Glued to my cell at the Westchester, I took daily calls from Irving, made futile attempts to contact Janice and spent an hour or two each evening with Leonard, who had received a special dispensation from the owner of the hotel, to "fraternize with our esteemed doctor".

The owner, Leonard informed me, was a seventy-five-year-old woman, a wealthy and eccentric Bohemian-type who found me "devastatingly handsome", "an American Peter O'Toole", a guest who finally added some "panache" to her hotel.

"She wants to meet you," Leonard concluded with a wolfish grin.

"Swell."

Between them, Irving and Leonard (my two-man PR team) had managed to convince nearly everyone that Mariela was really and truly nineteen-years-old. An article in the Times (citing sources at the Immigration and Naturalization Service, as well as the Cuban government) had made it official. In the eyes of God, the law and the world-at-large, my status had been formally upgraded, from "Pedophile" to "Dirty Old Man".

Halleluiah.

Seven days after our initial meeting Irving summoned me back to his office. Out of respect for my gluttonous attorney's sense of propriety, I shaved for the occasion, put on a freshly pressed suit, a tie and a pair of polished shoes.

"Well, well," Irving said, swallowing an amorphous chunk of protein and nodding his head with approval. "This is more like it. A little bleary-eyed. A little frayed around the edges. But, basically, presentable. You have been laying off the rum?"

"Cutting back."

"Good, good." Irving seemed uncharacteristically ill at ease. For several moments he sat shuffling the dozens of loose papers around on his desk, to no discernible effect. Then he said, "You, uh, have to go to the hospital."

"What for? Don't tell me they want me back?"

"Uh, not exactly. Karl, I got a call from some bull-dyke over there. What was her name? Dr. Mengle? Dr. Mangle?"

"Mercer, Edna Mercer. What did she want?"

"She wants you to remove your personal effects from your office. She says they need the space. I did my best to get you a reprieve, but the bitch wouldn't budge. The deadline is tomorrow noon. After that, everything goes in the dumpster."

"I can't send someone else?"

Irving shook his jowls. "I already asked. Tried to spare you the embarrassment, etc., etc. She said it's against hospital policy. I said, fine, in that case I am going to sue your flat fascist ass, just for the pleasure of seeing it squirm in court."

"You really said that? Those exact words?"

"Afraid so. She pissed me off, Karl."

"How did you know she has a flat ass?"

"Lawyer's intuition. Hey, did I just see you smile?"

"Possibly."

"Good. On the subject of being pissed off and lawsuits, I need to bring you up to date on a few matters. We are suing the *Enquirer*. For libel. Ten million dollars."

"Irving, the last thing I want is more publicity. I'm already…"

"They called you a child molester!" Irving bellowed. "On their front frigging page! We are suing. Or get yourself another lawyer."

"All right, Irving, if it makes you happy, sue the idiots."

"Idiots is right. Okay, next. The divorce. We have to contest."

"I've already told you, I don't want to fight. Janice has suffered enough. If she wants…"

"You do not understand," Irving snarled, his face turning salami-red with fury. "They want everything!"

"What's everything?"

"Everything is everything!"

I had once heard that same phrase spoken by a black jazz musician on a PBS documentary, when asked by the host how life was treating him. I hadn't really understood what he'd meant, but his demeanor seemed to convey a sense of peace and contentment. Irving, on the other hand...

"Can we be specific?"

"Specific? You want specific? Okay, here is specific: The house. The cottage on Martha's Vineyard. All liquid assets, including stocks, bonds, IRAs, savings and checking accounts. The cars—both of them. All her legal fees. And, last but not least, alimony to the tune of fifteen thousand dollars a month."

I saw his point. Their demands were unreasonably, insanely excessive. But I was determined to make the divorce, if that's what Janice wanted, as easy and painless as possible. "That's it?" I said.

Irving, whose nickname was the "Little Bull", snorted with such force even my brother-in-law would have been forced to settle for the silver medal. "That's it? That is all you have to say? Tell me, Karl, after the bodies have been carted off and the battlefield cleared, what does that leave you?"

"Not much," I admitted.

"Not much?"

"Well, nothing, actually."

"Do you want to be destitute, Karl? For the rest of your life? Is that what you want?"

"Of course not. But I won't fight. I've hurt her enough."

Irving slammed the top of his desk with both meaty hands, and took another bite of what looked like a long tube of orange rubber. "You schlemiel!" he sputtered. "You poor, guilt-ridden putz! You do not get it, do you? You do not understand what is happening here at all!"

"It seems," I said, wiping a moist protein particle from my face, "simple enough to me. I screwed up in the worst way possible, and now I'm paying the price. Crime and punishment."

Irving made a visible effort to calm himself. "Please, Karl, allow me the opportunity to explain what is really going on here, from a legal standpoint—from my standpoint."

My mind was made up, but I decided to hear him out. For his loyalty and his passionate concern for my well being, I owed him at least that much. And his fee, of course.

"All right, Irving, go ahead and enlighten me."

"Thank you." Irving stood up and began to pace back and forth behind his desk as if he were addressing a one-man jury. "Up until several months ago, and for more than twenty years, Dr. Karl Sanderson had always been an exemplary husband. But then, like many men, especially those who are passing through the grim gates of middle age, he began to experience certain urges. In his case these urges were exacerbated by the behavior of his wife, Janice—a fine woman by any standard, but who for more than a decade had displayed an all but complete lack of physical interest in her husband. A cooling of ardor over time is only natural in a marriage, but in this particular instance we are talking about an authentic Ice Age of Aloofness. An Epic Saga of Apathy. A veritable Vacuum…"

"Wait a minute, Irving, this is…"

"Shut up, I'm on a roll here. And so, Dr. Karl Sanderson, a handsome virile man in the prime of life, starving for affection, dying for the least tidbit of physical gratification, felt an irresistible compulsion to seek outside the confines of his arid marriage the warmth, the closeness he so desperately craved. But.

"But, being the decent fellow he is, he decided to do this in the most discrete manner possible, so as to minimize the risk of causing any injury to his wife, who he loved, but from whom he was unable, no matter how hard he tried, to eke out even a miniscule modicum of…"

"Irving, I can see where you're going with this and I refuse…"

"Quiet! So concerned was he with protecting his wife's feelings, that in order to satisfy his needs he travelled to another country, a foreign land where he judged the possibility of his sensual meanderings coming to light all but impossible—travel to said foreign country being proscribed by law.

"But then, as the song goes, 'He fooled around and fell in love.' And all his precautionary planning went out the window. He fell in love with a young woman living in the most difficult circumstances, and because Dr. Karl Sanderson was and is a decent human being, he felt compelled to do what he felt was the honorable thing. Honorable? Perhaps. But, in retrospect, highly foolish and completely contrary to his own self-interests. Risking everything, he…"

"All right, Irving, that's enough. I get the point."

"Which is?"

"That this is not a black and white situation."

"Correct!" my attorney said, resuming his seat. "Now, here comes part two. Please, pay attention. Janice has suffered and continues to suffer. That is an undeniable fact. But this, the situation you now find yourself in, is not about her suffering. This is what is called a hostile divorce, which means it is about revenge. It is about your brother-in-law and this vampire Bormann attempting (while Janice sits oblivious on the sidelines, or not) to destroy a human being. A decent human being, if I may be permitted to offer an opinion.

"The question you have to ask yourself, Karl, is not, are you going to pay for your sins? The answer to that is obvious. Yes, you are going to pay, and pay plenty. The question you should be asking is, are you going to allow these people to annihilate you? Because that is their intention. And what I am trying to tell you, Karl, is very simple: that punishment (your personal destruction) does not fit your crime. You are not Rashkolnikov. You did not kill anybody. You did not brutalize an innocent victim. You did not deliberately set out to hurt anyone. What you did was cheat on your wife. And that is not a capital offense.

"Therefore, you must, it is your duty, Karl, to defend yourself. To fight back! To take a stand against this gross injustice!"

Exhausted, Irving collapsed, along with all his chins, atop his littered desk, upending in the process a white carton container of potato salad.

Despite myself, I felt swayed by my attorney's eloquent, if over-the-top, performance. If I were a jury, I would have voted in favor of the defendant then and there. But I was not the jury. I was the defendant. And in my mind I was as guilty as hell.

"Bravo," I said, softly clapping my hands.

"Are we being sarcastic?"

"No, Irving. We are impressed with your logic, and your passionate concern for our well being. We'll think about it."

"Good. Just don't think too long. And remember, this is not a civil proceeding; it is an Inquisition. And the flames are already licking at your feet."

TWENTY-ONE

"This is some seriously good shit, man," Leonard said, firing up the purple bong.

"Not Mendocino Mindwipe, is it?" I asked, recalling with nostalgia those good old days when I'd had a family, a lover and something resembling a life. How long had it been—a month ago?

"Not that good, man," Leonard exhaled, "not on my salary. Hey look, you're on TV again."

I'd begun, as I suppose many people do, to leave the television on for long periods of time to help take my mind off my problems. Usually, I left it on a classic movie channel, one without commercials. But Leonard had changed the station and at this particular moment the brain-numbing tube was tuned to one of those "all-news" cable channels. And there, to my infinite distress, filling the screen was the now infamous photo of the mismatched couple snuggling in the round orange taxi.

From the photo, the screen switched to a full frontal shot of Nancy Drew, a bona fide lawyer and the host of the show. Nancy reminded me a little of Edna. Her sour face was set in a permanent scowl, and framed by a helmet of blond hair so stiff it looked as if it had been dipped in glue. Her voice was abrasive and her tone grating, like a nagging parent forever saying, "I told you so."

All in all she was a singularly unattractive individual, but there she was on television, playing the role of the avenging angel: tough, fearless and unswerving in her crusade to expose the slippery societal scum, who without her courageous intervention, would otherwise be getting away with murder. Her standard modus operandi was to zero in on a target and verbally beat it to death, until something juicier came along.

In the days immediately following the publication of the Enquirer and Post stories, Nancy had scooped up the "Prestigious-Doctor-As-Child Molester" saga and run with it for all she was worth, her ratings climbing with each sleazy installment.

"This man," she sneered, "just because he's a big-shot surgeon, thought he could get away with the alleged crimes of kidnapping and abusing a child? He thought he could get away with allegedly snatching some poor desperate girl from the bosom of her family and locking her away in a seedy hotel, where he could, with impunity, indulge his allegedly perverted tastes? No, sir! I don't think so. Not in this country. Not if I have anything to say about it!"

Once it had been proven beyond any reasonable doubt that the "child" was nineteen-years-old, Nancy, like a bull terrier that's got its teeth into another dog's neck, only dug in deeper. Onto her show she summoned various experts, including today's guest, an "Age Expert", a class of specialist created especially for the occasion. As Leonard and I looked on, zoned-out on the potent cannabis, this guest, a forty-something female pediatrician with jet black hair who bore a striking resemblance to the Wicked Witch of the West, was soon seen pointing her pointy nose at the viewing public.

"So, you tell me, Dr. Armstrong," Nancy demanded, "after all your years of experience treating children of all ages, looking at this photograph, taken only a few months ago, is there any way you can believe that this girl is nineteen-years-old?"

Dr. Armstrong, staring into the camera with an expression so implacable it would have put fear into the heart of the Grand Inquisitor himself, said, "Ab-solutely not."

"As an expert on age," Nancy said with a straight (albeit sour) face, "what exactly leads you to draw that conclusion?"

"Nancy," Dr. Armstrong began in somber tones, "I have been treating children of all ages for twenty years. I can determine a child's age within three or four months with only a cursory look. Bone structure, skin tone, demeanor, posture, degree of bodily development—they all play a role. And of course," she paused to bark once like a sarcastic collie, "when you see a young girl dressed in a school uniform…well, the conclusion is obvious, isn't it, Nancy."

"What a crock of bull," Leonard said.

"Leonard," I asked fearfully, "are there people actually watching this? Besides us?"

"Afraid so, man. This bitch has a bigger following than Mick Jagger."

"All right," Nancy announced, "on my show, we are nothing if not fair and balanced. So I have invited the author of the New York Times article which has been so widely cited in the media as so-called 'proof' that the girl in question is actually (Nancy smirked briefly at the camera) of legal age. Mr. Jacobs, welcome to the show."

A middle-aged man's weathered face filled the screen. "Thank you, Nancy," he said in a bored voice.

"Mr. Jacobs, you have just heard Dr. Armstrong, an acknowledged expert, deliver her verdict that, contrary to the view expressed in your article, this girl, Mariela, Dr. Karl Sanderson's alleged sex toy, could not possibly be of legal age. What is your response?"

Mr. Jacobs' first response was a stifled yawn. "Well, Nancy," he said, "my reaction, frankly, is one of incredulity."

"Incredulity?" Nancy asked in apparent amazement. "Does that mean you don't believe Dr. Armstrong is being truthful?"

"No, Nancy, that means that I don't believe there is such thing as an age expert," he drawled. "And I also don't believe that Dr. Armstrong has ever seen the young woman in person. Have you seen her in person, Dr. Armstrong, or are you basing your judgment solely on a photograph reproduced on low quality newsprint?"

"Dr. Armstrong?" Nancy said.

"I have been treating children for over twenty years, Mr. Jacobs, and…"

"Yeah, you already said that," the journalist cut in.

"Right fucking on!" Leonard exclaimed, passing me the bong.

"My point is," Dr. Armstrong persisted, "it becomes second nature to…"

"To make erroneous judgments," Jacobs interrupted again, "which fly in the face of known facts, which demonize an innocent man, based solely on a…"

"I would hardly call Dr. Karl Sanderson innocent," Nancy Drew overrode her guest.

"What a cunt!" Leonard exhaled, coughing most of his lungs out.

"As a journalist," Jacobs said, "I am compelled to deal with facts. For example, in Cuba even freshman university students, like the young woman in question, are made to wear school uniforms. That's a fact, not some subjective baseless judgment. Every single fact I've uncovered proves the young woman is nineteen-years of age."

"Well, then, Mr. Jacobs," Nancy said venomously, "we seem to have a difference of opinion. And we'll leave it at that for…"

"Excuse me, Nancy," Jacobs broke in, "I would like to make one more comment."

"So would I," the Wicked Witch of the West said.

"All right," Nancy ruled. "Dr. Armstrong, you first. But please be brief, we are running short of time."

"The corruption of an innocent child," Dr. Armstrong stated, "is one of the most heinous crimes anyone can commit. Despite Mr. Jacobs' so-called facts, if there is the shadow of a doubt as to the girl's age, then Dr. Sanderson must be brought to justice!"

"Amen!" Nancy said. "Dr. Jacobs, you have three seconds to respond."

"I'm not a lawyer like you, Nancy," Jacobs drawled with disgust. "Nor am I an age-expert. But I have always labored under the assumption that in this country a person is considered innocent until proven guilty in a court of law.

When you start 'convicting' people on low-brow TV shows, using bogus self-proclaimed experts desperate for publicity, then you are…"

Jacobs was cut off in mid-sentence, as he disappeared from the known Universe, to be replaced by an even more pugnacious Nancy Drew, who said furiously, "That's all we have time for today. And so, the controversy boils on. Is Dr. Karl Sanderson in fact a child-molesting felon? Or is he merely a pathetic pervert who thought he was having sex with a child? Tomorrow night we will be joined by Dr. Henry Sinclair, a man uniquely qualified to answer this question. Dr. Sinclair is an expert in the fields of abnormal and criminal psychology. He has testified countless times in child molestation cases, both for the prosecution and for the defense, so we know that he will give us a fair unbiased opinion as to whether or not Dr. Karl Sanderson is in fact a dangerous pedophile. Until then…"

I hit the off button, threw a shoe at the screen, missing badly, then followed with Leonard's bong, which went wide of the mark, as well.

"Careful with the bong, man," Leonard advised. "Those things cost money."

"Sorry."

For quite a while we both sat staring in silence at the blank screen, reminding me of my last quality evening with Janice.

TWENTY-TWO

And then the other shoes began to fall, so many they seemed to be flying off the feet of some vengeful centipede floating over my lumpy head.

Irving, a bit of a history buff, likened it to a Blitzkrieg, with yours truly standing in for Poland, Austria and France. Leonard, who was currently working his way through the Classic Comics version of the *Iliad*, remarked, "You know, Dr. Sanderson, it's like the gods are using you for fucking target practice, man."

The next forty-eight hours went as follows:

The day after my evening with Nancy Drew I drove out to Sands Point, determined to see my wife. For all I knew she might actually want to reconcile, but I'd never know until I'd bypassed the impenetrable barrier erected by Charles, the psycho psychiatrist, and pleaded my case in person.

The coast was apparently clear. My brother-in-law's Mercedes was not in evidence. Nor was Brenda's brand new Sentra—hopefully she'd worked up the courage by now to return to school. Janice's Volvo was also out of sight, but it might well be tucked away inside the garage. Trembling with apprehension, I took out my key and attempted to open the front door. For the second time in as many days (Edna had changed the lock on the door to my office as well) a key which for years had served me faithfully refused to do its job. Two dysfunctional keys in two days: a troubling trend to say the least.

Thus was I reduced to knocking on my own door. In short order it was opened from within, and there was Janice. She did not seem surprised to see me. In fact, she was remarkably composed. "It's you," she said. "Come in, I've been wanting to speak to you."

"Janice," I began, encouraged by her serene demeanor, "I can't tell you how sorry I…"

"Yes, yes," she said impatiently, "I'm sure you're quite sorry, especially for yourself."

"Janice," I tried again, "if there is any possibility that you could forgive me, I can promise you that…"

My wife cut me off with a curt laugh. "Forgive you? Don't be absurd. What I wanted to tell you is that I will never forgive you. Never," she repeated with icy (Xanax-induced?) calm. "The divorce will proceed. You may fight it or not. My attorney has assured me that the outcome is a foregone conclusion. I intend to strip you as bare as those maple trees you used to be so fond of contemplating outside your study window. Just as you have stripped me of my dignity."

"Janice…"

"To be mortified on a daily basis on television, in newspapers, in magazines. Seeing my photo, side-by-side with your little brown harlot, on the cover of that filthy scandal sheet at every checkout stand in every supermarket in town."

I'd missed that one.

"Janice, all I can say is how…"

"With the words 'HUMILIATED WIFE' printed in bold type directly over my head. Do you have any idea how that makes me feel?"

"No, Janice, how could I. But to throw away twenty-five years of…"

"Brenda, of course, will have nothing further to do with you. Ever. Thanks to you, Charles has had to put her on Prozac."

"He put Brenda on Prozac? That's like, like hosing down Lake Ontario!"

"As for Candace," Janice continued in her automated voice, "she still seems to possess a small smidgeon of affection for you. But I will encourage her to follow her older sister's example with all the weapons at my disposal."

"Candace…"

"Candace has severe emotional problems," Janice proclaimed. "Most of which I blame on your irresponsible behavior. And Charles agrees."

"That's not fair, Janice. I've been…"

"If we happen to see each other again, it will be in an attorney's office, or a court of law. Outside of that, please do not attempt to speak to me, or see me ever again. I will never forget what you have done to me, and to my children. As long as I live. Please leave my house, and don't even think of coming back. And stay away from Candace. My attorney is preparing a restraining order just in case."

It was a set speech which Janice must have composed and then memorized. I could even picture her practicing it in front of a mirror. Having said her piece she stood ramrod straight glaring at me with undiluted contempt. Though I had no right, no right at all, I became angry. I felt that I deserved, like any man, no matter what his transgression, the opportunity to say I'm sorry. And the bit about the restraining order—that was nothing but pure spite.

"All right, Janice," I said with a bitter smile, "do your worst. Skin me alive, if it satisfies your injured pride. But as for Candace, you could not be more mistaken. If anyone has emotional problems in this family, it is not her. Just because she has a mind of her…"

"Get out of my house. Now."

Deciding that a reconciliation was probably not in the cards, I left my former home and returned to my current one, where I poured myself a drink and put in a call to Irving.

"I just got back from Sands Point," I told him.

"And?"

"I don't think there's going to be a reconciliation."

"Was she hostile?"

"You could say that."

"So?"

"Carte blanche, Irving."

"Fire at will?"

"Be my guest."

"Good. I have some news myself. They've assigned us a judge. The Honorable Marsha Fielding."

"What's she like? Fair minded, I hope?"

"Once divorced. Never remarried. They call her the Man Eater."

"That doesn't sound good, Irving."

"No, it is not good, Karl, but it is not a worst case scenario, either."

"Irving, what could be worse than the Man Eater?"

"I don't know, Karl. Adela Eichmann?"

TWENTY-THREE

The very next day I was informed by the New York State Board of Medicine that my license to practice said profession in said state was, effective immediately, suspended. Pending the outcome of their own investigation, as well as unspecified civil and criminal proceedings, my license would either be reinstated or not. I would, they added almost as an afterthought, be permitted at some point in the proceedings to testify on my own behalf.

This news, though not unexpected, was a blow nonetheless. My intake of rum, which I had with a heroic surge of self-control reduced to only two shots a day, spiked upwards at once. Halfway through the third spike someone came knocking at my door. I assumed it was Leonard. He'd been up only minutes earlier to hand-deliver Irving's fax confirming the latest bad news, and now he'd returned bringing word of some additional calamity my attorney had neglected to mention the first time.

But it was not Leonard standing there when, reasonably sloshed, I opened the door. It was in fact a fellow hotel guest, a preternaturally pale young woman with long shapely legs, short black hair and hot pink lips. Displaying the "vampire-slut" look, de rigueur at the Westchester, she wore a scandalously short black leather skirt, black gloves, black boots, a leather top and enough bracelets to sink a corpse.

"Are you the famous doctuh?" she asked in a comical Brooklyn accent.

"Infamous is more like it. What do you want?"

"I'm staying here, just down the hall."

"You don't say?"

"Can I come in?"

"What for?"

"I want to see you in a professional capacity," she said, sliding past me into the room.

Not certain whose profession she was referring to, hers or mine, I closed the door and offered her a chair.

"I think I have bweast cansuh," she said matter-of-factly. "That's why I need to see a doctuh."

"I'm not that kind of a doctor," I said, polishing off my third rum. "What you need is an oncologist."

"I don't have any insurance," she said. "Or money."

"I'm sorry to hear that, but unless you've also got a strained ligament—and your ligaments, I must say, look fine to me—I don't see how I can help you."

"You're a doctuh," she said, rising from the chair and stripping to the waist. "I want you to feel my bweasts."

"Well, they are…very nice breasts," I said, taking a step back. "But, like I said, I'm not that kind of doctor."

"Even so," she said, "you could tell bettuh than a normal poyson if I had dangewous lumps. I need my bweasts. They are essential for my caweer."

"And what career would that be?"

"I'm an actress," she said. "Off-Off-Off Broadway."

"Off-Off-Off? I hadn't realized they ran all the way to three Offs. Where do you perform, in the East River?"

"Lately, I haven't been puhfoaming at all," she admitted. "That's why I can't afford a doctuh. Even when I do work, they don't pay much."

"That's a pity."

"Please, doctuh, feel my bweasts."

"Might as well," I muttered to myself. "My new career: from hotshot surgeon, to bweast palpitatah. All right, dear. Take a deep breath, and…ah, don't move," I instructed her pointlessly.

"Weady, doctuh," she said, shutting her eyes and holding her breath.

"Maybe I should wash my hands first."

"Oh no, doctuh," she said without opening her eyes, "you look quite clean to me."

"All right, then. Here we go." Reaching out with my right hand I squeezed first one breast and then the other. They were, both of them, firm, upright, well-formed and, as far as I could tell, free of lumps. When I'd squeezed for what I felt was a reasonable amount of time, I said, "They feel perfectly healthy to me."

"Thank God!" she cried. "Oh, thank you, doctuh! Thank you! I'll pay you now."

"I thought you said you didn't have any money."

"I don't," she said, unzipping my fly. "I was gonna pay you with a blow-job, if that's all wight?"

"Well…"

Taking me in her gloved hand, she looked up and said, "Do you think I'm a hypochondwiac? That's what my husband says."

"Your husband?"

When she'd finished paying me, with enthusiasm and proficiency, she swallowed once, gave me a quick affectionate squeeze and left.

Almost at once, another knock sounded on the door.

She must have dropped a bracelet, I thought. Or maybe she wants me to take a quick peek at her cervix. But when I opened the door there was a strange little man standing there dressed in a green suit. In a small squeaky voice, he asked me if I was Dr. Karl Sanderson.

Assuming he was another hotel guest, I said, "What's wrong with you, strep throat?"

Glancing down uncertainly at my exposed lipstick-smudged manhood—I'd forgotten to put it back where it belonged—he favored me with a lewd smile, whipped out a piece of paper and thrust it into my hand. "This is a summons, Dr. Sanderson, to appear before a federal grand jury. Please," he added cheerfully, stealing another look at my pink penis, "continue having a nice day."

TWENTY-FOUR

Robert Zimmerman, though a member of the same New York State Bar as Irving Waxman, might well have belonged, judging by his appearance and demeanor, to an entirely different genus of mammal. Tall, slender, neat and soft-spoken, he sat behind his immaculate desk, and regarded me with a look of frank concern.

"Something odd is going on here, Dr. Sanderson," he said.

"How so?" I asked. The tidy attorney had already explained to me that when a federal grand jury is called, an indictment is likely to follow; and that no prosecutor is anxious to indict unless he is fairly certain that the odds of obtaining a conviction or a satisfactory plea bargain are in his favor.

"Technically, you may have violated a couple of laws," Mr. Zimmerman began, "but under ordinary circumstances, your 'crimes', if you could call them that, would never be prosecuted."

"My circumstances are not ordinary?" I asked fearfully.

"That's what puzzles and alarms me. You've never crossed paths with Jack Davidson, the U.S. Attorney, have you?"

"Not that I know of."

"It doesn't add up," Zimmerman said with a frown. "If our government doesn't encourage Cubans to emigrate to the US, they at least tolerate it, as a matter of official policy. The so-called Dry-Foot, Wet-Foot rule. So then, why should they not tolerate your aiding and abetting Miss Gomez? She's over eighteen. She came here willingly. Even if your motivation was not, shall we say, altogether altruistic, I fail to see what could be compelling Mr. Davidson to pursue this—unless he is being pressured."

"You think someone is forcing him to prosecute me?"

"Nothing else makes sense. By prosecuting you he has, from a political standpoint, little to gain, and a good deal to lose. You are, after all, the man who saved Brian Westin's career—twice." Zimmerman allowed himself a small smile. "Yes, you cheated on your wife, but that is not, as they say, a federal offense. And from a certain point of view, what you did was rather heroic. Tell me, Dr. Sanderson, do you have any powerful enemies?"

"In truth, Mr. Zimmerman, I have only one enemy in the entire world, and he's hardly powerful. He's just a psychiatrist. He…"

"What is it?"

"Is there any way we can find out if Davidson has ever been under the care of a psychiatrist?"

Zimmerman saw where I was headed at once. "You think a psychiatrist may be blackmailing a former patient, who happens to be a U.S. Attorney, into prosecuting you? That seems a little farfetched."

"Mr. Zimmerman, let me tell you about Charles Meredith, my brother-in-law."

When I'd finished the ten minute exposition, Zimmerman said, "This man is a psychiatrist? You make him sound more like a mental case."

"Can't he be both?"

Later that day I called Irving and filled him in on the latest revolting developments. "What do you think?" I asked my primary care attorney. "Am I being paranoid?"

"When you think someone is out to get you," Irving said sagely, "and someone really is out to get you, that is not paranoia. Blackmailing a former patient? In my estimation, your whacko Nazi brother-in-law is capable of far worse. Let me check around, see what I can dig up. In any case, I don't believe, at the end of the day, that there is going to be an indictment. For what? For helping a young woman escape from Cuba so you could continue to have sex with her in a more convenient location? For crossing state lines with a political refugee?"

"I like how you put that, Irving."

"Where is the proverbial smoking gun? Do not lose any sleep over that one, Karl. The divorce—well, that is another matter. That is where you're really going to take it up the tuchus. And maybe on your medical license. Those things are always a crapshoot. But the grand jury? I do not see it as a problem."

"So I lose my family, almost everything I own and possibly my career, but I won't go to jail. Does that about sum it up, Irving?"

"Remember, Karl, it is always darkest before the dawn."

"And will the sun be rising anytime soon, Irving?"

"I don't know," Irving sighed, "I'm your lawyer, not the fucking weatherman."

TWENTY-FIVE

Without any further ado, matters went from worse to horrific. The only ray of sunshine was the news that Brian Westin, while skiing (an activity expressly proscribed in his contract) with an Italian supermodel in the Swiss Alps, had run over a tobogganer and badly mangled the healthier of his two knees. Fortunately, the tobogganer, a precocious eight-year-old, escaped with only minor injuries.

Aside from that wee silver lining, it was all dark clouds and stormy weather. Subpoenas were raining down upon my head like hailstones: subpoenas from the US Attorney, from Janice's legal team, the IRS, the Secret Service (I'm still not sure what that was about) and the New York State Medical Board. My bank records for the past year were in especially great demand. Everyone wanted to know where and how Dr. Karl Sanderson had been dispersing his funds. As for the dispersal of my seed, that would be looked into as well.

I appeared in due course before the grand jury with Mr. Zimmerman sitting silently by my side. One's attorney, I discovered, plays a limited role in these proceedings, leaving the client exposed and helpless. I was not permitted to plead the Fifth Amendment. I could not refuse to answer any questions. And I could not lie. I was, however, perfectly free (duty-bound, in fact) to incriminate myself to the best of my ability.

"Tell the truth," Zimmerman advised me. "As far as I can see there is no offense they can charge you with more serious than perjury. In fact, that may be the government's primary goal, to get you to perjure yourself. It could be their only hope of bringing charges against you at all."

In this assumption, that no serious charges would ever be brought against me, my two attorneys would prove to be something less than prophetic. Of course, at that time they had no way of knowing how Byzantine and brazen the conspiracy against me would turn out to be, or the improbable lengths to which the U.S. Attorney would go to keep the dirt Charles was holding over his head from becoming public knowledge.

My grilling was long, grueling and entirely predictable, except for one bizarre line of questioning towards the end.

"Dr. Sanderson," I was asked, "did you at any time after your return with Miss Gomez to the United States, urge her, or pressure her in any way to perform acts of prostitution, with yourself as the financial beneficiary?"

"Of course not."

"Are you certain?"

"Absolutely."

"And are you certain that you understand the question?"

"Yes," I snapped. "You're asking me if I acted as her pimp, and the answer is no!"

After I'd been dismissed, my attorney and I held a short confab in the hall.

"What do you think?" I asked.

"So far, so good. No surprises. Except those questions at the end. You're not holding anything back from me, are you?"

"Mr. Zimmerman, I told the whole humiliating truth, and nothing but the humiliating truth. The idea of my being Mariela's pimp is beyond absurd. I'm a wealthy man, or at least I was. And I loved that girl. I may still love her, in spite of the blackmail and everything else."

My attorney's ears twitched with alarm, like a deer's at the sound of a broken branch. "Blackmail? What blackmail?"

"Oh, it was nothing. Nothing relevant."

Naturally, I did not want to get into the details of my relationship, arm's length though it may have been, with Pedro's friends' friends' friends. Zimmerman was, after all, an officer of the court.

"Let me be the judge of what is relevant and what is not. What happened?"

"She dumped me for someone her own age. A petty criminal. They made a weak attempt at blackmailing me. When that failed, they sold the story to the tabloids. I suppose I should have paid them off. I could have avoided this entire mess."

"Giving in to the demands of blackmailers or extortionists is never a wise course of action," the attorney said judiciously. "Ten times out of ten I would advise against it. You were smart to turn them down."

"Smart? No one's called me that for a while."

"Well," Zimmerman said with lawyerly precision, "in that one particular instance."

TWENTY-SIX

On the divorce front, after a deposition in Irving's office (highly unpleasant), there had followed a preliminary hearing (your basic nightmare) before our dour unblinking judge, the Honorable (Field Marshal) Marsha Fielding.

I presented myself for this hearing carefully shaved and neatly dressed, but looking something less than robust and alert. The stress of fighting three seemingly lost causes simultaneously, combined with my new vegetable-free/doughnut-and-rum diet, had left me suffering from third degree heartburn, insomnia and category five constipation.

It was in this lamentable state, nerves shattered and exhausted unto death, that I was set upon without mercy by Judge Marsha, a large Teutonic woman with the put-out, no-nonsense demeanor of a contract killer having a bad-hair day.

"Dr. Sanderson," she said, once she'd settled herself, with a few duck-like wiggles, comfortably on the bench, "you don't look very well. Are you all right? If you are too ill to proceed, we can postpone this hearing, though I would prefer to proceed."

"My client," Irving leapt into the breach, "is understandably distraught over this whole tragic business. He has not been sleeping well, but is otherwise as fit as a fiddle, and ready to proceed."

"Is that correct, Dr. Sanderson?" she asked with a frown. "Are you, in fact, as fit as a fiddle?"

"That might be overstating the case somewhat, Your Honor," I admitted in a hoarse voice. "But I believe I can soldier on."

"Bravo, Dr. Sanderson."

I stole a quick glance over my shoulder at Janice and her attorney. Mr. Bormann, who I'd had the misfortune to meet at the deposition, was not a young man. He looked, in fact, like a retired grave robber. His eyes had a dark sunken look, not unlike mine, but his did not suggest ill-health or even fatigue, but rather an insatiable thirst for human blood.

Janice was wearing an uncharacteristically feminine dress, and her posture was odd as well. Instead of sitting ramrod straight, as was her custom, she sat in something of a defensive slouch, practically cowering in her chair.

"They're trying to make her look vulnerable and victim-like," Irving whispered in my ear.

"This," the Man Eater proclaimed with a mirthless smile, "is what I like to call a 'getting acquainted' hearing. An opportunity to obtain a sense of where we're all at, sort of feel our way around. So. I see here that we seem to have a small difference of opinion as to the precise nature of the financial settlement. Who knows," Judge Marsha said with obvious sarcasm, "maybe both sides can bend a bit and we can get this all wrapped up today. So as not to waste too much of the Court's valuable time."

She glared in turn at each attorney.

"Your Honor," they said nearly in unison, "we would love nothing better than…"

"Yes, yes, yes," she cut them off. "But miracles can happen. One never knows. I have a motion before me. Let's get that over with first. Mr. Bormann, your motion to freeze all of Dr. Sanderson's assets, liquid and non-liquid? The Court has already frozen most of them, pending the outcome of these proceedings. Is it your aim, Counselor, to starve Dr. Sanderson into submission? This, Mr. Bormann, is a divorce case, not a medieval siege."

"Your Honor, according to Dr. Sanderson's bank records, as well as his own confession…"

"I object!" Irving cried.

"This is not a trial, Mr. Waxman. You cannot object at a preliminary hearing."

"Your Honor, I…"

"And for the record, Mr. Bormann, the appropriate word is testimony."

"Janice should have hired a woman," Irving whispered. "The judge seems to hate Bormann almost as much as she hates us."

"I am so sorry, Your Honor," Bormann said unctuously. "As he himself admits, Dr. Sanderson has spent in the last six months over $50,000 on Cuban prostitutes, including his 'mistress'. For all we know he continues to squander the family nest-egg on prostitutes, drugs and other related…"

"Your Honor!" Irving was on his feet, his face red, his veins doing the boogalu up and down his neck. "That is nothing but distortion, lies and innuendo! How can we be expected to reach a compromise when my colleague…"

"Prostitutes, Your Honor," Bormann cut in.

"All right," Judge Marsha ruled, "shut up, both of you. I have taken, believe it or not, a quick peek at the evidence. That Dr. Sanderson spent $50,000 in the pursuit of his extramarital activities cannot be disputed. The great bulk of it, however, was spent on smuggling his teenage girlfriend, who may or may not have been a prostitute, into the United States. No evidence has been brought to my attention that he spent any great sum on prostitutes in Cuba, or that he is spending any money on our own domestic variety at the present moment. By the way, Dr. Sanderson, how much money did you spend on prostitutes? While you were in Cuba?"

"Your Honor…" Irving began.

"Let him speak for himself, Counselor."

"Your Honor," I asked, "is that, ah, including what I spent on Miss Gomez, or…?"

"No, we'll give that poor girl the benefit of the doubt for the moment."

"In that case," I said, the numbers floating elusively around my fuzzy head, "I think it, ah, must have been around eighty dollars."

"Only eighty dollars?" the Man Eater asked, seemingly impressed. "And how many sessions of wanton pleasure did that pay for, Dr. Sanderson?"

Staring in deep embarrassment down at my trembling hands, I said in a small voice, "Well, I think, ah, four."

"So," Judge Marsha said, "that would come to about twenty dollars a pop, wouldn't it, Dr. Sanderson?"

"Yes."

"That's pretty darn economical, isn't it, Dr. Sanderson?"

"I, uh, suppose so," I mumbled.

"You see, Mr. Bormann," the Man Eater said, "why I am having a problem with the reasoning behind your motion? Dr. Sanderson, when it comes to paying for prostitutes, would appear to be something of a penny-pincher."

Bormann shrugged his vulture-like shoulders, conceding the point.

Once the subject of how much I had spent on, and how often I'd lain with Cuban prostitutes had been probed to her satisfaction, Judge Marsha asked me if I was planning to smuggle any more young women into the United States in the near future.

"No, Your Honor."

"There you have it, Mr. Bormann," she declared. "I would say that Dr. Sanderson's primary expense in the coming months is going to consist of legal fees, which he is certainly entitled to pay."

"He certainly is," Bormann said with a sickening smile.

"In as much as," the Man Eater ruled, "we have already deprived Dr. Sanderson access to the vast majority of his assets, motion denied. Now, why don't we talk about those assets, and their division. As I said earlier, perhaps we can reach some kind of compromise today. Mr. Bormann, I see that you are asking for, among other things, both Volvos. Don't you think that's a little harsh? Don't you think the doctor is at least entitled to keep his car?"

"I believe we could be persuaded," Bormann said, in an unprecedented display of generosity, "to forgo the second Volvo."

"There," Judge Marsha said grimly, "that was nice. And what about you, Mr. Waxman, is your side willing to bend a little as well?"

"Certainly, Your Honor. We are willing to match them concession for concession. As you know, we have proposed a standard fifty-fifty split, while the other side is asking for what amounts to ninety-nine per cent of the entire pie. In the spirit of compromise, we would be more than happy to tack the used Volvo's value (approximately .1 per cent of total assets) onto their end of the settlement. That would make it, let me see," Irving said, counting on his fingers, "50.1 per cent for Mrs. Sanderson, and 49.9 per cent for Dr. Sanderson."

Judge Marsha was not amused. Ever. "Are you serious, Mr. Waxman?"

"Why wouldn't I be?" Irving said stiffly. "Half and half is standard in this state, is it not?"

"In an amicable divorce, Mr. Waxman, where there is no injured party. Would you characterize this as an amicable divorce, Counselor?"

Irving glanced over at Janice and the outsized scavenger sitting beside her, looking famished as he seemed to sniff the air for carrion.

"No, Your Honor," Irving said, "amicable is probably not the word I would choose. But if we are going to discuss injured parties, then I…"

"Did you say parties, Mr. Waxman?" Judge Marsha pounced. "As in, more than one? My hearing isn't what it used to be."

"Yes, Your Honor," Irving said bravely. "Every coin has two sides, and this case is no exception."

"Really?" Judge Marsha said, her eyebrows arching in amazement. "Well then, go ahead, Counselor. I can't wait to hear this."

TWENTY-SEVEN

It was time for the Bong, Rum and Doughnut Hour, a new Westchester tradition. I paid for the comestibles and Leonard supplied the combustibles.

"So then, like, your lawyer went on the attack?" the ex-bass player asked eagerly.

"Well, he tired to, Leonard," I explained, taking a sizable hit from the purple tube, followed by a small swallow of rum, "but he was forced, in short order, to sound the retreat. Any more doughnuts in that bag?"

"Half a French cruller, man. So, in other words, the judge was, like, not buying?"

"She wasn't even kicking the tires, Leonard."

"Too bad you caught a woman judge. A man might've been, like, less hostile. Or at least, you know, more subjective."

"Objective."

"Objective. Right. I still get them mixed up. Mark was always on my case about that. Mark, from Mark and the Mandalas, my old group? That guy was sharp, man. A serious talent. Too bad he got into the crack. All those brain cells up in smoke. Lost everything: his house, his family, his career. A real waste."

"Sounds familiar."

"Huh? Oh, sorry, man. I didn't mean to, like…"

The telephone rang. Leonard picked it up. "Leonard here. Yeah? He does? What kind of girl? Man, you're shitting me." Leonard cupped the receiver. "Dr. Sanderson, you're, like, not going to believe who's downstairs."

If it'd been Lizzie Borden the axe murderess down there, waiting to chop off my limbs, I would not have been surprised. I'd tell Leonard to give her a number and have her wait her turn behind Janice, Judge Marsha, Edna and Nancy Drew. After all, what was one more estrogen-starved mammal clawing at my testicles? I'd hardly notice.

Even so, it was something of a shock to see, a few minutes later, Irving's "smoking gun", dressed in a bright yellow pants-suit, standing in the doorway of her old room.

"Mariela."

She looked, as I remembered her, good enough to eat, save for a sad wary look about those huge brown eyes. I did not invite her in.

"You must hate me," she said in a subdued voice.

"No, oddly enough, I don't." Seeing her, I didn't feel much of anything.

"You should," she said with conviction. "After everything that happened." When all I did was shrug, she said, "You don't look so good."

"No, I suppose not. Listen, if you came here looking for money…"

"I came here to say I'm sorry," Mariela said. "I've got plenty of money."

"From your journalistic endeavors? I hear they pay pretty well for that type of thing."

"No, not from that. Ricardo took all that money when he ran off. I have a job. I work on commission in a men's clothing store. They say I'm the best salesperson they ever had. I sell something to almost everyone I talk to."

"Do all the customers want to sleep with you?"

"Most of them. Except the gay ones. One gay customer told me that if I was a boy, he'd marry me."

"Well, I'm certainly happy to hear you're doing so well," I said bleakly. "And," I added, remembering my scene with Janice, "I'm glad you've taken the trouble to tell me you're sorry. But I'm very tired, Mariela, so…"

"All right," she said, "I'll go. But I have to tell you something first. I want you to know. They made me testify against you. I didn't want to do it. I've already hurt you so much. After you were so good to me. But I didn't have a choice. I…"

"Wait a minute. Who's making you testify against me?"

"Mr. Davidson, with the government. He told me if I don't say what he tells me, he'll have me deported back to Cuba. I can't go back. They might put me in jail. And I have a good life here. I'm saving money so I can bring my family over. I know it's not fair. I'm really sorry."

"What," I asked, "is Mr. Davidson making you say? It doesn't have anything to do with me forcing you into prostitution by any chance?"

Mariela nodded her head and burst into tears. "I'm so sorry," she cried. Then she turned on her three-inch heels, and left.

I watched her marvelous elfin figure retreat down the stairs, and still I felt no anger, only a faint longing for what had been but no longer was. There goes my little ex-lover, I thought with nostalgia as I stood, all but asleep on my feet, leaning against the door. There goes my wee ex-wife, I mused, recalling the ceremony in Eustacia's backyard. There goes Mariela, I concluded with a shudder, my pint-sized smoking gun.

TWENTY-EIGHT

"The call, Karl, came early this morning."

Bob (we were on a first-name basis now) was looking anything but his serene self. Even his normally placid desk appeared upset, three loose sheets of paper scattered willy-nilly about its surface. "Jack Davidson said he wanted to observe all the niceties," he said bitterly, "let you turn yourself in, in order to preserve your dignity."

"Well, Bob, it's not like we weren't expecting this," I told my attorney.

"Karl," he said, gritting his teeth, "Davidson is charging you with eight completely bogus felonies. And he's concerned about your dignity? Bull-shit!"

"The charges do seem somewhat redundant, Bob."

The news that I'd been indicted came as no surprise—not after Mariela's doorway confession. But it left me in a state of shock, nonetheless, like the victim of an automobile accident. I was further numbed by my two-bong, two-rum breakfast, which was why I appeared, for the moment at least, considerably more calm than my attorney.

"That's how they always do it," Zimmerman explained. "They charge you with eight, then hope you'll plead down to one or two."

"Still, Bob, it does seem as if they've gone a little overboard. Felony Number One: Doing this. Number Two: Conspiracy to Do This. Number Three: Hoping to Profit from Doing This. Number Four: Lying about Doing This. It'd be comical, if it wasn't my own ass on the line."

"I know it's confusing, Karl, but it's SOP—the same basic charges wrapped in different packages to make the case seem weightier than it actually is."

"Human Smuggling and Crossing State Lines for the Purposes of Promoting Prostitution aren't weighty enough, Bob?"

"They'll never get away with this, Karl. No matter how many supposed witnesses they have."

"Witnesses? They have more than one?" I croaked.

"Yes, Karl, they must have more than one; otherwise it's just Miss Gomez's word against yours. They'd never go with just that."

"Oh, thank fucking God!" I cried, finally coming unglued. "Thank fucking Jesus Christ On The Cross they wouldn't dare to go with just that!"

"Please, calm down, Karl. It's not as bad as it looks."

"No, Bob, you're right," I said hysterically, "it couldn't possibly be that bad. Not when it looks like my reputation has been destroyed forever, no matter whether I'm ever proven guilty or not. Not when it looks like…"

"Karl, listen. As your attorney, as someone you have hired to look after your interests, I have to ask you something. I'm not being judgmental. I'm just doing my job. It's ten o'clock in the morning, Karl. Have you been drinking?"

"Of course I've been drinking, Bob." This first name business was beginning to irritate me. "What the fuck do you expect me to do?"

"I expect you to fight this thing, not roll over like a beaten dog. I'm pretty darn good at what I do. But if we're going to win this, I'll need your help. We'll both have to be on top of our games, Karl."

"My game is repairing knees," I muttered. "But they won't let me play anymore. Bob."

Robert Zimmerman was not without sensibilities. For a full minute he sat silently staring at his manicured nails. It could not have been easy for him to watch a man, a man not unlike himself, being crushed, spindled and mutilated right before his eyes. He might even, at one time, have had a Mariela of his own.

"You've been dealt a crumby hand," he said finally. "It's rather ironic, if you think about it."

"Ironic?"

"The real conspiracy is being perpetrated by the prosecution. Too bad we can't prove it."

Irving had been able to confirm that after the tragic death of his young wife in an automobile accident, Jack Davidson, not yet the U.S. Attorney, had indeed sought the services of a psychiatrist. Apparently, he'd been suffering from depression, and who could blame him. This had been six years ago. Everything, Irving said, pointed to my bother-in-law as the shrink in question, but short of obtaining a subpoena (impossible without some solid evidence of wrongdoing), it could never be proved.

"Yes, Bob, that's certainly ironic," I said miserably. "What happens next?"

"Well," Zimmerman said, consulting his watch, as if we just had time to catch a plane, "we're due downtown in an hour. You present yourself. You're formally charged, and arrested."

"Will they put handcuffs on me, Bob?"

"No. Jack assured me that you will be treated with kid gloves."

"I see. Since he's already defaming and framing me, why not be nice about it."

"That's the idea."

"And then?"

"Mug shots, fingerprints, the usual. Then, I've been assured, you will be arraigned later today. We plead innocent, of course, and the judge sets the bail, which I have also been assured, will be low. Davidson is determined to appear kind, gentle and totally fair—as he slips the noose around your neck."

"Jail?" I asked, my voice trembling.

"One night. It's all been arranged. Unless the judge wants to be particularly severe, which I doubt."

"I don't know, Bob, I haven't done so well with judges lately. What's the jail like? Will I be in my own cell, or…"

"Don't worry about it. You'll be in and out so fast you'll, uh…" Zimmerman had noticed the tears beginning to run down my face. "Karl, I'm really sorry. You don't deserve this. You're no criminal. I've defended my share, and I should know. There's nothing criminal about you. Trust me. We're going to fight. And we're going to win. First thing, we go after their bogus witnesses and their phony testimony. We'll know everything they supposedly 'have' on you in a matter of days. I can't wait to see what they've cooked up. It should be interesting."

Interesting? It occurred to me that all lawyers have a little of the ghoul about them, even relatively human ones like Zimmerman.

"I can't wait, either. Bob."

TWENTY NINE

As advertised, I was treated throughout the entire process with consideration and respect; like a monarch, in fact, on his royal way to the guillotine. Everyone spoke to me in polite and reasoned tones, calling me "Doctor". Jack Davidson, a worried man if ever I saw one, was especially cordial, though he did have some difficulty looking me in the eye.

"You operated on a cousin of mine," he said by way of breaking the ice. "Did a damn good job, too."

The young man who took my fingerprints asked me what Brian Westin was really like. I said that he was a prince among men. The fellow who took my mug shots was concerned about Brian's recent injury. Would he be back for another run at the title, he wondered? Not likely, I said, the human body could only take so much.

And so it went, as I was carefully passed from one person to the next. Under different circumstances (Not being arrested, for example!) it might have been a not unpleasant way to pass the time.

Zimmerman had finally gotten one thing right. I was only made to spend a single night behind bars, in my own private cell. At ten o'clock they turned out the lights, allowing me to lay awake all night in the dark in a state of near total despair. If only they hadn't taken my shoelaces, I told myself, I'd really do it this time—if it was in fact possible to hang oneself with only a pair of laces, which I tended to doubt.

Upon my release I made straight for the Westchester, the bottle and the bong. The tabloids, I quickly learned, as well as the local television news stations, Nancy Drew and Herman Bormann, were all having the time of their lives at my expense. Someone, a grand jury member it was rumored, had leaked portions of the "testimony" to the media. The resulting headlines were impressively lurid:

"DOCTOR TURNED PIMP?" and "HE LIKES TO WATCH?" were two of my personal favorites.

What Charles and Davidson had, in my attorney's words, "cooked up" was so absurd, so unbelievable, so far beyond the realms of plausibility, no one, it seemed to me, could possibly take it seriously. But of course, in this, as in so many other things, I was wrong. The thrust of the prosecution's "case" went like this:

The moment we landed on the coast of Florida, I informed Mariela that if she wanted to remain in America, she would have to perform acts of prostitution in my presence. Apparently, money was not my sole motivation. I was, it seemed, a world-class pervert who derived endless pleasure observing my girlfriend/prostitute being banged by other men, as I sat nearby masturbating like a monkey.

I was particularly fond, according to Mariela's testimony, of watching her be demeaned, slapped around, peed upon, sodomized, spanked, etc. On one such occasion I'd insisted, to spice things up, upon having Carmen, her best friend, present. Carmen, who was now a witness for the prosecution. Under constant threat (by me) of being sent back to Cuba (Yes, that was ironic, Bob), Mariela had had no choice but to involve her friend, and Carmen no choice but to go along with the entire sick business; either that, or see Mariela deported back to the living nightmare that was her native country.

There were two other witnesses, alleged customers, who claimed to have paid me five hundred dollars for the privilege of sexually abusing Mariela in my presence. God knows out of what dung-heap Davidson had hauled these individuals, or what threats he'd used to garner their cooperation. And what difference did it make? As I imagined my daughters reading all this, the mechanics of my crucifixion seemed almost beside the point.

That the two male "witnesses" would both turn out to be "known" (as opposed to "unknown"?) child molesters, would only make, once you'd accepted the first false premise, the prosecution's case that much stronger. For who, after all, besides "known" perverts would agree to such an arrangement in the first place?

The times of these alleged encounters had been carefully chosen to coincide with occasions when I had actually been with Mariela in her room. That no one would be able to recall seeing the known perverts or Mariela's best friend going up to, or coming down from said room was, apparently, of little consequence. The prosecution would claim that any number of people came and went unnoticed at the Westchester, and they would be correct. The place was chronically understaffed, and Leonard was often forced to leave the front desk unattended.

The afternoon of my release I taxied up to Irving's office. My primary care attorney was naturally outraged by the gross injustice being perpetrated upon his friend and client, but was also, despite himself, impressed.

"You know why this far-fetched fantasy fuck-job might actually hang together?" Irving told me. "It is ingenious, diabolically ingenious, if you think about it. What those bastards are counting on is that no one is going to believe that a U.S. Attorney would dare to make something like this up; that a U.S. Attorney would threaten and bribe witnesses; that he would commit a dozen felonies in order to destroy a man he doesn't even know! It is a case of the incredible being trumped by the unbelievable. You know," Irving concluded, his voice tinged with admiration, "if everybody sticks to their story, this could actually work."

Another ghoul.

Bob Zimmerman was on more or less the same page (my obituary page) as Irving. "If all the witnesses stand up under cross-examination, and we can't find any chinks in their armor, this could be bad," he told me. "In all my years…a U.S. Attorney…I just can't believe it."

And neither could I. "A jury is really going to swallow this garbage?"

"Karl, it depends on the witnesses, how credible they are. The problem is, there is no denying the first part of their case, that you, a man of great professional and social standing with everything to lose, took a tremendous risk, went to an enormous amount of trouble and expense in order to smuggle Miss Gomez into the United States. The leap from that to the pandering and all the rest of it seems enormous to us, but might not appear so to a jury. I'm afraid, Karl, this is a good deal more serious than I first believed."

"How much more serious?"

"We go to trial on this, and lose, you could be looking at serious jail time. Five years, maybe more. It depends. That's what they have to hold over your head, to force you into a plea. I'm sure they'd prefer a plea; something can always go wrong, and in this case, something going wrong would be very bad news for Mr. Davidson."

"Plead guilty?"

"Plead guilty to one of the lesser charges. You'd do only a year, or maybe less. But…"

"My career?"

Bob shook his head.

"In that case I might as well be in jail."

"We'll just have to work that much harder," Zimmerman said with grim determination, "to break one of their bogus witnesses. We do that, and the whole thing collapses like a house of cards. We just have to keep digging until we've… uh…" Poor Bob had run out of clichés.

"Until we've dug me out of my living grave?" I offered helpfully.

"Be positive. This thing is a long way from over, Karl."

"That's what I'm afraid of. Bob."

THIRTY

"Pervert or not, you're still the best in the business."

"I am not a pervert!" I informed the maimed quarterback.

"Hey, take it easy, Doc; I didn't mean it, like, disrespectfully."

Brian had hobbled up three flights of stairs with the aid of two aluminum crutches and one plastic woman, who, if she wasn't a model, was surely wasting away from some mortal disease. Brian had a certain fondness for models, and went through five or six of them a year. Irving had given the lame narcissist my address. He'd thought a visit from Brian might be "therapeutic".

The handsome but defective couple had arrived unannounced, Brian levering me out of the doorway with one of his crutches, the model loaded down with an oversized envelope containing an entire deck of MRIs.

"Doc, this is Lise."

Lise, who if you turned her sideways might have disappeared altogether, regarded me with a mixture of fear and disgust, as if she'd just been presented to an enormous cockroach.

"Well, Lise, it is just so nice to meet you. Are you hungry? You look hungry. Would you like a snack?" I picked up a crumpled white paper bag from the floor, reached inside and fished out a half-eaten jelly doughnut.

"No thank you," she said, her worst fears confirmed.

"You're looking kind of haggard, Doc," Brian remarked.

"Haggard? Someone loan you a dictionary, Brian?"

Brian, impervious to irony, sat on the bed, patted a place beside him, and was joined by Lise, who continued to watch me warily, as if she feared that at any moment I would begin to crawl up her leg. For my part, I fixed my best bug-eyed gaze on her crotch, hoping to discomfort her to the point where she would insist on leaving.

Brian, of course, noticed none of this. Having dispensed all the small talk at his disposal, he went directly to the matter at hand: himself. "These bogus doctors," he whined, "they're telling me it's all over. They're saying I'm finished, that I'll never play again."

"Well," I said, leering evilly at Lise as I stuffed the remains of the doughnut into my mouth, "at least you'll be going out on a high note."

"But I'm not ready to go out. I'm only thirty-two."

"Here, let me have a look at those," I said, reaching out ambiguously—I could have been reaching for the MRIs, or I could have been going for one of Lise's deflated breasts. The model recoiled, sliding back on her boney butt out of reach.

Brian frowned. "Lise, what are you doing? Give Doc my x-rays. He's not going to bite you, for Christ's sake."

Lise did not appear to believe him. While she sat there, hesitating, I grabbed the white envelope out of her hands and took it over to the window.

"I wouldn't let that pervert touch me," Lise whispered, just loud enough for me to hear. "How could you let him operate on your knee?"

"Different strokes," Brian said. "One thing has nothing to do with the other. They say Leonardo de Vinci was a perv. Michelangelo, too. And what's his name—the guy who painted the soup cans? Another perv. But that doesn't mean they weren't geniuses. So, Doc, what do you think? Ready to put humpty dumpty back together again?"

"Perhaps you haven't heard, Brian, they've yanked my license. There's not a hospital in the country which would let me in the door, except as a patient."

"Then we'll go somewhere else," Brian decided, "like the Philippines. They love me in the Philippines, and I hear they'll let anyone operate there, regardless of his... whatever."

"Where did you hear that?"

"I read it in a magazine. An article about something they call Psycho-Surgery. These guys over there, they pull your liver out with their bare hands and wash it in a pail of water. It's amazing. None of them have licenses, either."

"I think we're reaching, Brian. In any case," I added with a smile, "looking these over I have to agree with the prognosis. The party's over. Time to hang up the cleats. Not even I could repair this mess; not to the extent that you could play football again. Unless it's from a wheelchair. Isn't that an event at the Special Olympics—wheelchair football?"

"But you'd try, wouldn't you, Doc? I know you. You'd take it as a personal challenge."

"Or maybe it's wheelchair basketball. Hard to imagine people in wheelchairs tackling one another."

"You'd try, Doc, right?"

"My advice, Brian, is take the money and run. Go back to Switzerland with your friend here. Or was that another friend? Are you listening, Brian? Forget football. You're done."

"That's not the real you talking," Brian said with infuriating smugness. "Doc, this mess you've got yourself into—it's got you down. But you're not out. Not if I have anything to say about it. I'm starting a campaign to get your license re-instated. Me and the whole team. They can't turn down the reigning Super Bowl Champions. Not in this town!"

"Brian, I wish you all the success in the world. In all your future endeavors. And I wish you an infinite supply of pain killers—you're going to need them." Then, turning to his escort, I said, "Miss, are you quite certain you wouldn't like something to eat? I'm sure I've got a chunk of something lying around here somewhere."

I began to root about under my chair until I found a twist of cinnamon bun wedged into the carpet. Plucking it from its fibrous prison, I raised the deformed piece of pastry triumphantly aloft. But by then, Lise was already on her way back to Berne.

THIRTY-ONE

It was time once again to confront Field Marshal Marsha Fielding, to be verbally eviscerated, judicially drawn and quartered. On the corner of Third Avenue and Twenty-Third Street I climbed into the back of a cab. The driver, the top of whose head was wrapped in what appeared to be an adult diaper, turned to ask where I was going. Actually, what he said was, "Djoutoweir?" Before I could respond, however, his eyes grew wide and he began to more or less foam at the mouth. "Dyou!" he declared. "Bed min!"

"What?"

"I hab door-tourz!" he shouted furiously.

"You have a tortoise?" I asked in confusion

"Bed min! Oot texi!" Reaching under the seat he grabbed a revolver and pointed it at my face. "Bed min! See dyou en dee Nancy Drew! Oot texi!"

Carefully, I climbed out of the car, walked a block (just for luck) and flagged down another cab. My new driver spoke excellent English, being a native of Astoria, Queens, and so was able to express himself with considerably more elegance than the previous fellow.

"You low-life pervert bastard!" he barked. "I hope they cut your dick off and shove it up your ass, you sick fuck!"

Somewhat taken aback, I said, "I assume then that you are unwilling, at this time, to take me downtown?"

"I'd rather eat rat poison," he replied.

The fourth cabbie (he must have lived in one of those allergy-proof bubbles) failed to recognize me, and before long I found myself in the fearsome presence of Judge Marsha Fielding, albeit fifteen minutes late.

"You're late!" the Man Eater snarled.

"Yes, I know. I'm sorry," I said meekly.

"I do not like to be kept waiting. I hope you have a good excuse."

Certain that Judge Marsha's last remark did not require an actual response, I cast my eyes penitentially downward and waited for the storm to pass—until I felt Irving prodding me in the ribs. Looking up, I saw the black-robed beast glaring at me, like an overfed cat waiting to see which way the trapped rat will scurry next.

"You really want to know why I was late?" I asked.

"Absolutely."

"Well, ah, the truth is…"

"The truth would be nice, Dr. Sanderson."

"The first three taxis I attempted to flag down refused to take me."

"And why was that?" The Man Eater was on a mission.

"Well, Your Honor, I'm not really sure, except they all seemed to be Nancy Drew fans."

"Nancy Drew?"

"Yes, Your Honor, you know, that horrid woman with the lowbrow television show."

"I know who she is," Judge Marsha said, "and I happen to be a Nancy Drew fan myself."

Irving and I exchanged a despairing look, like two men in a life boat watching their compass, their oars and their last quart of fresh water being washed overboard by a malevolent wave.

"Let's get down to business," Judge Marsha announced. "Under normal circumstances I do not entertain the same motion twice." There was that terrifying phrase again. Apparently, nothing about my circumstances was normal anymore. Irving, who realized at once what was coming, grabbed my wrist. "Mr. Bormann, however, has introduced some compelling arguments as to why I should reconsider my ruling on his motion to freeze all of Dr. Sanderson's assets."

I glanced over at the enemy camp. Bormann was looking especially thirsty today. Janice, slipping back into character, was perfectly rigid, her face an impassive mask. I noticed a hand resting supportively on her shoulder. Following the arm back to its owner, I saw that Charles was sitting directly behind his sister. Our eyes locked. Charles smiled, or rather smirked, slowly nodding his head with satisfaction.

My brother-in-law had once informed me, at a wedding I believe, that tennis was "a wonderful metaphor for life". Charles could not stand to lose at tennis. He'd throw tantrums, break rackets, make wild accusations against his opponents. Now, up two sets to none, and with match point a mere formality, Charles could afford to relax and enjoy the game.

"In the interests of fairplay," the Man Eater continued, sneering openly in our direction, "after Mr. Bormann presents his arguments to the court, Mr. Waxman will have forty-eight hours to present his counter arguments. After which, I will make my ruling. Any objections?"

Irving leapt to his feet. "Yes, Your Honor, I have several objections. We have just been blindsided. I was not informed of this…"

"You're being informed now," Judge Marsha cut him off. "And you will have ample time to prepare a response."

"Forty-eight hours, in my humble opinion, Your Honor, is not an adequate amount of time to prepare…"

"All right then, Mr. Waxman, I'll give you a week. Mr. Bormann, proceed."

Harry Bormann rose to his feet and raised his arms into the air, like a vulture sunning itself on a chilly morning. Then he proceeded to speak for nearly ten minutes, though all his legalistic verbiage came down to one single point: Dr. Karl Sanderson was currently spending "inordinately large sums of money" defending himself from criminal charges, money that would be "better set aside for the future use of his family".

"What about Dr. Sanderson's future?" Irving interrupted at one point.

"His future?" the Man Eater said, the implication being that Dr. Sanderson did not actually have one.

Bormann, also writing me off like a bad debt, chimed in with a cheerful, "Dr. Sanderson's future is, at best, ill-defined."

"What about innocent until proven guilty?" Irving shouted. "Is this not the United States of…"

The Man Eater once again, and with obvious pleasure, cut my attorney off at the knees. "That will be enough of that, Mr. Waxman. I've already told you that you will have your chance to respond. For the present I will ask that you behave yourself and keep your rhetorical mouth shut."

"But, Your Honor…"

"You are testing my patience, Counselor."

The hearing ended, as it had begun, badly. "Testing her patience!" Irving exploded in the safe confines of the elevator. "What a joke! That sadistic Nazi bitch is giving me a fucking castration complex!"

"What about me, Irving? What about my balls?"

"Your balls? They're long gone, my friend," Irving said with a sigh. "Send them, wherever they happen to be, my best regards."

THIRTY-TWO

As the foundations upon which I'd built my life continued to crumble, my state of mind deteriorated accordingly. Even the slightest hint of agreeable news might have helped to reverse this decline, but of good news there was none. In my pocket I now carried at all times a small vial I'd procured with the aid of my prescription pad, which technically I was no longer empowered to use. On the increasingly frequent occasions when the nightmarish nature of my situation threatened to overwhelm me, I would caress the vial and think: Twenty Phenobarbital and a glass of water—a few painless swallows, and I can kiss this whole train wreck goodbye.

That I was incapable of hanging myself or jumping off of a tall building, I was certain. But to swallow a handful of pills while sitting comfortably in the fading light at the end of the day, with several shots of rum under my belt and Handel playing in the background—that, I felt, was eminently doable, even for a coward like myself.

Of all the many factors contributing to my terminal malaise, the most demoralizing was the eager manner in which everyone seemed to be accepting my re-minted status. First, I'd been a child molester. Then I'd been upgraded to dirty old man. Now, I'd been downgraded to something in between. Nancy Drew had summed up the prevailing sentiment nicely: "No one," she'd snarled on her show, "could ever make up something like this. It's worse than the sickest porno movie. It turns your stomach. Thank God, Jack Davidson, the U.S. Attorney, had the intelligence and the integrity to listen to me, and put this alleged predator…"

No one could ever make up something like this. Not a grand jury and, certainly, not a U.S. Attorney with no apparent axe to grind. I'd been tried and convicted in the media, and condemned in the court of public opinion. I was a pariah, guilty of grotesquely embarrassing crimes, a monster who got his jollies abusing and watching others sexually abuse young defenseless girls. This was the public perception and nothing, it seemed, I could say or do would change it.

Thus was my situation growing less tenable with each passing day. I was so despised and my face so familiar that I could no longer go out in public. It wasn't a matter of mere humiliation anymore; it had become dangerous. Death threats arrived every day at Irving's office, many of them written in Spanish, which I found particularly disheartening.

And then that vindictive centipede, still hovering over my head like a poly-pedal Jehovah, proceeded to drop the cruelest shoe of all. The call came from Irving. An old friend, he said, wanted to speak with me. The old friend, Jeremy Morgan, had been a mentor to me in my younger days, and over the years we had remained on friendly terms. Now retired, he sat on the New York State Medical Board; was in fact one of its most influential members. If anyone was in a position to help me regain my license, Jeremy was the one. With trembling fingers, I punched in his number.

"Jeremy, it's Karl."

"Karl. How are you holding up?"

"Not well."

"So, I've heard. Listen, Karl, the reason I called." Jeremy was a great believer in brevity. "There are two things I must tell you. The first is this: I don't believe for one second these ridiculous accusations they're making. I can imagine you wandering off the reservation, certainly no crime. And, obviously, you've acted like a fool. But these outlandish stories of your involvement in prostitution—the whole business smacks of vendetta and conspiracy. I have no idea why, but clearly someone is out to destroy you."

Thank God! I thought. Finally, someone (someone not being paid to be on my side) who believed in my innocence.

"Jeremy, I can't tell you how grateful I am. This is good news, the first I've had in ages. Do you think there's a chance you can sway the board?"

"That's the second thing I have to tell you, Karl. Unfortunately, my colleagues on the board do not share my opinion. Their minds are made up. Even if you are found innocent of all those felonies, they will never reinstate your license. According to them you've besmirched—that was the word they used—the good name of physicians everywhere. And for the sake of 'Medicine Itself' you can never be readmitted into our holy fraternity. I'm sorry, Karl. I tried my best. But the publicity—I thought you should know what you're up against. It's a shame," he concluded, "to lose a man of your caliber."

So, that was that. I'd been flushed down the nearest drain. A man of my caliber. What a shame.

THIRTY-THREE

Most injuries are the result of a single traumatic event: a fall, a sudden application of force, a collision. But others are the consequence of a long slow process, an accumulation of stresses and strains which eat away at what was once a healthy joint to the point where, finally, it can no longer function.

My personal breakdown, or surrender, or emotional collapse, or whatever you choose to call it, was brought about by a combination of the two: a process of steady erosion on the one hand, and on the other a series of body blows, Jeremy's call not least among them. But in the end, it was a visit from Candace, the one person upon whose unconditional love I knew I could always count, which nudged me over the edge.

We'd spoken on the phone several times prior to her visit, short uncomfortable conversations with too much left unsaid. At the end of each call she'd told me she loved me, and that was all I needed to hear. Then the indictments came down, and there'd been no more calls.

It was her birthday. She turned eighteen today and I was desperate to speak to her. I thought of calling the house. If Janice or, God forbid, Charles answered, I would simply hang up. Candace might not even be home, but it was worth a chance. I sat in my room in the late afternoon gloom working up the courage to make the call. I had another drink, and was about to reach for the phone when it rang of its own accord. It was Candace. She was coming to see me. I felt, floundering amid the debris of my life, as if I'd been tossed a piece of driftwood upon which I could float a little longer.

"You look terrific, sweetie," I told her.

"You look…not so great, Dad. You been hitting the booze pretty hard?"

I'd rehearsed this scene in my mind numerous times, with every intention of putting up a strong façade, making light of my difficulties, being a model of stoicism under fire. But with Candace staring me frankly in the eye, I opted for the truth. "It's all I can do to get out of bed in the morning," I confessed. "The rum helps me get through the day. Otherwise…"

"Drinking isn't going to solve anything, Dad."

"How's your sister?" I asked, desperate to change the subject.

"Brenda is a self-centered cunt."

"Your mother said that Brenda would never forgive me."

"I don't know. She's just following Uncle Charles' script. Did you know he convinced mom to send me to an academy for troubled girls?"

"You're joking."

"No joke. They told me it was for my own good."

"What did you say?"

"I said, 'In as much as I'm about to turn eighteen, the two of you can stuff it.' I'm moving out. So is Steven. We're going to share a place with our rhythm section. It'll be kind of cramped, but I can't take it at home anymore. It's like living on a Gulag."

"I can imagine."

"Dad, tell me what really happened," Candace said with sudden urgency. "The stuff they're saying…"

A silent scream filled my head. I took a long deep breath, and then another.

"All right, Candace, this is what happened. This is the truth, I swear to God."

And with hoarse voice and red eyes, I told her. Everything. A complete confession. At several points I became too embarrassed to continue. It was, after all, my eighteen-year-old daughter sitting there. Candace, with the occasional, "Come on, Dad, I'm not a baby," urged me over the rough spots, until I'd told it all, from sweet beginning, to bitter end. Then I sat there, red with shame, timorously awaiting her verdict.

"Uncle Charles blackmailing a federal prosecutor?" she said after a while. "It's like a bad movie."

"That's pretty much what my life has turned into, sweetie."

"It was stupid to bring her back."

"I know, believe me, I know."

"I mean, you could have had your fun, Dad, and got away clean. Being married to an icicle like mom, who could blame you for fooling around."

"Yes, well…"

"You know, I used to think that you were kind of an icicle, too. I never would've believed you were so—but you never should have brought her back. Why'd you do it, Dad? You're not stupid."

"I was in love, sweetie. Not much of an excuse, but there you have it."

"Being in love makes you stupid?" Candace had never been in love, and honestly wanted to know.

"Not stupid, necessarily. More like, insane. Being in love—it's like a disease which eats away at your brain."

"But not everybody who falls in love," my daughter pointed out, "brings their girlfriend back from Cuba and sets her up in a hotel only twenty miles from his wife's house."

"No, sweetie, that's true. I must have come down with a particularly virulent strain. And I felt guilty leaving her behind. Who knows? Maybe it was the guilt that did me in."

"Is she as hot as she looks?" Candace asked with more than idle curiosity.

"Let's, ah, talk about something else," I said, blushing furiously.

Candace, who never found it convenient to disguise her feelings, sat there for a long time staring at me quizzically, as if she were attempting to figure out who this man, her father, really was. "Do you have any proof?" she finally asked.

"Proof?"

"Of the conspiracy. You think the U.S. Attorney was once Uncle Charles' patient, but can you prove it?"

I didn't like the way the word "conspiracy" sounded on my daughter's tongue. It was as if...

"It doesn't seem likely," I said.

"No one's going to believe it, Dad. Not without some solid proof. It just doesn't sound plausible."

I didn't want to ask the question; I was terrified of the answer. But I had to know. "Do you believe it, sweetie?"

"I know Uncle Charles and what he's capable of," she said evasively.

"And?"

For the first time, she looked uncomfortable, confused. "It's all so out of character, Dad. Sneaking off to Cuba. The prostitutes. Risking your life to bring back a nineteen-year-old hooker."

"Yes, I agree. Even to me, it was all one big surprise. But what about the rest of it?"

"The rest of it?"

"Yes. Forcing her into prostitution. The perversions. The cruelty. That's even more out of character. Do you believe all that, too?"

"I don't want to believe it, Daddy," she said, her eyes filling with tears.

And there it was. The last nail. There is no hope, I realized, no hope at all. I looked at this beautiful brilliant young woman who wanted to believe that her father was not a monster, and I gave up. I died.

So. What next? The vial? I was ready. Only, there was something I had to do first. Before I killed myself, I needed to kill Charles. For the children's sake. And for my own. The thought of him pontificating at my funeral ("A tragedy. He was a very sick man. Naturally, I begged him to seek help. But, of course, he wouldn't listen. They rarely do when they're that far gone. A great loss.") was more than I could stand.

In a sense, Charles saved my life that night. For the first time I truly hated someone, and that hatred kept me alive, kept my hand from reaching for the Phenobarbital.

PART V

ONE

The bewildered individual at the Immigration counter regarded me with what I felt was a certain lack of friendliness. Déjà-vu all over again, I thought, recalling Yogi Berra's famous redundancy.

"Señor," he said, "what are you telling me? That this is not a valid passport?"

"*Correcto*," I replied with a smile. "It's a fake."

Eying me warily now, certain that he was dealing with a lunatic, the official said, "Why have you travelled to Cuba on a forged passport?"

"Because," I said with a straight face, "I am a political refugee."

The man's head jerked back, pigeon-like, on his thick neck.

"You are an American seeking political asylum in Cuba?" he demanded.

"Exactamente. I'm also a close personal friend of the Minister of Health, Dr. Villaseñor." A slight exaggeration, although I was nearly certain that the minister would, at the very least, remember me.

Once again, the officer's head jerked backwards. At any moment, I thought, he will begin to coo and peck at the papers on his desk.

"The Minister of Health?" he repeated helplessly.

"Yes. Before you take any further action, you might want to give him a call. My real name, by the way, is Dr. Karl Sanderson."

To be on the safe side, I handed him a card.

The official picked up his radiophone and repeated

more or less what I had told him. Within minutes we were joined by a small army of his cohorts who, en masse, led me to a small windowless room. Then, chattering like a troop of excited monkeys, they went away, after locking me inside.

I was left alone for almost two hours, allowing me to consider from every point of view the wisdom of my present course of action. This might work, I thought, or it might not. I put my hand on the vial. It was still in my pocket. If they decide to send me back, I reasoned calmly, it will probably be to San Juan, the city from which I'd flown in. More than likely there would be U.S. Marshals waiting for me there on the tarmac. But long before they could put the cuffs on, I would have taken my pills, and all they'd get to extradite was a corpse.

Oddly enough, I didn't seem to care a great deal one way or the other. I'd reached a point where my own fate was largely a matter of indifference to me. I might die in the very near future. Or I might live in Cuba for another two or three dreary decades. Either way, it didn't seem to matter. With the breeziness of a man flipping a coin into the air, I'd tossed my future to the Cuban authorities. Heads, they catch me, and I live. Tails, they bobble the ball, and I die. I closed my eyes, yawned once and fell asleep.

I awoke with a start sometime later to discover two men standing over me: the Minister of Health and a man who, judging by all the shiny insignia hanging from his fatigues, had to be a colonel at the very least.

"Dr. Sanderson?" the Minister of Health said, his eyes wide with wonder. "It's really you? What in Ché's name is going on here?"

"Dr. Villaseñor," I said, shaking his hand, "so good to see you again."

"Yes, it is good to see you, too, Dr. Sanderson. But I am a little confused. The Immigration people say that you—but surely, they must be mistaken."

"I have come to Cuba, Dr. Villaseñor," I proclaimed formally, "seeking political asylum. Refuge, as it were, from the corrupt ruthless gangsters who run my former country."

"Political asylum? You can't be serious."

"I am completely serious, *Sr. Ministro*. In fact, it would not be an exaggeration to say that my life is now in your able and compassionate hands."

"But why?" the Minister spluttered. "A man in your position. With all your wealth, your prestige. What, what could have made you take such a step?"

"You haven't heard," I asked carefully, "about the conflict with my government?"

"Not a word. You know, we are kind of insulated here," he said apologetically, as if in my absence he should have been keeping abreast of my every move.

"Yes, well, the government of the United States and I have reached what you might call, an impasse. I've decided to renounce my American citizenship, and become a Cuban. If you are willing to have me," I added humbly.

"I see. No, I don't see. I am shocked. But honored," the nervous man nattered away. "Of course, this kind of decision is only made at the highest levels. Not by me, I am afraid, though I will be delighted to give you my personal…" The Minister paused, realizing that he might be jumping the gun. "Come with me, please. We have been summoned."

"Summoned?"

"Yes. *el Comandante* has requested our presence. Or yours. I'm not certain if he wishes to actually see me. Of course, we are very close, but *el Comandante* is such a busy man."

"*Comandante*? You mean, Castro?"

"In Cuba there is only one *Comandante*." Then, putting his arm around my shoulder, he said, "The car is waiting. We must hurry. Your timing, Dr. Sanderson, I must say, is…interesting. You have arrived at a time of great national crisis. This is purely coincidence, I suppose? No, don't tell me. If I was meant to know, I would have been informed."

"Informed of what?"

"You have arrived at a potentially tragic moment in our nation's history."

"Oh? I'm sorry to hear that."

"Don't be. If you really want to live here in this fu—in our Worker's Paradise, then this crisis may be just what the doctor ordered."

"Very good," I said, emitting a polite chuckle.

"What?"

"The joke you made. Very good."

"I made a joke?"

"Didn't you?"

The Minister of Health cast a furtive glance at the security camera. "I don't think so," he said uncertainly.

TWO

I was blindfolded for the last half of the ride, which ended in the driveway of an immense colonial mansion. Before being allowed to enter the white colossus, I was professionally patted down by a massive man with a thick black beard who everyone called *el Sargento*. Holding my vial of Phenobarbital as if it were a dangerous insect, *el Sargento* said, "What are these?"

"Sleeping pills," I replied. "I suffer from insomnia."

"They are not poison?"

"No, but if you took all twenty of them, you'd be dead in an hour."

"I will hold on to them for you," he said politely, "until your interview with *el Comandante* is over."

Fidel Castro, for a man dealing with a grave national crisis, seemed remarkably relaxed. Dressed in a powder-blue track suit, with his boots propped casually atop his desk, he held an unlit cigar in his hand as he stared out a large window at the ocean.

Seeing the famous leader face-to-face was, despite everything, an electrifying experience. Of course, he'd aged since his glory days. His beard wasn't as thick as it once had been, nor did he have exactly a full head of hair. But the man was still remarkably intense, charismatic, larger than life. And mad as a Hatter.

Fidel spent a frighteningly long time staring at the water, a faraway look on his face, deciding, one assumed, important matters of state. I sat in my chair, saying nothing, *el Sargento* looming over me, his garlic-laden breath making my eyes water. Finally, the aging despot turned to me and said in an accusatory tone, "You are Dr. Karl Sanderson, the famous surgeon."

"It is an honor to meet you, *Comandante*."

"You haven't met me," he said. "Perhaps, at a later date. What are you doing in Cuba?"

"*Comandante*," I began my prepared speech, "I am a victim of political repression. I have been forced to flee my country, and seek asylum in your Worker's Paradise."

"You," Fidel said severely, "helped a young daughter of the revolution emigrate illegally to the United States."

El *Comandante* appeared, unfortunately, to be somewhat better informed than the Minister of Health.

"Yes," I said.

"Why?"

"I was in love with her, *Comandante*."

"Love…love…" For a full two minutes Fidel went away, lost in some reverie—he was said, even at his age, to be a man of strong and vigorous passions. When he came back, he was scowling. "What about the prostitution?" he demanded.

El *Comandante* was very well informed, and I prayed that in the event of an unfavorable ruling, *el Sargento* would return my pills before I was booted from the country.

"An official conspiracy," I said, playing to Fidel's reputed paranoia where the American government was concerned. "The witnesses were bribed and intimidated. The entire case, a fabrication. The only crime I committed was falling in love with someone who was not my wife."

"Perhaps," Fidel said, reaching into a drawer and withdrawing a magazine. "They say," he went on, holding it up for my perusal, "that you are the best knee surgeon in the world. Is this true?"

The magazine was the Spanish language edition of Sports Illustrated, featuring myself and Brian Westin on the cover. Fidel, I later learned, was a subscriber.

"Who can say who is the best at something, *Comandante*," I said modestly.

Fidel reached into another drawer and pulled out the infamous issue of the National Enquirer. "She is very young, but you have good taste," he said, nodding his head with approval.

"Ah, thank you." Fidel's abrupt jumping from subject to subject was making me dizzy.

"My doctors no longer let me smoke," he said, waving the unlit cigar. "They call me a dictator, but doctors are far more bossy than I ever was."

"Yes," I agreed, "we are rather a tyrannical group."

From still another drawer Fidel removed an MRI featuring eight views of a knee. Holding it in both hands, he said with great urgency, "This belongs to the future of Cuban baseball. This could represent one of the great tragedies in the history of our nation. This is the only reason you were not sent packing the minute you landed in my country with your bullshit story."

There was another unnaturally long pause. Was I expected to say something? With Castro it was hard to tell. Finally, I could contain myself no longer. "Well, *Comandante*, may I be permitted to see it?"

His mad dark eyes locked onto mine, Castro solemnly passed me the MRI. I held it up to the light for a minute and said, "Torn anterior cruciate ligament. Torn medial meniscus. Slight rupture of the patellar tendon. A bit unusual for a baseball injury, *Comandante*."

"The moron was playing basketball! Against my express orders!"

"Yes, well, young athletes are full of…"

"He threw," Castro thundered, "three consecutive one-hitters!"

El *Comandante*, even from a range of six feet, managed in his enthusiasm to spray my face with a fine mist of saliva. I remained motionless in my chair, not daring to wipe it off.

"His fastball is a bullet," Fidel proclaimed. "His sinker has no bottom. And his curveball is an enigma. In two years he will surpass even Sendme Gofucks!"

What?

After another excruciatingly long pause, he added, "If… if…if someone can fix (he indicated, with a wave of the unlit cigar, the MRI) this lousy mess! Can you fix this lousy mess, Dr. Sanderson? Can you make the Cuban Sendme Gofucks as good as new?"

Ah, now I had it: Sandy Koufax! So this was the national crisis. No wonder the Minister of Health had called my timing interesting. "Probably," I said. "I'd have to examine the actual knee to say for certain."

Fidel nodded. *el Sargento* went to the door of what turned out to be a closet, opened it and led a young man, hopping on his uninjured leg and dressed only in a pair of bright red boxer shorts, out into the room.

"Here it is," Castro said, "examine it all you want."

The injured pitcher couldn't have been more than twenty-one. He was very tall, a shade darker than Mariela and completely terrified. "*C-c-Comandante…*" he began in a pleading voice.

"Don't talk to me, you undisciplined goat!" Castro seethed.

"Where do I, ah, put him, *Comandante*?" The room contained only the large wooden desk and our two chairs. I needed something I could use as an examination table.

"Put him on my desk," Castro snarled. "Put him on the moon, for all I care. God, how I long to light this fucking cigar!"

"*Comandante*," the young man whimpered, "I promise I will never…"

"Quiet!"

I spent twenty minutes moving the pitcher's leg this way and that, asking him how much pain, if any, my various manipulations were causing him. Then, from force of habit, I said, "You can get dressed now."

"I will tell him," Castro thundered, "when he can get dressed!

"Of course, *Comandante*."

"So, what is the prognosis?"

"I don't see a problem, *Comandante*, as long as the young man does exactly what I tell him. The post-operative therapy is every bit as important as the…"

"He will do what he is told," Fidel assured me.

"In that case, we can have him pitching more one-hitters in about a year."

"Six months," Fidel said.

"I beg your pardon?"

"The Caribbean World Series is in six months. He must be back in peak form no later than that."

"Impossible," I said.

"What!"

El *Sargento* placed a warning hand the size of a catcher's mitt on my shoulder.

"I could never allow him to pitch in six months," I said.

"You? Who gave you the right to decide anything? You, a perverted Yankee fugitive, you think you can come to my country and make decisions? He pitches in six months, and that is the end of it."

"Then send me back to where I came from, *Comandante*. Because if all you want to do is destroy this young man's career, you don't need me."

"If I send you back, they will put you in jail," Fidel said.

I shrugged. Castro, it seemed to me now, was just a cranky old man. I feared neither him, nor prison, nor anything else. It was really quite remarkable. I felt as if a chemical transformation had come over my brain, annulling my most basic instincts. Throw me to the sharks. Put a bullet in my head: I, the detached observer, simply did not care.

The balding dictator and I locked eyes. After a while, his lips curled up in a rueful smile. "You are a brave man, Dr. Sanderson."

"Actually, *Comandante*, what I am is a man with nothing to lose."

"You could lose your life."

"Everyone loses that," I said, "sooner or later."

"Yes." Castro nodded his head. "Did you know that eight gold medals—eight gold medals—were stolen from our valiant Cuban boxers by your corrupt government, in consort with their lackeys the International Olympic Committee, in the 1968 Olympics in Los Angles? It is a perfect example."

A perfect example? Of what? The man made sense only to himself.

"*Perfecto*," I agreed.

"Eight gold medals!" he shouted in a hoarse voice. "Stolen from around their young brave necks by those thieving, lying, cheating capitalist pigs! What do you say to that?"

"As I said, *Comandante*, a grave injustice."

"Are you fond of chicken livers?" Castro asked.

"What? Uh...who isn't?"

"All of our boxers are fed chicken livers on a constant basis. You will notice that none of them have injured knees."

Poor Cuba, I thought, they might as well have Daffy Duck running the country.

"Of course not," I agreed.

"When will you operate?"

"On his knee?" I asked, glancing at the trembling pitcher.

"No, on my hemorrhoids."

"Your hemorrhoids, *Comandante*?"

Castro returned his gaze to the ocean. "*Puercos capitalistas degenerados*," he muttered, "*ni saben distinguir entre sus culos y sus rodillas*." ("Degenerate capitalist pigs, don't know their asses from their knees.")

And with that, my audience with the world's longest reigning dictator came to an end.

THREE

"El *Comandante* likes you," *el Sargento* told me on the ride into town.

"He does?"

"Yes. And I, too, admire your *huevos*, Dr. Sanderson. We could have used you at La Mercedes."

"I'm not really brave, *Sargento*, just indifferent."

"Indifference to one's fate," *el Sargento* proclaimed, "is the foundation of courage. I've heard," he added, patting me affectionately on the knee, "that you get an enormous amount of pussy, Dr. Sanderson. Is this true?"

"Well, I, ah...do you think we can remove my blindfold now?"

"Of course. Virility, my friend, is nothing to be ashamed of. *el Comandante* admires virility. As do I."

"Oh yes," I agreed, "virility is a wonderful thing. Especially in a man."

"Especially in a man?"

"Yes," I said, wishing *el Sargento* would remove his massive hand from my knee, "that is, as opposed to, shall we say, in a dog?"

El *Sargento* nodded his approval. "I know what you mean. I have a macho bull terrier at home, and he leaves all the bitches breathless. You should see the size of the balls on that dog."

"Nothing, *Sargento*, would give me greater pleasure."

"Nor me," he replied with a troubling smile.

Now, I decided, would be a good time to ask *el Sargento* to return my pills. Though things seemed to be going my way, one never knew, especially with Captain Ahab at the helm. To my great relief *el Sargento* handed the vial over at once. For this, I nearly forgave him his intense garlic breath which, in the close confines of the limousine, was making me increasingly nauseous.

"By the way," I asked, "where are we going?"

"We have requisitioned a suite for you at La Havana Libre. But if there is somewhere else you would prefer to stay?"

"Yes, there is. My old room. Where I stayed on my first visit?"

El *Sargento* favored me with a lewd wink. "Correcto," he said.

Eustacia stood in the doorway of her small stucco home dressed in her frumpy housecoat. I stood directly before her, blocking her view of *el Sargento* and our heavily armed driver. It took Eustacia a moment to recognize me, whereupon her welcoming smile collapsed into a fierce scowl.

"Oh, it's you," she said. "If you're looking for a room, I'm all booked up. Even if I had a room, I'd rent it to you over my dead body. I had half the whores in Havana coming around here after you left. The neighborhood was scandalized. And I didn't like the way you ran out in the middle of the night, like a criminal, without even so much as a good-bye. And your room was a mess. A pair of pigs would have left it cleaner. And my knee still hurts. And…"

"Dr. Sanderson wants his old room," *el Sargento* announced, stepping onto the small porch and shouldering me gently to one side.

Eustacia's rheumy eyes went wide with astonishment as they finally fell upon *el Sargento* and our skinny driver, who was standing at attention, holding my suitcase in one hand and an automatic rifle in the other. *el Sargento*, I would learn, was well-known and well-feared throughout the country.

"Dr. Sanderson?" she croaked in dismay.

"Eustacia," I said, "so nice to see you again."

"Take us to his room," *el Sargento* ordered. "It is hot out here in the sun and we do not want Dr. Sanderson to be discomfited."

"I…I'm afraid the room is occupied," Eustacia said. "A German gentleman. Very respectable. I don't think he would…"

"Ask him to leave," *el Sargento* said.

"Leave?" Eustacia swallowed once with great difficulty. "He is, um, occupied, too, at the moment and I don't…"

"Tell him to leave," *el Sargento* said. "Now!"

Casting confused and fearful glances my way, Eustacia led us all back around the side of the house to my old room and knocked, rather timidly, on the door.

"Go away!" an annoyed voice barked at us in heavily accented English. "I am busy."

"What did he say?" *el Sargento* asked me.

"He said," I replied with disappointment, "that he is busy and that we should go away."

El *Sargento* rolled his eyes, turned to his driver and frowned. Still holding my suitcase and the machine gun, the soldier assumed a karate stance and effortlessly kicked open the door.

Inside, the scene was grotesque. The pot-bellied middle-aged German tourist was dressed, if you could call it that, in only a black brassiere. The girl, of course, was dressed in nothing at all, but wasted no time in donning her skimpy outfit (minus the brassiere) and sprinting out the door.

Meanwhile, the German, who reminded me of an embarrassed walrus, was not so agile when it came to dressing himself and took considerably longer. When he was almost done, he turned to face the soldiers, put his beefy hands on his beefy hips and said, "My embassy shall hear of this!"

"Tell him to pack up and leave," *el Sargento* told me.

"Pack up and leave!" I ordered the German.

"Why for!" he shouted. "I am paid the room. I am going no place!"

"What is he saying now?" *el Sargento* asked.

"He's calling you," I replied in astonishment, "a filthy black pig."

This was, perhaps, a bit extreme, but I'd never been fond of loud kinky Germans, and this one had had the Teutonic temerity to occupy my room.

Before hauling the mostly-dressed German away by the scruff of his neck, *el Sargento* ordered Eustacia to get my door fixed. "And be sure," he added, "that the doctor is not charged for the room. He is *el Comandante's* personal guest."

"*El Co-Co-Comandante?*" Eustacia stuttered.

"We will be in touch," *el Sargento* told me. "I hope you are as good as they say. For your sake," he added somberly.

Once we were alone, Eustacia recovered some of her old bravado. "You're travelling in some high company," she said, watching me warily out of the corner of her eye as she changed the sheets. "Since when are you a friend of *el Comandante?*"

"That's enough for now," I said. "I'm very tired."

"But the room is dirty," she protested. "And you haven't given me your passport."

"I don't have a passport. You can finish cleaning the room later. I need a nap."

"No passport?" she croaked. "That's against the law!"

"Well then, Eustacia," I suggested with a yawn, "perhaps you should inform the authorities."

"The authorities?" she moaned. And then, like a lame mouse limping for its life, she scampered from the room.

Exhausted, I lay down on the lumpy bed and listened for a while to the familiar and somehow consoling flu-like symptoms of the old Russian air conditioner. God only knew I could do with a little comforting. My former life was gone, irretrievably lost, as if I'd actually gone ahead and swallowed my precious vial of pills. With Pedro's help (another friend of another friend had provided the false passport), I'd fled the United States of America with the last thousand dollars I'd been able to extract from my account before it had been slammed shut in my face forever by Judge Marsha—a woman who had, almost single-handedly, destroyed my faith in the American judicial system.

I'd spent my last night in America with Leonard, passing

the purple bong and watching Nancy Drew. Nancy's guest that night had been, of all people, my brother-in-law, the self-declared, "World's leading authority on the mental pathology of Dr. Karl Sanderson".

Obviously, I'd opted not to murder the man, a decision for which I knew his wife and son would never forgive me.

Charles had all sorts of unpleasant things to say about me, all couched in convincingly technical psychobabble. His last words of the evening were, "In his mind, Karl was a pedophile. He wanted to be a pedophile. He would have been a pedophile. But he was afraid of being caught."

"In other words," Nancy said impartially, "a gutless pervert."

And that was how I'd left the United States, and how I would be remembered there forever, as a "gutless pervert". In Cuba, oddly enough, where only *el Comandante* and a select few seemed to know my secret, I was still regarded as a prestigious surgeon. It was comical, really, but I was too tired to laugh. I closed my eyes and went to sleep.

Several hours later, as had occurred so often in my homes away from home, I was awakened by a loud insistent pounding on my door, the one which communicated with Eustacia's house. For a few moments I lay there, dazed, uncertain of my surroundings. Then la doctora Eva burst in like a vengeful goddess and proceeded to tear my head off.

"What in God's name have you done to her?" she demanded. "She's hysterical. Practically hallucinating!"

"Eva," I said, "what a pleasant surprise."

"She says you came here," Eva seethed, "accompanied by Castro's personal bodyguard, who threatened her life. What are you doing here, anyway?"

Even more beautiful than I remembered her (and I remembered her as being the most beautiful woman I'd ever seen), Eva stood in the center of the room, a living statue, a force of nature, glaring at me with withering fury.

"Believe it or not, Eva," I said, twisting the truth just a little, "I have been summoned by *el Comandante*. Eustacia is not hallucinating."

"So the rumors are true," she said. "Ramos did tear up his knee."

"Someone has a bum knee," I said cautiously. "I'm not sure if I'm allowed to say who. Sorry Eustacia got so upset."

"Well, at least she's not hallucinating," Eva said with relief. "I had to give her a sedative. Did *el Sargento* really threaten her?"

"No, not at all. He didn't seem like such a bad fellow."

"Not a bad fellow?" Eva shuddered. "By the way," she added unkindly, "whatever happened to your little friend?"

"Mariela? Oh, she, ah…"

"Dumped you for someone half your age?"

"How did you know?"

"Predictable. And now you're looking for another teenage lover, I suppose?"

"No, I'm through with all that." Or, was I? The suite at *La Havana Libre* would have been far more comfortable.

Eva laughed. "Oh, I'm sure. How long are you here for? A week? Two?"

"Forever. I've decided to spend the rest of my life in Cuba."

"Very funny."

"It's true. I'm going to renounce my American citizenship and become a Cuban. If they'll have me."

"That's a bad joke."

"I'm perfectly serious. From now on, it's 'Death to the Yankees!', and 'Viva la revolucion!'"

"You are serious. What happened? Did they throw you out?"

"Not exactly, but I had—I can't go back. Let's leave it at that."

Eva thought this over for a minute. "You're really here for good?"

"Yes. Maybe we could continue this conversation later, Eva. It's been a long day. I'm tired."

"How tired?" Eva asked, removing her blouse.

"Well, I'm not sure. On the one hand…"

"Shut up," Eva said, "and take off your pants."

FOUR

"Is it a little cramped in here? Or is it my imagination?"

"If you need to unbend a limb or two," I advised my daughter, "there's always the backyard."

We were sitting, somewhat ill at ease, in a pair of ancient chairs in what had once been Eustacia's micro-parlor. Since the old woman's timely demise a year earlier, the coffin-sized room, along with the rest of the house, "belonged" to me. Fidel himself, overriding the claims of a dozen irate relations, had by presidential decree made me the nominal "owner". I'd even been encouraged (ordered, actually) to keep up the mini-bordello business—as long as the government continued to receive its ninety per cent of the gross.

Candace and I spent some time studying the floor. Our relationship, once so close, seemed to have grown a little rusty with time. We hadn't seen each other for more than two years, and only spoken once, the previous month, on my problematic Cuban telephone. The operator had claimed that the call was "person-to-person", but in reality it was more like "asteroid-to-asteroid". At one point Candace had asked me to turn down the volume on my television; she thought I was watching a science fiction film. The connection was so bad that even after twenty minutes of fractured dialogue, I had little idea why she was coming to see me. Did she feel duty-bound? Was this the reluctant daughter forcing herself to visit the disgraced father in exile? Or was she compelled by affection alone?

As we sat there in our stiff-backed chairs in the wee parlor, I wondered if we'd grown too far apart to recapture that rare bond we'd shared in our cannabis days. Not that much time had passed, but we'd both changed. Candace had grown into a stunning and self-possessed, albeit eccentric, young woman. And I'd…grown older.

After the third or fourth aborted attempt at conversation, she said, "You still a binge drinker, Dad?"

"Hardly. I like an evening cocktail now and then, but I've left all that melodrama behind me in America, along with…a lot of other stuff."

"Like me?"

"No—well, yes. For whatever it's worth, Candace, as far as regrets go, leaving you behind pretty much tops the list."

Another short but uncomfortable silence ensued.

"So, how about a nice cold mojito, Dad? It's hotter than hell in here."

"My aged Russian air conditioners," I said, heading for the kitchen. "They're all on life-support."

I returned with the drinks and we toasted our mutual health. I could no longer afford the ten-year-old Havana Club, but with an extra dozen mint leaves thrown in, it was tough to tell the difference. I took out a cigar. I couldn't afford them, either, but every now and then a grateful patient would give me one or two (presumably stolen) as a gratuity.

"Dad, you're smoking."

"I don't inhale," I said defensively.

"You have another one?"

"You want a cigar?"

"Why not. Cigars, rum and sex—isn't that what everyone comes to Cuba for?"

"Well, they do have some nice beaches. Or so I hear."

We sat for a long while, as the day faded, sipping our cocktails and puffing on our Cohibas, like a pair of Hollywood producers taking lunch.

"So tell me, Dad," Candace said, expertly trimming the ash from her cigar, "how did it all come down? You got here on a fake passport, and then what?"

"From that point on, it was all Marx Brothers: *A Day at the Dictator's*."

I told her about *el Sargento*, the injured pitcher, Castro's obsession with sports and the devil's bargain I'd made. I explained how, eleven months after his surgery, the young left-hander had returned to the mound and thrown an impressive three-hit shutout. I'd been at the game, sitting at Fidel's side, so that he could congratulate me personally if everything went well, and order my God-only-knew-what if it didn't.

A month later I was officially made a Cuban citizen and given the directorship of the Jose Marti Hospital for Orthopedic Sports Medicine. Fidel, who was something of a sadist, had me working like a slave, operating on what seemed like every injured knee in Cuba, while a gaggle of star-struck surgeons followed my every move.

"And there you have it," I concluded. "You see before you a man working himself into an early grave for the astounding sum of thirty-five dollars a month. But I'm a free man, more or less, and I'm doing what I love. So I can't complain."

"Wait a minute, Dad. You're making thirty-five dollars a month?"

"That's ten dollars above the going rate, sweetie. I'm probably the best paid surgeon in Cuba."

I didn't go into any great detail about the manner in which I supplemented my income; somehow it didn't seem appropriate. "What about you," I asked, "how's your life going?"

"Me? I'm cool. Since the band got reviewed in *the Voice* we have paying gigs almost every weekend. They're calling me a 'Guitar Wizard', whatever that means. And it looks like we've got a recording deal. Mom sends me a check once a month. Sometimes I cash it, sometimes I don't. But all that mundane crap aside, Dad, I've got some news you might find interesting."

"Really? What's that?"

"Our favorite person," she said with studied nonchalance, "the world's biggest shithead? He's in jail."

"Charles?"

"Yep."

"You're joking."

"No joke. Sure is hot in here. How about another mojito, Dad?"

There had always been something a little frightening about my daughter. Mainly, I'd put it down to her hyper-intelligence. But sometimes, I wondered.

"All right, Candace, cut out the cat and mouse routine, and tell me what the fuck happened!"

Apparently pleased at my violent reaction, Candace broke into a wide grin. Then, her voice charged with excitement, she said, "It was right out of Dostoyevsky, Dad: Slime and Punishment! When I told Steven what you said about Uncle Charles blackmailing the US Attorney, he went Biblical—totally nuts: 'Charles is the Devil. I'm the Avenging Angel. The Evil Father must be destroyed.' Then, it was Revelations, The Apocalypse, The Ides of Freaking March. You name it. Finally, I had to give him a valium."

"*So, he believed me.*"

"Completely. So did I, Dad. Kind of. Anyway, Steven became obsessed. All he'd talk about were the f-f-f-f-iles."

Steven, as Candace told it, decided that his father must have a cache of "s-s-secret f-f-f-iles", and even if it took him all Eternity, he was going to find them. He began his search with the assumption that Charles would not have hidden the files in his office, since that was where his records were supposed to be, and anyone looking for them would search there first. That left the cavernous co-op. It took Steven eighteen months, but in one of the dusty rooms dedicated to "deep storage", behind a sliding panel in the wall, the Avenging Angel struck gold.

Several hundred tapes were hidden there, all meticulously catalogued and accompanied by detailed handwritten notes. Some of these notes were wonderfully incriminating: "Sell short Wetzger Chemical—arthritis drug off market." "Dump GM—massive recall." "Buy Systems Tech—anti-trust suit settled their favor."

In addition to the insider information garnered from sessions with CEO'S and CFO'S, there were scores of humiliating and/or incriminating admissions made by influential citizens of every stripe. And last but not least, there was the dirt on Davidson. Steven made copies of everything and gave them to the *New York Times*; the originals, he turned over to the Manhattan DA.

Davidson, when confronted with the tapes, broke down and confessed everything. It had been more than grief over his wife's tragic death in an automobile accident which had sent him rushing into Charles' villainous embrace. It turned out that Davidson, not his wife, had been at the wheel, and he'd been drinking. Davidson being one of their own, the authorities had willingly bought his bogus story, and the entire business was soon forgotten. But Davidson could never forgive himself. The guilt was crushing him. Being an Episcopalian, confession was not an option, so he had done the next worst thing and sought the services of a psychiatrist.

Charles, as a matter of course, had recorded his patient's "privileged" confession and filed it away for future use. Then, when the time was ripe, he'd taken it out and ordered the US Attorney to do his bidding, or else.

Denounced by the American Psychiatric Association for breaking a dozen sacred taboos, including several they'd had to invent on the spot, Charles was summarily expelled from the fraternity of witchdoctors and, soon thereafter, indicted on multiple felony charges. With no hope of beating the rap, he'd copped a plea, and was sentenced to five years in prison.

And thus was Charles shoved nose-first into the grave he had so carefully prepared for me. His keepers had even placed the psycho psychoanalyst on "suicide watch". (Now that, Bob, was an irony I could appreciate.) And I won't lie, or feign a generosity of spirit I did not feel. The news of Charles' wretched fate filled me with immense joy.

But then the residual guilt I myself carried around like an irritable bowel turned my thoughts to Janice. Though any feelings of affection were long gone, I still felt responsible. My betrayal had pushed her to the brink, and this second blow might well have impelled her over the edge.

"How is your mother taking all this?" I asked.

"To be honest, Dad, she and I don't communicate much. Brenda says that mom is a wreck. She hardly leaves her condo.

And, guess what? She wants you back. Everybody wants you back. Even that bitch at the hospital. You've been exonerated, Dad. You're officially a victim—practically a hero. You can go back home anytime you want!"

I hated to disappoint my daughter. Having handed me a full pardon she expected me to fly home at once, back into the arms of everyone who'd rejected me. This had been the entire point of her trip to Cuba. She wanted her father back; back home in America; back where he belonged. It was an appealing idea, going home. But going back? Was it possible to go back? Somehow, I didn't think so.

The sound of the front door opening and closing echoed in the parlor. "Sweetie, I'm afraid it's not that simple, this going back business. For one thing, I've remarried."

"Remarried? You're shitting me."

"No, it's true."

"Wow. What's she like? Is she having periods yet?"

"Very funny. Here she comes now." And into the room walked Eva, dressed in doctor's whites and looking, as usual, too good to be real.

Candace gasped, audibly.

Eva frowned at the cigars; I wasn't supposed to smoke in the house.

"Candace, this is my wife, Eva. Eva, this is my daughter, Candace."

"I am delighted to meet you," Eva said with a warm smile. "Your father has told me all about you. You're even more lovely than I imagined."

Candace, who had three years of high school Spanish, stood up, took Eva's proffered hand and said, "You're really married to my father?"

"Yes." Eva laughed. "Why would you doubt it?"

"Well, it's just that…"

Candace, for one of the few times in her life, was struck dumb. Eva had that effect on people, although typically the people she rendered speechless were men.

FIVE

That evening the three of us went out to "dinner" at Los Viejos Tiempos. Candace wanted to hear some live Cuban music. And it was about all we could afford.

Mario the midget strutted up to our table, took in my two companions and said, "Whoa! The Gringo Stud rides again!"

"Hello, Mario."

All but drooling, the midget said, "One wasn't enough? You had to have the two most beautiful women in Havana? That, my friend, is true capitalist greed."

"Mario, this is Eva, my wife. And this is Candace, my daughter."

"Sure, Doc, whatever you say. He turned to address the two women. "That's what *el Comandante* calls him—his 'Gringo Stud'. Now, I know why."

"Three mojitos, Mario. The cheap ones, please."

"Wait a minute, Dad. Fidel Castro calls you his Gringo Stud?"

"Only once. At a baseball game. Somehow, it got around."

"Actually, he's my gringo stud," Eva said, placing a possessive hand on my arm.

Mario shook his head. "And I thought midgets had it good."

"Dad, why is everyone staring at us?"

"Well, the men, I imagine, are staring at you and Eva."

"And the women," Eva said, "are staring at your father. Some of them still think he's rich," she added with a laugh.

"The Gringo Stud? Gee, Dad, who would have guessed?"

"I believe," I said, turning various shades of crimson, "el *Comandante* was referring to my prowess as a surgeon."

Mario returned with our drinks. I asked him what was good tonight.

"Good to eat?" he asked. "You joking?"

While we were attempting to ingest the odd-colored "pizza", Candace said, "Now that the stud here can return to America, why don't the two of you live in New York? You'd have a lot better life there. You could even eat real pizza."

"We are content here," Eva said, "aren't we Carlos?"

"Yes, I suppose. Though my situation has changed, Eva, and if we wanted to, we could live in America now."

"We don't want to," Eva said, ending the discussion.

Later that night, after Eva had gone to bed, Candace and I sat up for hours talking in the kitchen, almost like old times. All we lacked was a little Mindwipe, and some room deodorant.

"What do you think of Eva?" I asked her.

"She's unreal," Candace said. "I mean, I've never even seen a woman that beautiful. But—don't take offense, Dad—she seems a little on the bossy side."

"A little?" I laughed. "The woman is a total tyrant."

Especially in bed, I wanted to add, but it was my daughter sitting there, after all.

"I bet," Candace said eagerly, "she's a real dominatrix in bed."

My little girl, all grown up. I felt a sense of loss so intense it brought tears to my eyes. My old life, regardless of what anyone said or did, was gone forever. "What about you, sweetie? Have you finally settled on one gender or the other?"

"Yeah, Dad, I've definitely opted for tits. I gave the hetero thing my best shot, but, I'm sorry, dicks make me nauseous."

"Well…as long as you're happy. You have someone special at the moment?"

"At the moment, I've got several."

"Several?"

"I'm going through my promiscuous phase. There is one, though, this really rich dyke in the Village? She's the heir to some shaving cream fortune. Or dental floss. Something to do with personal hygiene. Anyway, she wants to buy me a townhouse."

"That's nice."

"She's cute, but I told her I'm not ready to settle down."

Infinitely out of my depth, I said, "Yes, well, good move."

Candace took a few leisurely puffs on her cigar. "So tell me, Dad, if I'm not being too personal, does Eva look as good naked as she does with her clothes on?"

"Well, ah, actually..."

We were interrupted, thank God, by someone knocking on the door to my old room. I excused myself and went to see what the fellow—a greasy Frenchman—could possibly want at that hour. As it turned out, what he wanted was a condom; his own, manufactured in China, had split open in his hands. I told him in broken French to go to hell, and slammed the door in his flushed face.

"What was that about, Dad?"

"Oh, one of my demanding tenants. A smelly little Frenchman."

"What did he want, a condom?"

"Candace, please stop reading my mind—it's unnerving."

"I was just using logic, Dad. Foreign men, or so I've heard, only come to Havana for one thing. And at this hour, I figured he didn't want a glass of water."

"It wasn't my choice," I said defensively. "The government insisted I carry on the, ah, family business."

"It's okay, Dad. I mean, making thirty-five dollars a month, I could see how you'd need to supplement your income. Nothing to be ashamed of. Being a pimp must have been your destiny all along."

"Candace!"

"Just kidding. So, tell me the truth—are you ever coming back to America?"

"Who knows. The government might not be all that anxious to have me back, even if I'm no longer a multiple felon.

Did you know that I've renounced my American citizenship?"

"Yeah, I saw the video. I thought it was pretty good. Especially the part where you called the President of the United States a 'lying, gutless, homicidal thug'. That made you real popular with the mom-and-apple pie crowd."

"I had no choice. The video was part of my deal with Fidel."

"But you could still go back," she insisted, "if you really wanted to. I guess what it comes down to is, are you happy here?"

Not for the first time, I thought about what my ex-friend Burt said to me at the hospital that day: "Life goes on. Until it doesn't. Then you're dead, at which point, who gives a shit."

"Happy? I suppose, in a perverse sort of way, I've grown to like it here. Though I'll admit, being poor takes a little getting used to. But I'm working, doing what I love. And of course, I've got Eva."

"Lucky you. I guess I'll just have to come and visit whenever I can scrounge up the bread."

"That would be great, sweetie. You're about the only thing I miss here. Besides food. I never realized how much I enjoyed edible food. At any rate, you know you will always be welcome in my home, wherever it is."

"Don't be too sure, Dad. I could provide you with some serious competition."

"Competition? For what?"

"I think," my daughter said grimly, "I'm in love with your wife."

THE END

www.ingramcontent.com/pod-product-compliance
Lightning Source LLC
Chambersburg PA
CBHW021037090426
42738CB00006B/122